Consumer
Information Systems
and
Consumer Policy

Consumer Information Systems and Consumer Policy

Hans B. Thorelli
Sarah V. Thorelli

Ballinger Publishing Company • Cambridge, Massachusetts
A Subsidiary of J.B. Lippincott Company

This book is printed on recycled paper.

International Standard Book Number: 0-88410-271-8

Library of Congress Catalog Card Number: 76-48925

Printed in the United States of America

Library of Congress Cataloging in Publication Data

Thorelli, Hans B
  Consumer information systems and consumer policy.

  Bibliography: p.
  Includes index.
  1. Consumer education—Information services.   2. Consumer protection—Information services.   I. Thorelli, Sarah V., joint author.   II. Title.
TX335.T47   640.73   76-48925
ISBN 0-88410-271-8

Contents

List of Figures

List of Tables

Preface

We hear a lot about the information explosion in science and industry—indeed, in all walks of life. Yet our demands for information seem to grow even faster than its availability. In the marketplace, in particular, *effectively* available data about the proliferating flora of products and services is insufficient. We are faced with a *consumer information gap.*

This is serious. Only informed consumers can make intelligent decisions. Only when consumers are at least capable of making intelligent decisions among competing offerings can we meaningfully speak of consumer sovereignty. What is more, only when at least some consumers are making intelligent decisions some of the time can an open market economy serve the needs of modern society.

This is a book about systems for the delivery of independent consumer information—present and future. Such data are supplied by organizations that themselves have no direct interest in the sale of the products and services about which they disseminate information. The largest body in this area is the Consumers Union of the United States, publishers of *Consumer Reports.* Other comparative testing organizations—private or public—exist in most industrially advanced nations. Independent consumer information (CI) is also disseminated by information labeling and quality certification agencies. *The testmakers* is our collective term for all these organizations.

Our concern includes both content and context. The nature, anatomy and operating problems of CI programs are examined in detail. The contextual analysis is multidimensional. CI programs are related to other mainsprings of product information, notably advertising and other commercial sources, and to personal experience and contacts. They are then related to other aspects of consumer policy. For this purpose a systematic overview of the entire consumer policy area is developed—possibly for the first time. Next, an ecologic approach is applied to the examination of interaction between CI programs and the economic, social and political environment in which they operate. Ecologic analysis gives the background for a discussion of internation transfer of CI technology and experience. Finally, a synthesis of content and context is attempted in a strategic planning framework for future CI systems.

The students, makers and administrators of consumer policy in government, consumer organizations, business and academia are those to whom this work is primarily directed. It should also be of interest to students of organization theory and to cross-cultural researchers. Not least, it will interest business executives—and marketing men in particular.

The book is the last of three volumes representing the output of a seven year research project, the International Consumer Information Survey (ICIS). The first book, entitled *Consumer Information Handbook: Europe and North America* (cited throughout text as *Handbook*), published by Praeger in 1974, is a detailed survey of comparative testing, informative labeling and quality certifying organizations in the North Atlantic community of nations. There are well over forty such agencies in the fifteen countries represented, plus another ten or so at the international level. In addition the book deals with relevant aspects of related groups concerned with consumer policy, such as consumer lobbies, standardization bodies and public regulatory agencies. If the present book deals with the forest, the *Handbook* deals with the trees.

To make CI available may be praiseworthy. To make it useful, there must also be an audience of consumers willing to assimilate the information and make use of it in the buying process. The second ICIS volume, *The Information Seekers—An International Study of Consumer Information and Advertising Image*, co-authored with Helmut Becker and Jack Engledow and published by Ballinger in 1975, undertakes to identify this audience, comparing its characteristics in Germany and the United States, with extensions to Norway and other countries. It also compares this cosmopolitan group of consumer sophisticates—the Information Seekers—with average consumers in the countries studied. As advertising for better or worse probably constitutes the single most important source of product information in the advanced democracies, consumer attitudes to advertising are also examined and compared with consumer views of CI.

As the capstone of the ICIS project, this book is squarely based on the data and conclusions emerging from the first two volumes. However, it also brings additional theoretical and analytical material to play. Although the three volumes are companions, each book is written to stand on its own. This makes a certain amount of repetition inevitable; we believe it has been held to a minimum.

An important final comment must be made regarding the nature of this final volume. It is in part a treatise in political economy. That is, it deals with socioeconomic problems from the point of view of the public interest as this is interpreted by the authors. In our opinion, the reader by this time has a right to know how we feel as experts, rather than merely what we have observed as scientists. Thus, in part the discussion is normative (what should be done) rather than positive (what is being done). It stands to reason that in such a context the biases and predilections of the authors will enter more than in a research monograph. A statement of the author's personal viewpoint is contained in the introduction.

The ICIS project is finished, but far from dead. An offshoot project, undertaken by Hans B. Thorelli in association with Dr. Gerald E. Sentell and staff of the National Institute of Development Administration (NIDA) in Bangkok, has been sponsored by MUCIA, the Midwest Universities Consortium for International Affairs. This is a pioneer study of consumer policy and consumer problems in a less developed country (LDC) based on a field survey of the Thai experience. The research is premised on the notion that modern marketing in general and what may indeed be called "consumers' liberation" in particular are indispensable and yet sadly neglected instrumentalities in LDCs wishing to achieve that difficult combination: economic development *cum* political democracy. Our findings will be reported in a separate monograph.

At this time, too, Drs. Engledow, Becker and Ronald Anderson of Indiana University are engaged in a partial "update" study of *The Information Seekers.* The object is to establish to what extent the patterns in attitude and behavior of German and American consumers reported in that volume are stable over time (1970-76) and in what respects they may be changing. Our guess is that the original findings will have a high degree of validity over time.

In formally concluding the ICIS project we again wish to extend thanks to the persons and organizations that made the work possible. They were acknowledged in some detail in preceding volumes. At this time we wish to single out our longtime collaborators on *The*

Information Seekers, Drs. Jack Engledow and Helmut Becker, for invaluable intellectual stimulation and criticism. The grants in aid of publication of the first two volumes given by the Consumer Research Institute (CRI) of Washington will always be gratefully remembered. The economic and moral support of the Graduate School of Business of Indiana University during the last seven years has been simply indispensable. It hardly needs saying that none of the persons or institutions named here or in the companion volumes is in any way responsible for the policy conclusions or any factual shortcomings of this work.

Hans B. Thorelli
Sarah V. Thorelli

Bloomington, Indiana
September 1976

Consumer
Information Systems
and
Consumer Policy

Executive Summary

This summary is in the form of a policy memo prepared at the request of the Consumer Task Force of Jimmy Carter, candidate for president of the United States at the time of writing. Thus, of necessity, it focuses more on public than private consumer information policy measures. In the aggregate, the book will demonstrate that we place greater emphasis on private and pluralist efforts in this area than on governmental ones. Non-American readers will understand that the origin of the summary means that it is oriented to United States conditions, while the book itself is written with all affluent nations in mind.

This executive summary is more condensed than those of the companion *Handbook* and *Information Seekers* volumes, as the last chapter of this book in effect presents a "summary and conclusions" in the form of a strategic planning manual. For concentrated background briefing the reader may consult the executive summaries of the other two volumes.

Informed consumers are protected consumers—more than that, they are liberated consumers.

1. Right to Know, but Information Gap.

In a democratic society freedom of choice is a basic consumer right. The key to freedom of choice is the consumer's right to know; however, there is a yawning product information gap. The prime reason for the gap is the very richness of our markets, with product and brand proliferation, increasing complexity of the average product, and rapid change. Too, Plains, Georgia, and other nonmetro areas,

1

due to the narrow selections of local stores, are removed from much of this richness, as a great deal of information is lost when the actual product is not at hand. Commercial information is sometimes deceptive. Consumer expectations as to product performance seem to grow exponentially with the level of affluence. No doubt, the gap is there—and growing.

2. Information Sources, Consumer Information Programs.

Consumers rely on commercial, personal (own experience, friends) and independent information sources. Currently, commercial and personal sources dominate, but the existence of a gap shows that they need supplementation with independent consumer information (CI) programs. Thus, CI here stands for information about consumer products and services provided by a party with no direct commercial interest in the promotion of these offerings. The most well-known CI program in the world is Consumers Union. Vigorous CI programs by example and osmosis will raise quality of commercial information.

3. Consumer Policy and Policymakers.

The total range of consumer policy may be divided into consumer information, education and protection. In a general sense, consumer information comprises all data about individual markets and offerings. Consumer education is "consumer civics"; it provides the insight necessary to develop citizens into intelligent consumers. Consumer protection consists of measures taken by other than the individual consumer to safeguard consumer rights. It ranges all the way from antitrust via complaints handling to product safety.

Consumer policymakers include consumer organizations, other citizen groups, business, government, educational institutions and the mass media. There are almost infinite tradeoff and reinforcement possibilities between information, education and protection, and between various makers of consumer policy in the struggle to enforce consumer rights and stimulate consumer responsibility. For a capsule view of consumer policy and policymakers in the context of consumer rights and responsibility see the diagram in Figure 2–2.

4. CI Program Types.

In terms of product coverage there are some fifty broad spectrum CI programs in the twenty-nation North Atlantic community. Currently, comparative testing (CT) programs issuing detailed test reports (e.g., *Consumer Reports*) dominate the field. There are also a number of voluntary informative labeling (IL) and quality certification (QC) programs. In IL programs an organization, after establishing norms as to the nature of information to be given about relevant product characteristics to be declared on the label, will permit interested producers to attach the informative label to their products. For a sample label see Figure 7-1. Each participating producer guarantees that his product lives up to the level of performance he has declared. QC indicates that the product carrying the seal at least measures up to a minimum norm (threshold) of performance established by the certifying agency. Again, products may carry the seal only so long as they comply with, or exceed, the minimum norm.

The United States does not have broad-scope IL or QC programs; rather, we have many narrow-scope IL and QC programs: energy labels, wool product labels, nutrition labels, etc. Fairly well-known among narrow-scope QC programs is Underwriters' Laboratories, Inc. Quite notorious are the grading schemes of the U.S. Department of Agriculture (their terminology must be unified!). IL and QC both have the great advantage of giving point-of-purchase information. A combined IL-QC scheme should be the objective of the future. A quality mark in the corner of a label gives a consumer assurance of a minimum threshold of performance; the label itself gives details for comparative shopping. A producer may elect to use either or both.

5. The Information Seeker (IS), Average Consumer (AC) and Underprivileged Consumer (UC).

CT programs reach mostly the Information Seekers, cosmopolitan, middle and upper income, college-educated consumers in professional and managerial jobs. Both the Information Seeker and average consumer find IL useful. The underprivileged consumer will generally be content to settle for quality marks. In many cases, the time-pressured Information Seeker or average consumer is also a potential audience for QC.

Vocal socialists (the so-called consumer radicals) in Sweden have put a stop to CI programs there, with the argument that it is mostly the Information Seekers who make use of them, and Information Seekers are overprivileged already. The same reasoning could be used to abolish universities and national parks. It is especially short-sighted in the CI case, as Information Seekers are the vigilantes of the marketplace. Information Seekers are the people who enforce consumer rights on behalf of all consumers and keep suppliers on their toes by pinpointing poor service, deficiencies in products, out-of-stock conditions, misleading advertising and other malpractices. In the U.S., they voluntarily finance the world's greatest CT program. They disseminate information and advice to fellow consumers, and in some respects serve as proxy purchasing agents for many less information-conscious and planful citizens.

6. The Role of Government.

The consumer policy diagram shows that government plays a vital role as policymaker in the protection and, at least potentially, consumer education areas. Our concern here is limited to CI, an area in which programs managed by consumer groups or by consumer and business organizations jointly may be preferred. In this area we view the role of the U.S. government as primarily stimulative and supportive rather than administrative or continuously regulative. Specifics follow in points 7 through 10.

7. Initiate Unified IL-QC Program.

Public bodies could stimulate consumers, business, standardization bodies and other interested parties to create and run a unified IL-QC program. Adherence by producers is to be strictly voluntary. Experience shows that large-scale promotion is indispensable; government must supply these funds. Government is to be represented in such a program to foster credibility, to safeguard the interests of underprivileged consumers, and to prevent possible (but unlikely) antitrust abuse. If necessary the secretariat—but not policymaking—may be provided by a government agency, such as the National Bureau of Standards.

It is critical that a unified IL-QC scheme comes *soon*. We are daily proliferating product-unique, narrow-scope schemes, adding noise and confusion instead of information.

8. Product Testing.

The CU does does a fine job of comparative testing—no reason for the government to compete. On the other hand, CU resources are limited. Exploratory testing of products untried by consumer testing organizations might be done by the NBS, or contracted out to private labs when this would be helpful to the IL-QC program.

All CI programs are based on tests. A key bottleneck is the lack of SMMPs—Standard Methods of Measuring Performance—for many products and many characteristics. Government should play an aggressive role in developing new SMMPs in cooperation with consumer, business and standards groups. Government should defray out-of-pocket expenses of consumer representatives on standards and IL-QC committees.

9. Computerized CI Utility.

This has the great charm of adding local price, service and availability data to "nationwide" product test information. Technical feasibility is already proven. Organizational and financial problems remain. Government should support aggressively experimental work in this area.

10. Consumer Advisory Centers.
A few exist in the U.S., many more in Britain, Germany. They combine education, advice and information, tailoring all to the needs of the individual. This is of special importance to underpriviledged consumers. There is ample room for government initiatives, and for decentralized, pluralist orchestration.

11. Consumer Education.
At present only Norway and a handful of states in the U.S. have obligatory consumer education in public schools. Yet education is critical in today's complex marketplace. It is also critical to make consumers information-conscious. This will generate many more Information Seekers, promoting the social circulation on which a democracy thrives. The government should do what it can to promote both obligatory consumer education in high schools and adult education programs, especially for the underpriviledged consumer.

12. Health and Safety.
Protective regulation has been the motto regarding products potentially affecting health and safety. For protective reasons obligatory minimum standards of information clearly have a legitimate role to play here next to minimum performance standards for the products themselves. What we need is more consumer education and information programs in this area to reinforce—or often even obviate the need for—direct protection. That the Consumer Product Safety Commission in its early years has focused on direct intervention is understandable. There was a pent-up need for this, and direct intervention provided a publicity platform badly needed in such a period. Education and information programs could not have served the latter purpose (as discovered long ago by more vocal consumer advocates). The time has come, however, to provide a more balanced mix between education, information and direct intervention in matters of health and safety.

13. Metrication.
Perhaps the single most important consumer policy measure the U.S. government could take in the consumer policy area at this time would be to mandate a conversion to the metric system within a five year period. Changing measurement systems is *not* a voluntary matter—standardization is far too important here. Studies have demon-

strated that comparative shopping is greatly facilitated and much time saved when units are in tens rather than twelves and sixteens. Increased market transparency is what CI is all about. Of critical significance to consumers is that converting to metric results in limiting the number of standard package sizes. This is a consumer concern as much as an industry matter.

14. Cost.

In dealing with CI programs we are in the bargain basement of consumer policy measures. Exceedingly worthwhile government contributions to CI programs, as outlined in points 7 through 9, could be made at less than $10 million a year. The Information Seekers are voluntarily subscribing another $20 million per year for CT reports. Industry costs are harder to estimate. Much of the testing necessary for an IL-QC program would be an integral part of strong ongoing quality control in production, even in the absence of labeling. In the European experience, the costs of printing and affixing labels and/or seals to products have been marginal. They are certainly trivial as compared to the costs of advertising and sales promotion. Incidentally, an important point in favor of CI programs is the possibility of using them (or at least labels and seals) as integral parts of the firm's market information strategy.

We are more uncertain about the costs of items 10 through 13. Although probably just as significant as elements of consumer policy, these measures are a bit removed from the core of CI programs.

15. Philosophical Premises.

In capsule form, the premises of these recommendations are: Consumer sovereignty, as reflected by consumer rights on our consumer policy diagram, is a seminal objective in democratic society. So is the viability of the open market system. So, too, is the right to information when it can be produced without undue cost. So, finally, is equality of opportunity in decisionmaking. The reinforcement of all these values calls for CI programs bringing greater transparency in the marketplace.

The autonomous and self-reliant citizen is an age-old ideal of Western civilization. That ideal is promoted more by education and information than by protection. It is also promoted by decentralized, pluralist and voluntary CI systems more than by centralized, unified and mandatory ones.

Introduction

PURPOSE OF THE BOOK

The purpose in hand is an analysis of consumer information systems.

A hot topic in management and computer literature these days is Management Information Systems (MIS). These are information systems designed to facilitate decisionmaking and control by producers. A large part of any respectable MIS is focused on feedback from the marketplace: data on sales and market share, on competitors and their products, on the effectiveness of advertising campaigns, on changing consumer preferences, and so on. It is obvious that consumers, too, make decisions—and that consumers, too, need information about products, brands, prices and other aspects of the market. Some of these needs will be detailed later. Ideally, of course, one would envisage a market information system generating all the data needed for marketing decisions, be they made by consumers or producers. Such an all-comprehensive data system is not a realistic proposition at this time, though the subject is broached in the final chapter. In the meanwhile, little has been written on Consumer Information Systems (CIS)—that is, information systems designed to facilitate consumer decisionmaking in the marketplace. This book is written to report on some exploration and analysis in this area, to increase public and business awareness of the problems and opportunities in it, and to stimulate discussion among private and public policymakers.

All systems consist of interacting components. Systems may be classified in a variety of ways, some of which are relevant here. They may be single purpose or multipurpose. Open systems interact continuously with their environments, while closed ones do not. Systems may be well-defined or ill-defined. They may evidence varying degrees of internal coordination and competition. Systems may also be grouped along the centralization-decentralization axis, depending on how the coordinative influence is exercised. In principle, the performance of any system can also be evaluated from various points of view.

The principal components of CIS are the consumers in need of information, the sources of information, and the information disseminated by these sources. The manner and degree to which consumers use various sources of information, and their evaluation of information from different sources, were the subject of the companion volume, *The Information Seekers.* Our findings in these regards will be utilized in this work, which is more oriented to the sources of information and the nature of the data they disseminate. Information sources are traditionally divided into personal, commercial and independent—and frequently these epithets are also given to the information generated by them (although in that context the terms easily become misnomers).[1] Commercial sources and information have been studied extensively in marketing, advertising, mass communications and consumer behavior literature. Considering their importance, personal sources and information have received relatively limited attention. Scanter still has been the research devoted to independent sources and the data transmitted by them. Thus it is that although our interest here is with CIS as a whole a large part of the work is devoted to an examination of independent consumer information (CI) programs.

CIS are multipurpose in that they serve two related but distinct functions: informing consumers and enforcing the open market system. CIS themselves are open systems in the sense that they are conditioned by and interact with their environments. Thus it is but natural that ecologic and cross-cultural analysis of CIS and CI programs will be a major focus of attention. It turns out that in most cultures the total CIS is quite ill-defined. Indeed, it involves some stretching of the imagination even to view the massive network of personal, commercial and independent product information as a system. We shall submit that bringing about a more deliberate systems approach is one of the major challenges of the future. As indicated by the sections on the local CIS at the end of each country study in the companion *Handbook*, it is even true that the subsystem represented by various CI programs is quite ill-defined in most cultures.

As might be expected from ill-defined systems, there is little or no internal coordination in most CIS. There is very little deliberate mutual supplementation and reinforcement among the parts. While there is some conflict between subsystems, in that representatives of CI programs tend to be critical of advertising and vice versa, there appears to be relatively little overt competition between them. Competition is mainly found inside subsystems, notably between advertisers, but to some extent also between CI programs (as in Belgium, France, Germany and the United States). An outstanding characteristic of all CIS before 1973 was their extreme decentralization. In 1973 the State Consumer Board was created in Sweden with the deliberate purpose of centralizing consumer policy in general and independent CI programs in particular. At about the same time, central control of advertising was considerably heightened. Elsewhere, decentralization is still the rule, although centralizing influences are unmistakable in several countries.

Pending further research on such matters as the degree of informedness of consumers and the impact of personal information sources, no attempt will be made here to evaluate the performance of CIS as a whole. In *The Information Seekers* we did obtain a rich body of data on how consumers themselves evaluate both CI programs and advertising, which we shall draw upon in an evaluation of CI program effectiveness. That evaluation will also include CI program impact on producers, distributors, governments and international trade.

INFORMATION NEEDS AND THEIR SIGNIFICANCE

To comprehend the nature of product information, to understand the operations of CI programs, and to evaluate the performance of a CIS and its personal, commercial and independent subsystems, it is necessary to inventory the main needs for information in the consumer buying process. Let us assume that you are an Information Seeker. Assuming further that you have identified your problem as that of getting music reproduction at home, you need information about the alternate products that will solve the problem (do the job, perform the function). This is basically an educational need, though not typically provided for in educational programs, except maybe in home economics. Unfortunately, neither commercial nor CI sources have done a very good job of filling the breech. The consumer may have to learn about the eight or ten different ways of obtaining music reproduction in his home on his own or through "cultural osmosis."

Assuming that you conclude that a portable tape recorder will meet your needs most effectively, you now need information about the things to look for in such a machine. You also need information to clarify your own values, so that you can develop your buying criteria, your set of priorities (it must have good music reproduction and be able to shut off automatically, but it need not necessarily be light weight; it must cost less than $100). Personal, commercial and independent sources are all helpful in this regard.

Of rapidly increasing importance is the question of how the product will do as a unit of a larger need-fulfilling system. You may be asking, will the recorder be able to tape programs directly from my radio? Can I use my high-fidelity speakers with it? How will it look on the sidetable next to my rocking chair? By and large, it seems fair to say that CI programs have rendered only a modest contribution in the product systems area. Personal information—obtained through experience, contacts, search or physical inspection—and commercial information sources would seem more effective here.

We are finally ready for the type of product-specific information that is of prime concern in this work. You are looking for data about the many different brands and models of tape recorders that may meet your buying criteria more or less satisfactorily. Among these are physical characteristics (dimensions, weight, materials and components of which product is made, etc.), and perhaps the processes by which it has been manufactured. The most critical category of information is performance data. These include functional characteristics (in the tape recorder case such attributes as faithfulness of reproduction, amplification, tonal range, number of speeds, constancy of speed, mono versus stereo versus quadraphonic, etc.), as well as dysfunctional ones (distortion, hum, inconveniently placed or sized controls, parts subject to premature breakdown, etc.). Durability, economy, energy consumption, relative need and ease of maintenance and repair, features endangering health, and safety are other important performance aspects. You may also be interested in the impact on the environment of the product in use or at the time of disposal.

No man—or woman—is, or has ever been, a pure functionalist. Thus, you also want to be posted on such matters as beauty and style. And for most of us, some products have other psychosocial characteristics, and our selection of brand or model may be influenced by this. In any culture, certain versions of the product will express individuality while others express belonging; some will indicate that you are "in" with fashion, others that you are "out" of it; some that you are (or think of yourself as) a sportsman, etc. If you are interested in keeping up with the Joneses (or the Durants, Schmidts, Erikssons), or are determined to keep down with them, there are ways of expressing these ambitions in your marketplace decisions. It is not part of the purpose of this book to argue for or against the desirability of psychosocial characteristics in products, nor to engage in the polemics as to how these characteristics originate. We do believe, however, that it would indeed be foolish to deny that they are important, or to overlook them simply because they cannot be tested by engineers.

That you need price information is self-evident, including such matters as credit, discounts, and trade-ins. Finally, you will wish to know about local outlets for the product, the reputations of maker and seller, and the availability of parts and service.

Table I-1 gives an overview of some of the main categories of product information, and the relative capabilities of personal, commercial and independent sources, *as they are currently operative*, to satisfy the respective needs for data. The table is not based on research—the rankings are subjective. It is our hope that the research needed to evaluate the capacities of various sources of information needs in a more factual manner will make more rapid strides in the future than hitherto. In the meantime, the table makes the simple but vital point that, being parts of a total CIS, the different sources of information supplement each other. The table further suggests that each source may have certain built-in advantages and disadvantages in any given economic, technical, political and cultural environment. We had the United States in mind in preparing the table. In a country with legalized resale price control by manufacturers, the

Table I-1. A View of Current Information Source Capability Rankings by Type of Information

| | Information source | | |
Information type	personal	commercial	independent
Alternative market offerings	3	2	1
Physical characteristics	3	1	2
Performance characteristics	2	3	1
Style	1	2	3
Psychosocial characteristics	2	1	3
Price	2	1	3
Local availability, service, parts, seller reputation	1	2	3
New product developments	3	1	2

Legend: Independent consumer information (CI) programs are given highest rank as a source of product performance data. Personal information comes next, while commercial sources appear to be lagging in this area. On the other hand, commercial sources are clearly preeminent as regards price information, this area being one of manifest weakness among CI programs.

capability of CI programs as a source of price information would give independent sources a ranking of 1—as a single firm price could be readily inserted for each brand in any comparative survey.[2] Examining the table, the reader should further bear in mind that no CI programs have anywhere near the effective spread enjoyed by personal and commercial sources, although CI impact on the Information Seekers as a group may well be comparable to that of any other source. An analogous table could clearly be prepared for information in the services market.

The inherent needs for product information before any given purchase will vary considerably between individuals as well as societies. Generally speaking, the needs would seem to be more significant:

the more expensive the product relative to the consumer's budget
the more complex the product
the greater the functional distance between consumer and producer
the greater the bias exhibited by any single source of information
the less the personal experience of the consumer
the less well-educated the consumer
the less the public protection of consumers

There will be reason to discuss the interrelations of consumer information, education and protection later. The individual consumer may or may not perceive his needs for information, and he may or may not be able to give a fair evaluation of his own degree of informedness at any stage in the decisionmaking process. Even though aware of a need for additional information, he may not be willing to spend the additional time, money and nervous energy necessary to get it. This is a vital observation, as it demonstrates the critical need for simplified CI programs, such as quality marks certifying a minimum standard of performance.

BRIEFING THE READER

In the preface we said that the relationship between this book and the prior volumes of the ICIS project is somewhat analogous to that between the forest and the trees. It would be unfair to readers of those volumes to be overly repetitious here. Yet it will be necessary to illustrate our general points with specific examples from our earlier work. We shall freely cite names, or abbreviations, of CI organizations and journals with which the reader may not be familier. To help out in such instances, a listing of abbreviations and names of these institutions by alphabet and country appears in Appendix A. The reader who would like some background without total immersion in detail is recommended to acquaint himself with the executive summary and Part I on prototype CI programs in the *Handbook* and the executive summary and the epilog of *The Information Seekers*. Again, we emphasize that this book is written to stand on its own feet.

The briefing of the reader also includes the statement of our personal predilections and prejudices that follows.

The Authors' Viewpoint

This being a policy-oriented book, there is special reason for the reader to be wary of the personal values of the authors. We have a basic faith in the merits of an open market system predicated on the interplay of market forces and the private and collective initiatives of consumers as well as producers. We share the view that the open market system is vaguely but inextricably linked to political democracy. We think that abuses of competition as well as monopoly should be prevented or tempered by public policy, notably antitrust and consumer policy. What is called pluralism in political life we think of as *alternativism* in the market economy. We imagine that a Milton Friedman and a J.K. Galbraith, both in their own "wrong," are about equally far removed from both what is and what should be in the economic system.[3]

More directly germane is our belief that the consumer information gap referred to earlier represents a serious challenge to private and public policymakers. The growing gap implies an erosion of consumer sovereignty. It also threatens the viability of the open market system, tied as it is to informed consumers making intelligent decisions at least a fair part of the time. We see independent consumer information programs—and preferably a variety of them working in decentralized orchestration—as one means of meeting this challenge. We also feel that individuals have a right to as much information about market offerings as they please, as long as the cost of supplying the information is not prohibitive. Freedom of information is part of a great Western tradition. Moreover, research strongly indicates that the Information Seekers are the true vigilantes of the marketplace.

Organization of the Book

This book is arranged in four main sections:

Part I is devoted to a discussion of the purpose of the book and the theory and philosophy of CI programs. Chapter One analyzes the emergence of the consumer information gap in affluent and postindustrial societies. Chapter Two develops a rationale for CI programs against the background of consumer sovereignty and open market policy, as well as an overview of the total field of consumer policy seen in the context of consumer rights and responsibilities.

Part II is concerned with the content of CI programs. Chapter Three examines the operating aspects of such programs in detail. Some matters potentially within their scope are also taken up. Chapter Four focuses on the particularities of comparative testing, informative labeling and quality certification and examines the potential for the interaction of such programs in CI systems. In Chapter Five the impact of CI programs is discussed. Such an evaluation is necessarily tentative due to the methodological problems involved.

Part III deals with the context of CI programs. Chapter Six develops a theoretical framework for such analysis, based on an ecologic view of organizations. In Chapter Seven the theory is applied to an analysis of the dynamics of CI programs in Sweden in the 1940–75 period. Chapter Eight undertakes a cross-cultural comparison of the ecology of CI programs in the North Atlantic community of nations. It is also concerned with international cooperation.

Part IV deals with the futurology of CI systems. Against the background of environmental trends and future information needs, a forecast is made of the development of personal, commercial and independent product information. New types of CI programs are predicted, based on computerized databanks, possibly supplemented by videophones and/or home TV sets with dialogue capability. Decentralized CIS based on concerted action among commercial, personal and independent consumer information programs are outlined, based on the premise that such systems are at once plausible and desirable. The extension of such systems to the international scene is viewed in a similar light.

NOTES

1. Thorelli, Becker and Engledow, *The Information Seekers*, ch. 2, uses the terms buyer sources, commercial sources and neutral sources.

2. Please note that we are not advocating resale price control by manufacturers.

3. German-speaking readers may find some similarities in viewpoint in Gerhard Scherhorn, *Gesucht: der mündige Verbraucher* (Düsseldorf: Droste, 1974) and *Verbraucherintresse und Verbraucherpolitik* (Göttingen: Otto Schwartz, 1975).

Part I

Consumer Information (CI) Programs: Philosophy

Chapter 1

The Consumer Information Gap

THE GENESIS OF THE INFORMATION GAP

Picture yourself as an average consumer at the end of the eighteenth century. You are enjoying every minute of life, and looking ahead a couple of hundred years you realize that the generation then around will refer to your era as "the good old days." Why? Because you do not have a consumer information problem. You only buy maybe a score different products in a year. You buy them locally—a trip to the next town takes a day or more and is apt to be expensive. When you buy something—a pair of shoes, let us say—there is always a specialized outlet to go to. As a matter of fact, there are only one or two shoe shops in your town. There is certainly no problem of getting a grasp of the market.

What is more, the man in the shop is a true expert on shoes. He *has* to be, because as master cobbler he personally makes the shoes he sells. Indeed, if you are well-to-do at all, chances are that he will custom-make them just for you. You spend quite a while getting all the information from him—after all, what else is there to do with your time? How shoes function is not hard to understand—and, come to think of it, all other products you come in contact with are really pretty simple. So your discussion centers on issues of size and price. As your cobbler has a near monopoly, the price is high, and you also find his everyday assortment narrow. But that, again, simplifies information handling. It is also wonderful to know that if you do have a complaint you will always know to whom to go! In addition, the rate of change in markets is close to zero. What you learned about shoes the first time you bought a pair is valid for a lifetime.

To be sure, this is a simplified (as well as glorified) view of craft and guild society. But it shows that consumer information could not possibly be a social issue. The customer orientation about which we hear so much today was never discussed, simply because it was an automatic, built-in feature of that type of economic system. Indeed, the cobbler almost literally put himself into your shoes.

Now hop into your time machine and make it stop at 1977 (if you can)—in an affluent, postindustrial society such as Switzerland or the United States. The contrast is almost overwhelming.

1. There is *a product, brand, and model proliferation* of bewildering proportions. *Test*—the journal of Stiftung Warentest of Germany—in January 1969 reported on thirty-two brands and types of "ordinary" 60 watt light bulbs. The same year the *Guide de l'acheteur* of the French standardization organization, AFNOR, listed 1,060 different types, models and brands of refrigerators meeting French standards. Any big supermarket now stocks 6,000–8,000 different items, which may well be more than the total number of different products 200 years ago. Dr. Charles C. Edwards, a former U.S. Commissioner of Food and Drugs, estimated that nonprescription drugs on the American market may number half a million different items.[1] The proliferation process has been accelerated by the emergence of private brands, the use of several brand names for many generically identical products (synthetic fibers, drugs), and differences in a single branded product as you cross national borders (Kleenex, Nescafé, Philips TVs in Europe).

2. The *space between products* is forever getting narrower. Between the refrigerator and the freezer is the two door combination, between the maxi and the mini is the midi. We are rapidly becoming faced with one continuous market, where all products are competing with each other. Certainly, for almost any everyday need there are now several generically quite different products that will do the job. In addition, multipurpose products are on the increase, such as refrigerator-freezer and recorder-amplifier-radio combinations. We may yet see the day when to be a true shopper you should compare not only all brands of a given product but all brands of *all* products each time you make a purchase!

3. We justly marvel at modern technology. But even while it is making life easier and richer it makes it more complex—because *products are so much more complex*. Compare your car with a horse and buggy, the TV set with the crystal wireless of fifty years ago, or the sewing machine with your great grandmother's needle and thread.

We find a vast amount of capital equipment in the home. A modern home may have a dozen electric motors or more, from the washing machine and recordplayer to the electric carving knife, razor and toothbrush. Running the household is increasingly like running a firm.

4. *Product characteristics* are subject to rapid change. Think of the change from eyeglasses to contact lenses, from mini to maxi, from the DC3 to the Concorde SST, from products made of wood, glass and a host of other materials to plastic. New York supermarkets added some 3,500 new items and dropped another 3,900 in 1971.[2]

5. Our society is one of *mass production and mass consumption.* The essence of industrialization is the use of economies of scale and specialization in production. This in itself was sufficient to create a vast functional, geographic and communications distance between producer and consumer. Lately we have added mass *distribution,* with its emphasis on self-service and removal of the last vestiges of personal contact between seller and buyer. This anonymization of the distribution process has naturally served to reduce the sense of personal responsibility to customers among sales personnel. It becomes more and more difficult for an intelligent buyer to accept the notion that he can substitute trust in the establishment for information about the products it purveys.[3]

As mass distribution must accompany mass production, so *mass promotion* is the inevitable companion of mass distribution. The problem with mass promotion is that, to the individuals in the market for a given product, most of the advertising for all other products he sees in his paper or on TV or hears on his radio merely raises the general noise level around him. Indeed, it may even make it harder to find the information relevant to the specific good of interest to him.

6. *Nonmetro areas are only semimarkets.* It is a fact of life that only a part of the enormous range of selection brought about by product and brand proliferation in most markets is represented in cities below, say, 100,000 inhabitants and in rural areas. Such a state of affairs is "natural" in simple economic terms. However, it does mean that consumers in such communities are underprivileged in the sense that they will lack a considerable fund of comparative product information.

7. *Time is at a premium.* As so imaginatively portrayed in S.B. Linder's *The Harried Leisure Class,* time is the ultimate constraint in postindustrial society, taking precedence over all others.[4] Nowadays, time is not merely money but also a scant resource of whose irreplaceability affluents are getting ever more conscious.

8. *The rise of discretionary income* is the main characteristic of an

affluent society. The very essence of it is that great numbers of consumers are no longer preoccupied with the problem of subsistence; instead they have found that relative prosperity has brought the challenge of choice, including difficult questions of resource allocation and brand selection. "The consumer" has traditionally been the housewife purchasing on behalf of the family. In the last thirty years her husband has been taking an increasingly active part in the shopping process; and today, the consumer is typically *all* family members, from the young child with his allowance to the retiree on a pension. In addition, increased well-being is daily bringing more buyers of sophisticated goods, including great numbers who have little prior personal experience of these goods and are less well educated than the traditional middle class.

9. In the wake of discretionary income and the premium on time has followed a *diversification of buying criteria.* My car is not just a means of transport, it must be sporty to express my youth, contain a radio and tape stereo hi-fi center, have air conditioning and have extrastrong rear suspension to handle the vacation trailer. The score of additional options permits *the individualization of demand,* so characteristic of postindustrial society, some chance of expressing itself. You see what this leads to: further complexity, even further difficulty in penetrating and comprehending the real—or alleged—differences between alternatives.

10. In addition, well-being has brought a more acute *social awareness.* This takes at least two different expressions of relevance here. It adds further to our buying criteria: not only do we have to know whether the product will meet our own needs, but also whether it is ecologically sound in design and packaging. We are also more sensitive to the needs of the underprivileged groups of society, and we are becoming increasingly aware that *one* of their problems is that they are underinformed, at least by our own standards.[5]

11. *Commercial information is sometimes deceptive.* Advertising in particular has become the whipping boy of critics of commercial information. Many FTC cases in the U.S., many complaints to advertising ethics boards in a dozen countries, as well as private and public studies,[6] indicate that a fair amount of deception in modern advertising does indeed exist. It is also conceivable that the very complexity of the contemporary marketplace facilitates unfair practices, although in the absence of any real documentation one may seriously doubt that such practices are on the increase.[7] Being of an ecological bent, we subscribe to the school of "situational ethics." In this view, a given society tends to have the business ethics it "deserves"; that is, there is no particular reason to assume that in the long run the stan-

dards of business are very much lower (or higher) than in society at large.

However, this does not exclude the possibility of a "cultural lag" existing between business ethics and social expectations at any given time. That business ethics may indeed be lagging—or at least perceived as lagging—is suggested by *The Information Seekers* and other studies of the social reputation of advertising in several countries.

12. Finally—and this is the real clincher—*consumer expectations with regard to product performance seem to grow exponentially with the level of affluence.*[8] To a fair extent this revolution in expectations is accompanied by rapidly increasing aspiration levels regarding product information among the Information Seekers, the elite group of consumers.

To sum it all up: the proliferation, change and complexity in products and variants has created a veritable explosion in the amount of total information needed to keep on top of the market. Incidentally, the information explosion is not limited to products, but affects politics, economics, science, sports and all other fields of human endeavor, meaning that product information has a greatly intensified competition with all other types of information to contend with. As if this "info explosion" were not enough of a problem, we have two major exacerbating factors to reckon with. First, personalized information sources—whether in the form of knowledgeable salesclerks or of prior personal experience of the buyer himself—are steadily losing in significance,[9] while such new sources as TV advertising really fall short of meeting the same need. Second, the price we subconsciously place on our time is rising at a fast clip, meaning that the cost of information gathering—or search, as decision theorists would say—is getting higher every day. These forces have conspired to create a social and economic problem complex that we may aptly call the *consumer information gap*. The present work is devoted to important types of social action that have been or may be taken to deal with this problem complex.

THE REAL GAP AND THE PERCEIVED GAP

It is important to make a distinction between the "real" (objective) and the "perceived" (subjective) gap. The real gap would be a measure of the difference between the omniscience of the consumer in regard to a given product market assumed by classic economic theory and the actual knowledge[10] he possesses. While in some sense, the closing of the real information gap might be an ideal symbol of the consumerist movement, it is hardly attainable. There are several good reasons for this statement. First, while the average producer, by being a specialist in his particular wares, is likely always to remain better informed about them than is the average consumer,[11] it is a commonplace experience that producers and distributors do not know "everything" about competitive offerings. Indeed, often they have a rather distorted view of what happens to their *own* brand in the hands of the final consumer—knowledge that might well be of critical importance to its long-term survival in the marketplace. To expect the average consumer ever to know as much about television sets as the average producer or distributor of such sets would clearly be to expect too much. The further projection of this idea, that the average consumer should know as much as the average producer of *every* product that he buys, is a staggering one.[12]

Second, if it were seriously attempted to "pump up" the consumer with enough information to close the real gap completely, he would probably burst at the seams in the process. Indeed, even if this heroic briefing activity were confined to those markets of personal relevance to him, it would most likely demand so much time that there would be no room for him to make any practical use of the information, let alone to indulge in any interest other than shopping. Third, the costs of such an information program would be truly astronomical; most likely they would be well beyond the resources even of postindustrial society.

Thus far we have assumed that the typical consumer is aware of the real gap and anxious to close it—or at least receptive to efforts in his environment to ameliorate the situation. Actually, however, the most serious problem facing product information programs is that the information gap as *perceived* by most consumers is rather modest—indeed, for most convenience goods it is a rather trivial matter. While surprisingly little research has been done to find out how well informed consumers really are about the marketplace,[13] it seems clear that the average consumer considers himself fairly well informed,[14] and thinks that he is able to fill the perceived gap in any new product market he might enter without much difficulty. That consumers think they are fairly well informed about product markets is no more remarkable than the fact that most farmers in underdeveloped countries think they know whatever is worth knowing about agricultural practices. Yet the explanation of growing numbers of consumer complaints and the tide of consumerism is likely to be found in part in underinformation.

It would seem that consumers consciously or, more often, subconsciously adopt a strategy of "satisficing" with regard to information. That is, they care only for a certain level of market knowledge (varying by product, to be sure), without any greater ambition than achieving a reasonably satisfactory purchase in a plurality of cases. A principal premise of ours is that the current market information system is deficient. We believe that this system may be improved to the extent of yielding more information for less input of consumer time and money. We also think that this system, if left unimproved, is not likely to provide the market transparency base needed to maintain "workable competition" in the still more complex markets of tomorrow.

INFORMATION OVERLOAD AND INFORMATION STRESS

It stands to reason, and has long been assumed in psychomedical literature,[15] that an individual may be overstimulated as he accumulates more and more information in a specific choice situation. A popular notion is that the average individual cannot effectively handle more than three or four alternatives in making a reasonably complex decision. Beyond this point, information "overload," frustration or even outright stress will set in, and the decision is apt to suffer. Information stress is also used in a different manner, referring to the perpetual overstimulation many people feel subjected to in our complex society with its high level of background "noise" or static—much of it originating in the marketplace.

Thus far, little research has been done on information overload in consumer buying situations. What little has been done does suggest that the conventional wisdom in the field is realistic.[16] On the other hand, the realism and validity of these laboratory studies with college students (simulating detergent purchases!) has been seriously and, to our mind, justly questioned.[17] To the specific points raised by other critics we would add that the effects of subjects likely having minimum thresholds on certain performance criteria and of their possibly changing their preferences under the impact of the *educational* experience provided by CI was apparently disregarded. In any case, as a consumer in real life himself determines how many brands he will consider, this type of experiment has little or nothing to say about how much or how little information should be contained in CI programs (which constitute only a small share of total available product information in the first place). The fact that over two million Americans pay $11 per year to get *Consumer Reports* does suggest that as far as the Information Seekers are concerned we still have not reached the point of overload.

For average consumers we still do not know how much information is "enough." We do know, however, that different consumers look for different characteristics in products. Further, CI programs in large part are not aimed at adding new information, but are to be viewed as instruments of transforming, supplementing and systematizing information from commercial and personal sources. Finally, there is the philosophical issue of the consumer's right to know, as long as costs of information provision are within reason (see Chapter Two).

The possibility of information overload does, however, serve to remind us of three important influences on effectiveness of information programs—namely, motivation, education and the packaging of information. By and large, an individual will assimilate and/or make use of information only if he is motivated to do so. In a free society people cannot be "pumped up" with information against their own will. True, they may be subjected to a barrage of facts and "angles," but everything not perceived as pertinent will pass into the oblivion of background noise almost automatically. This is precisely where education in general, and particularly consumer education, comes in. Its prime purpose is to make us information conscious and intellectually curious, and to assist us in gaining whatever control over our own lives we can. In a truly basic sense, consumer education is the most important marketing instrument for CI programs. But the overload issue also reminds us that people have different degrees of information-mindedness and tolerance for information stress. This means that a variety of CI programs should be available to suit varying needs, a matter extensively discussed in this volume. It means also that information packaging—the use of standard formats, simplification, efficient presentation techniques and so on—is a matter of crucial importance to the use and usefulness of the information disseminated by such programs.

CONSUMER POLICY: INFORMATION, EDUCATION AND PROTECTION

Consumer policy is a helpful concept more widely used in Europe than in the United States. Broadly speaking, consumer policy includes the familiar threesome: consumer information, education and protection. To position our work properly it is necessary to provide working definitions of these terms and to discuss briefly how the three types of policy relate to each other. In a general sense, consumer information comprises all data about individual markets and offerings.[18] It is oriented to specific buying decisions. By contrast, consumer education may be thought of as "consumer civics": consumer education provides the knowledge foundation necessary to develop citizens into intelligent consumers, or at least to make their self-development into intelligent consumers possible. Thus consumer education extends all the way from conveying an understanding of how the market economy operates, of the consumer decisionmaking process, and of consumer rights and responsibilities, to such pragmatic matters as the properties of different textile fibres and dietary concerns.[19] Consumer protection refers to measures taken by others than the individual consumer to safeguard consumer rights. Consumer protection ranges all the way from competition (antitrust) policy to maintenance of open markets via the control of deceptive practices and the handling of consumer complaints to standards and other rules and regulations for maintaining consumer health and safety.

Clearly, the distinctions between consumer information, education and protection are not hard and fast. For instance, the same information may have multiple uses. Americans will find the phrase "The Surgeon General has determined that cigarette smoking is dangerous to your health" on each and every cigarette package. That the message is intended for consumer protection is self-evident. But it could also be viewed as educational. And it could also be regarded as consumer information about any single brand you might happen to select. As regards the border area between consumer education and information we may say that the more "generic" the data are in terms of product or consumer characteristics, the more likely it is that consumer education is the appropriate term; and that the more specifically they are related to individual offerings (brands) or to the needs of individual consumers, the more appropriate it is to speak of consumer information. As regards product information, this distinction is illustrated by Figure 1-1. The information labeled "generic" for some purposes might be labeled as consumer education rather than consumer information. Similarly, information about an entirely new product may be viewed as consumer education just as well as consumer information. Although no part of the matrix is beyond the purview of consumer information programs, their main thrust is in the lower right hand field of cross-brand comparisons. This, incidentally, is what we shall call the *brand decision*, logically preceded by the *product decision* in the upper part of the matrix.

In spite of the areas of overlap, there is a core area of difference between consumer education, information and protection. Perhaps in the end these differences spring from the distinct underlying philosophies of the three. It would seem that the rationale of consumer education is "help to self-help," while consumer information assumes that the consumer is ready to help himself. Consumer protection, on the other hand, proceeds from the notion that the consumer needs a

Type of information	Market offerings covered	
	one	several
Generic	*product type* (characteristics of reel-to-reel tape recorders)	*cross-product* (casette, 8-track cartridge, reel-to-reel recorders compared)
Specific	*single brand* (features of Roberts reel-to-reel recorder)	*cross-brand* (Roberts, Sony, Tandberg, Viking, etc., reel-to-reel recorders)

Figure 1–1. Product Information Matrix

guardian angel (or at least a policeman) to keep the market open, to enforce his rights and to protect his health and safety. There will be reason to return to these variants of consumer policy in the next chapter.

CONSUMER INFORMATION (CI) IN A TECHNICAL SENSE: PRODUCT INFORMATION SOURCES

It would be foolhardy indeed to set out to study the total flow of consumer information in the broad sense of data about market offerings stemming from all conceivable sources. Our research was focused on consumer information in a more restricted and technical sense. Under this definition consumer information (CI) is information about consumer products and services provided by a party with no direct commercial interest in the promotion of these offerings. The project was further limited to broad-scope CI programs in the North Atlantic community of nations—that is, programs aimed at consumer goods in general, and thus not confined to one product or group of products (such as appliances). A great number of single industry programs exist, generally created by trade associations or industry-sponsored research institutes but sometimes by law, as in the case of wool products labeling in the U.S. We have no doubt that in some countries such programs provide more CI in the aggregate than do the broad-scope organizations, although the independence and objectivity of single industry programs at times may be subject to question.

Having thus delimited our study, it still behooves us to relate these

Type of source	Offerings covered	
	single brand	several brands
Commercial	most advertising exclusive dealers manufacturer, catalogs, manuals	comparative ads multi-brand stores auto shows, trade fairs
Personal (past experience and friends)	had brand X before	had several brands before
Independent	American Dental Association endorses Crest toothpaste Government approves a new drug Consumers Union reports on a new product	market overviews computerized CI bank comparative testing informative labeling quality certification

Figure 1-2. Principal Sources of Specific Product Information

CI programs to the total consumer information flow. This flow of more or less accurate product information is of course enormous in affluent societies. In Figure 1-2 the flow is broken down by sources of information and by single versus multibrand coverage. In a sense, Figure 1-2 is a breakdown of the lower half of Figure 1-1 by types of information source. We note that commercial sources, primarily in the guise of advertising and sales promotion in all forms, play a critical role in providing product information—notably about single brands. The problem here is that promotion also has the purpose of persuasion, which is, of course, perfectly legitimate in itself.[20] The multipurpose nature of advertising may, however, result in biased, sometimes outright misleading information, and its mass communications, repetitive character often results in our receiving the information when we neither need it nor want it. Nor is past personal experience always a good guide to future purchases. Advertising and personal experience are the prime information sources we have relied on in the past. Both have grown vastly in quantity if not necessarily in quality; and, in any case, they have not been able to bridge the yawning information gap. Again, this is a prime reason for our interest in independent programs permitting comparisons between several brands of a product, as indicated in the lower right-hand cell of the figure.

TYPOLOGY OF CI PROGRAMS

This work is focused on what we have called *the testmakers*,[21] i.e., organizations carrying on comparative testing, informative labeling and quality certification programs and not themselves having any commercial interest in the offerings covered. Among independent sources of product information including many brands of the same product Figure 1-2 also names market overviews and computerized CI banks. Market overview here connotes comparative reports based on information from trade sources (rather than comparative tests) gathered by an independent organization. Among others, most testing organizations publish such overviews from time to time as well as test reports. As market overviews are a great deal cheaper to execute than comparative tests, such digests provide an efficient means of increasing product coverage. Long a feature of photographic and high-fidelity journals, such overviews can clearly be of considerable interest to consumers. Here as elsewhere in the information field it would seem important that the origin of the data as well as the interests of the organizations publishing them are also made clear to the consumer whenever these matters might not be obvious.[22]

Not yet more than a highly exciting image on the consumer information horizon, computerized CI banks are briefly discussed in Chapter Nine.

In our parlance, *comparative testing* denotes a special kind of market survey carried out by an independent body. This organization selects the individual samples of the brands of a given product (or products, if the focus is on substitute products) to be tested, and also prescribes the characteristics to be tested, and the test methods to be used. The results obtained for each brand are reported, and are frequently cross-tabulated. A generalized judgment about the whole product—usually including a consideration of price and often of non-testable but relevant features—may be added in the form of an overall rating or a categorization in terms of relative recommendability ("best buy," "not acceptable," etc.) as a consumer counseling device. Such conclusions are almost invariably reached by most of the comparative testers nowadays.[23] A small and declining number of organizations prefer to let the tests of individual characteristics and products simply speak for themselves, and hence generally do not include any overall product ratings. Comparative test reports tend to be fairly lengthy and technical. They are generally published in special journals focused on subscribers rather than on newsstand sales.

Informative labeling here denotes an activity in which an organization, after establishing certain norms as to the range and depth of information about product characteristics to be declared on the label, will permit interested producers to attach the informative label of the organization to their products. The label on a certain brand of a given product will state where on the scale established for each characteristic (color fastness, proportion of wool contents, etc.) that particular brand is to be found. This is determined in advance by tests. A manufacturer may continue to use the label only as long as his products comply with the information given on it.

Labels generally give ratings for testable properties only. Wherever possible, the characteristics selected are those deemed important from a consumer and performance point of view. There is no overall rating, but separate ratings for each of the selected properties. In theory this enables practically any product to be labeled, irrespective of its quality. The idea is that a label allows the consumer himself to judge whether the product is suitable for him. Under labeling, *information* is standardized rather than products, declares a brochure from the Swedish VDN, until recently the pace-setting organization in the field.

Quality certification, as the term suggests, indicates that the product carrying the seal at least measures up to the minimum norm or the threshold level of performance or the materials contents established by the certifying agency. Again, advance tests are performed and products may carry the seal only so long as they comply with, or exceed, the minimum norm. As regards both labeling and quality certification, routine control that performance levels involved are in fact attained is often entrusted to the producers themselves. However, all organizations retain the right to undertake control tests ex officio, and several will do so on an intermittent basis. The leading quality certification bodies are the RAL of Germany and the Qualité-France. Some of the quality seals of the latter organization incorporate informative labels.

An important practical distinction should be observed concerning sponsorship of CI programs. Comparative testing organizations tend to be sponsored either by consumers subscribing to test reports or by governments. These organizations generally maintain an arms length relationship to manufacturers. Economywide labeling and certification schemes—thus far voluntary in nature in all countries—on the other hand, are clearly dependent on producer cooperation. Government is typically giving at least a financial assist. While consumer interests are always represented, consumer organizations have lately played a less prominent role in these types of programs. By and large, CI programs of the types discussed here have not in and of themselves provided a sufficient basis for commercial ventures in recent years, although at one time the journal *DM* (Deutsche Mark) was quite successful.[24] However, several well-known general consumer magazines—

such as *Quattrosoldi* in Italy and *Good Housekeeping* in the United States—will include reports on comparative testing or quality certificates among their materials.

INFORMATION AS A PUBLIC GOOD

Experience from the U.K., the U.S., Germany, the Netherlands and Belgium indicates that it is indeed possible to make the publication of comparative testing (CT) journals a financially self-sustaining venture. This is true even in fairly small, though affluent, countries. Note, however, that such journals will always have a limited audience of Information Seekers. Indeed, for many years CT organizations tended to avoid disseminating popularized or condensed versions of their reports via the press or the broadcast media for fear that they would be cutting into their own potential market.[25] The German experience of disseminating summaries of test reports from the journal *test* via hundreds of local newspapers and several radio and TV stations does indicate, however, that as long as a significant market potential remains untapped, such activity may be an effective promotion device in building the stock of paying subscribers to the journal. Beyond this, a social contribution is being rendered to millions of non-subscribers.

Suppose we now try to reach average consumers by another route, by publishing a suitably condensed version of our CT journal in the form of a comic magazine sold at, say 25 cents. Would it be a success? Although a definite answer cannot be given, there is some reason for skepticism. The trouble with information is that you do not know whether you want it until you have it. It is also irreversible—you cannot buy it and then return it, expecting to get your money back. Average consumers tend to hold CI in fairly low esteem in the first place, and the difficulty of assessing its value in advance is probably why many do not get it by comparative shopping or otherwise, even though the cost involved might be just a few minutes or dimes.

What we have just said applies even more in contemplating informative labels or quality certificates affixed to products at the point of purchase. These are truly *public goods* in the sense that they are available to every individual, whether or not he has borne any of the costs of providing them, and in that the information obtainable in this way is not diminished by an individual making use of it. Simplified information of this kind is also easy to transmit from person to person at close to zero cost. Under these circumstances, individual consumers cannot be expected spontaneously to pay for it.[26] Thus it is that the costs of all labeling and certification programs are defrayed by business and/or government. In either case, of course, ultimate consumers will have to foot the bill in higher prices and/or taxes. But at least the individual will have the satisfaction that he and his neighbors are "all in the same boat."

NOTES

1. U.S. Office of Consumer Affairs, *Consumer News* (January 15, 1972): 1.

2. A report by Sales Area Marketing, Inc., quoted in the *New York Times* (December 24, 1971): 37.

3. Paradoxically, this development in consumer marketing is taking place at a time when the role of trust in the supplier is a buying criterion of strongly increasing importance in industrial marketing.

In personal services such as dentistry, law and medicine, licensing of the professions involved has been the typical way of "guaranteeing" the service, thus ostensibly removing the need for these professionals to provide consumer information. It is, of course, a commonplace observation that the faith of the public in the sanctity of this system is rapidly eroding in our time.

4. S.B. Linder, *The Harried Leisure Class* (New York: Columbia University Press, 1970).

5. Underinformedness need not stem from lack of information in an absolute sense. It may result from information not being available in the right form or at the right place and time, from culturally conditioned lack of receptivity to information and from a variety of other causes.

6. See, e.g., studies commissioned by the Royal Advertising Commission in Sweden 1971–74 and the study of misleading advertising in Britain and Germany sponsored by BEUC in 1974.

7. For a discussion of business practices in the United States seventy to one hundred years ago, see Hans B. Thorelli, *The Federal Antitrust Policy* (Baltimore: John Hopkins Press; and London: Allen & Unwin, 1955): ch. 1.

8. The mechanism underlying this process has not been adequately researched. It may be a reflection of a more general process conceivably underlying the entire consumerist movement. It might be hypothesized that in affluent societies consumers, having found that "material satisfaction is not everything in life," are making market institutions the scapegoat for what is really a much broader sense of frustration.

9. It is a fair assumption that many modern salesclerks learn more about their products from their customers than from the employers and manufacturers they represent.

10. By "knowledge" we mean information assimilated for decisionmaking purposes.

11. Compare the statement attributed to Richard H. Holton: the consumer is a part-time amateur buyer facing full-time professional sellers. We might add that no one sells by mistake, but many buy by mistake.

12. Note that here we are not commenting on the desirability of making information *available*.

13. What advertising effectiveness surveys suggest in this regard would seem to be relatively discouraging.

14. See, for instance, the surveys of French consumers sponsored by Institut National de Consommation and conducted by l'Institut Français d'Opinion Publique in 1968, *L'information des consommateurs* (December 1968), and in 1971, *Consommation Actualité* (December 1971).

15. James G. Miller, "Information Input Overload and Psychopathology," *American Journal of Psychiatry* 116 (1960): 695-704.

16. The most well-known researcher in the field is Jacob Jacoby. See, e.g., Jacob Jacoby, D.E. Speller and C.A. Kohn, "Brand Choice Behavior as a Function of Information Load," *Journal of Marketing Research* 11 (February 1974): 63-69.

17. See, e.g., John O. Summers, "Less Information Is Better?" *Journal of Marketing Research* 11 (November 1974): 467-68; J. Edward Russo, "More Information Is Better: A Reevaluation of Jacoby, Speller and Kohn," *Journal of Consumer Research* 1 (December 1974): 68-72; and William L. Wilkie, "Consumer Info Processing Research: Product Labeling," Marketing Science Institute, Rept. 75-104 (March 1975).

18. In our research it was necessary to employ the term in a more technical and restricted sense, see below: p. 26.

The word "offerings" is used in the definition above as referring to both products and services.

19. The Canadian Consumer Council defined consumer education as follows: "Consumer education is the development within the individual of the skills, concepts and understandings that are required for everyday living and that help him, within the framework of his own values, to participate fully and effectively in the market place." *Survey of Consumer Education in Canada* (1970): 3.

20. Indeed, experience indicates that even freely available consumer information from independent sources needs aggressive promotion to reach an audience. It is to be noted that the distinction between persuasion and "objective" information is nowhere nearly as ironclad as many a critic of advertising would have us believe. See Chapter Four: 124 f.

21. Hans B. Thorelli, "The Testmakers—A Non-Comparative Study of Organized Consumer Information in Europe," *Proceedings of the American Marketing Association* (Fall Conference, 1965): 51-71.

22. Some European testing organizations—such as UFIDEC in Belgium—on occasion publish market overviews in a format confusingly similar to comparative test reports.

23. An unkindly observer might well say that the State Consumer Board in Sweden starts from conclusions.

24. For a detailed discussion of *DM* see *Handbook*. According to the editor, *DM* was again breaking even in 1975.

25. Until recently the media were not interested in paying for the information and, as we have discussed in the *Handbook*, in many countries and instances there has been a problem of retaining control of the integrity of the information redistributed. "In 1974, Consumers Union sold three-minute spot features, incorporating CI and advice, to more than 50 TV stations . . . . By the end of 1975

this venture had yet to become self-sustaining financially." E. Scott Maynes, *Decision-Making for Consumers* (New York: MacMillan, 1976): 147.

26. Mancur Olson, Jr., *The Logic of Collective Action—Public Goods and The Theory of Groups* (Boston: Harvard University Press, 1965). It is a different matter that Information Seekers might be willing to buy a catalog listing all the labeled or certified brands, as this might save a good deal of shopping around.

Chapter 2

Consumer Information in the Context of Consumer Rights and Responsibilities

THE CONSUMER INTEREST AND THE PUBLIC INTEREST

This chapter positions consumer information in a setting of consumer rights and responsibilities. It represents a search for a philosophy of consumer information—for its skyhooks and moorings, if you will. Adopting a funnel-type approach, our quest might well begin with a consideration of the relationship of the consumer interest and the public interest.[a]

It may sound trite to say that the public interest manifests itself in what the public and/or its representatives do by way of passing (or not passing) laws, rules and regulations, and taking (or not taking) decisions and actions in matters of political concern. For our purposes this is a sufficient definition, however, and volumes of political philosophy indicate that it is actually difficult to give the concept much more meaning and still retain a broad acceptance. The consumer interest, on the other hand, is perhaps most readily identified with established, or at least articulated, consumer rights. Paradoxically, the most important consumer right is hardly ever mentioned. This is the "freedom to consume," a right that is greater than and antecedent to the four consumer rights enunciated by John F. Kennedy in 1962 and since quoted thousands of times around the world.

We need to do no more than contrast the freedom to consume

[a]We are aware of but not discouraged by the fact that in the end the very notion of "interest" is metaphysical. So is "marginal utility" and "quality," but they are still indispensable concepts.

with the public interest as manifested in laws and official action to realize that the consumer interest and the public interest are *not* identical.[1] This is easily seen in a country like the USSR where consumption has been deliberately restricted for decades in favor of military and industrial development, and in the rationing systems artifically restraining private consumption in Western countries during World War II.[2] It is no use protesting that "we are all consumers." Everyone wears several hats and plays several roles, and, by definition, no single role (except perhaps that of the voter) can adequately express the public interest. Indeed, conceptually most consumers are also producers—and few have had the temerity to suggest that the producer interest is equal to the public interest.

The consumer interest, like any "special" interest, is a subset of the public interest. What is good for the consumer may not *always* be good for the country. Nevertheless, as it concerns everyone, the consumer interest is clearly a subset of grand importance. And to those of us who believe that inextricable links exist between political democracy and free markets, the consumer interest is a matter of paramount concern.

It must be admitted, however, that to define "the consumer interest" in specific situations tends to be a task fraught with ambiguity. The fractionalization of the consumer interest begins right in the marketplace. Preferences with regard to style, quality and price, as well as the total bundle of products desired, vary greatly among consumers of different income, age and educational groups and frequently even within these groups. The open market is the equilibrating mechanism among all these consumer "interests." Beyond the marketplace, some consumers are ecologically oriented in the process of consumption and the disposal of refuse while others are not, etc. Indeed, it is precisely because our role as consumers is such an all-pervasive aspect of life that the consumer interest is so differentiated. No doubt this is why it has proven impractical to bring about a unified consumer movement of major proportion in most countries.

In view of the preceding discussion, it is not self-evident that "more" or "better" consumer information is in either the consumer or the public interest. The legitimacy of such an assertion becomes especially doubtful when the costs of production and distribution of improved information are laid alongside the benefits. Thus, it is not surprising to find that a number of consumer radicals in Sweden are opposed to publicly sponsored comparative testing programs, claiming that such programs address themselves to a privileged few. We must also keep in mind that many, perhaps a majority, of consumers think of themselves as well informed, and thus most likely would not perceive any interest in CI programs. It may be objected that these consumers do not really know what their "true" interest is. This is, however, a somewhat dangerous rationale, used in the past to legitimatize both such noble ideas as compulsory education and such base ones as political dictatorship.

We must conclude that the notion of the "consumer interest" is insufficient to yield a categorical imperative in favor of improved consumer information. Somewhat paradoxically, however, we may still find that improved CI is in the public interest, even though not in the immediate interest of all—or even a plurality of—individual consumers. There will be reason to return to this proposition in later sections of this chapter.

CONSUMER SOVEREIGNTY

While not explicitly using the term, Adam Smith made a first approach at defining a state of consumer sovereignty: "Consumption is the sole end and purpose of all production; and the interest of the producer ought to be attended to, only so far as it may be necessary for promoting that of the consumer."[3] More recently, a keen British marketing writer observed that consumer sovereignty "signifies that it is the preferences of consumers, as shown by the ways in which they spend their money, that determine what merchandise is produced and which services supplied."[4] Jerome Rothenberg, in one of his classic articles on the subject,[5] reminds us that the simplest definition of consumer sovereignty is that "the customer is king." Sincere traders (and some not so sincere ones as well) are wont to declare that "the customer is always right." We note from the outset that the term may be used both in a descriptive and a normative manner.

Before we examine the consumer sovereignty concept and its implications in some detail we should observe that it may also be used to apply both to consumers as a group (the macro level) and to consumers as individuals (the micro level). At the macro level it would seem clear that consumer sovereignty has been increasing rapidly indeed in the more affluent nations around the North Atlantic.[6] Two important reasons for this rise in aggregate consumer power are increasing levels of education (bringing consumer sophistication and consciousness) and of discretionary income. Indeed, the very word "discretionary" is a symptom of sovereignty, implying resources that can be either withheld or spent in any manner and on any offerings consumers see fit. Another major lever bringing up consumer power relative to that of producers is the vastly increased cross-product competition referred to in Chapter One.[7] While there is little reason to worry about consumer sovereignty at the macro level this is not true with regard to the micro level. Paradoxically, individual consumer sovereignty has not increased—if anything, it has, rather, been reduced under the impact of the increasing complexity of the marketplace analyzed in some detail in the beginning of Chapter One. For this reason, it seems only natural to limit the following discussion to the micro level.

Rather than steep the analysis in conventional—and artifically rigid—economic terms, we will proceed from our own definition: *Consumer sovereignty at the individual level is the freedom to consume and the consumer's freedom to make intelligent choices to serve his needs.* We have already had reason to emphasize that freedom to consume is logically antecedent to any other consumer rights or freedoms. It implies two things: the right to spend our money on whatever we want[8] and the right to consume whatever we bought at whatever time and in whatever manner we want.[9] To be sure, there are some governmental and cultural restrictions on these rights.[10] In many countries there are restrictions on the right to buy drugs, prescription medicines and guns, for example.[11] To play your high-fidelity equipment at full volume after midnight would not be considered acceptable behavior in most cultures; we are enjoined from driving the family car over the neighbor's lawn, and so on. Yet it is surely fair to say that Western democracies display a high degree of freedom to consume.

Turning to the part of the definition dealing with serving consumer needs it would seem apparent that sovereignty implies (1) that the consumer is able to articulate his needs and (2) that they arise after some independent cogitation rather than from mere outside manipulation. With regard to articulation, consumers would seem to have this ability so far as needs that may be met by existing products are concerned. It is well known that we frequently lack this talent, however, when it comes to latent rather than manifest needs. While the thought apparently terrifies some radical observers, we have relied extensively on producer initiative to draw latent needs to our attention—and largely at their risk.[12]

Whether or not consumers identify their needs after independent cogitation or as a result of outside manipulation is, of course, a highly controversial question. According to Vance Packard our needs are "pre-determined" by "hidden persuaders," and if we are to believe J.K. Galbraith, "consumer wants are created by the process by which they are satisfied."[13] These views are shared by a great many people. The position here is that it is most realistic to think in terms of an interaction process.[14] Some of our preferences are specified by inherited characteristics; others are derived from friends, opinion leaders (Information Seekers and others), the educational process[15] and the general cultural environment. A third group are no doubt inspired by advertising and sales promotion by sellers. Finally, one set of needs are generated by ourselves as a result of interaction between our own personality and all these social influences. A number of the producer-sponsored wants are no doubt trite and contrived by most standards, as are probably a few of those originating elsewhere. But, as Harry G. Johnson points out,

> . . . it is not possible, contrary to what Galbraith assumes, to dismiss wants as valueless simply because they have been acquired under the pressures of social emulation and advertising. All economically relevant wants are learned. Moreover, all standards of taste are learned. It is therefore both arrogant and inconsistent to assume that those who have acquired their standards from general culture and advanced education can choose and pass judgments according to standards possessing independent validity, while those who have acquired their standards from social pressures and advertising can neither understand nor learn to understand the difference between good and bad taste.[16]

There are two important points to be added here. First, sellers compete, and hence give off messages that are conflicting perhaps as often as they are reinforcing (buy premium gasoline for a faster getaway versus buy regular gasoline for economy's sake). These conflicting messages are bound to emphasize the relativistic nature of promotion and thereby put any thinking person on notice he had better sort his priorities. Not only that: the conflicting messages also imply that it is indeed both possible and legitimate to have different tastes, which cuts the edge off of Marcuse's argument that advertisers are producing a unidimensional man.

One may still have reasonable doubts about the ability of consumers to withstand the pounding of sellers with sufficient alacrity to maintain "consumer sovereignty." This is where our second point comes in. We see the key to increasing the ability as well as the desire of consumers to form independent judgments in the interaction with advertising (as well as other social forces) as lying in consumer education and consumer information. Here, indeed, is a prime rationale for CI programs administered independently of individual producers.

In conclusion, consumer needs are shaped by an interaction process between the individual consumer and surrounding social forces.[17] There is no absolute independence—and in an absolute sense sovereignty will never exist. Certainly there is no complete dependence either, as indicated by Figure 2-1 summarizing our discussion. The

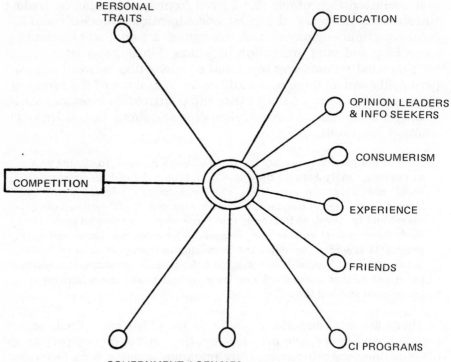

PERSONAL
TRAITS

EDUCATION

OPINION LEADERS
& INFO SEEKERS

CONSUMERISM

COMPETITION

EXPERIENCE

FRIENDS

CI PROGRAMS

GOVERNMENT AGENCIES

Figure 2-1. Major Determinants of Consumer Sovereignty

degree of consumer sovereignty may be increased in several ways. One of them is by raising the quality of advertising. Another is by consumer education and information programs.

The words "freedom to make intelligent choices" constitute a critical part of our definition of consumer sovereignty. We mean freedom of choice in the sense of freedom to select within a range of viable alternatives. There will never be an absolute freedom of choice in the sense that every consumer could expect to get his ideal product for his every need[b]—as indeed the choice of political parties hardly ever corresponds to anyone's personal ideal in the market for votes. We have to satisfy our desires within the realm of the practically and economically feasible.

Rothenberg maintains that in a command economy one might have consumer sovereignty without an open market—nota bene if the

[b]We are assuming for the moment that every man would be able to articulate what these ideal products would look like.

central planners were able through marketing research perfectly to define consumer needs and then to have the production system proceed to make products matching these needs. Without denying the theoretical validity of this point, let us merely observe that such a development has not yet occurred in a world that has sixty years of experience of communist government in various countries—and centuries of experiences of other varieties of dictatorship.[18]

For the foreseeable future, therefore, consumer sovereignty *will* presuppose reasonably open markets of the type encountered in the "mixed" economies of the West. Only in these countries do we find a range of viable alternatives in most markets. And only in these countries are the forces—cultural, social, economic, commercial and so on—in interaction with which the consumer defines his needs, in themselves sufficiently variegated to make for an emancipated consumer.

Two further observations should be made about the "freedom to make intelligent choices." First, we interpret "freedom" in this part of our definition to mean "opportunity." Clearly, a part of my consumer sovereignty is that I should have the right to make poor choices, and the right not to have to worry whether or not my choice was a clever one, if I so desire. Second, to have an opportunity to make intelligent choices the consumer must be well informed. Here is another powerful rationale for CI programs striving to improve the amount, veracity, availability and timeliness of information about market offerings.

How would one try to measure the degree of consumer sovereignty obtaining in a given country? As the concept is multifaceted, we would suppose that multiple indicators would have to be used, as is the case in the measurement of "business climate" or "degree of economic development." One would have to look at restrictions on the freedom to consume established by governmental fiat or social mores and at the number of distinct alternatives available in each market, as well as consider the total number of product and service markets in the economy, the sensitivity with which markets adjust to changes in consumer preferences, the independence of the consumer in terms of education and income, the degree of differentiation among the social forces interacting with him in the needs-specifying process, and so on. Not least, one would have to look at the quality, quantity, timeliness and cost of the market information available to him from CI programs as well as from all commercial and personal sources. Perhaps there should even be an informedness test applied to him at the moment of purchase!

Presumably, consumer satisfaction is also a dimension of consumer sovereignty. In a sense, consumer satisfaction is an expression of the ability of the market system to meet buyer needs. Satisfaction is, however, a much more complex and dynamic psychological phenomenon than it may seem at first sight,[19] and progress in the establishment of measurement techniques in the area has been modest. To be a true indicator of sovereignty, satisfaction measures may also have to be related to consumer awareness of available alternatives—there is clearly a link between satisfaction and free choice. All in all, it will be a while before we have a measurement system for consumer sovereignty. It is even understandable that many people have doubts as to the usefulness of the entire concept.

We do not feel this way. Even though it may never be possible to give the term fully operational meaning, the very notion of consumer sovereignty provides certain guidelines for consumer policymakers, be they private or public.

In conclusion, consumer sovereignty implies that the object of production is to satisfy consumer needs. A critical ingredient of consumer sovereignty is the opportunity and ability of consumers to make intelligent choices among a range of viable alternatives. To paraphrase Abraham Lincoln, while you might be able to fool some consumers all of the time, and to fool all consumers some of the time, in a society of consumer sovereignty you cannot fool all the people all of the time. To enhance consumer sovereignty by increasing the opportunity and ability of citizens to make intelligent choices in the marketplace is the prime rationale of CI programs.

CONSUMER STRATEGY

In the classical economics of perfect competition neither producer nor consumer had need for any strategy in the marketplace. The reason: total information about all market conditions and offerings was assumed to be available at zero cost in money, time and energy to all parties in the market. But, for better or worse, we live in an uncertain world; all we really know is that we don't know everything there is to know. To cope in such an environment man develops strategies, rules governing purposeful behavior in the face of uncertainty.

The literature is rich in dealing with the strategy of producers. Typically, almost all writings on "marketing strategy" are written about (and often in the interest of) sellers. One of several likely reasons for this state of affairs is a lingering notion of consumers as a mass of passive agents abiding the initiatives of sellers and opinion leaders—incapable of independent thought or action. Another reason is that the burgeoning field of consumer behavior research is relatively thin in strategic content. Yet it is clear that most consumers rely on more or less sophisticated strategies to govern their activity in the marketplace. Some of them involve very active conduct on the part of consumers.[20] This may begin by a conscious setting of objectives—diagnosing needs and preferences and relating them to budgetary and other priorities. Analyzing what alternative types of products meet a given need may follow. After deciding on product type the consumer is faced with the brand information. He may have a strategy for search, e.g., the more "important" or "expensive" the product is for him, the more search. Or, "the less prior experience I have of this product, the more search."[21] He may also have a strategy to avoid overload or stress, such as "consider seriously only three alternatives."

There are a great number of strategies to select from in order to arrive at the final choice of brand and supplier. Here are some illustrations:

You get what you pay for—price and quality move together.[22]
An old firm is reliable, or it would not still be in existence.
If my prior experience of Brand X refrigerators (cars, etc.) is good, it
  is probably a good idea to buy Brand X again at this time (which
  may be five to ten years later).[23]
General Electric refrigerators are good, so when I need a TV it is
  probably a good idea to buy a GE model.

These and similar strategies are drastic short cuts governing the conduct of millions of consumers. Both sober reflection and the fairly scant research on the subject indicate that these strategies are highly imperfect.[24] Yet, in the absence of better alternatives, their superficial plausibility will continue to attract myriads of new followers. We submit that consumers will have little interest in applying more rational approaches to decisionmaking (such as "highest expected value"[25]) until the quantity, quality and comparability of product information has been considerably improved—a different way of saying that modern markets call for modern CI programs.

CI PROGRAMS ASSUME OPEN MARKETS, OPEN MARKETS ASSUME CI PROGRAMS

Our discussion in a preceding section indicated that consumer sovereignty assumes a range of alternatives—alternatives perceived as *viable* by consumers. A range of viable alternatives is the outstanding characteristic of a great many markets in the highly industrialized Western democracies. In these cultures, alternatives are generated in the play of decentralized market forces. Whatever the theoretical merits of the case, no command economy in the history of man has come anywhere close to realizing similar degrees of consumer sovereignty. For practical purposes a philosophy of alternativism (to which we admittedly subscribe here) seems to be realizable only in market economies, or what is often called open market systems.[26] In an economy of chronic scarcity or very limited alternatives CI programs would tend to be of secondary interest. The prime concern of the consumer is to get hold of the product in the first place, or to avoid being "stuck" with the poorest alternative.[27] That alternative is frequently known through the jungle telegraph of sardonic folk humor. CI programs have their greatest meaning only in a world of viable alternatives;[28] in fact, past and current experience suggests that they assume open markets.

The prime criterion of open markets is the existence of active competition. CI programs and competition policy are intimately related. They not only share the same aim of promoting consumer sovereignty but also, when working in harmony, reinforce each other in the process. Only informed consumers are able to play fully their role as equal partners in the marketplace and by their buying decisions to promote the generation of better alternatives through competition. Referring to our discussion of the information gap in the first chapter, we may now turn around and say that in the complex economies around the North Atlantic open markets assume CI programs.

This is not the place to develop in detail the requirements of a modern competition policy. A few points seem appropriate, however. In some cultures—and most notably in the United States—market competition is in itself a premium socioeconomic value. As competition tends to be relatively aggressive in most markets, the prime focus of open market policy is antitrust—that is, the prevention of monopoly and collusion among sellers. In other cultures—and we would include a few West European countries in this group—legislation against monopolies and cartels in and of itself is not necessarily sufficient to guarantee workable competition in many markets. In such situations a more active procompetitive policy may be called for, such as the elimination of international trade barriers,[29] special credit facilities for new ventures, public support of research and development, competition from public enterprise, and so on. Certainly in the less developed countries the need for procompetitive policies is a crying one.

In all highly advanced economies (such as those in most of the countries studied here) it behooves policymakers to observe that the

nature of competition and cooperation in business is forever changing. Thus, the space between products in the marketplace is increasingly being filled by other new products. For instance, in music
reproduction we may have our choice between TV, radio, high-fidelity
sets and tape recorders. We are gradually approaching a continuous
spectrum of products. In some markets cross-product competition is
probably even stronger than the rivalry between different brands of
the same product.

New varieties of competition stem from new types of organizational arrangements among sellers. Examples include franchising and
such other varieties of vertical systems as supermarket chains, representing a new type of competition next to traditional forms of distribution. Large retailers, such as Quelle in Germany, or Sears, Roebuck
in the United States, inject a new element of competition by usurp-
ing from many manufacturers their old role of governing distributive
relationships. And while we do indeed agree with Edwards[30] that industrial conglomerates may represent a concentration of economic
power greater than the parts of which they are composed, and that
frequently there is in this power the potential of monopolistic abuse,
we would also emphasize that in many markets they have added a
new dimension of actual or (and this may be no less significant) potential competition.

We would also count ourselves among the growing number of observers who maintain that sometimes competition between the few
can be more beneficial to society than competition between the
many. Oligopoly—that is, competition between the few—has reigned
in the chemical, drug and computer industries, all of which seem to
have made rapid progress to the ultimate benefit of consumers. Conversely, the textile, shoe and saw mill industries in many countries
are represented by scores or hundreds of firms—and yet the only major "happening" in these industries often seems to be that they are
becoming increasingly depressed relative to other parts of the economy. The point is that atomistic competition in the classical textbook
sense seems less and less worthwhile as an ideal aim of public policy.
On the other hand, there is certainly no guarantee that oligopoly will
yield the type of competition we desire.

Finally, one must be cognizant of a new emphasis on cooperation
in business. This is evident in standardization programs, industrywide
management information systems, and consumer complaint systems.
Indeed, the trend is evident in industry cooperation in such CI programs as informative labeling and quality certification. We may also
note cooperation in research and development, joint ventures for
king size problems (the Concorde), for ecological action, community

enhancement, export promotion, and so on. Clearly, it is not always easy to draw the line between constructive cooperation on one hand and conspiracy against the consuming public on the other.

The philosophy of alternativism may provide *one* important guideline in our attempts to establish what constitutes workable competition as contrasted to undesirable restriction. That is, we would empirically attempt to establish whether in a given market the customer—be he a distributor, retailer or end consumer—has realistic and viable alternatives at his disposal. Other guidelines will surely be needed. We mention that of alternativism because of its obvious relation to CI programs. Indeed, in economies increasingly characterized by oligopolies and conglomerates, one of the key roles of CI programs is to work as an integral part of competition policy itself: by increasing the transparency of the marketplace they enhance the likelihood of these organizations serving the consumer interest.

CONSUMER RIGHTS AND CONSUMER POLICY: A SCENARIO[31]

This section is concerned with consumer rights and responsibilities and with consumer policy and policymakers. The graphic representation in Figure 2–2 will serve as a point of reference. The matrix arrays aspects of consumer policy in the left-hand column and of consumer rights and responsibilities in the right-hand columns. As a book page is not suitable for three dimensional diagrams, the reader is left to use his imagination for our third dimension, namely, the principal makers of consumer policy: consumer organizations, other voluntary groups, business, government, educational institutions and the mass media.

In outlining our concept of consumer policy[32] we noted that the distinctions between education, information and protection are not hard and fast.

The classification of consumer rights by now is pretty traditional. We have also noted that logically the specific rights identified in the matrix are preceded by the more general and basic "freedom to consume" (or not to consume, for that matter).

The matrix tries to make two vital points, namely:

that the enforcement of literally every consumer right logically depends on all three types of consumer policy, that is, education, information and protection, and
that for every consumer right there is a corresponding consumer responsibility.

Consumer policy	Consumer rights			
	1. Choose freely	2. Be informed	3. Be heard	4. Be safe
A. Education	decisionmaking budgeting nature of market economy, rights and responsibilities	generic product and materials data, information sources	how to assert consumer rights	importance of health and safety, user manuals and training
B. Information	buying criteria buying advice	models and brand data, independent consumer information programs	market research two-way market dialogue	safety certification, care and maintenance data
C. Protection	maintain open markets, antitrust; stop high pressure and deceptive tactics	truly informative advertising, product claims substantiation	complaints handling machinery	minimize health and accident risks
Consumer responsibilities	Choose wisely	Keep informed	Sound off	Safety first

A third dimension of the matrix would show the makers of consumer policy. These policymakers include consumer organization, other citizen groups, business, government, educational institutions and the mass media.

Figure 2-2. Consumer Policy and Consumer Rights and Responsibilities

The lesson here is simple and crucial: no matter how aggressively we may use consumer policy, it will not in itself suffice to enforce consumer rights. In the end consumer rights will exist only if at least *some individual consumers* really exercise *some of their rights and responsibilities* at least *some of the time.*

Positive and Negative Rights and Responsibilities

The last statement suggests a few remarks on positive and negative rights and responsibilities. Rights and responsibilities are inherently two-faced. The positive right to choose between viable alternatives (including having access to suppliers of the brands in question) corresponds to the negative right not to have choice imposed (such as by some central planning authority, or by overly well-meaning consumer "protectionists").[c] The right to be informed corresponds to the right not to be deceived.[33] The right to be heard corresponds to the right to privacy.[34] The right to safety corresponds to the right to take some safety risks—such as smoking cigarettes or driving without a safety belt—at least as long as we are aware of the risks and are respecting the rights of other consumers.

Consumer responsibilities present us with an analogous situation. The positive imperative to choose wisely is negated by our freedom to choose what we know is "wrong" for us, or to spend our money foolishly.[35] The positive duty to keep informed corresponds to the "negative" phenomenon of impulse buying, or of taking a deliberate chance at an auction, and no voice has as yet been raised to prohibit these types of behavior. The duty of sounding off corresponds to the urge to keep quiet, to avoid the unpleasantness and the waste of time involved in asserting our rights. And instead of battling for safety first at all times some of us at least occasionally will put performance[d] or, indeed, even fun[e] above safety. Or we may use a product for another purpose than that for which it was made.[f] Or we may simply neglect maintenance, which in and of itself may be enough to create safety hazards. The point of all this is that we cannot expect most consumers to be vigilantes of the marketplace most of the time.

It may be observed that most of us have quite positive—often adamant—feelings about what here is loosely termed the negative rights and responsibilities of consumers. Indeed, they all seem to represent

---

[c]The right to choose is listed first in the figure as without it the other rights lose much of their meaning.

[d]In operating an electric saw, for example.

[e]Smoking in bed, for example.

[f]Using a razorblade for a knife, for example.

widely embraced Western ideals. For the enforcement of positive consumer responsibilities society relies almost exclusively on voluntarism among consumers themselves. On the other hand, positive consumer rights, while perhaps self-evident in theory, seemingly need to be constantly reasserted to stay alive. Even though the reassertion of these consumer rights is logically the prime responsibility of consumers, governments and other groups are having to add their weight. The market economy may create the *potential* for the realization of positive consumer rights (indeed, in our personal view, it does), but in a complex society there is no automaticity about their actual realization. This implies cost and effort on the part of individual consumers and consumer policymaking organizations in the struggle to enforce the rights.[36] There is no need to develop this theme here except with regard to the right to be informed. We know that *some* product information will always be forthcoming, because it is in the self-interest of sellers to provide it. No matter how subversively persuasive in a Galbraithian sense a seller's intentions, he will find that, over the long pull at least, any line of argument must have some basis in fact to gain credibility. But, as detailed in Chapter One, commercial information and personal experience are no longer sufficient. Experience indicates that millions of well-to-do, well-educated consumers are willing to pay for additional information in the form of comparative test reports. It becomes a cost-benefit problem for consumer policymakers just *how much* additional CI it is worthwhile to provide in *what form* and to *what target groups of consumers*. We will return to this question in the last section of this chapter.

Consumer Policy Measures

While the cells in Figure 2-2 give some examples of consumer policy measures, they serve illustrative purposes only. There is nothing sacred about the arrangement; and in several instances it is a matter of taste and emphasis rather than principle. This is almost inevitable given the overlaps between education, information and protection as well as between the several consumer rights. The right half of the matrix would seem fairly self-explanatory. We shall comment on the left half in terms of consumer rights (and corresponding responsibilities).

The effective implementation of the right to choose freely assumes a mature consumer. This is a consumer who through a process of formal or informal education has acquired some degree of understanding of personal and household decisionmaking and budgeting and who has developed a sense of judgment in making buying decisions. As indicated by cell A1 he will also have some insight into the nature of the market economy and an attendant awareness of consumer rights and responsibilities. His chances of making use of his freedom to choose wisely will be enhanced if he is also aware of how his needs will change over the life cycle and of such basic notions as cost-benefit analysis, discounted cash flow, the economics of information and the value of his time.[37]

To make a choice on any basis other than pure whim or impulse the consumer has to articulate (at least to himself) what his major criteria in buying the product really are. He needs information inputs (B1) to help him define what his requirements in the product should be, given his own set of values and circumstances.[g] Should the consumer be unable or unwilling to digest abstract information for these purposes, such agencies as the Verein für Konsumenteninformation (VKI) in Austria and the Citizens' Advice Bureaux in the U.K. may provide him with more concrete—and, by inference, more directive— buying advice. (Should this go as far as quoting brand names we are moving to cell B2.)

The intimate connection between competition (and antitrust) policy and CI was the subject of a prior section of this chapter. The open market policy serves the purpose of maintaining viable alternatives in the marketplace. Thus, when it is viewed from the perspective of consumer policy it logically belongs under consumer protection (C1). Here we also find regulation of such practices as high pressure and door-to-door selling and sundry varieties of deception in trade that obscure or undermine freedom of choice.

Proceeding to the right to be informed, we observe the need for generic product and materials information as a logical prelude to the choice among models and brands. This type of information (What will a tape recorder do that a recordplayer will not? What is the difference between nylon and cotton in men's shirts?) in our conceptual scheme falls under the heading of education (cell A2). The furnishing of data about models and brands is the purpose of information policies implementing the right to be informed, as indicated by cell B2. The focus of this work is on independent CI programs, principal exponents of this kind of policy.

As indicated in *The Information Seekers*,[38] there is a broadly felt need in Western countries to safeguard the integrity of product information. In several countries there is mounting pressure—within industry as well as without—toward more informative advertising (cell C2). Without going into the merits of its policy, we may note that the U.S. Federal Trade Commission is a pioneer exponent of the view

[g]Typical question: What should I look for in a freezer?

that advertisers should be prepared to substantiate specific claims made for their products, or to retract false or misleading claims.

Tradeoffs and Reinforcement

These are characteristics that apply to both consumer rights and consumer policies.[39] A tradeoff relationship exists when one item is more or less a substitute for the other (rice and potatoes). Items reinforce each other when their joint effect is greater than the total effect obtainable if they are used in isolation (a cake as contrasted to its ingredients).[40] Some examples from consumer rights: if the consumer were informed he could choose wisely (reinforcement). If he chose wisely he would most likely not need to complain or to worry about safety (tradeoffs). Similarly, if the pleasure boat owner about to buy a life vest does not wish to take the time to be informed about the market offerings he may simply get a vest with a safety certificate, but may later find he has to complain about the fabric fading in the sun (tradeoffs). If I have taken time to ferret out my buying criteria I will more likely make an informed choice (reinforcement).

With regard to consumer policies the most dramatic examples of reinforcement occur between consumer education and information. While the reinforcement works both ways, it is far stronger in going from education to information than vice versa. Indeed, one may say that effective consumer information *presupposes* consumer education. Properly conceived, consumer education provides the citizen with the mental apparatus required to receive and evaluate consumer information. Not only that: we have every reason to expect that well-planned consumer education will provide the stimulus needed to get a ravenous and cumulative information-seeking process going among ever-wider circles of consumers. At present, this type of process is active only among a rather small minority.[41] As will be seen (Chapter Four), there are also numerous possibilities of reinforcement (and some of tradeoff) between different types of independent CI programs.

Conversely, the most dramatic tradeoffs in the consumer policy area occur between consumer information and education on the one hand and protection on the other. This is only natural in view of the fact that the former policies aim at developing the decisionmaking capabilities of the consumer, while the emphasis in protection frequently is to substitute the judgment of policymakers for that of the individual. For instance, a high level of general consumer education would obviate the need for legislation for a period of regret after the signing of door-to-door sales contracts. If there were more CI, advertising would almost surely be more disciplined, and there would be little concern about substantiation of product claims in promotion messages. If drivers were better trained and behaved there would be less need for traffic regulations and auto safety devices (a somewhat self-evident observation, the point of which seems to have been lost in recent agitation about automotive product safety). If more citizens were well trained and informed as consumers, markets would certainly function better, and there would be less need for public intervention in the form of antitrust and competition policy. There are some tradeoffs between education and information as well. Thus, if consumers were better educated (or self-educated) in the characteristics and use of various products (cells A2 and A4) there would be less need for certification of product safety (cell B4).

Policymakers

This third dimension of Figure 2-2 was left to the imagination of the reader. In a basic and pervasive sense individual buyers making the myriad day-to-day decisions in the marketplace are the crucial makers of consumer policy. As long as we wish to retain a high degree of consumer sovereignty (and the concomitant open market system) this must be so. Our diagram, however, focuses on organized efforts to educate, inform and protect the consumer. In this view, the policymakers include consumer organizations, other citizen groups, business, government, educational institutions and the mass media. In view of the fact that reinforcements and tradeoffs are characteristic of consumer rights and responsibilities as well as of consumer policies, it is hardly surprising to find that the same thing applies to the policymakers.

This is especially evident in the area of key concern in this work, the implementation of the consumer's right to be informed. From a tradeoff point of view, if business did a better job of informative advertising there would be less need for independent CI programs. If business (or the educational system) did a better job of providing generic product and materials information, there would be less need for CI programs in this area. Similarly, in countries where consumer organizations have not been created (as they have in the U.S., U.K. and Benelux countries) to engage in broad-scale CI programs, this function has tended to gravitate to government (Scandinavia), or to women's, business and labor groups (Switzerland, France). Reinforcementwise, consumer information can have a multiplier effect if CI program test reports, labels and quality seals are used in business promotion programs, or discussed on public radio and TV. While there are always possibilities of abuse, we would optimistically point to the favorable experience of the Swedish VDN as an indication that this cost—at least in a well-disciplined environment—can be held quite low relative to the benefits of large-scale dissemination. As regards labeling and certification programs, it would appear that multiparty cooperation between policymakers is a well-nigh indispensable prerequisite to secure both viability and credibility.

A type of consumer organization deserving special mention in discussing consumer policy is the coop. Cooperatives play a great role (more so in Northwest Europe than elsewhere) in the area of consumer education and, in some respects (by providing competition, by revealing deception, etc.), in consumer protection. By and large, however, relative to their great financial resources, coops have taken a surprisingly modest interest in CI programs. In the end this may be due to some conflict of interest (with attendant credibility problems) stemming from their second role as producers and/or distributors. The Swedish coops had a kind of split loyalty to their captive labeling program and to the economywide VDN program. The Belgian coops withdrew from UFIDEC following the publication of an unfavorable test report. Another reason for the lukewarm interest of coops (and labor unions) in CI programs may well be a realization that the initial beneficiaries of such programs would be middle class, highly educated consumers rather than average citizens constituting the core of coop (and union) membership.

In speaking of conflict of interest problems among consumer policymakers one could hardly neglect the mass media. The German *DM* and the Italian *Quattrosoldi* are consumer information and education magazines that unabashedly accept advertising—seemingly without any gross loss in either integrity or credibility. The daily press, while doing an increasingly creditable job in the consumer education and protection areas ("hot lines" and other complaints columns, consumerist-oriented articles, etc.), is not doing well when it comes to CI. May we suggest that this is due to two fairly weak reasons: that comparative product reviews (typically confined to theatre and screen) would incur more advertiser wrath than such reviews are worth, and that such reviews would not generate enough reader interest. The latter is probably a mistaken notion. The newspapers could at least start with market overviews based on manufacturer data, which are a cardinal ingredient of innumerable hobby magazines. With regard to TV and radio the tug of war between media producers and CI organizations for program control had by the end of the sixties led to victory for the former in most countries—without any doubt to the detriment of consumer information.[42] By 1970 the so-called consumer information programs emitted by radio and TV in England, France and Sweden were not deserving of the name.

Educational institutions play a role essentially confined to the consumer education area. (This is not to say that they are entirely without potential as regards information and protection.) Unfortunately, however, one may seriously doubt that schools are doing what they should. Conventional home economics courses in no way meet the agenda implied by the cells in the education row of Figure 2-2. By 1976, as well as we could ascertain, obligatory consumer education courses (including, as a matter of course, students of both sexes) only existed in some states in the U.S. and in Norway and even these generally did not nearly fill the needs indicated by the diagram and our prior discussion of education to implement the right to free choice.[43] Experimental work is going on in several countries. For reasons that by now should be abundantly clear, we strongly favor the introduction of obligatory consumer education of the type sketched here at the high school level. We do this even though aware of the fact that there is a tendency afoot to simply push problems to the school system whenever other social institutions have proved unable to solve them. It would seem natural that universities and home economics institutes should cooperate with business, consumer groups and governments in the planning of such a curriculum. It is also important that the effort be undertaken from the perspective that while such courses would lay the basis, consumer education, like learning in general, is a lifelong process.

Trust in the Marketplace

The reader will have noticed that we have placed more emphasis on education and information than on protection. This is simply because there is no logical end to protective measures, just as there is no logical end to paternalism.[44] In the end, protection means that products will have to pass the test of the bureaucrats instead of the test of the marketplace.

It used to be that the austere rule of caveat emptor defined the place of consumers. Many Western countries are now moving at supersonic speed in the opposite direction, toward caveat venditor (let the seller beware). Open markets with a high degree of consumer sovereignty thrive between the extremes. They are based on trust and on respect for mutual rights and responsibilities. Like all institutions of liberal democracy, trust in the marketplace is a delicate thing that must be fostered with care. Yet there is some reason for optimism: that producer and consumer in the end have more interests in common than in conflict is no more remarkable than the fact that employers and employees do.

CI AND THE COUNTERCULTURE

The quest for improved market information is right in the main-stream of consumerism. Consumerism is sometimes ridiculed by representatives of the "counterculture" (or, more appropriately, countercultures). Although it requires considerable material resources to sustain them, counterculturists profess to be antimaterialist. One may surmise that their disdain for the Establishment and "corporate liberalism" would extend to courses in consumer education as well as to CI programs, and one might suspect that they would hardly be open to any attempt by others to present what would seem to be clear-cut merits of such arrangements even from a counterculturist point of view.[45]

Yet it might be fruitful to contemplate what consumer policy-makers and counterculturists could learn from each other. The consumer policymaker must beware of emphasizing concerns with malfunctions in the marketplace to the point where he lays himself open to the counterculturist accusation of excessive materialism. Some perspective could be brought to bear by introducing in consumer education courses discussions about social criticism of the "market culture," about "real" versus "false" needs, about "quality of life" and so on. Somewhat paradoxically, stream-of-consciousness III and other counterpoint thinking would also reveal what is already a crying need for improvement of CI programs: to extend compara-tive product research and information to the psychosocial character-istics of market offerings, thus recognizing their immense and possibly even still growing importance relative to purely functional perfor-mance. Policymakers in general must get out of the trap that psycho-social dimensions are somehow unworthy of attention, and CI program leaders in particular desperately need to increase their awareness and use of the behavioral sciences.[46] Another lesson could be learned from the Latin type of *personalismo*, which constitutes such a prominent element in much counterculturist behavior. For better or worse, one of the principal means of "doing your thing" will always be to indulge in forms of behavior or styles of life mani-festing themselves in the consumption of more or less individualized goods. (The notion of a stampede to an age of contemplating our navels is not to be taken seriously.) Individualization means greater product differentiation—and a greater need for market transparence.

On the other hand, counterculturists may some day become aware of the potential benefits to be derived from consumer education and information. Resistance to manipulative tendencies of the Establishment would seem to call for more mature consumers (the ultimate alternative of nonconsumption also means nonsurvival). Then there is the uncomfortable fact that most reforms in vogue among counter-culturists—environmental cleanup, natural resource conservation, health and welfare measures—would call for vast economic inputs. While the term productivity may be anathema to many a young fighter against the current system, he is apt to wind up wanting more of the same if he is at all serious. By increasing productivity in consumer behavior, education and information help free resources for other uses. Finally, from a personal point of view the counterculturist may learn to relish the fact that high quality market information will permit him to discharge objectionable buying chores with maximum dispatch and minimum loss of time out from Marcuse.

CONSUMER ORGANIZATIONS AND CONSUMER REPRESENTATION

In the history of political theory it has long been a bone of contention whether one person can ever "truly" represent another. Without taking a position on this issue, it seems worthwhile in the context of consumer rights and responsibilities to discuss briefly some typical patterns of representation of consumer interests on the current scene. We have singled out broad-scope government agencies, nonconsumer organizations, consumer organizations[47] and a group of consumers we shall label the Information Seekers.

Government Agencies for Consumer Affairs

The enormous diversity of consumer interests is reflected by the fact that in all countries a multiplicity of government bodies are in some respect real or at least supposed guardians of consumers. For examples we need only to think of food and drug inspection, health and sanitation control, weights and measures authorities, the enforcement of competition policy or the training of home economics teachers. Besides the fairly specialized offices that handle such specific functions we find an increasing number of general purpose agencies for consumer affairs, such as Institut National de la Consommation (INC) in France, the State Consumer Board in Sweden and the Office of Consumer Affairs in the United States. These multipurpose institutions are of special import as their prime duty is to "represent" consumer interests across all other governmental agencies and, frequently, also to the executive branch and to the legislature. In a sense it is difficult to understand the lingering opposition to such bodies in some countries and quarters. After all, ministers of labor, commerce and agriculture often do analogous things for other interest groups. And it might be said with some justification that the fragmentation and diffusion of consumer interests makes such a focal point especially desirable.

On the other hand, it must be understood that this very dispersion also creates a major problem: How do we know that such a body really "represents" consumers? It would seem clear to us that with the possible exception of INC—which has made large-scale opinion surveys among French consumers at least twice—most of these agencies are making too modest an effort to gauge how many consumers they are really representing on any particular issue. While these organs would indeed be justified in saying that there is no such thing as an "average" consumer, this is no great rationale for not trying to establish what degree of support there is for a given measure. As long as this is neglected there is always the possibility that these agencies will become "political kickballs."[48]

The main merit of a central consumer unit is certainly not an ability to represent all consumers before all government bodies. On the contrary, the day-to-day consideration of consumer interests in government agencies is more effectively handled by *direct* consumer representation in such agencies—that is, by a decentralized approach. Of this one of the authors became convinced when, as member of the President's Consumer Advisory Council in 1976, he undertook a review of the consumer representation plans of seventeen cabinet level federal agencies in the United States. The prime appeal of a central unit is its ability to bring a consumer point of view to bear in matters cutting across many government bodies.[49]

On Professional Consumers and
Two-Way Representation

Many public bodies principally or tangentially concerned with consumer affairs make use of advisory groups with varying quotients of consumer representatives. Typically, these representatives are university professors, scientists from testing laboratories, or delegates from consumer, labor, women's or family organizations or the political parties. Whether these persons are really "representative" of consumers may be doubted. Rather, they tend to be "professional" consumers even before being named to such bodies as the Consumer Advisory Board of the Office of Consumer Affairs in the U.S., the Belgian Consumer Council or the innumerable standardization committees in most countries—and to become even more so while grappling with the questions coming before these agencies. This development is probably not to be regretted. Even if the "average" consumer existed, it is not necessarily the case that consumers in general would be well served by having him represent them in today's extremely complex policy matters.[50] The fact remains that the age-old issue of experts versus laymen has been resolved largely in favor of the former when it comes to representation in consumer affairs.

Without denying the usefulness of expert consumer representatives, we should point out an additional problem. Frequently, not being directly accountable to any outside organization, and working closely with the agency with which they are serving as consumer representatives,[51] these experts will tend to acquire an understanding of the many practical and tactical obstacles making certain measures "infeasible" that might benefit consumers.[52] Thus, we tend to get a situation of two-way representation, where the experts may begin to represent the agency (or the government) to consumers, in addition to their original task of representing consumers to the agency. A certain amount of two-way representation is of course also characteristic of most public consumer agencies themselves (this is not surprising in view of the lack of identity between the consumer and the public interests).[53]

No doubt general purpose government agencies of consumer affairs and the consumer representatives appointed to them have done a fair, if nowhere near sensational, amount of good. Yet it is hard to avoid contrasting their impact with that of a free agent like Ralph Nader. Of course a great deal of Nader's success is due to his catching the fancy of journalists and receiving, consequently, a Jacqueline Kennedy type of press buildup. Quite apart from the fact that even such an accomplishment is unusual, the fact remains that Mr. Nader has picked up a groundswell of popular acclaim and support far beyond that of most public agencies and private consumer organizations around the world. As no one else, Nader and his Raiders have demonstrated that consumer causes can indeed catch the public's imagination—and notably the enthusiasm of youth—as much as any other single set of issues on the contemporary scene. His influence is observable in every one of the nations studied in our work.

The Role of Nonconsumer Organizations

In many countries labor, family, women's, associations of home economics teachers and similar groups, either singly or in unison, have sponsored or participated in CI programs. Sometimes they have been joined by consumer coops. In retrospect, the dependence on nonconsumer organizations has been a mixed blessing. It is true that in some instances a certain CI program (e.g., Qualité-Belgique) might not have been started at all without this kind of sponsorship. Yet in most cases CI programs have been a secondary activity for the sponsoring groups. In this situation they are rarely the kind of effective promoters at the grassroots level that these programs so desperately need. Labor has really done very little for OR.GE.CO. in France, for instance. Or, even worse, if the baby shows a tendency to begin to walk on its own, the parents may try to place a harness on it to keep it under control (as, for example, UFC in France before the merger with Belgian AC). Occasionally, sponsorship of CI programs by other than consumer organizations may have forestalled the emergence or growth of such organizations. The sour attitude of German AGV toward Stiftung Warentest in the critical first five years of the Stiftung can best be described as that of a loser in a powerplay. It is refreshing to note two instances of strong offspring-parent cooperation to the apparent benefit of both: that of the Dutch IVHA quality certification program and of the Austrian Verein für Konsumenteninformation.

Whenever a CI program is sponsored by one or several other organizations, the program itself becomes an "organization of organizations," or what we shall call a second order organization. The contact with consumers and, in a critical sense, with reality tends to become especially esoteric when CI programs become third or fourth order organizations. OR.GE.CO., for instance, is a fourth order organization. Its main sponsor is a trade union confederation composed of national unions, which are in turn composed of union locals. If the AGV had sponsored an "independent" CI program, it would have become a fifth order organization. The problems of joint ventures and pyramid holding companies in business seem to reoccur with exponential impact in higher order organizations of voluntary groupings.

Industry groups and trade associations are also sponsoring or cosponsoring CI programs (such as Qualité-France and most labeling programs). In this case the conflict between the mainstream of sponsor activity and the CI program could potentially become even greater than when labor or similar groups are the sponsors. Certainly, a key question immediately becomes: Is there sufficient consumer representation in the program? Yet we would suspect that if producers and consumers were to actively cooperate in CI programs they would become more effective than when run by labor, family and other non-market-oriented groups.[54]

The Role of Consumer Associations[55]

All nations around the North Atlantic except Germany and the Nordic countries have consumer associations of at least some prominence.[56] In France and Switzerland the main associations are regional.[57] From our vantage point there is reason to distinguish between three types of consumer associations: consumer lobby organizations, associations exclusively concerned with CI and dual purpose associations.[58] Although in the main we are not concerned with the first group, it seems natural in a section on representation of consumer interests to raise the issue of representativeness of these organizations. Leaving aside the question of internal democracy of these associations—a topic on which we are admittedly poorly informed—we may observe that the membership cadre is nowhere impressive relative to the total number of consumers, (which these associations seemingly claim to represent). Even so, it is difficult to take the membership figures claimed by a Federacion Nacional de Asociaciones de Consumidores of Spain or a Consumer Federation of America (CFA) with any degree of seriousness. Both of the above-named groupings are also higher order organizations whose direct rapport with individual members is tenuous at best. Indeed, the CFA to a fair extent seems to serve as a career ladder for its own and affiliated union officials and an opening wedge to the centers of power in Washington. There is little grassroots activity, and these groups appear to have problems building aggressive local chapters. Indeed, experiments carried out by CA in the U.K., by FRD in Denmark and under the auspices of the former Consumer Council (KR) in Sweden[59] suggest that even when local groups are challenged by a broad consumerist charter of activities the direction of support—in these cultures at least—tends to be from the top down rather than from the bottom up. The Italian UNC would seem to be a fairly rare example of a balanced interplay between central and local initiatives.[60]

While questioning the representativeness of most general consumer lobby organizations, we are neither denying their usefulness nor their right to arrange their affairs as they see fit. These groups do however raise a credibility gap in our mind when they appear to pretend to represent all consumers. In some instances they may not be much more representative of consumers at large than the public officials whom they serve as advisers. For a well-rounded view of consumer interests legislators and public administrators are well advised not to limit their "consumer pipeline" to these organizations.[61]

Turning to the second type of association, we may note initially that quite a few CI programs have a single-minded devotion to the great job of providing consumers with useful and unbiased information about products and services. Notable examples are Warentest, all the labeling organizations and such certifying bodies as IVHA of Holland and SIH of Switzerland. However, none of the bodies mentioned is a subscriber-based consumer association. Examples of such associations exclusively devoted to CI programs are becoming increasingly rare. It may well be that in 1976 Association des Consommateurs of Belgium was the only case.

Clearly, as long as an organization does not engage in lobbying (or if it does so without any pretense of universality) there is no public question about its representativeness. Consumer associations and other bodies solely devoted to CI programs may, however, wish to become more representative (oriented to their market) for reasons of their own (such as the desire to grow). They may increase the degree of internal democracy (although one may seriously doubt whether this will contribute much to the specific goal of growth).[62] Or they may try to reach categories of consumers currently "underrepresented" among their users or subscribers. Finally, they could vastly increase their use of modern marketing and survey research techniques—an area in which there is room for much improvement in virtually all CI program organizations (see Chapter Five).

Finally we come to the CI-cum-lobby associations. Confining our attention to member- (or subscriber-) based associations we may observe that several of them have from the outset assumed varying degrees of lobbying or other broad spectrum consumer affairs activity. Here we find Konsumentinnenforum and Fédération Romande of Switzerland, Consumers' Association of Canada and the Dutch Consumentenbond.

Yet another sizeable number of CI associations have entered the broader areas of social action on behalf of the underprivileged, consumer protection, ecology, quality of life, etc., more cautiously—responding to environmental impulses more often than initiating them, but unmistakably becoming increasingly involved in what might be termed consumer conglomerate activities. In this group are such heavyweights as CA and CU. At least in the CU case it is probably correct to say that the leadership always wanted to do these things, but felt that economic reasons prompted attention to "first things first": i.e., providing the comparative test reports subscribers were explicitly paying for. The fact that in recent years CU has felt freer to move into consumer affairs in general is an example of what may be called "transformation of goals"—that is, the tendency on the part of any successful organization to broaden its objectives. CA, well into general consumer affairs even before the abolishment of the Consumer Council in 1970, has intensified its activities in this area since then in spite of occasional financial strain.[63]

Whatever the motivation in each case, the manifest tendency of many CI organizations to broaden their objectives beyond those associated with product information will inevitably give rise to some interesting questions. A philosophical issue thus far not much discussed among CI groups is to what extent it is practically feasible to combine information and representation (lobbying) without losing the spirit of objectivity and circumspection required in testing, labeling and certification. Purely pragmatically, this is ultimately a question of credibility.

Again, there is the question of representativeness. It does not seem to us a serious problem in subscriber-financed organizations (so long as they do not insist that they represent all consumers), as the subscribers (members) can stop their subscriptions if they do not like the opinions voiced. There is only one residual and comparatively minor question in this area: a fair number of consumers may be subscribers because they want CI and while they do not care for the consumer politics part of the journal or of the association's activities they are willing to tolerate this "nuisance" for the sake of obtaining the product information they really care for. This matter is not entirely academic, as our U.S. field survey suggests that the views expressed by CU and its *Consumer Reports* may be just a shade more liberal than those of average members.[64] Others, even though in sympathy with the views, may simply feel that it is not the business of a CI organization to engage in broader issues of consumer policy.[65]

Superficially, CI organizations also might appear to have something of a problem acting as representatives of consumers in general since their subscribers do not constitute a representative sample of consumers at large. We may also note that only in a few CI organizations are subscribers actually members. They certainly represent active consumers, however, as suggested in the following sections of this chapter.

Conflict and Convergence of Consumer Interests

From a fiscal point of view the fact that consumer information to a large extent is in the area of public goods or externalities is one of the major problems of CI programs. At least conceptually, a conflict of interest obtains between consumers who pay for CI and the "free-loaders" who also use it.

There are many other conflicts of interest among consumers. Different consumers are interested in different products, and those interested in the same products frequently are interested in different characteristics of these products. It was mentioned that some consumers interested in product information are not interested in lobbying.

An equally important problem facing CI organizations broadening their objectives to encompass the presumed interests of consumers *in general* in such areas as ecology and the quality of life is to what extent these collective needs are compatible with the equally well understood interests of *individual* consumers in convenience, fun, the reduction of household drudgery and the saving of time. If the collective and the individual may indeed have different interests (as suggested, for instance, by those left-wing thinkers who claim that ecology is the gospel of the privileged classes or by those underdeveloped countries that at the 1972 UN environment conference in Stockholm claimed that ecology is the gospel of the privileged nations), then, one might ask, is it proper for a CI organization to go any further than objective statements such as "Nonreturnable bottles damage the environment while they may save you time and trouble"? One is reminded of the *New Yorker* cartoon reproduced in Figure 2–3.

"Notice how bright and white Brand X gets your clothing because of the harmful chemicals and enzymes it contains. Pure-O, on the other hand, containing no harmful ingredients, leaves your clothes lacklustre gray but protects your environment."

Figure 2–3. The Consumer and the Environment

Drawing by Dana Fradon; © 1971 The New Yorker Magazine, Inc.

A major challenge to all consumer organizations is presented by the fragmentization of our very role as consumers. In the words of one observer:

> ... I don't believe that the consumer movement can ever develop the organization and power of labor unions. Work involves face-to-face human relationships sustained through common activity and discussion of the task. Consumption rarely involves discussions beyond the immediate family. Work for any person is a rather comprehensive activity toward which he has a certain outlook, complex as this may be. There is no parallel to this in consumption. Picking up the morning paper, making the weekly trip to the supermarket, paying the monthly electric bill, going downtown to buy a spring suit, deciding to buy a new car—all represent acts of consumption, but none of these acts are linked together in people's minds. ... It is hard to find any common basis on which people can react to issues that involve consumption per se.[66]

Adds the executive director of Danish FRD: "One of our main problems is to teach people to consider themselves as consumers."[67]

There is a practical dilemma facing consumer organizations. Our observations indicate that a certain minimum size relative to its environment is necessary for a consumer group to have any degree of effectiveness, regardless of its specific purpose. To attract a sufficiently large clientele to have an impact there is a temptation among small organizations to become multipurpose, thereby risking the dissipation of their energies. More specialized organizations, which are already above the threshold, tend to branch out in the process of "transformation of goals" that is seemingly characteristic of all organizations. Even a large organization may, however, find that in the process of diversification it is spreading its resources dangerously thin.[68] Maybe one solution is indicated by the CU's 1972 procedure of "spinning off" a separate organization—the Consumer Interest Foundation—for special purposes. This may facilitate access to new sources of funds or a partially different clientele, or the engagement of personnel with special motivation and talent, and will automatically tend to produce a more functional accounting system.[69] Conversely, there is every reason to point out the urgent need for closer cooperation among consumer organizations to achieve economies of scale in resource use and impact (see Chapter Four).

The plurality of consumer interests does indeed call for a pluralist, decentralized, experimental approach, a system involving several organizations in countries of any size.[70] But opportunities for synergy exist. And in the end there is a core of commonality and convergence: the implementation of consumer rights and responsibilities.

The Information Seekers

Consumer information is for consumers. And all consumers have the opportunity to avail themselves of the output of CI programs, be they test reports, labels or quality marks. The usage rate does, however, differ significantly among various groups—at least as regards comparative test reports. Our own survey data include representative samples of members of CU and of subscribers to the two German as well as the Norwegian testing journals. This includes a member-based association, two journals published by government bodies (Stiftung Warentest and Forbrukerrådet) and one private enterprise (the German testing journal *DM*). The demographic data are amazingly similar across countries and types of sponsoring organizations. The typical subscriber to test reports is middle-aged and is more likely to be married than is the average consumer. Furthermore, beyond any doubt subscribers constitute an elite of high education, high income and high occupational status. Quite similar data exist from at least half a dozen other North Atlantic countries.[71]

Other data of ours demonstrate that these subscribers tend more than average consumers to search for information from other sources (labels, hobby magazines, exhibits, friends, etc.) as well. That is, test report subscribers are typical of an important social group that we have named the *Information Seekers*. It is characteristic for this group that "the appetite grows while eating"; their information processes to some extent seem to be self-reinforcing or cumulative.[72] The Information Seekers also turn out to think of themselves as opinion leaders and advice givers in matters of buying much more often than do the general population, although they are not necessarily themselves the earliest adopters of new products. At least in Germany and the United States subscribers are more often traditional liberals than ultraconsumerists.

No similar representative studies of usage of labels and quality marks are known to us. While the findings just reported indicate that we would encounter a heavy concentration of our Information Seekers again, it is also legitimate to assume that a fair number of other consumers would be checking labels and quality marks. This is because these means of CI are both more digestible and more easily available (affixed to the product at point of purchase). In the meantime we may observe that the number of nonfood, nondrug consumer products labeled or certified under broad-scope CI programs is limited wherever these programs exist, and that at least outside of Scandinavia they have not even been promoted to the point where the average consumer is aware of their existence.

Our findings suggest that CI may never acquire mass appeal. This would indicate that a certain "concentration of information power" in the hands of the Information Seekers is inevitable. From our point of view there is no reason to be discouraged. The active part of this elite group differs for different products (the writer will gladly read a twenty-page test report about tape recorders, but would never spend that time on an equally detailed report on fishing equipment; my friend does the reverse). For each product, too, the "local" information-conscious elite almost surely includes a sizeable number of consumers who are not generally among the Information Seekers. Observe, too, that we are talking not about an oligarchy in the classic sense, but about an open-ended elite based on free circulation—which is about as far as one can get in liberalization as long as no two human beings are identical. After all, there is equal opportunity to make use of the information.

As everyone knows, it is possible to draw the wrong conclusions from statistics. This is what some—by no means all—Swedish consumer radicals have done. What we have labeled the elite of Information Seekers they call the overprivileged minority, and demand that government-financed comparative tests be stopped. The crucial fact overlooked by these critics is that the Information Seekers are also the opinion leaders of the marketplace. They, rather than the average consumer, are keeping producers on their toes, and they, more than others, fight the battle for better products, for honesty and decency in business practice, and for more truthful and informative advertising. In effect, their role relative to the average consumer is that of St. George, ombudsman and proxy purchasing agent, all in one. The idea of removing from their arsenal the weapon of comparative testing is radical only in its reactionism.

Policywise this does not mean we should rest on our laurels. In democratic societies based on the open market economy we have a moral obligation to stimulate ever-widening circles of citizens to avail themselves of the opportunities to become better informed about the marketplace. To provide motivation, we need consumer education. In the meantime, the reach of CI can almost surely be vastly increased by supplementing comparative testing with more easily available and digestible information (labels, quality marks) and with dialog-type CI programs (advice centers, computerized databanks; see Chapter Nine).

CONSUMER INFORMATION: A RATIONALE

Chapter One demonstrated the existence of a growing consumer information gap. The purpose of this chapter has been to establish whether there is a rationale for independent CI programs and, if so, what it is. It was quickly found that the consumer interest and the public interest are not identical, and that, therefore, to justify such CI programs it is not sufficient merely to refer to the public interest.

A philosophical fountainhead of CI programs was found in the concept of consumer sovereignty: the freedom to consume and the consumer's freedom to make intelligent choices to serve his needs. Such programs will fortify the formation of independent judgment among consumers and make them more resistant to overstimulation by producers and to other social pressures. CI programs will also enhance consumer sovereignty by increasing the opportunity and ability of citizens to make satisfying choices in the marketplace.

Choice presupposes the existence of viable alternatives—that is, options that are subjectively perceived as "real" by the consumer. "Alternativism" is a prerequisite not only to the exercise of consumer sovereignty but also to the existence of CI programs. In practice and to date alternativism is associated with open markets. No surprise, then, that CI programs assume open markets. It was also found that open markets require CI programs—another cornerstone in a philosophy of such programs. This rationale is societal (macro) rather than individual (micro) in nature.

A different perspective on the role of CI programs is provided by our discussion of consumer policy in the context of consumer rights and responsibilities. The three graces of consumer policy are education, information and protection. Of these, too much protection fosters too much dependence—i.e., too much in the sense that it undermines consumer sovereignty and discourages independent judgment. To a fair extent CI may take the place of protective measures. Education lays a foundation, but intelligent decisionmaking in any given real-life situation assumes additional information about the alternatives at hand. Again, we find a rationale of CI programs in their interaction with consumer education and protection. Indeed, it was found that the enforcement of every consumer right depends on some combination of all three types of consumer policy.

It stands to reason that the right to be informed is the most vital of consumer rights affected by CI programs. We have argued that consumer rights will live only as long as at least some consumers really exercise some of their rights and responsibilities at least some of the time. Fortunately, the Information Seekers constitute a group of consumers in all the North Atlantic nations that is taking the time and trouble and spending the money and energy to keep informed. The typical Information Seeker is a highly educated person who also tends to have higher income and higher social status than the average consumer. The elite of Information Seekers is, however, a marvelously open-ended one: the opportunity is there for everyone to join, and for any one product it is true that many consumers not otherwise members of the group will make the effort to be equally well informed. Not only that: willingly sharing their know-how, the Information Seekers more often than average citizens are opinion leaders and advice givers to fellow consumers. In effect, they serve as proxy purchasing agents and ombudsmen for many fellow citizens, they keep sellers on their toes, and they more than others are the safeguards of open markets.

To raise the degree of informedness of consumers at large we need to have obligatory consumer education and to supplement comparative testing with convenient, point-of-purchase-oriented information in the form of labels and quality marks. We also need more personalized CI programs, such as advisory services and computerized CI databanks—and much more experimentation. The plurality of consumer interests with regard to both information and product needs calls for a pluralist, decentralized approach involving multiple organizations in countries of any size.[73]

Let us finally note that an integral part of the philosophy of CI stems from its effect on producers and, thence, on market offerings. It stands to reason—and has been documented in an ad hoc fashion in many countries—that producers whose products receive poor ratings have an incentive to improve their offerings. Furthermore, in cases where reports display that all brands in a market are close to identical, rational producers will inevitably ask themselves whether they might not improve or lower the cost of the product, specialize on some particular variant of it, or maybe move on to something else. In either case, the consumer and the open market system are also likely beneficiaries. CI programs also interact with commercial and personal sources of data. The net effect of such interaction almost surely is an upgrading in the quality of these information sources.

In an open market system everyone has the right to spend his money foolishly, but no one should have to do this due to ignorance. How much information, then, is sufficient? There is unfortunately no easy answer to this question, except that growing aspirations surely mean that what might be sufficient today will not be enough tomorrow. Yet we cannot have perfect information about products—as indeed we do not have perfect information in any area of human experience, from medicine to gardening. Cost-benefit analysis is not likely to give us the answer (see Chapter Five). Maybe all we can say is that consumers have a right to whatever information about the market they deem relevant, as long as it can be generated at a cost within reason. Studies of the costs of implementing unit pricing in supermarkets and our own research on the costs of existing CI programs (Chapter Eight) suggest that we are far from that limit now. Certainly the total cost of consumer-controlled and other independent information programs today is trivial relative to advertising and other commercial communications.[74]

NOTES

1. This is even admitted by as engaged a writer as Jean Meynaud in his *Les consommateurs et le pouvoir* (Lausanne: Etudes de science politique 8, 1964): 120.

The point was well made in a lecture by then Commissioner Mary G. Jones of the U.S. Federal Trade Commission: "The consumer interest is a special pleader interest, no different from that of business and labor. The public interest, on the other hand, is that interest which is served by seeking to understand and find equitable trade-offs between each of the myriad of interests involved in the decision-making processes of public policy." "The Consumer Interest—The Role of Public Policy" (Lecture at the University of California, Berkeley, May 25, 1972; mimeographed release from the FTC): 19.

2. Some authorities predict that we may find ourselves saddled with governmentally imposed overall limits on individual consumption—such as gasoline rationing—before the end of this century for ecological reasons.

3. *An Inquiry into the Nature and Causes of the Wealth of Nations.* Book IV, Chapter VIII. Edited by James E. Thorold Rogers, Vol. II, 2nd edition. (Oxford: Clarendon Press, 1880): 244.

4. Christina Fulop, *Consumers in the Market* (London: The Institute of Economic Affairs, 1967): 11.

5. Jerome Rothenberg, "Consumers' Sovereignty Revisited and the Hospitality of Freedom of Choice," *American Economic Review* (May 1962): 269-83. See also his "Consumer Sovereignty," in *International Encyclopedia of the Social Sciences* (New York: Macmillan, 1968) 3: 326–35.

In coining the term William H. Hutt in his *Economists and the Public* (London: Jonathan Cape, 1936) related it to free markets and the public interest ("social will"). The former relationship will be discussed above; the discussion in the first section of this chapter suggests that the latter relationship may be a cul-de-sac.

An interesting and in some ways unorthodox treatment of consumer sovereignty is given by E. Scott Maynes, *Decision-Making for Consumers* (New York: Macmillan, 1976): 249-349.

6. While some political philosophers would maintain that sovereignty is "absolute," we hold that such an interpretation makes the concept useless in the real world. We believe that like other social phenomena sovereignty (of consumers as well as of nations) is situationally or "ecologically" conditioned, and hence is a "relative" concept.

7. As will be evident in the next section, we do not believe that the concen-

tration of production into a few firms (oligopoly) in a number of industries in and of itself has reduced either competition or the viability of alternatives available to the consumer.

8. Incidentally, neither consumer sovereignty in general nor the freedom to consume in particular assume equality of income among consumers, just as equality of educational opportunity does not assume equal intelligence among citizens. Equalization of income is an issue of social welfare policy in a broad sense, and measures in this direction would rely on governmental powers of redistribution (taxation, subsidies) rather than the market mechanism. William H. Hutt saw this, and so does Abba P. Lerner, "The Economics and Politics of Consumer Sovereignty," American Economic Review (May 1972): 258-66.

These points may seem self-evident to most readers. They are restated here because a contrary opinion was voiced by a number of participants in a consumer research seminar arranged by the Nordic Committee for Consumer Questions in 1968. See Leif Lundvall, ed., Konsumenten och samhället (Stockholm: Rabén & Sjögren, 1969).

9. Freedom to consume has also been related to self-actualization, which, however, is a good deal more elusive a concept. Peter Meyer-Dohm, Sozialökono-mische Aspekte der Konsumfreiheit (Freiburg: Verlag Rombach, 1965): 28.

10. We also have at least one basic obligation to consume: namely, public education.

11. Basically, however, consumer sovereignty must also imply freedom to make choices independent of government.

12. Professor C. Northcote Parkinson in a talk entitled "Parkinson's Law of Advertising" used the introduction of pepper by East India Company traders as a telling example of sellers identifying a latent need that has since developed into an everyday necessity.

That competitive risk taking means precisely what the term implies is evidenced by the high rate of failure of new product introductions. While no definite statistics exist, it is probably safe to say that at least one in three new product or brand launchings fail the market test. Many observers believe the rate is higher than 50 percent. The evidence shows that market failure befalls large corporations as well as small. Clearly, business is not omnipotent.

For a compact summary of product failure studies, see Maynes, pp. 269-71.

13. John K. Galbraith, The Affluent Society (Boston: Houghton Mifflin, 1958): 269. Galbraith has never made clear whether this and many similar statements of his were meant to apply to his own writings.

14. This position is anchored in the ecologic view outlined in Chapter Six, introductory section.

15. If higher levels of education have any generalizeable impact at all it might be in fostering logic in thinking and independence in judgment.

16. Harry G. Johnson, "The Consumer and Madison Avenue," Current Economic Comment (August 1960): 3-10; reprinted in Lee E. Preston, ed., Social Issues in Marketing (Glenview, Ill.: Scott, Foresman, 1968): 253-59, 257.

To strengthen the argument that the consumer is manipulated by commercial interests, Galbraith and others make a distinction between physical-economic (functional, tangible, material) needs met by a product and sociopsychological ones, claiming that advertising is especially adept—and insidious—at moulding the latter. Indeed, explicit or implicit in the argument is also the notion that psychosocial needs in consumption are somehow artificial and contemptible in the first place (presumably excluding the snobbishness of a Galbraith). This notion is pure nonsense. Sociopsychological considerations in consumption have been with us since Eve picked up the fig leaf (as, incidentally, has persuasion). These needs are just as real as are those associated with the physical performance of a product. What the proper balance between physical and social aspects should be in general and with regard to any given product in particular is in itself eminently a question of taste. The fact remains that the exact degree and nature of the impact of advertising (as distinct from other social forces with which it interacts) on taste remains empirically unclear.

17. The trouble with Galbraith is his narrow obsession with advertisers and salesmen: "He writes as though these other agents in value formation do not exist" (Maynes, p. 279).

18. Conversely, according to the same author, "Freedom of choice can be supported without consumer sovereignty where a central authority itself decides what the basic goals should be, independently of what it thinks consumers want, then employs resources to produce in accordance with its own goals, but allows the output to be distributed by means of market choices on the part of consumers, setting prices so that all markets clear." We would be hesitant to concede that this situation would represent "freedom of choice" in any meaningful sense. Indeed, the case is much more reminiscent of total manipulation in the Galbraithian sense. Rothenberg, "Consumer Sovereignty," pp. 327-28.

19. See, e.g., *The Information Seekers*, ch. 2.

20. This is amusingly illustrated in the novel by Emile Zola, *Le Paradis des Dames*, depicting the competitive scramble among the ladies at a yesteryear department store sale. Incidentally, the novel also demonstrates that not all unethical behavior in the marketplace is on the part of sellers.

21. We may note that the conventional categorizations of convenience, shopping and specialty products are based in large part on assumptions concerning consumer willingness to search for various goods.

22. Arthur G. Bedeian, "Consumer Perception of Price as an Indicator of Product Quality," *Michigan State University Business Topics* (Summer 1971): 59-65; André Gabor, "Price and Consumer Protection," in *Proceedings of the Second Workshop on Consumer Action Research, April 9-12, 1975* (Berlin: Wissenschaftszentrum, 1975); E. Scott Maynes, "Consumerism: Origin and Research Implications," in E.B. Seldon, ed., *Family Economic Behavior* (Philadelphia: Lippincott, 1973): 281-83; and Ruby Turner Morris and Claire Sekulski Bronson, "The Chaos of Competition Indicated by Consumer Reports," *Journal of Marketing* 33 (July 1969): 26-34, as well as other studies referred to in these items. Also several papers in *Foundations of Consumer and Industrial Buying Behavior* (New York: American Elsevier, forthcoming) and Maynes, *Decision-Making*, pp. 4-7.

23. Ruby Turner Morris, "Major Firms Comparatively Evaluated?" *Journal of Consumer Affairs* (Winter 1971): 119-39.

24. Ruby Turner Morris, *Consumers Union—Methods, Implications, Weak-*

nesses, and Strengths (New London, Conn.: Litfield Publications, 1971). Some of Morris' studies lack methodological rigor, but then such rigor is not easily achieved in a field that includes overall evaluations of product quality as a major variable. As far as we know, no one has gone beyond her work except in the price versus quality area.

25. Maynes, *Decision-Making*, ch. 7.

26. There is no need in this work to go into the vexing problem of whether it is possible to simulate open markets in command economies or otherwise to combine central planning and free consumer choice. Cf. note 18 above.

27. Note that we are not necessarily talking about less developed countries here. In many LDCs alternatives are plentiful; the problem is the lack of consumer resources. The most critical need in consumer policy in this kind of situation is likely consumer education and protection more than CI (Chapter Nine). Cf. also Chapter Five at note 31.

28. They could also have a meaning in hybrid command economies as a means of stimulating the emergence of such alternatives. In such a situation the primary addressee is really producers rather than consumers.

29. The emergence of the enlarged Common Market and the sixteen-nation free trade area is probably more significant in stimulating intra-European competition than any other possible array of procompetitive measures.

30. Corwin D. Edwards, "The Significance of Conglomerate Concentration in Modern Economies," in Helmut Arndt, ed., *Die Konzentration in der Wirtschaft* (Berlin: Duncker und Humblot, 1971).

31. This section is based on Hans B. Thorelli, "A Concept of Consumer Policy," in *Association for Consumer Research Proceedings 1972:* 192-200.

32. See above, p. 25.

33. Louis L. Stern, "Consumer Protection Via Increased Information," *Journal of Marketing* (April 1967): 48-52, 49.

34. Why should consumers have to listen to the producer-oriented chatter between taxi drivers and taxi dispatchers? Why should we have to put up with five by twelve meter billboards and skyscraper heighth gasoline signs along the highways?

35. Whether this "negative responsibility" is better looked upon as "right" or "freedom" is a semantic nicety that we fortunately do not have to discuss.

36. Some negative consumer rights, such as the right not to be subjected to deception, also call for enforcement effort.

37. We are very much in favor of an obligatory consumer education course at high school level. It would, however, take us too far beyond the frame of this work to develop our ideas on this score here.

38. See *The Information Seekers*, especially Ch. 9.

39. Indeed, we shall see that they apply to consumer policymakers as well.

40. A technical term for reinforcement is synergy. Somewhat vulgarly, one may say that synergy obtains when $2 + 2 = 5$.

41. Hans B. Thorelli, "Concentration of Information Power Among Consumers," *Journal of Marketing Research* (November 1971): 427-32.

42. Germany is a notable exception.

43. See above, pp. 49-50.

44. We emphasize, however, that the needs of less developed countries and underprivileged minorities elsewhere may call for strong consumer protection measures.

45. One of our counterculturist friends is fond of asking, why study deodorants while the world burns? The obvious counterquestion is, why *use* deodorants while the world burns? (We would guess that a majority of counterculturists do.)

46. Pending this development, the testmakers are a legitimate object of the countercultural criticism that contemporary scientism is entirely too obsessed with what is physicially measurable. See also note 16 above.

47. For the sake of simplicity we are disregarding a number of "mixed" organizations here. There will be reason to discuss mixed sponsorship and multiple influences in organizations in Chapter Four.

48. Had the U.K. Consumer Council been more directly anchored in the mind of consumers it might never have been abolished for a smalltime political cause.

49. The reader interested in probing further into the case for and against a central government consumer unit with strong executive powers is referred to the shelf-size literature concerning the bills to establish an agency for consumer advocacy which have been before the U.S. Congress during the last several years. See also Chapter Seven below.

50. It is symptomatic that Germany's AGt has found it desirable to arrange special courses for consumer representatives on standardization committees. This is probably all to the good so long as a healthy quota of participants retain some of the freshness of the layman's point of view.

51. Indeed, if they perceive advising the agency as a prestigious appointment they may gradually come to feel that they are accountable to it—an ironic and yet understandable twist.

52. Similar tendencies have sometimes been observed among labor representatives implementing co-determination on corporate boards and top management in France and Germany, even though the lines of accountability tend to be much clearer in those cases.

53. A certain amount of "reverse representation" may also become a fact of life in voluntary consumer groups accepting grants-in-aid from government or industry.

54. One might evoke the labeling organizations as an example. However, government plays at least an ancillary role in most of these, and there is no basis for comparison in this area with non-industry-sponsored activity. Voluntary labeling by definition requires industry cooperation. At least we may say that when it comes to (voluntary) labeling no program can be effective without industry participation.

55. We are confining this discussion to consumer groups other than coops. As to the role of cooperatives in CI, see above, p. 53.

56. The Finnish consumer association is very small. FRD in Denmark has permitted individual membership only since 1968, and is still essentially a higher order body.

57. UFC in France at least until 1975 did not qualify as a consumer organization; it was a higher order organization of nonconsumer groups.

58. All consumer associations to varying degrees engage in consumer education.

59. None of these three groups, however, are consumer lobbies in the same sense as CFA or the Italian UNC.

60. UNC has other problems. In 1974 it was revealed that the organization had been secretly soliciting and accepting subsidies from industry, apparently in a manner smacking of extortion.

61. See Christa von Braunschweig, *Der Konsument und seine Vertretung* (Heidelberg: Quelle & Meyer, 1965): 74–81, for a more abstract discussion of representativeness, arriving at similar conclusions.

62. This route is of no relevance in the case of governmental agencies and of little interest in multipartite bodies and second order organizations typically conducting labeling and certification programs.

63. The change in outlook is well illustrated by the tone of remarks of Chairman Jenkins in the 1968–69 and 1970-71 CA annual reports.

64. See *The Information Seekers*, ch. 4 and 6.

65. We are not excluding the possibility that a small minority of CU adherents are attracted to the organization primarily due to its broadened scope.

66. Leo Bogart, "Customers, Not 'Consumers,'" *The Conference Board Record* (May 1972): 37.

67. Helle Munch-Petersen, quoted in: *Consumer Rights—A World View* (Proceedings of the 5th Biennial Conference of the IOCU, The Hague, 1968): 11. The same problem in a different perspective: "Man is both consumer and producer; his interest as producer is immediate and obvious, but his interest as consumer is distant and diffuse" (Fulop, p. 11).

68. This apparently was the experience of CA in 1971 when hit by a postal strike crisis. Compare our prediction at the end of the CA story in *Handbook*, written a year earlier.

69. Earlier steps in this direction by CA would not appear to have been as clear-cut as in the CU case. Since the above was written the Consumer Interest Foundation has been discontinued for reasons not directly relevant here.

70. "It is impossible to imagine fully the diversity of consumer interests, a diversity that justifies a broad range of organizations" (approximate translation from Meyer-Dohm, p. 333).

71. For details, see *The Information Seekers*, ch. 4-7, and Chapter Eight, below.

72. In an overly polarized way one might formulate these propositions: (1) If a consumer does not consult a given information source it is likely that he will not consult another given information source either; and (2) on the other hand, if a consumer does consult a given information source, it is likely that he will also consult another given information source. The latter consumer is an Information Seeker.

73. Note that such arrangements in no way prevent systems planning; see Chapter Nine.

74. Again we refer to Chapter Eight.

Part II

Consumer Information Programs: Operations

Chapter 3

Consumer Information Programs in Action

OPERATING ASPECTS OF CI PROGRAMS

Comparative testing, informative labeling and quality marking programs face many common or similar operating problems in their attempts to cater to consumer information needs. Adopting a systems view we might say that decisions must be taken in four general areas that may be broadly grouped as input, processing, output and program support or maintenance. The first three areas are the subject of this section; the fourth will be treated in the next.

What product to test when
What types to test
What brands to test   } Input
What models
Number of units
What characteristics

When to test
What testing methods to use } Processing
Evaluation of test results

Ratings of products
Reporting mode   } Output
Marketing strategy: promotion and pricing

Product Selection and Definition

The first problem faced by all CI organizations is the decision of what product to test, label or mark. A few of the comparative testing organizations based on broad consumer membership consult their subscribers or a sample of them through questionnaires, open-ended or otherwise, as is the case of Consumers Union of the U.S. (CU). Government-financed Stiftung Warentest of Germany requests and evidently gets suggestions from the public at large. Others rely on their advisory service or complaint bureau as guides. Another possibility would be the use of panels, though no instances of this are known to us. Some second order organizations such as Qualité-Belgique claim to get suggestions from their member organizations. Taking the comparative testers in the countries examined it appears that most of them consider themselves amply capable of deciding what products to select. It is often hard to convince the professional consumer of the need to consult the average consumer. The usual answer is that limited resources can be better spent elsewhere. Incidentally, in no case did we find a publicly available long-range testing plan.

Voluntary labeling and certification programs have at least initially waited for enough manufacturers or large manufacturers to request marks or labels on any given product. This is due to the simple fact that in the past these programs have lacked sufficient funds to conduct aggressive promotion to the manufacturers of targeted products. A promotional advantage of labeling many small everyday items is that the consumer becomes aware of the labeling or certification body's symbol.

In the absence of direct consumer determination of the product selection it seems important—certainly more so than most CI organizations would admit—to discuss factors that influence the selection as well as factors that perhaps should influence the selection more than in the past. In a gross way, we may distinguish factors associated with the product itself, with consumers and with the CI organization.

Among product-associated determinants we find that organizations consider whether a product's basic character is that of a necessity of life or a luxury. In the Swedish discussion it is often stated that CI should focus on necessities. On the other hand, what is a luxury for one consumer (a freezer, say) may well be a necessity for another (a gainfully employed wife with a large family). And of course television sets went from luxury to necessity in most North Atlantic countries in a period of less than five years. As a matter of observed fact, most CI organizations—knowing that their prime clientele is middle and upper middle income groups—do test a range of "luxuries," such as trips to the Mediterranean, fancy cars, high-priced skiing equipment, and movie cameras and projectors. There is also the point that a magazine has to maintain reader interest. This might indeed be difficult if it only carried reports on detergents, mousetraps, pantyhose and canned peas. It is frequently claimed that CI should concentrate on big and expensive items, as these involve a higher degree of risk to the buyer. As with most suggestions for CI programs, we feel that this criterion should not be applied to the exclusion of others. The right kind of kitchen knife, can opener or clothes hanger can actually make a considerable difference in the everyday life of consumers. Yet once an item like this has been acquired, many people will stay with their purchase though it may not meet their particular needs.

Similarly, many critics object to CI program resources being spent on small, habitually bought items such as toothpaste, soap or canned foods. Their view is that with such "convenience goods," each shopper can easily afford to be his own tester, especially as taste and other subjective criteria often play a major role for these items. On the other hand, this is also an area where most consumers become habituated, buying by reflex rather than reflection. To the extent that these markets offer real alternatives—as most of them do—we fail to see why these choices should not be drawn to the attention of consumers. Indeed, if the "alternatives" are in fact "all the same," this is of interest as a signal to shop only for price or subjective criteria or as a reconfirmation that one might as well stay in the old rut. Moreover, when polled, consumers appear to want inexpensive items included in comparative testing programs. In a 1966 survey of the Berlin population 20 percent of the requests were for food items.[1]

To the extent that comparative tests and related evaluations influence producers and distributors, tests of small items are clearly as relevant as those of large capital goods in cases where the small item is sold in mass volume (i.e., consumers have a big total resource commitment), and product improvement or reassortment can be brought about at relatively modest cost.

The need for different types of CI programs during the life cycle of a given product market is discussed in the Ecolore section of Chapter Eight. While compulsory government pretesting prior to new product introduction is an idea sometimes advanced in the Swedish debate, currently no CI organization (except some elements within Sweden's KOV; see Chapter Seven, last section) is advocating this idea. Excluding such items as electronic heart pacers we are very much opposed to it as involving an injustifiable restriction on consumer sovereignty, which calls for the test of the marketplace rather than the preferences of self-appointed consumer substitutes. Clearly, voluntary and confidential pretesting, as practised by Swiss SIH for instance, is an entirely different matter.

CI organizations frequently select for testing products showing a broad spectrum of performance or price. This is clearly desirable. As implied earlier, brands of products showing little or no difference in performance or price may be of considerable interest, indicating to consumers and distributors that choice in this case is a trivial—or highly subjective—matter, and to producers that improving the product or, in some cases, exiting from the market might be the desirable course of action. Many testing and labeling agencies search the market for products that may compromise consumer health or safety. Indeed, the main object of several certifying organizations is to establish and apply norms for safety and health. Manifestly, this activity is of prime consumer interest, though its relative significance in CI programs may decline somewhat as nations increasingly establish government agencies with regulatory powers in this area.

Among general consumer concerns that should be helpful in selecting products in CI programs is the desire to avoid or at least reduce mistakes in buying, to minimize consumer dissatisfaction. (To maximize consumer satisfaction is hardly a realistic goal as long as CI programs largely neglect psychosocial aspects of consumption.) The importance of the product in the consumer's budget should be taken into account, preferably including operating and maintenance as well as acquisition costs. If some brands of a product appear to require a lot of service while others seem to be relatively trouble-free, the product deserves attention, as is also the case when a product draws numerous complaints. It also behooves the CI agency to examine how good a job alternate sources of market information for consumers are doing with regard to candidate products. If advertising for electric drills seems more informative than for average products, if hobby magazines seem to review such drills without obvious bias in favor of particular producers, and if personnel in hardware stores and other outlets selling the product appear less incompetent than most retail salespersons, consumers might well be better served by the CI agency focusing on a product for which these conditions do not obtain. An area deserving more attention than in the past is products of special interest to particular categories of consumers, such as gainfully employed women (and their husbands), newlyweds, teenagers, oldsters, and so on. The TEEN pages of Norwegian *FR* represent an effort in this direction. The fact that most CI journals do not reach the very young and the old no doubt is partly explained by the fact that they have made no effort to do so. Labeling and especially certifying schemes must not forget products of special interest to underprivileged consumers.

Among organizational factors influencing product selection is clearly the availability of special in-house expertise or laboratory capabilities. Financial resources also count, both in buying products to test and in financing the testing activity—be it performed in-house or on contract. The availability of testing methods—preferably SMMP—is a crucial concern in any serious CI organization. As uniformity of brands may develop over time during the product life cycle so do the methods and testing capabilities of CI agencies, so that differences in less important characteristics become clearer. Here, again, if the consumer is informed that all brands function about equally well on major criteria, his time can be spent on those aspects of the products of personal interest to him.

The fact that other agencies have tested the product has often been a stimulant. Thus, it became a fad to test dishwashers in one European country after another at a time when less than 5 percent of the households had this appliance. Another determinant of major importance recently has been the possibility of sharing experience and cost in joint testing activities.

After selecting the product classification, agencies must grapple with the age-old problem of defining it operationally. Most agencies avoid this problem by accepting trade association definitions (the SIC code is too broad). Some of the home economics research institutes face it head on by studying functions and needs and not products—that is, home cleaning, not vacuum cleaners or brooms or dusters or carpet sweepers or mops or brushes separately. As the product spectrum gets filled, these interproduct or cross-product comparisons become an increasingly important part of the total consumer information. A broad definition may make the test meaningless, a mark too specialized (as each subproduct category would require its own quality specifications) and a label noncomparative. Too narrow a view may exclude worthy competitive products: for instance, only agitating type washing machines, not tumbling type; one-speed hand mixers; clear soups.

The testing of services held great promise when it was first introduced in the late 1960s. It has numerous problems, however. Many service establishments are only of local interest. The performance of many services is still tied to the relative skill of individual operators—too small a unit of observation in most service tests. There is also a high turnover of employees, establishments and the functions they perform, sharply limiting the time period for which the consumer can expect any given test to be valid. Nevertheless, considerable success has been scored in certain areas, such as financial services—illustrated by CA's *Money Which?*—and travel—illustrated by CB's *Reisegids* and the VDN labeling scheme for continental hotels. Public service testing has been given inadequate attention, though CA— sometimes through its affiliate, Research Institute for Consumer Affairs (RICA)—has made some progress, and IOCU coordinated a comparative study of public telephone service in various countries. Conflict-of-interest issues may appear when and if government-sponsored CI organs begin testing public services. Nevertheless, there can be no doubt that CI activities in the services field will become increasingly significant.

Statistical data concerning the distribution of comparative testing activities on various product groups and services are given in Tables 8–3 and 8–4. For similar data concerning individual labeling and certifying organizations the reader is referred to the *Handbook*.

Brand Coverage

Perhaps the fairest criticism of the work of the comparative testers is that they can only rarely test every brand and model of a comparable group of products. Note, however, that the criticism has been advanced by producer interests—not by the consumers for whom the tests are made. It may be debated whether private organizations have less of a moral obligation than do public ones to include all brands, if one were to accept full coverage as a norm. Perhaps public agencies should have the obligation to include at least one model of every brand whose manufacturer insisted on it. This would require advance notice to the trade of a pending test. Norway's FR commendably tells consumers briefly about additional brands available but not tested—a practice we deem highly desirable in the interest of all market parties. The reverse complaint can be lodged against some other testers. In attempting to be inclusive, they test brands available in only a small part of the country, or available only in exceedingly small numbers, or, worse still, items no longer available in the market—either discontinued or not imported. Another facet of coverage is that, in comparing too many brands, the consumer gets lost in the welter of data. Disinterest or boredom may set in. How many consumers read the German reports on 117 irons and 98 lamp bulbs?

Financial constraints are always present. Does it serve the consumer better to test all brands of a product, but fewer products, or vice versa? Due to the lack of adequate testing facilities it may not be possible to get the job done in a reasonable time if all brands are to be included. New brands or models also come on the market after tests have begun.

Faced with these limitations, the comparative testers usually take the national brands, then narrow the list by taking categories defined by price or other major characteristics such as size or type. If there are still too many they take the market leaders, including one or two brands or models that in the pretest data appear to be interesting, very good or very bad value for the money, or with unusual design features. CU claims to go out of its way to report on little-advertised but excellent products. At the other end, heavily advertised brands are included by most testers on the theory that they will have drawn the attention of consumers, who will want to know whether these brands "measure up." In choosing an individual model of a brand it is important to establish whether it can be expected still to be on the market when the test report is published. If the model has been replaced, this is a source of irritation to consumer as well as producer. In selecting what models to test, most agencies will again be keen to include varieties whose safety or effect on health may be in question.

Assuming that major brands and models of special interest have already been included, we are still faced with a large collection of fairly anonymous small brands. Our budget will not permit us to test them all. The most reasonable procedure in this case is to take a probability sample among these small brands.

Many manufacturers have more than one brand name for the same product. The testers learned quickly to research the brand area thoroughly, and to avoid possible pitfalls by the pert comment "x is similar in all essential respects to y." This information in itself is of great value to the consumer, as one of the brands may be of the discount or "house brand" variety. The reverse problem has also appeared. FRC of Switzerland published in 1969 an examination of washing powders in which two brands were analyzed and found to be quite different. The manufacturer claimed later that they were identical. The laboratory, which revealed when and where the products were bought, showed that some ingredients degenerate over time and that differences appeared at the time of testing. The manufacturer was further embarrassed by the fact that the so-called identical products had directions calling for different amounts of powder, a difference of seventy grams.

In case of a market that is so homogeneous that there are no significant differences between the brands, the CI agency might simply inform consumers to this effect and abstain from costly comparative testing. Comparison between brands (models) is meaningful only so long as the differences between observed mean values for the brands (models) tested is—or can be expected to be—statistically significant, and distinguishable from the inevitable variations between units of one and the same brand (model).

Whatever principles of brand and model selection are used in comparative testing, they should be accounted for in the report. Consumers as well as the producers concerned also have a legitimate claim to know the names, or at least the number, of brands and/or models excluded.

Coverage is an especially sensitive question for the labelers. Unless at least the leading manufacturers of a product are party to the scheme, the system defeats its purpose of allowing the consumer to compare the similar characteristics of different brands of a product class. In quality markings, if too many products qualify in a class, the mark itself becomes only mildly informative. The quality marker IVHA claims that most of the bed linens sold in the Netherlands bear the IVHA mark. This leaves the consumer without any real basis for selecting among them. To alleviate the dilemma IVHA introduced marks of two colors, gold for top quality and green for standard quality.

Sampling

In comparative testing, the size of the test sample is often criticized. This may very well remain an unresolved issue. The size of the sample from a consumer testing point of view depends on the variability of the product and not on the number being produced. Also, comparative testing carried out for the information of consumers are very different from the tests made in factories for the purpose of quality control.

Production quality control is engineered to achieve that degree of consistency of output desired by the manufacturer, usually weighing quality and economy with market factors in mind. The tolerances within which a particular product is made are compromises between reliability and economy of production based on self-imposed standards. Comparative tests are designed to bring out significant interbrand and intermodel distinctions. Theoretically, as Belgian AC puts it in its journal, the testers only need a sample of one unit to establish design characteristics important to the consumer. And clearly, if one is only interested in the capacity of washing machines (as expressed in the volume of clothes finding room in the container), it is sufficient to observe one copy of each brand. It is equally clear that it would be absurd to compare the durability of various models of washing machines on the basis of tests of only one copy of each. Recognizing that different characteristics inherently call for different numbers of tests, the scientifically oriented former State Consumer Institute (KI) of Sweden, in examining vacuum cleaners, made practical tests in one unit per brand-model, made aerotechnical tests (suction power, etc.) on three units and recorded remaining technical data from one of these units. If the aerotechnical data differed appreciably between the three units of a brand-model, the institute bought additional units for testing. Durability tests of cleaner motors were performed on ten units of each brand-model.

However reasonable such an approach may be from a scientific viewpoint, it could not be used by most CI agencies for reasons of both economy and time. Only in the case of inexpensive products subjected to reasonably simple tests (detergents, canned peas) will they generally test several units of a given brand obtained from different stores and regions. In view of the exigencies of modern technology and human factors in production, a single unit of a given model sewing machine cannot possibly be identical with all other units of that model even in its most essential respects. There is also the phenomenon of manifestly poor units of a given model; in American parlance this is a "lemon," in Swedish it is "Monday made." How, then, can the use of a single unit for tests of most products be justified? For us, there are essentially four justifications, none of which is perfect.

First, branding a product is likely to prove a boomerang in the long run if the brand does not live up to its claims or reputation in an open market system. In the meantime, however, many consumers could get hurt.

Second, the tester can—and should—make an effort to determine that the unit to be tested is reasonably "normal." There are many ways of doing this: bring the unit up to manufacturer specifications before testing, if needed (CA is reportedly doing this with automobiles); alert the manufacturer in case anything unusual about the unit is discovered, and invite him to bring it up to specifications, or to comment; invite the manufacturer to the testing site to verify the normalcy of the unit (the procedure of Swedish KI). Some or all of these procedures are repugnant to many testers, who reject all contacts with producers. But the point is that such contacts seem vastly preferable to legitimate charges that tests of a single unit may be misleading. The integrity of the CI agency and the interests of consumers are satisfied if the procedure actually used is laid down in advance and incorporated in the test report, with details concerning any adjustments made.

Third, the use of single units for testing is increasingly justified as complaints and warranty systems are improved, taking care of unusual consumer experiences. CI agencies may well wish to supplement testing with surveys of consumer experience and satisfaction with different models, although in many cases model changes may very well occur before survey data are analyzed. Admittedly, consumer surveys are also expensive.

Fourth, the better the quality control system of the producer, the smaller will be the meaningful variations between the different units. This raises the question of linkage between CI programs and factory quality control systems. Private CT organizations can hardly be expected either to have resources to monitor such systems or to have free access to them. On the other hand, one might well envisage a future in which producers would submit to or even welcome quality audits by independent consulting groups or standardization bodies. If so, it would generally be in the producers' own interest to communicate the result with CI agencies (which might otherwise simply report that "nothing is known with regard to the level of quality control for brand X"). Alternatively, producers might publish their quality control standards as part of the text on warranties or informative labels. The tightening up of warranty legislation currently taking place in the U.S. and several other countries should in itself stimulate better quality control.

Based on cooperation by producers in the first place, certifying and labeling organizations have certain advantages over CT organizations with regard to quality control linkage. Quality marking agencies fairly uniformly, and labelers at least occasionally, have made factory visits to inspect quality control system an integral part of their programs. Such visits are undertaken in addition to conformance testing of the products involved.

Testing Methods and Characteristics Tested

These two matters are treated under one heading as the characteristics tested are in large part conditioned by the availability of suitable testing methods.

What characteristics should be tested, leaving availability of methods to the side? The answer is clearly: characteristics relevant to consumers. The problem is that different characteristics are relevant for different consumers.[2] Consumer input in the determination of relevant characteristics is frequently—and unjustifiably—a weak spot in CI programs. However, a number of areas of generic consumer concern have been given varying degrees of attention:

Performance
Safety
Convenience
Uses, applications (see Figure 7-1)
Durability
Dimensions
Energy use
Composition
Manufacturing process
Care and maintenance
Cost in use
Service and repair record

Speaking generally, a much better job has been done in the first three areas than in the following ones. CI agencies have shown much greater interest in characteristics testable by natural science techniques than features calling for economic or behaviorial research. Psychosocial product characteristics have generally been disregarded, or their relevance questioned.

There is no reason to comment on the list in great detail here. "Performance" for a complex product like a car may be a catchall term for twenty or more different characteristics. While convenience is clearly in part a subjective variable, testers should be commended for not neglecting its importance. Durability has not been given the attention it deserves, the reason being the expense in money and, frequently, in time that durability tests entail. As regards composition, CU deserves special credit for its analyses of the makeup of prefabricated foods. As regards care and maintenance instructions, CI organs have often contented themselves with reporting whether or not such instructions accompany the product. Labelers have incorporated standard fabric care symbols in their information. Cost in use and product service and repair records have not received much attention except from CU and CA.

Testing methods still constitute a major stumbling block. In 1972 the International Organization of Consumers Unions submitted proposals to the International Standards Organization for ground rules in comparative testing that stated that "whenever possible, tests should be based on national or international standards." There is still a dearth of such Standard Methods of Measuring Performance (SMMP), for which, in our opinion, CI organizations have to shoulder a fair share of the blame, though standards bodies—with which most CI groups cooperate on a lukewarm basis—bear the ultimate responsibility. Due to the lack of SMMP for the majority of all tests, CI groups spend considerable effort on developing homemade testing methods—not infrequently without much regard to vast industry experience. Nor do CI groups always exchange experience. In 1969 the executive director of Norway's FR did not know that KI in next door Sweden was developing test methods for toasters. It is also unfortunate that, like academics, CI organizations too often do not like to start out with someone else's results. Greater stringence would probably result if CI bodies were to discuss the test methods they are using more freely.

As in all research, test methods must themselves be able to stand up to the twin tests of validity ("Does the test actually measure what it purports to measure?") and reliability ("Would someone else repeating the test on the identical testing objects get the same results?"). The question of validity is especially important as most lab tests refer to a simulated world rather than the real one. In trying to test the wearability of floor covering in the 1960s, the testers in England got different results from two well-thought-of testing machines. Faced with this dilemma they rejected the machine tests as invalid and substituted hired rugwalkers. Yet continental laboratories at that time had apparently developed SMMPs for this.

Testing methods should be relevant, too. A test involving irons had as one of its aspects the dropping of the irons on a rugged floor. One of the irons lasted for fourteen drops. One broke on the first drop. Which was the better iron? The fact that housewives may iron in the kitchen on tiled floors was not considered. Nor was the fact that the one that broke first was manufactured with easily exchangeable parts, readily available and inexpensive. The other was totally built-in, and on the fourteenth drop was completely destroyed. Was the question of relevance given proper consideration? In fabrics, does more thread count per square centimeter invariably increase durability? Is there an optimum where more thread count does not matter? Is durability always desired? In the frequent cases when there is no acceptable testing method for a relevant product characteristic this should be reported to consumers. When this is not done, consumers may inadvertently be led to overlook the characteristics in question in their purchasing deliberations.

Timing and Testing Frequency
New products are of special interest to readers of test reports. A few CT organizations make an effort to review new products.

Such activity does, however, also have some risks. Consumer buying criteria may not yet have become firmly established, and the test or the evaluation may focus on the "wrong" characteristics. In this case, a very critical report might simply hold back development. In view of the opinion-leading role of the test report clientele, it would seem, however, that testing groups would do a service by increasing considerably their new product review activity.

The markers and labelers, too, are conscious of timing. If they mark or label too soon they may stagnate development by omitting from the label newly added designs or characteristics. If they label a product's characteristics too late, they have failed to serve all the consumers who have already bought the product. Sometimes other factors will cause problems in timing. For instance, by 1963–64 Sweden's VDN, after some twelve years of operation, had yet to create labels for such Swedish designs as vacuum cleaners, though they had developed a world-renowned test method and had been chosen to manage the Eurotest on this product for the purpose of setting up SMMPs. The bottleneck here was the absence of any local manufacturer interested in having his cleaners labeled. Sometimes the ease with which a test can be made or the accident of captive test equipment or expertise may become more important to the timing of tests than the desires of consumers might warrant.

Timing for testers may also be seasonal. If a test for cameras comes out before the Christmas season it can constitute a real source of information, as this is a traditional time for this purchase. Fishing gear and air conditioners are appropriate in the Spring, skiing equipment and electric heaters in the Fall.

Comparative testers have an additional problem: out of date reports. Of course, the reports are bound to be as obsolete as the products tested. In volatile product markets, with new products, different imports, discontinued models, and new substitute products, a product report may be "dated" at time of publication. Further, to retest a whole product group to take in a few changes in models may not be practicable. Some testers make do by undertaking tests individually on new models as they appear after the publication of a first report on comparative tests. Swedish KI did this with washing machines, for example. Several years lapsed between full rounds of comparative tests on such a product. CU finds it necessary to make a full round of automobile tests every year due to the enormous importance of the car in American life. It tries to test other major durables every other year.

Labelers and quality certifiers try to cope with changing consumer buying criteria and changing technology by incorporating in their agreements with subscribing producers that characteristics labeled, test methods and any minimum performance requirements be reviewed at specified intervals. The timing of conformance testing in labeling and certifying is considered in the section on special issues below, and in the section on ecolore in Chapter Eight.

Product Evaluation and Recommendations

The labelers have made their "evaluation" by the time the specifications are compiled and available. They have evaluated what the relevant testable characteristics are and decided on the terms in which performance is to be expressed. The certifiers by setting a certain threshold must evaluate a manufacturer's product to see that it meets these standards (see special issues, below).

The problem of buying recommendations has been a special challenge to comparative testers. From a classical liberal viewpoint it is, of course, as much of an infringement on the consumer's sovereignty to have a CT body tell him what is good for him as to have him spellbound by sellers. This is especially true if the agency speaks with the authority of government and there is no ready countervailing power. That the danger of manipulation by CI organizations is not idle talk is evidenced in the activities and philosophy of the new State Consumer Board in Sweden, analyzed in Chapter Seven. We freely admit that when first getting immersed in the subject of CI in 1965 we were quite skeptical about counseling activities by organizations in the field.

A decade later we find ourselves strongly in favor of such recommendations as long as they are given in a relativistic spirit and are surrounded by the safeguards of competition or countervailing power, or simply given off by an organization of modest standing in the community, such as Danish FRD or Swiss FRC. There are two principal reasons for this change of heart. Our extensive field research of German and American consumers with Becker and Engledow, as well as several other representative surveys, conclusively demonstrate that the vast majority of consumers strongly desire such recommendations in addition to objective reporting of brand and model characteristics. It would seem that to be useful consumer information had better be consumer-oriented! Experience also indicates that the needs of information-minded consumers vary with products. One person would hate spending time on reading "all" about weekend suitcases, much preferring to look up a recommendation, while he is prepared to spend any number of Saturday nights with detailed comparative test reports on tape recorders. The reverse is likely to be true about the next person. There is really no reason under the sun why every consumer should read every test report from beginning to end to benefit from the professional experience of the testing body.

It is, however, crucial that consumers be made aware of the short-comings inherent in any system of recommendations. There is no guarantee that the characteristics most relevant to a given consumer have been tested, or that test methods used were valid and reliable in each case. Even assuming this, there is the unavoidable problem of assigning weights to the results of tests on various properties in order to arrive at an overall evaluation of each brand or model. Ultimately all weighting systems are subjective. As pointed out by Dr. Hüttenrauch, the executive director of Warentest, a special com-plication in this context is caused by safety and any other property the tester may consider a sine qua non (such as a certain minimum suction power in vacuum cleaners).[3] Most testers would automatical-ly exclude from consideration for a high rating any model they con-sider nonsafe—yet there are many consumers willing to take certain safety risks if in doing this they can obtain superior performance.

No matter how "reasonable" the weighting system, it fails to take into account the Gestalt effect; that is, the whole is something else than a collection of parts or characteristics. A house is something more than a collection of bricks, boards and nails, a set of physical dimensions, a number of rooms, etc. If the rating system fails to take Gestalt into account it has a serious shortcoming; if it does, we are in effect adding one more layer of subjectivity.

Next, we have the problem that consumer needs differ; they may not use the product for the purpose or in the manner contemplated by the tester (or the producer, for that matter). A classic example is the tale of a threadbare young Parisian buying old bread for a few sous at the boulangerie. The salesgirl, taking pity on him, one day gave him freshly baked bread with plenty of butter. Shortly there-after the young man stormed in, blaming the girl for ruining his best painting. He had been using stale bread to clean unwanted marks and smudges from his canvas. In the area of product use the modest em-ployment of marketing research by testers is especially disturbing.

Having reviewed all these complications we may perhaps derive some consolation from the Warentest experience, which suggests that small groups of trade, technical and consumer representatives often arrive at surprisingly similar rating results. Indeed, according to the article just referred to, this often happens even if the relative weights of different characteristics are altered within reasonable limits.

We still have a major stumbling block, however. The attention thus far has been on the evaluation of the product and its characteristics per se. For each product there is a price the consumer has to pay. A traditional battle cry of the testmakers has been "value for money." Suppose the best model costs a lot more than the others. If we now want to take price into account before we decide what is the best "value for money," we clearly have added yet another layer of subjectivity. Becoming aware of this has been a disturbing experience to several testers; there is a manifest trend away from the agency weighing price against "quality" in lieu of the consumer. However, some CT bodies still describe certain brands as especially "price-worthy" (e.g., VKI of Austria). We prefer the rather ingenious solution adopted in quite a few instances, i.e., divide the brands (models) into price classes and then rank them within each class.[4]

Philosophically, this discussion has really centered on those age-old slippery concepts, quality and value. We have no ambition to contribute to the perennial debate as to their meaning. The European Organization for Quality Control (EOQC) defines quality as the degree of suitability of the product for its purpose. This is a good start, but as soon as one realizes that a product may have lots of purposes (including that of boosting my self-confidence or impressing my friend), we recognize its deficiencies. What is worse is that the definition suggests that quality can be reduced to something purely objective. This is simply not true. To us, quality is objectively good only if a majority of people would consider it good. To a great extent value, quality and price vary in the eyes of the beholder: thus,

$$V_s = f(P_s, Q_s, X_s, T).$$

V is value, P is price, Q is the evaluation of suitability in EOQC terms, and X refers to additional factors that may be of importance to the individual consumer (notably, though hardly ever exclusively, psychosocial ones). We add the subscripts to indicate that at the individual level every one of these items is ultimately subjective. T stands for the point in time at which the individual makes the evaluation, reflecting the fact that his criteria are likely to change over time. Note that we are not denying that a lot of subjective criteria or judgments may be identical.

A concluding note on the form of recommendations. There is a global trend at work away from singling out one or two brands as "best buys" and toward a greater differentiation in ratings. Warentest, for example, uses a five point scale of recommendation from "very good" to "not satisfactory." If the top brand in a test does not seem "very good" that designation simply is not used. In the

Warentest 1969 report on twenty-seven European ski bindings only one rated as high as between "good" and "satisfactory" (in large part for safety reasons). Unless there are clear-cut differences between brands, ratings had better be avoided. The trend toward multiple ratings is in line with the relativistic spirit in which recommendations should be used. We should not lose sight of the fact that in an open market system every model is the best buy for some consumer on some occasion. At the other extreme it is clearly subversive of that system to say (as the new Swedish State Consumer Board has been known to do) that "It doesn't matter what brand of product A you buy, they are all the same anyway"—when even superficial examination indicates an array of differences. Even observers skeptical of product recommendations will have to agree that ratings are preferable to such a statement—from both consumer and producer points of view.

Reporting and Delivery

Test results and evaluations constitute the raw material for reporting to consumers. It is clearly in the interest of all concerned —consumers, producers, distributors, CI agency and the labs to which tests typically are subcontracted—that the data are as thoroughly verified and are presented in as fair a manner as possible. A policy issue that arises here in CT organizations is to what extent producers should have an opportunity to comment on results, and hence have access to them before publication. The IOCU guidelines referred to earlier recognize that it is "desirable" that producers should be able to comment on the "specific results of tests on their own products before publication." Some CT bodies—including CU—have been sufficiently skeptical of cooperation with "the enemy" to resist advance circulation of results. Others permit producers to see only the technical report on their own brand. Still others give each producer a copy of the report on his brand plus reports on the other brands from which producer and brand names have been deleted. This would seem to be the preferable procedure in a balanced view of things. As far as we know, no CT agency permits producers advance access to the final comparative report intended for the journal. The varying policies among members is recognized in the IOCU statement, which ends on the somewhat anticlimactic note that "the degree to which this is done should be a matter for individual organizations to decide for themselves."

Another somewhat sensitive matter is the cooperation between technical and editorial personnel. This created sufficient friction in Sweden's KI to force a change in the bylaws by which control of journal content was for practical purposes completely delegated to the editors. Most other CT organizations have been able to bridge over disagreements without such drastic measures. It would seem that in the interest of credibility technical personnel must be de facto responsible for the contents, even if editors are responsible de jure. Certainly this is the kind of division of responsibility that CT groups themselves have typically insisted on in governing their own relationships with radio and TV (see Chapter Four).

Editors are necessary to insure readability and understandability, and while some CT journals are fairly "dry" (*Consumer Reports*, for example), we believe a sincere effort is made to find a balance between popularization on the one hand and informative detail and fairness on the other. A possible exception is the transformed *Råd och Rön* in Sweden (see Chapter Seven. It is true that the alleged lack of readability is a favorite target of critics of CT. Yet the evidence from journals manifestly striving for a popular image and variegated content is mixed. On the one hand we have the outstandingly successful *Forbrukerrapporten* in Norway; on the other we have such magazines as the Danish *Taenk* and German *DM*, both of which have been literally struggling to survive for a good many years. Our own research demonstrates that readability is *not* a concern of readers of *test* and *Consumer Reports*. The evidence from nonreaders is sufficiently divided and uncertain to make us doubt that popularization is a panacea strategy by which to increase circulation.[5] Clearly this does not mean that readability can or should be disregarded.

To facilitate planning and to secure total or partial financial independence, CT journals focus heavily on subscribers, who are attracted with special promotions and pricing. For smaller journals this may indeed be the only policy available, as a certain minimum volume is frequently required by newsstand chains and bookstores before they will handle a new item—an uncomfortable chicken-and-egg situation. Even for the large testing journals newsstand sales are typically only a modest proportion of total sales. Most readers of such journals are apparently habitual, in which case convenience and price differentiation induce subscription. (The experience of *Taenk* and *DM* again suggests that popularization is not sufficient to win the newsstand trade.) As many CT bodies are second order organizations (sponsored by women's, coop, or labor groups) one might expect that sponsoring groups would offer a ready outlet for CT journals, but this has generally not been the case (see Chapter Four). On the subject of circulation, we finally note with satisfaction that there appears to be a trend among the substantial minority of CT bodies who used to inflate circulation figures, or to with-hold them, toward honest and open publication.

Labelers and certifiers have an entirely different reporting and publications challenge. These groups determine the reporting for-mat, but the detailed information that goes on a label about a given brand or model is generally the responsibility of the producer. Readability studies by VDN and others have indicated that simpli-fication and graphic presentation is of the essence in accounting for individual performance characteristics. This is a topic calling for separate treatment. Here we shall only demonstrate one approach which illustrates what might well be called "the complexity of simplification." After naming a certain characteristic, the perfor-mance of the model at hand might be indicated in this way:

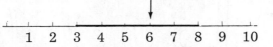

In this case, the yardstick covering the entire range of imaginable practical performance has been given a scale of 0-10. The values actually encountered in the marketplace are in the 3-8 range, and the performance of this brand is 6. Further simplification without major loss of information may be achieved by showing only the range in the marketplace and the performance of the brand at hand. Such presentation is also desirable when there is no specific upper limit, as in the case of vacuum cleaner suction power. There is always a question of how far to go in simplification, as a certain amount of information loss occurs at every step. (See Figure 3-1.)

This is well illustrated by the appliance energy-efficiency label-ing program in the United States. It was felt by many that to provide an incentive for prospective consumers to conserve energy the label should have energy cost data. But kilowatt-hour prices vary sig-nificantly between regions of the country as well as over time. In the case of air conditioners it was then agreed by the industry and the Department of Commerce (after some consumer input) that the label would carry only an energy efficiency rating (EER), derived by dividing cooling capacity in Btu/hour with electricity consump-tion in watts. It turns out, however, that energy efficiency tends to be inherently greater in larger units. Thus the efficiency range in-formation with which the EER of the unit at hand is compared is confined to models of the size of that unit only. The label suggests that "for information on cost of operation and selection of correct cooling capacity, ask your dealer" (or write the National Bureau of Standards) for an NBS flyer discussing these matters in detail. If the consumer does not wish to take that trouble he can at least compare

Figure 3-1. Non-informative Labeling

Drawing by Levin; © 1971 The New Yorker Magazine, Inc.

the efficiency ratings of models of the same size, as well as the EER ranges of various sizes available at the point of sale.

As member of an NBS evaluation panel, one of the authors has maintained that any labeling program focusing on only one characteristic, such as energy consumption, is apt to be dysfunctional. It can also be accused of being manipulative. The attention of market parties is drawn to only one aspect of performance. In their eagerness to improve EER producers may come up with more expensive designs, underpowered units, etc. It also does not seem quite fair to turn consumer attention away from such matters as ability to dehumidify and to circulate air, noisiness, etc.

Whatever the format of label or mark, there is a twofold challenge of publication. The first is the educational one of making consumers aware of the program and its value in making buying decisions. The second challenge is that of bringing the information about each model and brand to the point of sale. This is the responsibility of the producers (and cooperating distributors), who affix the label or mark to each unit of the product.

Marketing Strategy: Promotion and Pricing

Commercial or nonprofit, public or private, *any* program interested in gaining the allegiance of consumers (and in its own long-term survival) must develop a marketing strategy. Product and delivery system (just discussed), promotion and pricing are equally relevant to all organizations desirous of independent life. These statements may be self-evident to many readers. Yet CI programs for many years did not think in these terms; indeed a number of them still do not. Perhaps the idea of aggressive merchandising did not seem compatible with the spirit of altruism motivating many leaders of consumer causes. Certainly a major part of the tradition of little or no active promotion prevailing among CT programs until the mid-1960s is to be explained by an ingrained antipathy toward anything that would smack of advertising. Along with this, many CI leaders had the notion that an inherently good idea, such as theirs, will "sell itself"—needing no promotion. This part of the tradition is indisputably naive in an environment with as high a level of background noise as the North Atlantic community. Another element of traditional thinking—well illustrated by UFIDEC in Belgium—was a fear of experimenting with price coupled with a forlorn hope that a low price would attract the common man. Paradoxically, there was little or no marketing research among these groups ostensibly serving the consumer to identify the audience, and the various elements of the "marketing mix" mentioned here were never thought of wholistically: that is, as constituting a coordinated strategy to reach a target market, or a well-defined set of such markets.

Around 1965, a marked transformation among CT programs began. Although some programs—such as Consumers' Research, Inc. (CR) in the U.S. and UFIDEC in Belgium—remain unaffected, the results of strategic marketing are now there for all to see. In the product area Norwegian FR paved the way by a wholesale effort to popularize its journal—an eminently successful strategy in an environment that, at least at the time, was surprisingly poor with regard to women's magazines and hobby and special interest journals.[6] In the area of promotion the change was especially dramatic (if overdue). Here the pace was set by Belgian AC and by CU (see *Handbook*), which began spending 20–30 percent of annual income on promotion. These organizations enjoyed formidable increases in subscribers. Even more remarkable is the fact that AC and CU (and many other CT bodies) found that financial growth could be further accelerated by increasing price even as subscriber rolls were swelling. In view of CU research and the findings in our *Information Seekers* this is not surprising: the natural clientele for these journals is middle and upper middle income groups for which the elasticity (sensitivity) of demand to increases in price is low as long as the price and the increases therein are within reason and general consumer confidence is at reasonably high levels (see also Chapter Eight and Appendix D).[7]

For informative labeling (IL) and quality certification (QC) programs promotion is absolutely critical. This applies especially to the basic educational publicity aimed at generating consumer awareness and acceptance of the system. Ample experience indicates that unless sufficient resources are spent on this, the voluntary cooperation by producers and distributors on which most of these systems depend is not likely to be great enough to ensure survival and long-term growth. Pricing in IL and QC programs does not affect the consumer (most likely not even indirectly, as system costs are small to individual producers). The charges exacted by IL and QC agencies from industry members in the past have been modest—indeed, too modest. Had these programs been more aggressively marketed to industry, we have no doubt that charges several times larger than those typical in the past could have been applied. IL and QC programs have been notoriously underfinanced, as amply evidenced in the *Handbook*.

PROGRAM RESOURCES

Financial
Financial viability has been an almost constant challenge to most voluntary CI organizations, and financial constraints have plagued most government-sponsored or supported bodies. Tables 8-1 and 8-2 give comparative financial data for 1969, and some more recent figures appear in Appendix E. Even though, as we have seen, the picture has brightened for a number of CT agencies in the last several years, an OECD report stated as late as 1972 that "lack of finance permeates nearly all questions relating to comparative testing."[8] Even so, Table 8-2 indicates that CT groups generally have had a sounder financial basis than IL and QC programs. This is true even when one takes into account that the costs of testing, printing labels or certificates, and affixing them to products frequently are

absorbed directly by the subscribing companies, in whole or in part, in IL and QC schemes, and hence do not appear in the budgets of the administrative agencies. A number of CT programs have also applied a significant part of their funds to consumer action and lobbying activities. While they probably have attracted more readers in this manner than they have repelled, the net effect is almost sure- ly a significant reduction in funds available for comparative tests. In the case of CU—by far the largest of all CT organizations—there can be no doubt on this score.

What could be done to increase financial resources? In the case of CT programs no doubt the principal means is—and should be— attracting more subscribers by aggressive marketing programs. A possibility that as yet seems untried would be to sell condensed test reports to the mass media on a syndicated basis. The experience of the large-scale gratuitous programs of Warentest suggests that the net effect would not be a restriction in the growth of subscriber rolls. CT groups which have a bias against accepting outright govern- ment subsidies—a prejudice that we highly respect—might well seek government grants or payments for specific services, such as the development of SMMP, the testing of products involving health and safety, etc.

Given today's social values and political climate it would seem that voluntary IL and QC programs might stand to gain considerably by appealing to the sense of social responsibility among many busi- ness leaders. In other instances, support might well be forthcoming by reference to the fact that by taking voluntary initiative business might avert the trend toward compulsory and more bureaucratically administered governmental programs. Considering the remarkable achievements of numerous CI programs working with modest eco- nomic resources it seems obvious that the potential impact of a strengthened financial basis is promising indeed.

Expertise

CI organizations are often strong and sometimes outstanding in the areas of technical and home management expertise as well as in editorial skills. The larger organizations have also learned the im- portance of specialized competence in such areas as subscription fulfillment. Most CI programs are, however, seriously deficient with regard to marketing and behavioral science expertise. In the past the intuitive feel of general management was the substitute for the lack of specialized knowledge in these fields. It will not be sufficient in the future.

Laboratories

A minority of CI programs have their own laboratories. House-hold-oriented organizations such as Danish SHR, Norwegian SIFOV and Swiss SIH have well-equipped labs to test household appliances, utensils and supplies. CU and CA have large specialized automobile-testing facilities; Belgian AC founded a specialized lab for audio equipment, since spun off as quasi-independent Euro-Labo. Austrian VKI has a general laboratory of moderate size. Since 1969, CA has embarked on the development of large general lab facilities.

In general, however, the need for a captive lab has never been felt to be crucial in Europe. Experts abound, often with consumer-ist sympathies. The corps of technocrats has grown rapidly, opening new vistas of testing methodology. Independent labs, often operating with government grants, have earned the respect of all parties in the marketplace. A prime example are the large TNO labs in the Nether-lands. Warentest has used some twenty-five federal, state and uni-versity laboratories as well as a few independent ones, including at least three outside Germany.

By contrast, the American pioneers of the entire CI movement, CU and CR, forty years ago had to fight opposition from vested interests at every step. (Conditions certainly would have been differ-ent in Europe at that time, too.) Hence it was imperative to these groups to have their own facilities. CU has the largest lab of any CI agency, while CR's is medium-sized. Interestingly, several bills were pending in the Congress in 1975 on public certification of the capa-bilities and independence of unaffiliated laboratories.

SPECIAL ISSUES

Conformance Testing and Quality Control

In the absence of any formal linkage between CT groups and industrial quality control, these are issues concerning only IL and QC programs.[9] In conformance testing a distinction must be made between the initial test of his brand when a manufacturer joins an IL or QC program and subsequent routine tests to check that the brand continues to live up to specifications. Sweden's VDN, Fin-land's TSL and France's AFEI are unique (and successful) in per-mitting the manufacturer himself to do the initial test. All other IL and QC programs required pretesting by the agency itself or a designated representative (Qualité-France has a list of forty approved professional labs); routine conformance testing is then generally left to producers themselves. However, virtually all IL and QC agencies retain the right to undertake random control tests at any time—typically at the expense of the manufacturer. (For their use of this right see *Handbook*.)

An additional checking system is provided for by the majority of IL and QC organizations that undertake by themselves or through a representative to examine the quality control systems of participating manufacturers. In some instances, such inspection de facto may be confined to the occasion when the producer joins the scheme, but generally recurring inspections are made on a surprise basis. Occasionally—as in the former British Teltag scheme—the agreement provides in detail for the type of records that must be maintained by the quality control staff of the firm.

Minimum Thresholds

A hotly debated issue in IL and QC circles is that of minimum performance requirements. With regard to IL the issue is really a dual one: Should there be a minimum threshold at all, and, if so, where should it be? As QC by definition involves the certification of at least one certain level of quality, the only issue is where the threshold(s) should lie. Most labelers in the past rejected the idea of minimum thresholds in IL programs on the grounds that this was an undue infringement of consumer as well as producer sovereignty, and that there should not be discrimination against products at the low end of the range as an inexpensive low quality item will frequently meet a specific need. As a case in point the director of the former KI of Sweden used to relate how each spring she would buy an extremely cheap and low quality coat, which surely would fall below the threshold in any minimum requirement scheme. However, she wore it only to clean and paint her boat, and by buying the cheapest item on the market she could simply discard it rather than going through a semisuccessful coat-cleaning job every year. It is to be noted, however, that there were no objections to minimum requirements with regard to characteristics involving health and safety—for products such as motorcycle helmets and life jackets—whether the thresholds were set by the labeling agency itself or by governmental fiat. In the current German discussion—possibly critical to the future of labeling in the European Community—industry has declared its "unalterable" opposition to minimum thresholds.

The arguments against minimum requirements in labeling of non-safety-related products would seem especially strong in countries contemplating obligatory labeling. In that situation, lower quality models would be effectively banned from the marketplace. Under a voluntary scheme with minimum levels they could still be marketed, although not with the formal label. Consumer education could be relied on to make consumers aware that nonlabeled products typically might be "subgrade." An additional argument for minimums is that research has demonstrated that a significant minority of consumers believe that labels are, in fact, a kind of quality guarantee. Again, consumer education might appreciably reduce this misconception. The very idea of labels is comparison; from this point of view it would be undesirable to exclude certain brands or models by means of an artificial threshold. It is to be noted that a majority (but by no means all) of the buyers making use of informative labels are Information Seekers—i.e., consumer sophisticates.

Assume in the following illustration that we are operating a voluntary IL or QC program. An IL agency that wants to adopt minimum thresholds has a problem in common with all QC programs, namely, to establish the level of the threshold. Should it pertain only to some characteristics, or to the product as a whole? Should it be possible to pass the hurdle if some characteristics are a bit better, while others are a bit worse than the minimum? In any case, if we set the level too low, consumers may lose confidence in our concept of quality, and, at least in the case of QC, the makers of fine quality goods really have no incentive to join. Too, the lower the threshold is set, the less relevant the quality mark may be as an instrument of consumer information. Certainly, if the level were set at zero, the information value would also be zero. (In the case of IL, quality differences will still be accounted for.) If we set the level too high, we are discriminating against the makers of goods of middling or low quality. Dutch IVHA at first set their requirements for bedsheets so low that almost all manufacturers qualified for the quality seal. Faced with the dilemma that in this situation the green mark did not mean much, the organization introduced a second, higher quality threshold, assigning it the same mark in gold.

Voluntary and Obligatory Programs

This issue is generally irrelevant in CT programs. No producer can stop his product from being tested by an independent organization, nor can he insist that his particular brand or model be included. Although the process of clarification was not completed until around 1965, it is now the law in all North Atlantic nations that a producer also cannot resist publication of test results—or exact damages on the basis thereof—so long as the results have been fairly arrived at, or a misleading result is due to a pardonable human error. However, the recent Swedish debate (see Chapter Seven) has injected a new element: viz., the idea of compulsory pretesting of new products or improvements, with a committee of government gurus deciding whether the product is in the public—

or, alternatively, the consumer—interest. May we express the hope that this idea will have slow going.

In the case of IL and QC the issue of voluntary versus obligatory occurs at least at three different levels. First is the question of participation in the program. As yet we know of no general purpose IL or QC program calling for obligatory participation by all concerned. However, Norway has an enabling law authorizing the government to specify that a given class of products must be labeled by the Varefakta program if the government deems this desirable. Second, there is the question of obligatory minimum thresholds already discussed. At the third level, the question arises to what extent participants' use of labels and seals shall be regulated. In a voluntary system a producer may join but later decide not to use the label, or to affix it only to products sold in certain parts of the country or only to some of his models. As long as he reproduces the full label and adds no text inside the label frame he may also freely use it in advertising and sales promotion, but he is not required to do so. Some of the several official Swedish proposals for a future labeling system envisage obligatory arrangements at all three levels (Chapter Seven). If this were coupled with compulsory pretesting and approval, consumer information would simply become an element among many in a state-managed market system.

There are additional reasons to be skeptical about economywide mandatory CI programs. Any CI program requires two key inputs: *criteria* on which products have to be tested, labeled and certified, and *thresholds* of performance to serve as the basis of quality marks. The determination of these two inputs is ultimately a question of values, as is the selection of a *rating* scheme for any overall judgment or recommendation. Thus, no matter how objective the process of CT, IL and QC, these programs all involve a subjective selection of criteria or thresholds or ratings—or, generally, some combination of these. Ultimately we are faced with the staggering realization that there is no such thing as completely neutral mass information to consumers.

A heavy element of subjectivity is simply unavoidable in QC schemes, what with their built-in thresholds. But a dose of arbitrariness will also remain with CT and IL programs as long as we know as little as we do at present about what characteristics are germane in the minds of consumers, whether our SMMP (when they in fact exist) are valid and reliable, and whether our methods of presentation actually convey what we want them to convey. We do know that some part of the audience will think that a label implies a quality guarantee.

Of special concern are the dysfunctional effects of ill-conceived obligatory programs, such as that for energy labeling of appliances in the United States. When only a single characteristic is picked out for the special attention of producers as well as consumers, one may confidently predict that future product development will suffer from suboptimization. Indeed, this may be the case even in the area of energy itself, as appliances may be made in a more costly and energy-consuming way in order to bring down energy consumption in use.

We are not favorably disposed to so-called voluntary agreements between government bodies and business organizations, as they smack of blackmail and smoke-filled rooms. If it is deemed necessary to have the threat of mandatory programs in the background as a means of inducing more widespread adoption of an IL or QC scheme, we do think that the Norwegian approach has something in its favor. That legislation is open-ended as to product coverage and yet makes it clear that mandated labeling should be extended only to products for which such information is of special urgency to consumers. Again, we reemphasize the extreme importance of using a standardized format for the label (or mark) for all products to which an IL or QC program is extended.

We do not wish to be misunderstood as opposing any and all forms of affirmative information requirements. Clearly there is much to be said in their favor in the areas of health (drug labels, cigarette warnings) and safety (life vests, motorcycle helmets). Indeed, we happily endorse such requirements when founded on eminently social reasons, as in the case of truth-in-lending and nutritional labeling of packaged foods. Further, when the odds are overwhelming that the beneficial effects of a standardized information format will outweigh any dysfunctional effects we are also in its favor. As vice-president for public policy matters of the American Marketing Association in 1972–73, one of the authors was instrumental in securing the adoption of AMA resolutions in favor of obligatory unit pricing in large supermarkets and of conversion to the metric system. Sensible standardization of packaging falls squarely in the same area.

When all is said and done, however, it is clear that democracy and voluntarism go together. The truly great consumer-sponsored CT organizations in the United States, Britain, the Netherlands and Belgium are eloquent testimony to what may be achieved. So was the Swedish VDN labeling system. Given adequate promotional support from government (and experience shows this is indispensable), we are quite confident that voluntary IL, QC and IL-QC programs could be equally successful in their niches of the CI marketplace.

MISSING LINKS: MARKET FACTORS
BEYOND PRODUCT CHARACTERISTICS

Thus far, CI programs have emphasized physical characteristics of products measurable by the methods of natural science. In this section, we shall briefly discuss the areas of information in which the programs have fallen short. Such a discussion will demonstrate avenues of improvement in present programs as well as the need for new and supplementary approaches. It will also further demonstrate the need for those bodies that make buying recommendations, either explicitly or implicitly (as by a quality mark), to do so in a spirit of relativism, reminding the consumer of the many additional factors to be taken into account.

Usage Context

Consumers will use the same product for different purposes, in different environments, and often with widely differing frequency and care. CT organizations have not given different usage contexts systematic attention, although most of them will observe differences in use on a sporadic basis. In the last ten years, usage context has been the object of some concern as regards IL programs. The former British Teltag scheme in labeling carpets distinguished "light use," "anywhere except halls and stairs," and "anywhere in the home." Usage context as a key variable in IL has been strongly emphasized in the Swedish debate in recent years, with Dr. Hans Näslund as prime spokesman.[10] Näslund thinks of usage context as determined by user categories, place of use, occasion of use and means of use. An illustration in the case of shoes:

User categories: adults, children
Place of use: inside, outside
Occasion of use: cold-warm, dry-wet
Means of use: walk, sit

Many relevant characteristics may be derived from the contexts of use and also, if desired, suitable minimum thresholds for these characteristics for each type of use.

Clearly, usage context deserves more attention than it has been given traditionally. Again, however, it is no infallible key to the definition of all CI requirements (as some proponents seem to claim). Consumers are still interested in such things as the composition of materials—not least in the cases of shoes and furniture, as Swedish usage-context experimental labeling experience indicates. Frequently they are also interested in multiple usage, in which case the tradeoffs to be made (e.g., between practicality and elegance in shoes) become inescapably subjective.

Prices, Trade-ins

Price presents tricky problems in CI programs, due to its variability in time, space, between types of outlets, between brands (and certainly not necessarily in the order of quality, however defined), between customer categories, and so on. Trade-ins cause an additional complication. The introduction of standardization in this area by means of resale price maintenance or other forms of price control as a rule would be an undesirable tradeoff for the benefits of price competition.

QC and IL schemes generally disregard price. As long as such programs are focused on the point of purchase this may be reasonable, as the price will always be available at that point. CT organizations generally state at least the list price. CU indicates variations by stating whether discounts are generally available or may be available. At times they present a price survey, or state average prices paid by shoppers, or give a price range. Other groups increasingly do the same. Attempts by CA, Dutch CB and Danish FRD to rely on local consumer groups for data on regional price variations have had only limited success.

Availability

While CT organizations cannot be expected to list all stores in all communities, they could well indicate what type of channels carry the product. At least in the case of relatively unknown brands they might also indicate whom to write to for information on availability and/or state the number of outlets carrying the brand. In these respects hobby and other specialty magazines do a better job. IL and QC agencies might well consider keeping analogous information on file at least centrally.

Service

Pre-sale and point-of-purchase service (location, opening hours, parking facilities, display, assortment, information materials, credit, etc.) comprise a large complex of variables, each with many local differences. Consumer education will probably have to be relied on for generic discussion of the importance of these factors. In some instances, local consumer groups have been known to undertake surveys that include some of these matters. As regards opening hours, package sizes, and truth-in-lending, a certain amount of standardization has been brought about by private and public effort.

After sales service is important enough that it cannot be neglected by any CI program. Here we find such matters as handling consumer complaints, warranties, service during and after the warranty period, and availability of parts. IL and QC programs typically have not themselves guaranteed that products lived up to the performance indicated on the label or required by the mark. Instead, participating producers are required to do so, and to repair or exchange any item that does not meet specifications. In case a manufacturer fails to do so he may be expelled from the program. The procedure by which consumer complaints could be brought to bear here has not always been spelled out in sufficient clarity.

CT programs have not done a very good job in this area—and, of course, it is not easy to see how they could. Subscriber surveys of repair and service experience with regard to particular automobiles and appliances have been of value—and CU has been the pacesetter here. To some extent (though never fully), the problem may be alleviated by the trend toward legislated standards for warranties in many countries. Some after sales services (autos, watches, TV, etc.) have been deemed sufficiently vital by some CT agencies to be the subject of special comparative test reports. Again, such reports tend to be exploratory and "generic" rather than aimed at providing the impracticable mass of data necessary to compare all the specific establishments.

Ergonomics

Home-economics-oriented testing organizations for a long time have had an interest in bringing consumer viewpoints to bear on the "human engineering" of consumer products. In addition, CA sponsored an Institute of Consumer Ergonomics on the University of Loughborough campus, and agreed to meet "rather more than half of the cost to be incurred during the Institute's first three years, and CA representatives will form a majority of its governing body."[11] Speaking generally, however, CI organizations have not gone much farther in taking ergonomics into account than to make more or less subjective statements about convenience or comfort of products in use. By way of explanation, it is clear that a great deal more basic research is needed on man-machine systems and, not least, on methodology for evaluating their performance from a consumer point of view, before much progress can be made in CI applications. In this perspective the CA initiative seems especially commendable.

Environmental Impact of Consumption

As a number of CI organizations get involved with questions of environmental impact—including the rate of energy consumption in the use and, possibly, even in the production and disposal of consumer products and their containers—there is reason to ponder their proper mission in this new field. That the area of externalities may offer dramatic tradeoffs between collective and individual interests is dramatically illustrated by the New Yorkers cartoon reproduced in Figure 2–3. We stated in that context that objective education and information about the environmental impact of consumption may well be a function of CI bodies. But let promotion of conservation of natural resources remain the concern of naturalist and crusader groups, voters and governments.

Psychosocial Aspects

We include under this heading a vast array of "subjective" (or "expressive") factors influencing buying patterns and consumption. Among these are style, shape and other esthetic elements. Here are such strategies of social positioning as "keeping up with the Joneses," "keeping down with the Joneses," and the more recent "being different from the Joneses." Here are questions of taste and fashion, and of personality actualization. Other motives may have a religious or ethnic basis, or be generated by a concern about femininity or masculinity. Already long, this list could be greatly extended.

It may well be that some of the interest of consumers in psychosocial factors is due to an inability to judge more "strictly functional" product characteristics. Thus, the growth of functionally oriented CI programs may lead to a certain deemphasis of the more "personal" influences in buying and consumption. There is, however, no reason whatever to anticipate that they will disappear. Nor is there any reason to call for their demise. The psychosocial element of our lifestyle is certainly every bit as legitimate, and as important, as the purely functional. Indeed, it may well be that with growing affluence, discretionary income and leisure the significance of the "subjective" variables will grow even further.[12]

The neglect of psychosocial factors by CI organizations is understandable when one considers their origins in the depression of the 1930s or the wartime shortages of the forties, coupled with the early notion of "value for money" for the workingman. Also, until ten to fifteen years ago the methodologies of survey research, consumer panels and behavioral laboratories were not well developed. At this time, there is less justification in being evasive. CI programs need more initiative and imagination here. Certainly, little is gained by expressing or implying contempt for "subjective" factors in the buying process. If CI organizations find it too great a challenge— or too great an emotional obstacle—to incorporate such factors into their testing programs they could at least contribute frank and open discussion of psychosocial aspects.

Interproduct Tests

Cross-product tests are those comparing different types of products meeting identical or similar consumer needs. Such tests have not been the forte of CI groups. In fact the tendency has been to present, for instance, color TV separate from black and white TV (KI in Sweden, SKS-SKB in Switzerland), or zig-zag, flat base sewing machines separate from ziz-zag, free arm (CB in the Netherlands). An exception may be made for a few home-economics-oriented CI bodies concerned with household functions: ironing, comparing how mangels and irons handle new fabrics; dishwashing, comparing dishwashers with regular dishpan washing in terms of time involved, cleanliness of dishes, risk of damage; cutting frozen foods, comparing deep freeze knives with saws (SHR in Denmark). The results of such interproduct tests were usually presented as educational articles rather than as results of product tests. The editors of *DM* stated to us in 1970 that they viewed interproduct analysis as a melody of the future, and yet there does not seem to have been a dramatic increase of such material in *DM* in recent years.

Even in the realm of automobile testing, compact cars are usually presented as a group, luxury cars in another, estate wagons in a third and so on, without much discussion of the relative merits of these types of cars. No testers appear to have compared the motorcycle versus the automobile (a CA test of the two was largely confined to fuel consumption), the taxi versus the family automobile, or public transportation versus the bicycle. Still, as the product spectrum fills up, interproduct comparison is likely to gain in importance to consumers relative to the testing of various brands of the same product type.

Product and Service Systems

Interproduct tests involve "horizontal" comparisons between several products meeting the same need. Product and/or service system testing involves "vertical" examination of the degree of mesh: synchronization and compatibility of the several products and/or services that have to work as a team for a system to perform its overall function satisfactorily. To take a simple example: the successful toasting of bread is a function of both the type of bread and the type of toaster. The performance of automatic dishwashing is dependent on the washer, the detergent, the waterspot-preventing agent, the type of dishes, the type and extent of grime on them, the hardness and temperature of the water, and so on.

By and large this is an area where CI programs have been surprisingly weak. True, systems aspects have not been neglected in testing components of high-fidelity systems. But in such a case, how could they? And there will be other ad hoc examples of awareness of systems problems. *Consumer Reports* pointed out that the engine in early Ford Pinto models was underdimensioned in relation to the weight of the vehicle it had to move; *test* in their examination of ski bindings did consider the entire ski-binding-boot-leg system; and so on. Yet, considering the increasing importance—and complexity—of product and service systems in the lives of affluent consumers, it is still true that systems testing is a sadly neglected area. It is also an area in which the testers could accomplish much good with relatively modest resource inputs, and where their traditional capabilities provide a good springboard. Of the missing links in CI programs today this is one that could be forged with relative ease and one clearly capable of rendering an important contribution to consumer welfare, not to speak of manufacturer product planning.

NOTES

1. Institut für Market-und-Verbrauchsvorschung der freien Universität Berlin, *Repräsentativ-Befragung der Berliner Bevölkerung* (Berlin, 1966). It may be hypothesized that consumers are less interested in information about a product the cheaper, the more standardized, the more stylish, the simpler, and the more luxurious it is. However, the study just cited indicates the danger of preconceived notions about data consumers do *not* care for.

2. A relevant anecdote is ascribed to Stanley E. Cohen: "I recently received from our college-age daughter a card which pictures a man in laboratory gear, overshadowed by test tubes and other equipment. It reports: 'This birthday card contains vegetable fiber 95 percent, water 4.7 percent, glue 0.2 percent, ink 0.1 percent and my best wishes for a happy birthday 100 percent.' "

3. Roland Hüttenrauch, "Probleme um Qualität und Preis beim Warentest," *Markenartikel* 9 (1973): 434-44.

4. The former KI of Sweden did not give buying recommendations in test reports precisely because of the conviction that the consumer must weigh price, performance and more subjective criteria for himself. In its personal counseling activity the institute freely gave such recommendations after the consumer had *specified his requirements in these regards* and requested brand advice.

5. A recent Dutch study emphasizing low income consumers reports that "very few people express the view that the text is too difficult for them" in the CB journal. Seemingly somewhat inconsistently the study also found "that the attitude towards written information has a big influence on the opinion about the readability." Our own studies suggest that a majority of low income consumers tend to be listeners and lookers rather than readers. Quote from B.H.G.M. Grubben, J.H. Hörchner and T. de Vries, *Consument en Voorlichting* (Wageningen: Landbouwhogeschool, 1974): 32.

6. The stage had been set a few years earlier by German *DM*, whose early success in retrospect seems due to the novelty of product testing and, indeed,

freewheeling criticism of the business establishment in Germany at the beginning of the 1960s. While *DM*'s fortunes had already turned two years before the arrival of Warentest, its tumultuous history in the last ten years is heavily influenced by competition with *test*.

7. R.J. Smithies, director of the Consumers' Institute of New Zealand, symbolizes the new "frontier spirit" among managers of CT organizations in his monograph *How to Double and Treble Your Membership* (Wellington, Consumers' Institute, 1974). A couple of quotes: "I believe we must maintain the highest sophistication in our marketing techniques" (Foreword). "Beware that your subscription is not too low. There's no room in a $1 subscription for advertising costs."

Smithies' focus is solely on subscribers. He soundly points out that a high renewal rate is at least as important as new members, and urges substantial discounts for three-year subscriptions. Renewal rates in 1969 varied between 50 and 90 percent among CT groups. Smithies is also against newsstand-type sales, fearing that this would undermine subscription sales (people would turn to buying only those issues of special interest to them). We feel strongly that at least as regards the Information Seeker clientele around the North Atlantic such fears are without ground. The net effect of newsstand sales is almost surely to attract more subscribers.

8. Reports by the Committee on Consumer Policy, *Labelling and Comparative Testing* (Paris: OECD, 1972): 100. Note that the *Handbook* gives financial data for some forty individual CI organizations in 1969.

9. The reader interested in operating details of prototype IL and QC programs is referred to the *Handbook* surveys of Swedish VDN and of Qualité-France, respectively (chs. 3 and 4).

10. Teltag carpet label is reproduced in *Handbook:* p. 178. Compare Figure 7-1 below. See also Chapter Seven on IL in Sweden and for reference to Näslund's work.

11. Consumers' Association, *Annual Report*, 1969-70 (London, 1971): 5.

12. Cf. Olof Henell, *Konsumtion och sådant* (Stockholm: Bonniers, 1973). Thus far, this area of testing has been approached by CI programs only with regard to wine tests, cinema and music recording ratings, and the like, subjects on which it would be impossible to say *anything* meaningful without entering the realm of taste.

Chapter 4

CI Programs in Interaction

INTERACTION AMONG CI PROGRAMS

The testmakers

Comparative testing, informative labeling, quality certification—all three major contemporary types of CI programs—are based on tests. That is why twelve years ago we first applied the collective rubric "the testmakers" to them all.[1] There is also an array of common prerequisites with regard to operating environment necessary for the effective operation of all CI programs:

Alternatives in the marketplace, such as those generated by competition in an open market system;

Brand identification by trademarks, hallmarks or other means, enabling testmakers and consumers to identify available variants;

Reasonably stable quality, such as may be expected from a decent quality control system at the factory level;

Some stability of design;

Wide availability of the alternative brands;

Some commonality in buying criteria among consumers;

Some stability in buying criteria;

Availability of SMMPs;

A standard of living high enough to make the consumer feel he has a choice;

A level of general and/or consumer education sufficiently high to generate information consciousness among consumers

By and large, these infrastructure requirements are all met in the North Atlantic community of nations.

Against the background of these basic commonalities are naturally a great number of interaction possibilities among different program types. We shall discuss them in some detail, as they are generally overlooked not only by consumers but, more surprisingly, by most administrators of CI programs as well. Major overlapping, competitive and mutually supplementary characteristics are suggested by Figure 4-1. At first sight the differences may appear great. However, we shall see that in many respects the various programs may be made to emulate each other.

As regards *amount of information:* as more product characteristics are included, IL moves closer to CT. Admittedly, there are practical limitations to how many characteristics can be effectively declared on a product label. Comparability is also limited by two other factors: (1) in but few trades in any country are a majority of producers (or producers representing the lion's share of the market) participating in labeling schemes, and (2) few retailers will carry all the labeled brands.

Conversely, if CT reports decrease the number of characteristics tested and minimize commentary, or if they are accompanied by a condensed summary, CT moves closer to IL. A beautiful example of this effect is provided by the "test kompass" used to summarize all reports in the German *test*. The technique is illustrated in Figure 4-2. By adding an informative label to a quality mark, QC moves closer to IL.[2] If several quality levels are introduced, QC moves closer to CT.

As regards *degree of brand comparison:* if retailers carry many brands of a labeled product, or if the labeling agency issues a comparative label catalog, IL moves closer to CT. At the present time only the French AFEI has published such a catalog. This may be due to the fact that IL bodies have perennially been short of funds or per-

Program type	Program characteristics				
	amount of information	degree of brand comparison	counseling	convenience	prime clientele
Testing Labeling Certification	high medium low	high medium low	medium low high	low medium high	Information Seekers average consumers underprivileged consumers

Figure 4-1. Some Characteristics of Comparative Testing, Informative Labeling and Quality Certification

haps to the fear that not all producer-users would welcome such comparison. Similarly, if a QC scheme has several classes of quality (such as the green and the gold seals of Dutch IVHA), the degree of interbrand comparison is enhanced.

As regards *counseling*: testers abstaining from best buy or similar ratings are no more "directive" than labelers. The lower the minimum quality threshold required by a QC plan, the less directive it becomes. Conversely, if labels are issued only when products meet certain minimum specifications, IL gets closer to QC. This development is taking place in several countries as regards the health and safety characteristics of products for which minimum health and safety standards are obligatory. IL occasionally approaches QC in a more oblique manner by the designation on the label of a "suitable range of use" of the product, or even by strict definition of the product itself (i.e., what products may be labeled frankfurter sausage). Indeed, a fairly common experience is that 20–25 percent of consumers perceive a label as implying a minimum level of quality in the manner of QC. For this reason, and as a quality mark easily can find space on a label, the authors are in favor of combination IL-QC schemes whenever practicable.

As regards *convenience:* as labeling information is simplified or made more readable, IL will approach QC in convenience. Similarly, if comparative test reports are made available at the point of purchase, CT gets closer to IL. CT reports may already be found in a modest number of consumer corners in department stores and large supermarkets. What is remarkable is not the idea of furnishing test reports at the point of sale but rather that this has been done on such a trifling scale in the past.

If CT reports were commonly available in the stores there would still be two differences between CT and IL systems: test reports are generally much more detailed than labels could ever hope to be, and test reports are not backed by producer guarantees. The former difference, albeit important, is one of degree. The latter is a product of history in the field; there is no inherent reason why producer guarantees could not be made part of a CT system. As warranties and consumer complaints systems become more standardized (a clear trend), and as factory quality control systems hopefully improve, the significance of producer guarantees linked to CI programs may diminish. This would be an example among many of the interaction of CI programs with the broader environment in which they find themselves.

Domestic Interaction[3]

Most Western countries at this time have at least two types of CI programs. Denmark, France, Germany and Holland have or have had

STIFTUNG WARENTEST
test-kompass   STEREO-KASSETTENRECORDER

Bewertung	Preis in DM von/bis a	Mittlerer Preis b	Aus-stattung c 5%	Bedienung d 20%	Mechanische Eigenschaften e 40%	Elektroakustische Eigenschaften f 35%	test-Qualitätsurteil g
Akai GXC-40 D	698– 828	798	o	o	o	–	zufriedenstellend
Akai GXC-65 D	948–1322	1268	o	o	–	–	weniger zufriedenst.
Hitachi TRQ-2000 D	658– 798	678	+	o	–	–	weniger zufriedenst.
National Panasonic RS-263 US	688– 775	755	+	o	o	o	zufriedenstellend
National Panasonic RS-271 US	946– 995	975	+	o	–	o	zufriedenstellend
Philips N 2510	580– 748	698	+	o	o	+	zufriedenstellend
Pioneer T-3500	590– 798	698	+	+	–	o	zufriedenstellend
Sanyo RD-4300	868–1105	944	+	o	–	–	weniger zufriedenst.
Sony TC-134 SD	789– 898	898	+	+	–	+	zufriedenstellend
Sony TC-161 SD	895–1198	1162	+	+	–	o	zufriedenstellend
Tandberg TCD 300	1120–1298	1198	+	o	–	–	weniger zufriedenst.
Teac A-250	758–1050	942	o	o	–	–	weniger zufriedenst.
Toshiba PT-415	698– 798	725	+	o	+	o	zufriedenstellend
Uher Compact Report 124	798– 915	915	+	–	o	–	weniger zufriedenst.
Wharfedale DC 9	748– 998	898	o	o	–	+	zufriedenstellend

h **Reihenfolge der Bewertung:**
++ = sehr gut, + = gut, o = zufriedenstellend,
– = weniger zufriedenstellend, – – = nicht zufriedenstellend

i Die Preisangaben basieren auf der Umfrage eines von der STIFTUNG WARENTEST beauftragten Instituts bei 154 Geschäften in 30 Orten der Bundesrepublik. Die Umfrage erhebt keinen Anspruch auf statistische Vollständigkeit. Bei dem mittleren Preis handelt es sich nicht um den arithmetischen Durchschnitt, sondern um den Medianwert. Dieser teilt das gesamte Angebot eines Gerätes in eine teurere und eine billigere Hälfte auf der Preisskala.

Source: test, September 1973.

Percentages at head of figure indicate weighting scale for different characteristics; they add to 100.

Translation:

a = price range in DM
b = median price
c = design
d = convenience in handling
e = mechanical characteristics
f = electro-acoustic characteristics
g = overall quality evaluation
h = ++ = very good, + = good, 0 = satisfactory, - = less satisfactory, - - = not acceptable
i = the price data are based on a survey by an agency commissioned by Warentest. The survey included 154 outlets in thirty West German communities. It has no claim on statistical rigor. The price in column b is not the arithmetic average but the median price. The median divides all prices quoted into a more expensive and a cheaper half.

Figure 4-2. Stiftung Warentest. TEST-KOMPASS Summary of Comparative Test Report on Stereo Cassette Tape Recorders

all three types. We may note that while the United States has in Consumers Union the largest comparative testing organization in the world, it is not equally well represented as regards other CI forms. While informative labeling of drugs, many textiles and certain other products is prescribed by law, no general labeling or quality certification scheme exists. In the last six years the comparative testers have enjoyed spectacular growth in the North Atlantic Community. As will be seen, IL and QC programs have not been equally successful of late. However, in years ahead, labeling and certification programs are also likely to grow in importance.

Interest here is on actual and potential interaction between CT, IL and QC or between any two of the three. In some countries we have observed virtually *no* point of intersection, as one or the other type of program thus far is insufficiently developed to build up an interface with other programs. The Kitemark certification of the British Standards Institution, for example, is still of two little consequence to be comparable in the minds of consumers with the widely known comparative testing reports published in *Which?*, the organ of CA. The same thing is true of the labels and quality marks of RAL relative to the well-known *test* and *DM* journals in Germany. In Switzerland the proliferation of competitive efforts in the testing and certification fields has generated considerable heat between the organizations involved from time to time, while it may be questioned whether most consumers are in fact even aware of the existence of these programs. The same thing was true in France until the beginning of the seventies. In Denmark and Norway, on the other hand, where CT and IL programs exist side by side in a state of flowering development, the points of intersect and interaction at the organization level as well as in the minds of consumers are gradually becoming more evident.

At the organization level a certain amount of competition is to be expected, as organization executives tend to identify their own future with that of the organizations whose fate they are guiding. Organization theory does not as yet provide any clear-cut guidance as to the circumstances under which competition between nonprofit organizations is constructive and when it is likely to be wasteful. No doubt dysfunctional consequences *may* occur, for instance, when organizations have to rely on a common central source for their financial support. Even when this is not the case, bureaucrats in different organizations may spend too much time outwitting each other in jurisdictional disputes or on subtle points of interorganizational conflict of little real interest to the clients the organizations exist to serve. Organizational morale and/or effectiveness may suffer from imagined threats ascribed to actually or potentially competing organizations. Certain tendencies of this general type were indeed observed among the CI organizations in a number of West European countries.[4]

To a fair extent, however, such dysfunctional consequences may actually well be worth the price. There is no good reason why a certain amount of competition could not be a constructive influence even between nonprofit organizations engaged in the same activity, especially in cases when the aggregate market potential is nowhere nearly exhausted. The competition between Consumers Union and Consumers' Research in the United States is almost certainly to the good. So, probably, was the rivalry between *Which?* and the defunct *Shopper's Guide* (supported by the British Standards Institution). The coexistence of both during the critical pioneering years of the British CI movement almost certainly hastened the development of the *total* market for CI services.

Similarly, thus far the competition between UFC and INC in France has probably been of benefit to consumers, although feelings were running high on both sides during the early 1970s. Certainly their journals have had parallel and explosive growth. The ultimate problem here, of course, is that the competition is not on an equal footing. INC has the power and financial resources of the French government behind it, while UFC, as a private consumer group, has to be a largely self-sustaining organization.

Even when the market is small, competition between equals may provide a healthy stimulus, as indeed it has in Denmark and Holland from time to time. Yet the coming and going of many splintered organizations in a setting where none of them singly is resourceful enough to build a viable market following could hardly be functional. Past experience in Switzerland is a case in point.

A principally important—though generally overlooked—advantage from the competition of CI organizations of the same type stems from the fact that overall conclusions as to the relative merits of products will necessarily contain elements of subjectivity, as long as products involved possess more than a single characteristic of relevance to consumers. It is certainly no accident that *Shopper's Guide* and *Which?*, as well as *Consumer Reports* and *Consumers' Research* magazine, have frequently arrived at different conclusions as to the relative merits of products tested.

Interaction between dissimilar types of CI programs at the conceptual level was discussed in the prior subsection. That discussion demonstrated numerous possibilities of cooperation and coordination. With the empirically based observations concerning coexistence and competition added here we have a background for a discussion of *systems development* in the CI area. We shall turn to this topic in the last two sections of this chapter, after an examination of international interaction of CI programs and of their interaction with other groups, forms and medias of product information.

International Interaction

International cooperation in the CI field proceeds at two distinct levels. One is the creation and operation of international bodies such as the IOCU for the promotion of common interests at the level of general principle. The other is the cooperation between CI groups in different countries "at the business level"—that is, in the conduct of testing activities or the harmonization of national norms for labeling or certification of specific products or services. International bodies were discussed at some length in the *Handbook*; developments in the last few years are highlighted in Appendix E.

It is fair to say that the record of international cooperation at the business level before 1970 was fairly mediocre. In recent years there has been a resurgence of activity in this area. Cooperation may take a great variety of forms. At a modest level it may involve the use of an internationally approved SMMP, or of a SMMP developed in another country, or the reprinting—with or without due credit—of a test report published in another country. At the other extreme are international mergers of CI programs, such as that in effect between Belgian AC and French UFC in 1969–74 (Appendix E). In between are different forms of joint testing. The European Testing Group has been the focus of activity in this area in the last few years. This is a highly informal organization working in a highly pragmatic way, and without the fanfare surrounding the earlier Eurotests. There is not even a formal membership. It seems that the group comprises comparative testing organizations in Belgium, Holland, France, Germany, England and Scandinavia, with Austria apparently about to join. Representatives meet three to four times a year to outline the plans of their own organizations, to identify possibilities of joint testing and to hammer out arrangements for such activities on a case-by-case basis.

Costs of a joint test are shared. The organization initiating the project is responsible for the sample costs of all models it has chosen. Each participating organization then pays for the sample costs of any additional models it wants included. Laboratory costs are shared in proportion to the number of samples for which complete results are published by each participating organization. This system tends to encourage joint testing by making it financially worthwhile to participate in any organization's project. It does, however, depend on a leading organization that may bear a large share of the cost of the total samples tested.

Table 4-1.   European Testing Group in 1974

Subject	CA	CB	FR	SHR	STIWA	UFC	AC
Calculators, electronic, small	X	X				X	X
Cassette decks, stereo	X	X				X	X
Cassette recorders, mono, portable	X	X					X
Cassette tapes	X	X		X	X	X	X
Chip pans, electric		X					X
Cine projectors	X	X					X
Dinghies	X	X					X
Food adulteration: heavy metals		X				X	X
Frying fats and oils		X				X	X
Headphones, stereo		X				X	X
Hearing aids and hearing aid batteries	X	X					
Lipsticks		X			X		
Loudspeakers	X	X				X	X
Motorcars, four small		X	X		X		
Records: Berlioz's *Fantastic Symphony*		X ·				X	X
Records: Vivaldi's *Four Seasons*		X			X	X	X
Roller skates		X			X		
Rust preventives		X	X				
Safety seats, children's		X			X		X
Screwdrivers	X	X					
Sewing machines		X			X		
Shoes, children's (booties)		X			X		
Ski bindings		R			X		
Television, color		X			X		X
Wide angle and telephoto lenses	X	X					
Number of joint tests	10	24	2	1	10	9	15
Number of reprinted tests		1					
Total participation	10	25	2	1	10	9	15

Source: IOCU *Consumer Review* (April 1975).

Key

AC Association des Consommateurs
CA Consumers' Association (United Kingdom)
CB Consumentenbond (Netherlands)
FR Forbrukerrådet (Norway)
SHR Statens Husholdningsråd (Denmark)
STIWA Stiftung Warentest (Germany)
UFC Union Fédérale des Consommateurs (France)

X participating

R reprint (note that prime reprinters are Belgium UFIDEC and other smaller CI groups and the *DM* magazine in Germany, not here tabulated)

Countries participating in a given joint test will vary from time to time. Table 4-1 presents the joint activities of the European Testing Group in 1974. Judging by past experience, the number of tests reprinted is almost surely understated even among the members of the group. A fair number of reprints were also made by organizations outside the group, such as Belgian UFIDEC and German *DM*. The total engagement in joint testing activity by members of the group (excluding reprints) in the five year period 1970–74 was as follows:

Dutch CB	124
Belgian AC	75
German STIWA	57
British CA	42
Norwegian FR	7
Danish SHR	2

The AC data for most of the period includes French UFC. As in earlier years, there was also a fair amount of joint testing among the Scandinavian countries, including Finland; but in 1974 the Swedes more or less dropped out of the picture, due to the cooling of interest in CI generally in their country (see Chapter Seven).

Belgian Euro-Labo has found a good deal of international use in testing audio and TV equipment. There has also been a surge of joint activity in testing travel and tourist installations, an effort spearheaded by CB. A promising development is the exchange of local findings on holiday accommodations, tours and shopping. So, for instance, CA subscribers benefit from information on Holland, France and Norway based on the studies of CB, UFC and FR.[5] Joint testing has become important enough for the IOCU to issue a set of guidelines,[6] and for the EEC to contemplate the creation of a European comparative testing institute, though they concluded that such a move was "premature." On the other hand, relatively little international cooperation took place in the first half of the seventies as regards labeling and certification, due to the stagnation of these types of CI programs.

Interviewed by us in 1975, the chief executives of CB and Warentest—whose organizations have been more active than most in joint testing—emphasized both the advantages in cost savings, in building a broader experience base, and so on, and the limitations on such activity. Communications problems, prestige of local organizations, and variations in operating philosophies and in test priorities are some of the factors beyond the persistence of fairly dramatic differences in both styles of life and market structures within the European Community that currently mitigate against accelerated multinational testing. Nor are the language problems involved in precise translation of test reports entirely trivial, as anyone who has had personal experience of sophisticated translation work can testify. There is also the intangible but vital issue of trust. In the sixties there were the elementary questions of building trust in the professional competence of a "lead" organization executing a joint test abroad and in the good faith commitments of participants to adhere to a joint testing program to the end. A sign of the progress that has been made is that the issues of trust now tend to be more subtle, such as faith in the ability of the lead organization to abide by the programed test time schedule, which typically is a key concern to participants.

In view of the findings of *The Information Seekers* that the prime clientele of CT organizations is a cosmopolitan group with surprisingly similar cross-cultural characteristics it is clear that there is indeed an end user market for international cooperation among CI programs. The Information Seekers will increase in number with affluence, education and international travel. This overriding reason alone is sufficient to be optimistic about the prospects of international cooperation in the CI field.

STANDARDIZATION AND CI PROGRAMS

Standardization and CI programs interact in various ways. Indeed, product standards that are voluntarily applied are information in and of themselves.[7] While compulsory standards (for instance, for life jackets, motorcycle helmets) do convey some information, their prime policy purpose is consumer protection.

A few national standards bodies are themselves reasonably active in QC programs for consumer products. Prime examples are French AFNOR and British BSI (see *Handbook*). In recent years the American National Standards Institute (ANSI) has inaugurated a program for consumer products certification, but little of practical significance has been accomplished thus far. The importance of IL and QC has been formally recognized by the Committee on Consumer Questions of the International Standards Organization (ISO/TC 73), which in 1974 produced a draft guide for IL and in 1975 a guide for QC programs.

Standards organizations primarily have been interested in industrial products and in methods of testing them. Industrial and institutional buyers have had enough influence to bring about an interest in standards even among those suppliers who may have been reluctant. As industries in large part supply other industries, there has often been a commonality of interest in standardization between buyers and sellers. In industry, too, functional characteristics often predominate, while in the case of consumer products, style and other variables tend to play a substantial role. Serious work at the national and international levels as far as consumer products go is largely a phenomenon of the last fifteen years. The process has been a slow one, both as regards products and SMMPs. We have respect for the quality of what has been done—but it simply falls too far short in scope. Standardization and variety limitation is urgently needed for packages in most countries. The same thing goes for auto tires. The U.S. tire labeling scheme is literally worthless as long as the consumer has to contend with *hundreds* of types and sizes of tires. We do not object to their all being made, as long as they are categorized in a meaningful, managable number of classes. Definitions of products, characteristics and measurements in which their performance is to be expressed exist only for a couple of handfuls of consumer products at the international as well as most national levels. The development of SMMP is proceeding at a plodding rate. Little is heard of ISCA, the International Standards Steering Committee for Consumer Affairs, which was created largely at the behest of IOCU to bring about acceleration of the international standardization effort in matters of consumer interest.

Consumer representation is typically unsatisfactory, nationally and internationally. It must be underscored that consumer groups in general and CI programs in particular do not devote the energies to this cause that it deserves. From personal observation we are aware that CU in the last few years has permitted itself to be represented on a number of American standards committees largely in a figurehead capacity.

For such purposes as prestandards studies of products in use and the development of relevant product characteristics, consumer participation in the standards process may be ensured by the use of lay consumer sounding boards and by structured sample surveys. But it is imperative that there is also a *continuous* participation of consumer representatives in any standards project. Consumer representatives on standards committees should include both "unaffiliated" consumer sophisticates of the Information Seeker type and representatives of consumer organizations. It is truly important to have people of the first type to provide a certain "freshness," as the representatives of consumer organizations tend to be many of the same overly busy persons from one committee to the next. To entrust standards work exclusively to engineers and other technical experts is as absurd as entrusting all questions of war to the generals. Worse still is to jam such committees with producer representatives without an adequate counterbalance.

A key problem as regards consumer representation is that private citizens and representatives of nonprofit organizations cannot be expected to give freely of their time without a refunding of out-of-pocket expenses. In Germany and the United States, modest beginnings have been made to finance consumer representation out of public monies. This should be done on a much larger scale, although safeguards will have to be provided against favoritism and routine use of the same persons.

Standards may be abused to retard change, to favor certain producers over others, to facilitate cartel arrangements and to serve as invisible barriers to the free flow of international trade. In these areas constant vigilance of consumer and government representatives in standards work is needed. International pressure should be brought on national or regional (as in Europe) standards groups when their norms may create new barriers to trade.

INTERACTION WITH OTHER FORMS AND MEDIA OF PRODUCT INFORMATION

Advertising

In a fundamental sense, all communication conveys information. Thus, instead of saying that advertising typically furnishes both information and persuasion, we should rather say that it has an objective and a subjective information component. Discussions about product information often seem predicated on the twin assumptions that objective information is inherently superior to subjective, and that commercial sources—and notably advertising—are the only sources comprising a major subjective component. Neither of these assumptions is valid on closer examination. Throughout history and in all forms of human intercourse subjective information has played a critical role. All we can say, really, is that subjective information is different from objective information, (and that some of us might like to see the two more clearly distinguished in communication).

It is also clear that there is an subjective component involved in information emanating from personal sources and CI programs as well as from commercial sources. If on personal examination of a product we find we like it, the propensity is there to "rationalize" away any deficiencies it may have. What friends tell us about their experience with a General Electric or Frigidaire refrigerator tends to be subjectively colored indeed. CI programs have major subjective components by virtue of their emphasis on functional characteristics of a product at the expense of psychosocial ones and in their buying recommendations and/or minimum thresholds. While it seems difficult to generalize about the relative mix of objective and subjective components in personal and commercial information, it is probably fair to say that both of these sources tend to have a greater subjective component than does CI.[8]

In this discussion we are skirting at least two issues of some importance. It is well known that objective information tends to be subjectively interpreted by the receiver. How to present information so as to minimize misinterpretation is a question beyond our purview (although it is as relevant to CI programs as to other communicators). Similarly, what is (or seems to be) represented as objective information is often subjective information; the borderline between objective and subjective may be vague.[9] In addition, being advocates, many sellers display a strong interest in commingling the two. The borderline problem is especially noticeable in many trade association programs, walking a tightrope between providing objective generic information about the product (electric heating systems, say) and promoting industry sales.

The Information Seekers and other studies have established that consumers on both sides of the North Atlantic perceive advertising as a necessary part of the open market system. Indeed, to quote Dr. Colston Warne, the Grand Old Man of the international CI movement:

> We in the consumer movement are not in the slightest interested in attacking all advertising. Such an attack would be as ill advised as to seek to eradicate the free communication of ideas just because such communication has been extensively abused. Advertising is a valid mechanism for disseminating information.[10]

Let us, without being facetious, add that, *in general, consumers probably get the information that they want!* No doubt the reader (being an Information Seeker) cringes at this statement. But readers of this book—although admirable—are not average consumers. Recall that what evidence is available indicates that average consumers typically perceive themselves as having all the information needed in making their purchases. Applying our ecologic view of social institutions (Chapter Six, cf. discussion of consumer sovereignty in Chapter Two) we would rather assume that advertisers have more accurately sized up the perceived information needs of average consumers than have many well-meaning consumerist crusaders. After all, the advertiser does have to meet the test of survival in the marketplace. The first point on the agenda of those who feel the average consumer *deserves* "better" information is to motivate him to ask for it.

What has been said clearly does not mean that all is well with advertising. Dr. Warne depicts advertising as "an immensely potent yet neutral mechanism. It may be used to communicate truth or fallacy, to exaggerate or to understate. It reflects the emphasis of those who employ it—social or anti-social."

According to its critics, there are three major problems with advertising from a CI viewpoint: (1) a significant proportion of advertising is misleading; (2) advertising frequently does not give enough "relevant" information; and (3) the sheer volume of advertising is overwhelming, creating a high background noise level in Western society, generating intellectual pollution and invading privacy. This is not the place to explore these issues in depth. Some of the policy approaches attempted or proposed will be mentioned as illustrative of the actuality or potential of advertising as a medium of market information.

In *The Information Seekers* we found that on both sides of the Atlantic the prevention of misleading advertising was a key consumer policy concern among virtually all social groups. To this extent we *know*, then, that people do want better market information. (The sticky problem of judging just what is "misleading" remains.) Industry self-regulation by the adoption and enforcement of such codes as the rules of the International Chamber of Commerce has been fairly effective in many countries, but not sufficient to eliminate consumer concern. Britain's Trade Descriptions Act of 1968 cuts through the bureaucracy, issues of freedom of speech, etc., that go with any attempt at minute specification of what must not be said by simply stating, in effect, that a seller is responsible for whatever he says about his offering. Says CA in an internal policy document: "In our experience, since the passing of the Trade Descriptions Act, it is quite hard to find provable misstatements in advertisements, although there may be more than we realize."[11] In the United States the Federal Trade Commission has been conducting large-scale experiments in forcing advertisers to submit all necessary documentation to substantiate their claims. While we do not doubt the value of the principle that a seller should be prepared to substantiate his claims, experience indicates that it would be both impractical and monstrously expensive to require public proof of every claim in every ad. While policy experimentation proceeds, we would like to add an empirical and a conceptual observation. By far the greatest volume of misleading advertising and promotion measures are probably local rather than national phenomena. Surprisingly little has been done anywhere to combat misleading practices locally. At the conceptual level we may note that if the idea of "guaranteed ads" were ever fully realized we would actually have a new CI system of an effectiveness that neither governments nor private CI agencies could ever hope to emulate. Its only weaknesses would be lack of standardization and the direct comparability afforded by testing journals.[12]

The problem that advertising does not carry enough "relevant" (i.e., in the minds of critics, functional-performance-oriented) information can also be approached in various ways. We maintain that by far the most effective inducement would be consumer education that would raise popular expectation and demand for "better" information. Advertising could also become a great deal more informative (in the sense the word is used by critics) by more intense interaction with CI programs. Quality marks and informative labels may be freely reproduced in advertising. There would be many more products marked and labeled if advertisers more actively supported QC and IL programs. In Germany, one of the two largest mail-order firms is experimenting with its own informative labeling system, an integral part of which—with Warentest's consent—would be the overall evaluation given the product by *test*. A problem yet to be overcome is finding some means by which other CT programs might render active cooperation to industry efforts to make advertising more informative without endangering the perceived credibility and integrity of the CT groups themselves.

Beyond consumer education, more direct interaction with CI programs and "thou-shalt-not" regulation as means of making advertising more informative are governmentally enforced positive requirements that ads for certain products contain a specified minimum of information. Sweden is comtemplating major steps in this direction (Chapter Seven). Other countries have such requirements on an ad hoc basis, specifying, for example, that cigarette ads carry a warning about the health risk in smoking or that printed advertising for packaged or canned foods in which nutritional claims are made must include a label of all ingredients by weight, volume or percentage. Our view of compulsory information requirements in advertising is that there certainly is a place for them in the area of health and safety. We would, however, tread delicately in the unknown territory beyond, pending much more research on the average consumer's perceived needs for, and ability to absorb, information of the type specified by critics in each case. Compulsory regulations, when not clearly called for, are generally dysfunctional to the smooth operation of the open market system. There is a clear-cut possibility that requirements for "unwanted" information would contribute more noise and cost than benefits.

This brings us back to the problem of advertising as noise. Not only is this noise often irritating. It also makes it forever more costly for a new entry in the marketplace to make its voice heard—be it a seller or a consumer group. Further, the background static may be counterinformative. "The clearest case of negative information effect is the intensive advertising of products that are virtually identical with those of competitors in all characteristics in which consumers would be concerned—which is true of a good many consumer soft goods—aspirin and gasoline probably being good examples."[13] In cases where indiscriminate advertising would constitute an obvious invasion of privacy—as on the airwaves—most countries limit the permissible amount of advertising (some setting it at zero). Public regulation has also been used to limit the size of signs in cities and of billboards along highways to prevent obnoxious excesses. No reasonable person could quarrel with such restraints. Some countries have tried to dampen advertising by taxation. This may well be a more questionable device from the viewpoints of both the right to free speech and the effects on market structure and competition. One must avoid throwing out the baby with the bathwater. In the end we shall probably have to accept a certain amount of advertising "noise" as part of the price we pay for the benefits of an open market system and free choice.

The likelihood of greater interaction and reinforcement of advertising and CI programs in the future is discussed in the final chapter.

Individual Producers and Distributors

Marketing textbooks discuss advertising at great length as a competitive tool. However, they fail completely to discuss the provision of superior product information as a marketing strategy. Yet there can be no doubt that this is a melody of the future, in which Information Seekers will constitute a continually growing part of the population.

Already there are straws in the wind. Several American grocery chains have advertised the availability of unit pricing and open dating in their stores as a reason for shopping there. Federated Department Stores have experimented with informative labels of their own; Macy's of New York provides carpet and furniture customers with detailed information packets; and so on. No doubt considerations of information competition have also influenced the decision of firms to join (or not to join) IL and QC programs in many countries. All in all, however, it is probably fair to say that the golden opportunities of information competition remain largely unexplored. As we have remarked elsewhere, this is especially evident in the sad area of sales training. We foresee an explosive development in the area of information as a competitive strategy.

Hobby and Specialty Magazines

These magazines can do a very effective job of informing consumers in their product areas. Indeed, they may go into even further detail than CT journals. Many of their articles are broadly educational, and in the CI area they frequently carry non-test-based market overviews of products and models. Here they do a much better job than CI programs. Not unnaturally, they will often also carry more current information. Some of these magazines will do product tests. The trouble is that these tests frequently are not comparative, and the reader does not know what standards have been used in evaluation. Not infrequently, hobby and specialty magazines are fairly uncritical in their product reviews, and it is not uncommon to find mass reprints of favorable articles circulated at retail outlets of the products. It is to be hoped that greater sophistication of readers and increasing competition with CT journals will make for more of the integrity that seems to be lacking in some cases.

In *The Information Seekers* it was found that, for auto purchases, German subscribers to CT journals relied more heavily on auto magazines than on their testing journal. For American subscribers auto specialty magazines played no role at all. It should be noted that CU does a superb job of auto testing, and that German testing journals carried rather few auto reports at the time of the study. For other consumer durable goods purchases subscribers in both countries ranked their testing journals way ahead of specialty magazines. Average consumers—not very magazine-oriented in the first place—tended to rank specialty magazines about as low as testing journals as information sources in both countries.

The interaction possibilities between CT and specialty magazines are obvious. We have just mentioned the German auto example; and we pointed out earlier that one likely reason for the early and dramatic growth of the Norwegian FR testing journal was the relative poverty of the hobby, specialty and homemaker magazine market in that country.

Press, TV and Radio

In general, surprisingly little interaction between CI programs and the daily press exists. We would guess that this is due to the fact that comparative test reports as a rule are not sensational and to a perverted fear among many newspapers of incurring the wrath of individual advertisers. The occasional exposé, such as the UFC report on pollution of French Atlantic beaches, is another matter. The former KI in Sweden made news more as a controversial organization than for the information it generated. CA in England is part of the Establishment and as such is news.

It must be said, too, that traditionally most CI programs have been half-hearted in their cooperation with the press, in part due to a fear that publication of their test results by others would reduce their own subscriptions. That this fear is mistaken is strongly indicated by the great success of the aggressive press relations program conducted by STIWA in parallel with dramatic increases in the circulation of *test*. In 1973 alone the condensed test reports prepared by STIWA (including brand names as a matter of course) were published one or more times by over 350 papers and magazines in a total of well over 500 million copies. One cannot doubt that this was a significant contribution to the informedness of German consumers. Apparently it was also valuable publicity for *test*. Although a journal at a different stage of its growth curve might not have a similar experience, it would certainly seem that this example is worth considering by other CT bodies. Those that have to be more concerned about standing on their own financial feet than Warentest may well ponder the possibility of sales of condensed test reports to the press on a syndicated basis. If experience turns out as favorably in other countries as in Germany we may anticipate another desirable development: the more extensive preparation of product reviews (analogous to book, movie and music reviews) by the newspapers themselves. Should summary test reports prove to be of reader interest, the papers may well overcome their scruples regarding advertiser relations.

The relations of CI organizations to radio and TV has been a mixed blessing. Again, Warentest is in the lead. Characteristically, STIWA insists on retaining control of program contents. The issue of program control—as detailed in the *Handbook*—has been one of the major stumbling blocks on the road to closer cooperation between CT organizations and these media. Although most North Atlantic countries by now have some kind of consumer programs on radio and TV, these programs tend to focus on policy issues (muckraking being the theme in a country like Sweden) or matters of home economics. Yet data in *The Information Seekers* demonstrate that radio and TV would have to be used to a much greater extent if we desire to reach average consumers with CT reports.

Para-CI Organizations

In this group we include a great number of organizations unaffiliated with individual sellers that disseminate product information but do not meet our criteria for CI programs as regards continuous and broad-scale consumer representation, independence from producer interests, or publicity concerning test methods and standards of evaluation. Examples include *Good Housekeeping* in the United States and Britain, Underwriters' Laboratories in the U.S., the international Woolmark secretariat, the appliance exhibit and information centers maintained by many electricity and gas utilities, and so on. Standards groups in some respects are in this category, as well as hobby and specialty magazines.

Para-CI organizations of various types are here to stay. They can clearly play a valuable role in a total information system in between commercial and fully independent sources. At the same time, CI agencies probably should accept the mission of clarifying to the public (or, at least, to their own subscribers) the characteristics of para-CI organizations that distinguish them from CI programs. When para-CI bodies purport to speak with the voice of objectivity and independence, (as does *Good Housekeeping*, as well as standards groups, for instance), CI organizations might well campaign to induce the para-CI groups to adopt the institutional arrangements and policies that will indeed assure such objectivity and independence.

School System

Until now, interaction between CI and the school system has been exceedingly modest. Yet the potential for such interaction is of critical importance in the battle to maintain consumer sovereignty in an open market system. The first requirement in going from sounds to things is the institution of obligatory consumer education as in Norway and in some of the states in the U.S. The key part of any consumer education program of consequence is to foster student understanding of the decisionmaking process and of the value of information as a vital element of that process. The characteristics and costs of different information sources should also be analyzed. The types, extent and role of CI programs should be discussed.

Consumers Union and several other CI programs are providing materials for consumer education courses as a matter of public service. This is all to the good. It is even more important to realize that *CI itself is of educational value*—not merely instrumental to immediate purchases. Nutritional labels, for instance, will increase consciousness of a balanced diet and its significance to personal well-being.

It is true that prolonged exposure to any form of education tends to raise intellectual curiosity. Thus, it is no accident that a majority of the Information Seekers have way above average education. Yet the important point about consumer education in high school and in adult education programs is that it is a means of accelerating the growth of the cadres of Information Seekers—especially among the majority of the population who will never take postgraduate work in the universities.

INTERACTION WITH OTHER GROUPS

Second and Higher Order CI Organizations,
Special Interest Groups

Second and, even more, higher order CI organizations face the challenge of constructive interaction with the groups sponsoring the CI program. That this is not an easy task was pointed out in Chapter Two. Naturally sponsoring organizations can be of great value—occasionally financially indispensable—especially during the formative years of a CI program. Good examples occur in the history of comparative testing in Scandinavia. However, labor, coops and other organizations sponsoring CI programs frequently do so on a secondary interest basis; if the baby shows signs of aggressiveness and vigor he may even be placed in harness by the parents. French OR.GE.CO. is the best example, but there are many others, as evidenced in the *Handbook*.

Given this background, it is understandable that sponsoring organizations generally have not been effective distributors of the information disseminated by CI programs. Few subscribers have been generated by sponsor groups. Early co-sponsors of the VDN program, Swedish coops were ambivalent about using the labels even in their own marketing program. Feedback from members of sponsor organizations to CI programs is usually weak. Analogous problems tend to occur in cooperation on an arm's length basis between CI programs and consumer action organizations, labor unions, and other special interest groups. Sometimes one is reminded of the saying: "With such friends, who needs enemies?"

For relations with sponsors and collaborators to be of real benefit, experience indicates the urgency of aggressive educational campaigns concerning the nature and needs of CI programs. For maximum effectiveness such educational activities should be directed not only at the leaders of such other groups but at the membership as well. Occasionally it may even be necessary for second order CI organizations to emancipate themselves from the protection of their parent groups in order to realize their own true growth potential, as dramatically illustrated by French UFC (see *Handbook* and Appendix E).

Business

The attitude of organized business to CT agencies has been ambiguous, ranging from outright hostility to co-sponsorship of IL and QC programs. In some respects this may be a reflection of ambiguity at the level of the individual firm, which has frequently looked upon such programs solely from the viewpoint of what immediate competitive advantage or disadvantage might flow from the programs to it. Many business leaders have also questioned whether average consumers urgently crave CI. *The Information Seekers* data suggest that they may well have had a point here. However, the argument ignores the needs of the Information Seekers, that increasingly large group of consumer sophisticates. It also ignores the *consumer right to information*. In principle, the consumer is entitled to any information of relevance for which he is willing to pay or which can be produced without great cost. Business would be wise in recognizing this as a plain matter of social responsibility and in its own overall interest in the continued existence of an open market system.

In Chapter Three we discussed the patterns of limited interaction in the past between CT programs and individual firms. As a collective, business has often been skeptical. The skepticism has been based in part on genuine concern about the adequacy of testing methodology, the fairness of test journal buying recommendations and rejections, and other operational aspects of such programs. In part skepticism has been rooted in fears of "exposés," whether well or poorly grounded. In part it is a natural reaction to suspicion or hostility demonstrated by many CI groups themselves. There will be reason to discuss business reactions to IL and QC in some detail below, in a section on the relative failure of such programs in the past.

Our own view is that CI programs need not less but more interaction with business. It is indispensable both in any effort to develop voluntary consumer product standards and in the bottleneck area of SMMP. It is also clear that individual firms and business groups potentially have a major role to fill as distributors of CI program data, provided that forms of cooperation can be found that in no way endanger the actual and perceived integrity of such programs. Moreover, CI programs would do a more effective job if they were to feed back to industry suggestions for new product designs or improvements emanating from their testing activities or from consumer suggestions or complaints.

As suggested, business certainly has ample reason to do what it can to promote CI. Such programs constitute a clear-cut vitamin injection for the free market system. Likely alternatives would seem to be more regulation of advertising content, governmental monopolies of CI (with or without manipulative intent—cf. latest developments in Sweden), compulsory limitations on model variety, and the like.

To say that closer cooperation between CI programs and business is impossible or undesirable is tantamount to negating the possibility or desirability of democratic pluralism.

Government

Many CI organizations are virtually independent of government, such as CU and Consumers' Research in the United States, CA in Britain, AC in Belgium, UFC in France and *DM* in Germany. Government influence on CI programs may be exerted in a vast variety of concrete and subtle ways (see Appendix D). Financial contribution and direct representation on CI boards are the most generally used media of influence. However, a few CI bodies, such as Warentest and Danish SHR, are outright government agencies. Other government agencies engaged in broad spectrum consumer policy activities also run CI programs, such as French INC and Norwegian FR.

The relationship between independence and objectivity is highly complex. We regard German *DM* as a legitimate CI organization even though it is financially dependent on advertising revenues simply because in its fifteen year history no one has successfully demonstrated a lack of objectivity in its reports that could be related to advertiser preferences. Occasionally financial contributions from government may directly help to assure independence, as in the case of Danish DVN and the former VDN in Sweden, both IL organizations. And some wholly owned government CI agencies are noted for their objectivity. Interestingly, these are bodies whose *first* priority is CI or related scientific testing, such as Warentest and SHR. But it is naive indeed to believe that government influence or sponsorship is a guarantee of objectivity. Anyone living in that illusion is invited to read our examination of Sweden's new KOV in Chapter Seven.

Consumer information is one element in the triad of information, education and protection constituting consumer policy. We have discussed the many possibilities of tradeoff and reinforcement between these elements. Governments around the North Atlantic in the last decade or two have developed an array of consumer policy measures on an ad hoc basis, completely overlooking the interaction of these elements. As the need for a systems approach becomes more obvious, the path of least resistance is centralization. But in a centralized scheme in which CI is just one of many tightly coordinated policy instruments the risk is great that the CI program becomes manipulative. The polemic tone of *50 Millions de Consommateurs*, the organ of France's INC, also sets up a tension between the presumed objectivity and credibility of its test reports and its editorial material that may forebode future problems. In the long run, policy independence of CI programs may require the organizational independence of such programs.

Due to the inherent interaction potential of information, education and protection, CI bodies should indeed be heard at the preliminary stages of policymaking in related areas. They may also exercise a healthy influence on government in the information area itself. A beautiful illustration was CU's lawsuit against the U.S. Veterans Administration forcing that agency to make public its test reports of most brands of hearing aids, tests made with taxpayer money. Since then, the VA and several other U.S. government agencies have voluntarily published their reports of other tests of consumer products. It also behooves CI agencies to urge increased governmental support for the development of SMMP and product standards in the consumer goods area.

RECENT DECLINE OF LABELING AND CERTIFYING PROGRAMS

At the time the *Handbook* was drafted in 1970–72, the authors were optimistic about the future of IL and QC programs. In more recent years the overall picture in this area has not been encouraging, however. It is one of relative stagnation or decline as contrasted to the manifest prosperity of CT programs. Sweden's VDN, the pioneer and longtime pacesetter in the field, exists no more, and the future of voluntary IL in Sweden is bleak. The British Teltag program was discontinued in 1970. In 1975 the IL organization in the Netherlands was liquidated. Qualité-France and Qualité-Belgique have been making but little headway. German RAL achieved its long-desired independence from the DNA standards organization only to find its future in the labeling area obscured by a drawn out controversy among as well as within industry, government and consumer organizations (notably AGV) about suitable forms and frameworks for IL activity. The most important positive sign in Europe has been the appearance of the first labels from French AFEI, which has also pioneered in the publication of the first labeling catalog, an idea that we have long propounded (Appendix E). Denmark's DVN has also had a renewed burst of life.

On the other hand, the United States still does not have a broad spectrum IL or QC program of any kind. We would think that a prime underlying reason is the scope, size and heterogeneity of the American economy, which thus far has placed the practicality of a voluntary, broad gauge IL or QC program in question. The same characteristics of the economy have also thwarted the emergence of a national organization of business that might take a bold initiative in this area.[14] Consumers Union and various groups associated with the name Ralph Nader have shown no interest in the matter. At the time of writing the Department of Commerce has rolled out a poorly conceived voluntary labeling program greeted without much enthusiasm. The relative lack of progress in the voluntary IL and QC areas is reflected by the current shadowy status of the International Labelling Centre (ILC) and the CIPQ, its opposite number in the QC area.

Meantime, IL of the compulsory variety has gained some acceptance in many countries with regard to products affected by health and safety concerns, and in Scandinavia such compulsory programs may be extended to other consumer product categories as well when the government deems such information highly desirable for consumers.

One might well ask: Why the lack of progress? The answer is simple: insufficient support. Thus far, consumer activist groups have been fairly one-sided in their emphasis on protection, at the relative expense of education and information.[15] Why is this? First, it is much easier to protect and prohibit than to educate and inform, as every parent knows. Second, consumer advocates have a well-understood need for publicity and to demonstrate "instant results." It is characteristic that Ralph Nader has shown only incidental interest in CI programs. As a short-time board member of CU, he attempted to turn that organization into an agency for consumer advocacy. CT groups, although obviously sensitive to the need for better information, have shied away from support of IL and QC programs. In part this may have been due to the urge to conserve their own resources, although we have noted that several CT organizations have been investing heavily in much less closely related areas of activism. In part we believe that CT program executives have been lacking in imagination when it comes to other forms of independent information than testing. If they ever considered IL and QC, they may well have shied away simply because voluntary programs of this sort inherently require industry cooperation.

Industry has been the prime nongovernment supporter of IL and QC. But its support has been only half-hearted (even in VDN days in Sweden). True, industry has certainly preferred IL and QC to comparative testing. This is probably because IL and QC programs have been voluntary; each firm and each trade could decide whether it would participate. Industry has, however, resisted minimum thresholds in IL programs, except in some health and safety matters. As long as plans are voluntary, there would seem to be little rational ground for such opposition. Due to lukewarm support the programs outside Scandinavia have never had sufficient funding for the educational and promotional programs indispensable to making the average consumer aware of and interested in using the information provided. This tends to set up a vicious circle: as long as consumers don't seem to care, an individual firm has little incentive to join a program, as it will derive no competitive advantage from it. As a collective, business has lacked the insight to see that voluntary information programs might be a desirable tradeoff both to it and to the open market system for a great many regulatory measures of consumer protection.

In smaller part the lack of progress is due to inept administration of some programs (British Teltag, Dutch IE), and to IL programs not having devoted enough attention to the technical problems of presenting their information in a manner attractive to average consumers. In some instances, too, QC programs may have been unable to attain the degree of credibility necessary to public acceptance (QB, QF and Spanish Calitax come to mind). No matter how objective a program may be, it is its *perceived* credibility that counts. And the more condensed and simplified the information disseminated, the more important is credibility.

Yet is is crystal clear that simplified CI programs of the IL and QC variety are urgently needed. They provide independent point-of-sale information; they are of considerable potential use to average and to underprivileged consumers; and they provide valuable shortcuts to Information Seekers in the purchase of products about which they lack the time or interest to read CT reports.

One largely untried recipe for greater viability of IL and QC programs is to combine them. There is no reason why a label could not contain a star or other symbol of quality in cases where a brand meets or exceeds a certain standard. In this manner the consumer would be offered two alternative information programs in one. Administrative costs would be reduced (even in the case where the label text and the quality standard requirements might be worked out by different agencies). Above all, only one educational-promotional campaign would be needed to market the system among consumers.[16] By and large, IL, QC and IL-QC programs are not very resource-demanding for participating firms that have a decent quality control system in place. The cost of printing and affixing labels *is* fairly trivial.[17] The major cost is that of education and promotion to make the program known and used by consumers. Once established, the expense of maintaining awareness should be marginal, especially if a major part of this task were performed in consumer education courses. We confidently predict a resurgence of interest in this area.

CI SYSTEMS DEVELOPMENT TO DATE

CI Systems Defined

Technically speaking, a system is an arrangement of interdependent components which, acting jointly, produce an effect greater than (or different in kind from) that which could be obtained with the parts operating completely dissociated from one another. Systems may be tightly integrated; they may also be highly decentralized, based on the notion that independent operation and freewheeling creativity will best permit the parts to contribute to the whole. (An open market in many respects is a far more intricate and delicate system than a planned economy.) In this work the term Consumer Information System (CIS) simply refers to the totality of CI programs in a given country, regardless of the degree of coordination of such programs actually taking place.

Figure 8-1 indicates the size and composition of the CIS in the North Atlantic community of nations in 1969. The degree and types of interaction between the component programs in each country are discussed in detail in the *Handbook*, notably in the CIS sections at the end of each chapter.

CI Systems are Open Systems

A CIS is open in the sense that it develops and changes in interaction with the environment in which it operates. An intriguing question is to what extent the growth of a given CIS may be explained in terms of local environmental variables. We shall return to this question in later chapters. For the present we merely restate a few propositions for whose validity there is at least preliminary evidence in our data:

The more pluralist the environment, the greater the number of CI organizations.
The greater the middle class, the more diversity of CI organizations.
The greater the government share in the Gross National Product, the greater the degree of coordination of the CIS.
The greater the GNP, the greater the total CIS budget.

Being an open system, the CIS itself is also a component part of the total market information system (including commercial and personal sources, the media, and so on) and of the consumer policy system as discussed in earlier chapters. Both of the latter systems are more comprehensive than the CIS, and they tend to exercise more influence upon it than it does on them. That the role of the CIS may nevertheless be a significant one should by now be evident. This is spelled out in Chapter Five on the impact of CI programs and in examining the future of CIS in Chapter Nine.

Systems Experience to Date

In trying to examine the experience of CIS (as contrasted to individual CI programs) to date it is helpful to classify such systems from the viewpoint of internal cohesion. We may distinguish centrally coordinated systems, systems based on consultative coordination and decentralized systems. There are no sharp lines between the types, and there is ample room for diverging views as to how the CIS of a given nation should be classified. The centrally coordinated systems would, however, definitely include Norway and Sweden after 1972 or 1973. The Norwegian experience is somewhat limited, as neither the obligatory nor the voluntary Varefakta labels have been very effectively coordinated with the testing and publications programs of the Consumer Council. However, all forms of CI are presented in Norway's obligatory consumer education courses. In Sweden central coordination occasioned a general decline in the role of the CIS, as the radicals in charge of the new consumer policy did not favor information programs.

Consultative coordination on an informal basis is characteristic of the Netherlands, and since around 1970 it has been practiced on a semiformal basis in France under the auspices of the Institut National de la Consommation. This kind of system has not met with wild enthusiasm among participating CI programs; yet most organizations involved probably prefer consultative coordination to either a centrally coordinated or a decentralized system. It deserves mention that in France the UFC—the leading private CI program—has broken away from the consultative machinery of the INC. Consultative coordination was also a feature of the Swedish system before 1973.

Decentralized systems are found in the United States, Germany, Belgium, Switzerland and Britain (the last-named country might also be looked upon as one of consultative coordination). Intrasystem relationships vary from cordial cooperation via mere coexistence to artful antagonism. The most typical pose is one of mutual ignorance. This is certainly deplorable, but understandable in light of the fact that some of the smaller programs (UFIDEC in Belgium, RAL in Germany, Consumers' Research in the United States and several of the regional groupings in Switzerland) really play a very modest role on the national scene.

The general conclusion to be drawn here is that systems development in any strict sense of the term has been exceedingly modest thus far in the CI area, no matter what type of system may have prevailed in a given country. Thus, opportunities to divide labor and/or to gain cumulative benefits by programs supplementing one another in deliberate fashion were utilized poorly, if at all. Informal exchange of working experience appears to have been confined largely to systems within the Scandinavian countries and the Netherlands. Indeed, one is left with the reflection that international cooperation between CI programs of the same type—no overwhelmingly strong phenomenon in itself—with few exceptions was more intimate and generated more benefits for the participants as well as the consuming public than did domestic interaction between such programs, whether similar (two testing groups, let us say) or dissimilar. The opportunities for systems synergy and the likelihood that they will be exploited in the future will be evaluated in detail in Chapter Nine.

NOTES

1. Hans B. Thorelli, "The Testmakers—A Non-Comparative Study of Organized Consumer Information in Europe," in Peter D. Bennett, *Marketing and Economic Development* (American Marketing Association Proceedings, September 1-3, 1965): 51-71.

2. It is clearly not sufficient that the label accompanying the seal give information as to the thresholds met or exceeded by the product. The charm of IL is that the consumer is informed *just where* on the scale established for each characteristic a given brand is to be found.

3. This subsection draws heavily on Hans B. Thorelli, "Testing, Labelling, Certifying: A Perspective on Consumer Information," *British Journal of Marketing* (Autumn 1970): 126-32.

4. They are perhaps most evident in France. See, e.g., "Pourquoi les associations de consommateurs ne se groupent-elles pas . . .?" *Bulletin du Laboratoire Coopératif* (May-June 1976): 49.

5. Henk Nicolai, "Cooperative Testing for Tourism," *International Consumer* (Summer 1973): 10-12; and Jarmila Lentink, "Consumer Publications and Leisure," *International Consumer* (Summer 1973): 17-19.

6. International Organization of Consumers Unions, *Joint Testing* (The Hague: IOCU, 1974). Even the International Standardization Organization (ISO) has issued a *Guide on Comparative Testing of Consumer Products* (ISO/TC 73 Consumer Questions) which was presented to the general meeting of ISO in June 1975. It adheres closely to practice by that time adopted in the leading CT countries.

7. Dr. Howard Forsyth of the U.S. National Bureau of Standards in a paper delivered before the Association for Consumer Research, August 29, 1970.

8. Cf., however, the discussion of Swedish KOV in Chapter Seven.

9. I want to go sailing. My friend does not. He informs me that the weatherman predicts thunderstorms for the afternoon. We decide to go bowling. Clearly, the weather information, while objective, constituted a persuasive argument. Cf. the adversary process used in most court systems.

10. Colston E. Warne, "Consumers Look at Advertising" (Address before the Advertising Age Creative Workshop, Chicago, July 30, 1970; mimeographed).

11. "Advertising," CA Policy Document 585 (1974): 1-2.

12. A "patent medicine" about which we are skeptical is counteradvertising of the type obliging media to supply equal time or space at public or media expense for arguments against the allegedly misleading message of an advertiser.

There is no logical end to the rounds of claims and counterclaims that might be made, and the costs and politicking associated with enforcement present unpleasant perspectives.

13. Donald F. Turner, "Advertising and Competition" (Address before the Annual Advertising–Government Relations Conference, Washington, February 8, 1967; mimeographed.)

14. The aforementioned ANSI program has not really gotten off the ground.

15. In Holland and Belgium, housewives and family groups have sponsored or supported QC.

16. This kind of combined scheme has been advocated by the Consumer Advisory Council in the United States for packaged food products making use of the U.S. Department of Agriculture product grades.

The authors wish to recommend a piece of legislation that would stimulate the emergence of independent (as opposed to trade association managed) IL and QC systems. The law would provide that only when the CI agency had adequate consumer representation would the agency itself (as opposed to individual firms making use of its programs) be exempt from direct liability to end consumers for any products that failed to live up to its label or quality mark.

We would also like to see the mark on a certified product carry the year ('77, etc.) in which the product was manufactured. In cases where performance standards for quality marks have been changed, this would preclude disagreement as to which requirements a particular exemplar of the product has been built to meet.

17. The propensity of producers to join the program would be materially enhanced if the label (in the form of a hangtag) could carry promotional material on its reverse side. We see no principal objection to this idea, although it is thus far an untried one.

Chapter 5

Consumer Information Program Impact

Assessing the impact of any information program is difficult, as is well documented by studies of advertising,
political propaganda and education. It is especially difficult with programs as diffuse and as broadly directed as organized
consumer information. The exercise is nonetheless of utmost importance as societal concerns with the functioning and malfunctioning
of the marketplace increase. In the *Handbook* we presented in detail the consumer organizations engaged in product information generation. We gathered as far as available both quantitative and qualitative
measures of determining the extent of their work. Such materials
included number of tests and brands, informative labels, certificates
of quality, number of subscribers to testing journals, studies of
readership and the like. A recapitulation in comparative format is
presented in Chapter Eight.

Another companion volume, *The Information Seekers*, was solely
concerned with the individual consumer, both the subscriber to consumer testing journals and the nonsubscriber, who he is, what he
owns, what information sources he uses and his attitudes to them,
his views as to his possibilities in the marketplace, and what he
thinks about advertising and specific public policy questions. We also
related product satisfaction of subscribers to their use or nonuse of
test journal recommendations in specific purchases.

In this chapter we shall discuss the impact of consumer information programs on society sectors: consumers, manufacturers and
distributors, and government policies and agencies; the socioeconomic impact, including such matters as consumer democracy,

international trade, inflation, resources and physical environment; and the dysfunctional impact. An attempt will then be made to focus on key concepts in the area of impact: cost and benefits, performance planning and evaluation. The question of credibility will be treated briefly. We offer no simple inexpensive or scientific way of determining impact of any of the programs, either prior to their inception or after their adoption. We do offer, however, a recommendation that a clear and honest ordering of objectives is crucial to any effort at judging impact.

IMPACT ON SOCIETY SECTORS

Consumers

Labeling, marking and comparative testing of products are designed as information programs for consumers and presumably have their most important contribution in affecting buying behavior among them. The testing journals, by drawing attention to products and to their performance and usage, help define buying criteria, and in a general and indirect way aid in planning purchases. Long before purchase, a potential consumer has the opportunity to familiarize himself with available brands and their relative merits and demerits. His awareness of the products and specific brand recommendations may, in fact, become a part of the large body of his general knowledge of the market. The informative labels, by giving specific data on testable characteristics including content, ingredients and performance, allow the consumer at point of purchase to compare similar products. Quality marks, by assuring the consumer of controlled quality at or above a threshold level, reduce errors in purchasing.

To answer the question of what effect testing groups have, in fact, upon consumers, an extensive field survey of the American and the German consumer was undertaken in 1970 and reported in detail in *The Information Seekers*. The study was concerned with a "hierarchy of effects":

1. Awareness of the CI organization
2. Awareness of tests for specific products
3. Perceived usefulness of tests
4. Perceived use
5. Purchase satisfaction among users and nonusers

Twenty percent of all average consumer respondents in the Indianapolis survey named *Consumer Reports* spontaneously as a source of test reports. Seventy-two percent professed at least to have heard the name of *CR*. Under direct questioning 22 percent claimed either to be subscribers or to know a great deal about the magazine, and 29 percent said that the magazine was read or consulted in their households once a year or more. These percentages were even higher in Frankfurt. It appears that once information is published in a test journal it remains available for comparatively long periods of time, as subscribers and buyers of these magazines generally do not discard them the way we tend to do with most popular magazines.

Naturally enough, the impact of product tests was greatest among subscribers to journals both in their awareness of the information and in their use of this information source in purchases. In comparing subscribers and average consumers in actual purchases of durables it was found that 53 percent of the subscribers to *Consumer Reports* in the U.S. were aware of recommendations of the journal and 41 percent had used the recommendations in recent purchases. Twelve percent of the average consumers were aware of the recommendations and 10 percent used them. In Germany, where two comparative test journals were available, *DM* and *test*, 48 percent of the subscribers of the one and 38 percent of the other were aware of recommendations, and 44 percent and 35 percent respectively had used them in recent purchases. Among average consumers only 8 percent were aware of the recommendations of *DM* and only 6 percent had used them in recent purchases.[1] For these studies three groups of products were distinguished: durables, automobiles and convenience items. As we know, in these and other highly industrialized countries, the subscriber-consumer has a much higher income, education and occupational status than does the average consumer.

Based on analysis of the data from the two countries, a clear picture of the subscriber-consumer and the effect of consumer information in the form of comparative test reports emerged:

1. The more important the product to the subscriber, the more likely that the testing journal's recommendations will be considered.
2. The greater the amount of planning carried out for the purchase, the more likely the subscriber will use the testing journal.
3. The relation between past buying experience with the product and use of the ratings is not clear-cut, but there is some suggestion that greater purchase experience implies more use of test ratings.

4. There is high overlap of use of the test ratings in the U.S. Those who use the ratings to make durable purchases are more likely also to use them for convenience and automobile purchases as well.
5. Subscriber-users in any given purchase situation tend to be of higher income and educational levels than subscriber-nonusers.

As a measure of CI effectiveness, a comparison of the subscriber and average consumer satisfaction with purchases indicated that while U.S. subscribers were less satisfied with product selection, subscribers who used the ratings were better satisfied than those who did not. The German subscriber was more satisfied than the average consumer with the outcome of his purchases whether he used the recommendations or not. The differences between the two, although significant, are a matter of degree. Data from the study suggest that the average consumer in Germany is reasonably satisfied with his purchases and his information, even though he does not express his satisfaction as convincingly as the subscriber. The fact that American subscribers are less satisfied than their fellow consumers suggests that they have higher expectations for products.

A full scale, nationwide Norwegian study was undertaken by the Central Statistical Office in 1969 on behalf of Forbrukerrådet (the State Consumer Council) and our own project. Of the 1,817 households in the sample, 18 percent subscribed to the testing journal, and 19 percent—about one-fifth—had used its information in purchases. Awareness of the organization across the country was reported to be 87 percent of the sample. The Norwegian data showed unequivocally that subscribers are more intensive Information Seekers than average consumers not only by acquiring test information, but also in reading labels, visiting stores and talking with friends.[2]

Surveys of subscribers solely have been conducted by testing agencies in Sweden, Holland, England and Denmark. A 1968 Swedish study reported that 71 percent of subscriber households had used the test reports at one time or another for some purchase. The independence of subscribers is illustrated by a study of subscribers to the Dutch *Consumentengids* in which it was found that only 40 percent of the members who consulted the journal before a specific purchase bought the recommended model. Of course, the journal may have been just as useful to the 60 percent who read the report but bought other brands. In the group of products where the brand Philips was recommended it seems that 37 percent of the members bought a Philips, and of the products where Philips was mentioned but not recommended only 18 percent bought a Philips. The 1967 Consumers' Association survey reported that 95 percent of subscribers found "best buys" useful and 90 percent kept back numbers of *Which?*. In 1970 Statens Husholdningsråd in Denmark elicited subscriber views on format, coverage, readability, reasonableness of price and usefulness of their journal. Almost 90 percent claimed to check the journal before they bought an item.[3] A more complete presentation of other studies of consumer information views appears in Chapter 7 of *The Information Seekers.*

Some data on impact of labeling programs are available from Sweden, Norway and Denmark. At least two major studies were directed at the general impact of Sweden's Varudeklarationsnämnden (VDN) labels at the consumer level. A 1959 study involving a representative sample of 1,105 households indicated that 49 percent of the respondents had heard of, or personally observed, "informative labels marked off within a special box." The percentage of positive replies was appreciably higher for the young and the well-to-do. On recall, 58 percent of the sample said they recognized the VDN label. Experience from our Norwegian field survey would suggest that this percentage would have been much higher ten years later.

A 1966 study financed by the Swedish Consumer Council of awareness and impact of VDN labels among 194 customers in the bedding departments of three department stores revealed that 47 percent of all interviewees knew about the status of VDN and the significance of its labels. Some 25 percent of the interviewees, however, mistakenly believed that the label constituted a quality guarantee. Of those interviewees who had made a brand decision, 40 percent declared that the VDN label had been of significance in their choice.

In Norway in 1965 the Department of Family and Consumer Affairs commissioned a study of the informative labeling agency, Varefakta, and the Consumer Council, Forbrukerrådet. At that time, of the 1,403 persons interviewed nationwide, 72 percent had heard of Varefakta. Irrespective of geographical location, age or income, over one-half of the respondents stated that Varefakta was of "much help." In 1967 a smaller interview study was conducted to compare the knowledge and attitudes toward Varefakta among subscribers to the testing journal *F-rapporten:* randomly selected housewives, retailers (both owners and clerks) and home economics consultants. There was no significant difference among the first three groups, all of whom thought highly of Varefakta, but the professional home economists across the board gave Varefakta low ratings and further had quite a number of derogatory remarks to add!

The 1969 study of the Consumer Council and *F-rapporten* executed by the Central Statistical Office mentioned above included questions concerning Varefakta at the behest of the authors. It was found that public awareness of Varefakta was extremely widespread, some 80 percent of the nationwide sample of 1,817 households, almost identical with that of the Consumer Council. Fifty-eight percent of the sample stated that they regularly or occasionally bought Varefakta-labeled products, a surprisingly high percentage in view of the relative paucity of labeled products.

In 1973 the Danish labeling organization, Dansk Varedeklarations-Naevn, commissioned a study to analyze alternative designs and to evaluate the use of such labels on three items: record players, shoes and canned goods.[4] Small groups of consumers were interviewed clearly stunned by their findings. Generally, for recordplayers the information given was determined to be "too hard to understand for the average consumer." For shoes, they found that factors other than the information on the label played a more important role in purchasing: design of the shoes, price and previous experience. For canned goods, they noted a widespread use of the labels, with a slight preference for a design with no graphical symbols. The overall conclusion was that although the design of the label is important, the need to inform consumers about how to use labels may be even more so.

While there is no general informative labeling organization in the U.S., specialized labeling required by legislation or administrative rules is mounting fast. According to a study of nutritional labeling, availability of information increased consumer confidence.

> Consumers see informative nutritional labels as a part of general food industry accountability rather than an input to the purchase decision. . . .
> [They] see themselves benefiting from nutritional labelling because of the way it affects others—through advertising and through the accountability of food manufacturers for the nutritional quality of their food products.[5]

Somewhat analagous conclusions have been drawn in studies of open dating and credit information as required by truth-in-lending legislation.[6] Several studies have been made of the impact of unit pricing.[7] Due to the novelty of this practice, most past research in this area suffers from the fact that only immediate or short-term effects could be studied. Again, Information Seekers demographics were heavily prevalent among the reported users of unit price information. In a recent survey over two-thirds of all 700-plus shoppers interviewed reported that they used unit price data, and over one-third were observed apparently making at least moderate use of them.[8] To increase low income consumer use of unit prices, Isakson and Maurizi[9] have suggested that a brightly colored sticker be used to indicate the least expensive package per unit for a given product type.

A study of buying guide tags for small appliances supported the belief long held by labelers that more complete point-of-sale information helps consumers overcome the inadequacies of salesclerks.[10]

None of the quality marking programs has ever undertaken or, as far as is known, planned any full-fledged survey of the impact of certification. The data on Qualité-France's impact at the level of distribution and on consumer awareness and use are meager. On the assumption that QF-marked products would be well and conveniently represented among the famed departments stores of Paris, the authors spent each a day in two of the largest stores. We failed to uncover any products with QF marks. It is probable that had we brought our copy of the QF catalog and asked for the specific brands named there we would have had better luck. The fact remains that QF-marked products were not prominently displayed. According to a QF estimate, the mark is viewed between one and two billion times a year. Such estimates are necessarily vague, as no statistics are kept on how many licensed manufacturers are making use of the mark, the product units sold or on the use of the mark in advertising.

IVHA of the Netherlands during the period of our field study did not maintain any record of licensed manufacturers' market shares. Only in bed linen was it known that most of the market was covered as noted earlier. While IVHA has never undertaken or planned any survey of its impact, one study of consumer awareness of IVHA was conducted by Philips in 1962. According to the Philips spokesman, of the 500 families queried, 60 percent were familiar with the IVHA name and 50 percent had purchased items bearing the mark.

The NF mark of the Association Française de Normalisation (AFNOR) is apparently well known across France.[11] According to the director, this may be attributed to informational programs on TV. Of a sample of the general public in 1965, 64 percent of respondents said they had seen the mark before; 50 percent related it to such notions as quality, tests, safety, control and standards. No less than 44 percent declared that they preferred an NF-marked product. While any student of advertising effectiveness would be aware of the caution with which such data must be interpreted, they are still suggestive of respectable impact.

Manufacturers and Distributors

The potential of CI programs for influencing the policies and the success of manufacturers and distributors of products is substantial. Little data exists that might help evaluate the specific impact of test reporting on businesses, but logic suggests that some influence must exist and that the influence may be growing apace with informational activities.

Product ratings can directly affect manufacturers and distributors by changing the demand structure for their products, and occasionally even by causing major fluctuations in stock prices. Other less direct influences on the market resulting from businessmen's reactions to or anticipation of test reports might include modification of product features or design policies, changes in buying patterns by distributors, and promotional reactions to take advantage of good ratings or offset bad ones. Evidence to confirm the existence and magnitude of these influences is spotty and anecdotal.

Ratings by testers are apt to influence secondary demand (market shares of various brands) by giving information that allows buyers to discriminate among the various brands available. Sometimes, however, the test reports contain information and opinions that may affect primary demand (total demand for the product category) as well. For example, *Consumer Reports* has questioned the need for electric can openers, as inexpensive hand-cranked models open cans easily and efficiently.[12] *CR* was disappointed in the crusts, taste and high bacteria count on all but four brands of frozen pizza, and could rate even those brands only fair.[13]

Such statements have an obvious potential for influencing the overall level of sales for the product if heeded by a significant number of consumers. Several years ago a Swedish test report compared agitator and pulsator washing machines unfavorably to tumbler washers. Sales of agitator and pulsator washers dropped precipitously, and in the next few years they essentially disappeared from the Swedish market. In Germany, mail-order houses were said to have stopped buying some variants that got low ratings in comparative tests.[14]

Little solid data is available on the impact of test reports on brand sales and brand shares, but there is a great deal of conventional wisdom and a plethora of anecdotal case histories. It is infrequently said that good ratings have a strong positive effect on sales, but that poor ratings are much less likely to reduce sales.[15] Procter and Gamble recently stated that neither good nor poor ratings have much influence on the sale of the low cost convenience goods which they manufacture, since "consumers have an opportunity to make up their own minds with a relatively minor investment."[16]

Despite these disclaimers, good evidence exists that poor ratings are not ignored by manufacturers. A spokesman for the photographic industry put it this way: "If you don't do well in *Consumer Reports*, it's like having your throat cut."[17] It is within the authors' experience that one of the largest manufacturers of durables in the U.S. consistently invites executives responsible for low-rated models to "explain themselves."

Paradoxically, there is some evidence that any rating, good or poor, may be helpful to a little known brand by establishing brand awareness. The largest department store in Zurich noticed a substantial increase in the sales for a certain brand of shampoo after the brand received a very poor rating.[18]

Tales of success for products given the blessing of test ratings are numerous. Volkswagen's popularity in the U.S. is widely reputed to have stemmed in part from favorable treatment by *Consumer Reports* (though the original VW has fared less well in ratings in recent years). Westinghouse claimed a 20 percent increase in washing machine sales in the mid-1960s as a result of a favorable rating, and a Norge official is quoted as saying, "CU put us in the washing-machine business."[19] It is said about Philharmonic Radio (predecessor of the current Fisher Radio that Avery Fisher founded in 1937), "A favorable review in *CR* the following year helped get the company off the ground."[20]

Changes in the nature of demand as a result of product testing are not yet predictable, yet the above examples suggest that the changes are real, and that they are important to the economy in general and the involved manufacturers in particular.

In its July 1971 issue *Consumer Reports* had a special report on the oil additive STP that concluded in essense that the product was at best worthless and at worst harmful and in violation of new car warranties. When the report was released, STP stock dropped from $58 to $53 in one day, and the following day trading was brought to a standstill by a glut of orders. The stock of STP's parent company and the stock of companies with similar products also dropped immediately.[21] Within two years STP's profits had dropped rapidly, management had been reorganized, and the stock was selling at $6.

This is, of course, an extreme case, and certainly a great deal more was involved in the STP situation than a poor test rating, but it is also true that until the day of the report, STP stock was selling at record heights. The message is not that a poor rating can wreck a solid company, but rather that testing organizations are becoming more influential and influential in more different ways. In the case of Consumers Union, it has two million subscribers, and its press releases are widely published all over the country. When it speaks of issues critical to the succcess of products and brands it has the attention of the financial community as well as the consumer. The same is undoubtedly true of other significant testing organizations.

In testing and evaluating products, some CI organizations have come to examine the product generically with the purpose of determining whether the product as designed meets the need for which it was manufactured. Statens Husholdningsråd of Denmark was certainly among the first to attempt this, and consequently participated in the design of some kitchen utensils, such as potato peelers and egg beaters. The former Swedish Consumer Institute found all the wheelbarrows on the market physiologically at fault and together with medical researchers designed a totally new type. Consumers' Association in England through its affiliation with the Institute of Consumer Ergonomics and its work with consumer products for the handicapped has been concerned with product design. All the initiatives quoted are in the nature of setting examples, not attempts at forcing industry to accept the designs involved.

There is a substantial amount of testimony that manufacturers tend to change the design of products to eliminate competitive weaknesses identified by comparative testing, or to make products otherwise comply with criteria established by testing organizations. When producers withdraw bad models or improve them due to consumer testing activity, comparative testing clearly benefits all consumers.

A big test of ski bindings by STIWA revealed that only one or two of the dozens of European brands tested met reasonable standards of safety. The report created such a furor that the ski binding trade group got together to establish new standards.

Our associate Jack Engledow wrote to an executive friend at a lawn mower manufacturer to get an unofficial reaction to an unsatisfactory rating given one of that firm's mowers. The reply was that little attention was paid by executives, sales were unaffected, dealers agreed that the criticism was "picky" and, incidentally, the design had been changed so that the most recent rating for the product was favorable!

According to *Business Week*, Clevite eliminated a shock hazard from its headphones, Remington corrected a tendency for its electric knife to jam, and Westinghouse improved the design of its electric broiler, all directly as a result of product tests.[22] Robert Bosch redesigned their dishwasher on the suggestion of the Swedish consumer agency. Electrolux cut the height of their dishwasher when it was pointed out that the Swedish standard for kitchen counter height permitted a downward tolerance of 3 mm. The Cooperative Wholesale Society produced a detergent strong enough to create a corrosion risk on copper and brass parts in certain washing machines. After this fact was revealed, the detergent was made sufficiently milder.

The conclusion is clear. Despite the general claim that unfavorable ratings have a modest impact upon sales, there is ample evidence (though not statistically verified) that many manufacturers try to eliminate or improve product features deemed by test organizations to be unsatisfactory or weak. Beem and Ewing have suggested that corporate pride may be more involved than a fear of lost sales.[23] Whatever the cause, it is apparent that some product designs are substantively different because of the activities of testing groups.

In their haste to eliminate unsafe aspects of products in their modified designs, manufacturers may introduce other and different hazards or transfer the hazard from one group to another. For instance, by simply making the opening mechanism of a child's gate more secure without viewing the consequences the manufacturer may also make it so difficult to open that adults will step over the top rather than operate the mechanism. Studies performed in Sweden showed that the new drug bottle tops could be opened most easily by children, who had the time and took it as a challenge, a puzzle. For adults it caused frustration, or even an impossibility, as whimsically depicted in Bill Yates' cartoon (Figure 5-1).

Test reports have some influence on the extent of distribution of products. A study by Sylvia Lane made twenty years ago included a limited survey of department store buyers. Of the eighty-five buyers surveyed, two-thirds claimed they read *Consumer Reports* regularly, and of these, 67 percent found it "useful," 75 percent said it "guid-

Professor Phumble ® **By Bill Yates**

HOLD BOTTLE SECURELY IN ONE HAND, GRASP CAP IN OTHER HAND, AND WHILE FIRMLY PRESSING DOWN, TWIST IN A COUNTER-CLOCKWISE....

(c) King Features Syndicate Inc., 1975.

Figure 5-1. Consumer Policy Tradeoffs
The protection of one may be the undoing of another

ed buying," 66 percent said they "agreed with ratings most of the time" and 29 percent that they would "go out of the way to stock rated products." On the other hand, 54 percent said that they would buy certain products even if they had been rated unsatisfactory.[24]

The authors have personally spoken with a number of retailers and wholesalers who use ratings as one guide to what brands to stock. Particularly in specialized areas such as cameras and sound equipment retailers cite high percentages of customers who come to the store with a product-rating article as a shopping guide. Hardware stores claim to try to stock items highly rated by CU, especially products that are effective in areas having to do with household safety, such as insecticides and fire extinguishers. A survey conducted in 1963 in England by Business Research Associates, Ltd., of 400 electrical retailers, reported that 62 percent answered yes to the question, "Have you ever noticed *Which?* product tests having any effect on your customers' purchasing behavior?" Only 3 percent had not heard of *Which?*[25]

The implication is that distributors are frequently aware of the influence of ratings upon customers in some product areas, and that assortments and inventory of various brands at the retail and wholesale level are established with ratings as one significant input in a good (though unknown) number of cases.

It is obvious that firms would prefer to modify promotional programs to call attention to favorable ratings and to counteract unfavorable ones. At least in the case of *Consumer Reports* this is not possible, since firms are expressly forbidden from making explicit use of ratings for promotional purposes. CU has had this policy since its inception, in keeping with its general goal of keeping entirely free of any ties to commercial enterprises that might be construed as biasing its testing efforts. CU has vigorously and quite successfully enforced this policy both by suasion and by legal means.

Despite this ban on direct reference to the tests, there is little doubt that the tests still influence promotional strategy. STP attributed its drop in profits in the quarter subsequent to the unfavorable test reports to greatly increased advertising expenditures to counteract "unjustified criticism." Amana Refrigeration Corporation also moved vigorously to dispute CU's charges of excessive radiation from its microwave oven.

Another controversial aspect of the use of promotion was the nationwide publication of the results of the STP tests in large advertisements sponsored by the Foundation for Auto Safety. If firms are not allowed to make positive use of ratings when the tests are favorable, should third parties have the privilege of widespread use of unfavorable test information?

Not all agencies are as restrictive as CU in the use of their ratings. Stiftung Warentest, for example, makes its tests widely available to a variety of organizations both inside and outside of Germany, though with some restriction on commercial use. The result is widespread "borrowing" of the tests by *DM* and other agencies, and a multiplier effect on the dissemination of each of the expensive tests beyond Warentest's own magazine *test*.

While there is surprisingly little data as to actual cost savings to the individual consumer, in one dramatic instance a consumer organization triggered enormous savings to virtually all consumers by affecting the whole industry. In a test of forty-five brands of standard gasoline by STIWA it was found that the gasoline offered by independents was not basically different from that of the major concerns. In the several months following publication of this report the majors reduced their prices three times, thereby saving German motorists some DM 600 million, according to an estimate by the association of independent companies.[26]

As with comparative testing, the effects of informative labeling and quality certifying could be potent. Yet the statistics on number of manufacturers and distributors licensed indicate that the programs in existence have not captured the attention of most businessmen, whose cooperation is a sine qua non in voluntary programs. Even in instances where a label or mark has been approved, it does not always mean that any seller is using it. Further, typically little or no data exist on market share of brands labeled or certified, or even why the manufacturer decided to join the program.

One labeler under the defunct British Teltag system, Eastern Carpets, a major chain of carpet stores, signed an agreement to have all the brands it carried Teltagged, whether or not suppliers liked the idea. Eastern's prime motive for joining was to cut down on testing costs and to acquire a valuable means of disciplining suppliers. They also hoped that the Teltags would help to instruct their salesmen. Theoretically, with labels for capital goods, costs could be cut by reducing the amount of time per sale. As the director of testing at J.C. Penney stated recently, department store buyers are handicapped almost as much as consumers with regard to buying information.

It is precisely because labeling and certifying can help in both the stocking and the selling of items that distributors ought to be drawn to such schemes much more actively. Some labeling advocates, such as Dr. Walter Bodmer-Lenzin of Förderungsfonds für Konsumenteninformation in Switzerland, see informative labeling primarily as an aid to the small retailer, who still dominates the trade in many European countries. On the other hand, it is surely symptomatic that in both Germany and the United States it is large mail-order houses that have displayed the greatest interest in the idea of informative labeling.

It is sometimes claimed that distributors object to labeling if there is a chance that it might increase the demand for products where margins are low at the expense of high margin products. Private brand labeling is supposedly objected to by those retail chains who use the same producer or packer. On the other hand, some observers feel that labeling might induce a shift in the balance of power between manufacturers and retailers as a consequence of making private labels more competitive with national brands.[27] Some retailers—or their salesmen—have been known to remove labels, as they claim the labels encourage the consumer to ask additional questions.

Government Policies and Agencies

The relationship between government and testing agencies is a delicate one in private enterprise economies. Most discussion in this area concerns possible influence by government over agency procedure and outputs as a result of dependence on government financial arrangements by many CI programs.

The concern here is primarily with the opposite influence, possible impact of the agency upon government policy. In instances where the CI agencies are government bureaus, direct and official communication channels exist. No such formal arrangements are present in the United States. In Belgium, AC prefers a mutual hands-off relationship as a matter of policy. In England, Consumers' Association maintains close liaison with the Department of Prices and Consumer Protection and the Office of Fair Trading. In France, prominent members of the so-called testing agencies (except UFC) have participated actively in the functions of INC. In the Netherlands, Consumentenbond performs all tests for the heavily subsidized VW.

In the area of product testing, the most important direct influence at this time seems to be in establishing tighter safety standards for products. Consumers Union, in particular, has used its own findings and experience to urge new or more rigid minimum safety standards. CU has been concerned with toy and lawn mower safety standards, and has been active in pushing for tighter radiation standards, first in color television and more recently in microwave ovens.

The microwave oven situation is an interesting case of testing agency–government–industry interaction. Amana's microwave oven met government standards, but was rated "not acceptable" by *CR* for excessive radiation. CU pressured the Department of Health, Education and Welfare for more rigid radiation standards, claiming that the rules were "contrived to minimize the manufacturers' failure rates."[28] Amana filed a complaint with the FTC that the micro-wave test article in *Consumer Reports* contained false and mislead-ing statements, and demanded that *CR* be forced to conform to the same standards of confirmation of claims frequently being required of advertisers. Issues of this sort are not easily resolved, but the case may signal the beginning of a new, more complex and probably more heated era in relationships among testing agencies, government and industry in the U.S. As test agencies grow and expand their ac-tivities everywhere, these relationships promise to become even more involved with impacts more complex and difficult to assess. The debacle in Sweden a few years ago over a color TV test jointly administered by a handful of government agencies is another exam-ple of the intricacies in this area.

CU has also influenced government policy in the testing area by forcing the Veterans Administration by means of a law suit to re-lease the results of extensive tests on hearing aids. Apparently as an outcome of that suit, in 1970 the president issued an executive order that paved the way for the release of a broad array of theretofore restricted product information by the General Services Administra-tion, data obtained in connection with government purchasing of branded consumer goods or of products apparently identical with branded products.[29]

In Britain perhaps the most notable impact of CA on government has been the creation of the local Consumer Advice Centres serviced by CA (see Chapter Nine). CA has also achieved notable success in bringing about the Toy Safety Regulations of 1967 as a result of their toy testings. In 1971 the Unsolicited Goods and Services Act came into force in large part due to CA's lobbying activities.[30] Several years ago CA proposed to the Home Office that all electrical goods sold in the U.K. should conform to compulsory safety stan-dards, and in late 1970 the Home Office announced that such legis-lation would be introduced.

Forbrugerrådet of Denmark has shown imagination and courage by entering at least one legal case on behalf of consumers. A company selling imported appliances had applied for bankruptcy. FRD sub-mitted a petition on behalf of those consumers who bought ap-pliances to assure that their unexpired warranty rights would be placed on an equal footing with the claims of creditors. The Bank-ruptcy Commission accepted this point.[31]

Consumentenbond of the Netherlands makes regular representa-tions to the government on matters affecting consumers, most recently urging minimum requirements for safety, standard contract clauses and mandatory disclosure of interest rates.

The informative labeling and quality certifying bodies with few exceptions have not had any substantial impact on government and public policy. For many IL and QC programs survival has been a key concern. The labeling agencies in France, Denmark and Norway are indeed active ones, but their impact on government is quite limited.

The illustrations of impact on government of CI organizations chosen for this section have all stemmed from their activities in the consumer information area. Some of these organizations also have an impact as general consumer lobbies, an activity of less relevance here. Often such impact is also harder to evaluate, as there are typically several groups lobbying in the broader field of consumer policy.

SOCIOECONOMIC IMPACT

Open Market Systems and Consumer Democracy

The ultimate effect aimed for in all consumer information programs is greater market transparency. While this is very hard to gauge, the availability of adequate product information is a preservative of open markets. The supply of information has a direct relation to better-informed consumers and more "rational" purchases, the reduction of "mistakes" in purchases, the encouragement of "good" products and the discouragement of "bad" ones. By increasing the visibility of price, once quality is established, informative labeling and quality certification should promote price competition. Conversely, when prices are close to identical, CI programs would naturally tend to promote quality competition. It is a frequently encountered mistake to believe that the only effect of CI programs is to draw attention to price. By influencing the retailer to stock good buys rather than mediocre or bad ones, CI programs should in addition affect market channels. By inspiring the manufacturer to produce better products, or at least improve bad ones, such programs should promote higher standards in product performance and the marketing of goods that better satisfy consumer needs and wants.

All three current types of CI programs undoubtedly assist manufacturers by helping to develop standards for testing procedures in the industries concerned. Further, the comparative testing reports may serve as a source of competitive intelligence. All three systems may have a tempering influence on exaggerated advertising claims. Based as they are on brands, the comparative testers have engendered a healthy disregard for the inviolability of brands. This was especially evident in Germany in the early days of *DM* as consumers held a blind faith in brands. In markets where segmentation has been based on lack of information or on misinformation (deliberate or otherwise), an increase in objective information could lead to de-segmentation.

A problem of CT is that findings cannot be presented as simply and effectively as the advertising slogans of manufacturers. It is felt that much test information never reaches the lower middle and low income groups, presumably the groups who most need value for money. At the other end of the consumer spectrum, our research demonstrated that the availability and accessibility of product information has a highly significant impact on the Information Seeker, who as opinion leader, critic and proxy purchasing agent for less information-conscious consumers in turn has a vital influence in the marketplace.

If the recommendations of the markers and the comparative testers tended to cause consumers not to think, this would probably be a disservice, at least from the viewpoint of "consumer democracy." The slogan "buy by tests not by testimonials" would degenerate into a testimonial by the testers. We believe that the varying systems do not eliminate individual differences, but actually may intensify them by making it possible for the consumer to discriminate among products, by awakening his critical sense to form his own judgment. With CI a consumer can more readily select products with qualities especially suited to his own needs and wants. The filling of one information need tends to generate new questions, new needs for information in a cumulative process. The most critical problem for the labeler has been precisely on this point. The first labels of VDN exemplified this, as they were primarily concerned with ingredients, contents or specifications. It early became evident that on durables, performance, suitability, durability and economy in operation were characteristics rapidly becoming equally or more important to consumers in the 1960s.

International Trade

The testing of products that are distributed internationally and the attempt to utilize the same test results in more than one country have served both to raise some interesting problems and to identify some new uses for test reports.

One issue raised is comparability of models of the same brand sold in different countries or areas. CA found that the composition of a well-known U.S. brand of detergent varied substantially between London and Brighton. The company explained that difference in water necessitated the change in formula. A Swiss testing agency noted that a Swedish sewing machine cost more in Germany than in Switzerland. The company explained that volume was less in Germany and costs were higher. There have been other substantiated cases where the design of products varied considerably between countries, though the brand and model names were the same.

Should firms maintain strict comparability in product over regional or national boundaries, or should they be required to enumerate differences on labels or packages? Certainly if brand names do not signify a reasonably homogeneous product, international or even interregional use of product testing loses much of its potential usefulness. On the other hand, strict standardization not only places controversial restraints on managerial decisionmaking in private enterprise economies, but also limits a firm's flexibility in adopting products to very real differences that may exist in the market environments of different areas. Again, there is clearly a workable middle ground.

One unique use of test results revealed in interviews for this research was that firms seem frequently to use such reports to evaluate the competition when they are contemplating entry into a foreign market. Another possible impact of testing upon demand is bias against (or even for) testing of foreign products, or biasing of standards against design features of foreign products. The result would be an artificial "invisible trade barrier" for foreign products that might be quite significant in countries where CI programs are widely used by consumers.

The use of joint testing of products since 1970 by many consumer organizations in Europe has lead to an improved understanding in both directions, for the consumer groups, an awareness of market constraints of multinational corporations, and for the multinationals, a greater appreciation of the consumer's need for information. Since the activation of the EEC in consumer questions, the European consumer organizations, primarily through BEUC, may grow to have considerable influence on consumer policy in a number of areas, not least harmonization. They are also likely to make their viewpoints known on invisible trade barriers and international trade policy.

With the establishment of the CIPQ in 1958 and the ILC in 1966 it was hoped that both certifying and labeling would take on an international flavor. Labeled and certified products would supply a real impetus to increased trade. With standardized tests, procedures, identification of characteristics, measurements and labeling design the programs would be open to all. Buyers, both consumers and importers, would be able to compare offerings of foreign and domestic products. Sadly enough this has not transpired. A sufficient number of products was never labeled or certified to constitute a significant factor in any international market.

Inflation

Regardless of the economic times, most Information Seekers are not likely to abandon their support of testing journals, as witnessed by *CR's* birth and survival during the 1930s and by the ability of CT organizations to weather the 1973-75 recession. When money is short, informed consumers are clearly better equipped for ferreting out value. All three programs aid in weighing alternative buys as prices soar. In times of inflation, comparison takes place not only between brands and models of the same product but between products themselves as resources need stretching. The search for better buys inevitably helps to put a damper on rising prices.

Resources and Physical Environment

As noted above, consumer information may have an effect on aggregate demand, beyond the oft-noted surge following the publication of a test report recommendation or simply a type test of a new product. Actually, this effect could work in either direction. For instance, Consumers' Association, after testing baby pillows, questioned whether they should be used at all. Speaking generally, we definitely do not think CI programs on balance have any appreciable demand-push effect at the aggregate level.

Consumer information has a traditional emphasis on conserving scarce resources of all kinds—time, space, energy, money—by stressing functional characteristics of products. This built-in bias against wastage is seen most clearly in the testing agencies' discussion of the value of fashion ware. Institut National de la Consommation concluded its report on novelty watches as Christmas presents by stating that it was basically a question of "gaspillage" (waste). CI groups are slow in proclaiming the value of innovations in products. Almost all of the European agencies in the 1960s viewed dishwashers as a waste of money, energy and water, with no saving in time and adding little if any convenience. Some conducted long studies of the time and motion variety, proving the inconsequentialness of the appliance. These groups are learning to hold judgments on products heretofore viewed as gimmicks as the CI agency may lose more in credibility than the consumer wins in "good" advice.

Concern for the physical environment has caused some CI groups to sound like consumer advocates, attacking big business, conglomerates and multinationals. CI groups have an obligation to present tradeoffs in objective and meaningful ways: for instance, you can use less detergent if you increase the temperature of the water, or vice versa. The objection to printed color designs on household paper was that the printed part was not biodegradable. Considering that consumers have different views on these matters, we come back to the point that the legitimate business of CI programs is information rather than propaganda for a set of values.

The lasting influence of the energy crisis may be its emphasis on deconsumption or moderate consumption in all areas. Kotler predicts that consumers "will show a growing preference for products that offer economy, simplicity, and functionalism."[32] If they are, in fact, to do so, consumers are indeed in need of objective information from CI agencies.

DYSFUNCTIONAL IMPACT

If CI increased aggregate demand, the impact could be dysfunctional. If CI caused citizen-consumers to rivet their attention on products, it might breed materialism. Of course, if the citizen-consumer instead of weighing product information against his own needs is glued to the TV set eating and drinking junk food, his materialism is of a more insidious kind.

CI might cause manufacturers to emphasize only the characteristics tested or labeled. This may be a real dysfunctional effect in the labeling area. A case in point is the current rush to label energy consumption of appliances. A little information may be worse than none. Unless energy use is hooked to the many aspects of performance, it is meaningless, or worse, misleading.

That the testing, labeling and marking of products may lead to uniformity in product planning and overstandardization seems a vague and farfetched proposition. In fact, the reverse seems to be a more probable outcome. The realization that his brand is no different from the next may logically induce a manufacturer to engage in some meaningful product planning to differentiate his product and to segment the market by introducing specialized products. Also farfetched is the claim that CI programs may degenerate into information overload (Chapter One). For the foreseeable future this seems a rather remote risk as a general proposition.

In Sweden there has been some evidence that recent consumer information has had an overemphasis on price at the expense of quality. By selecting suction capability as the only single characteristic of relevance, the State Consumer Board concluded that all vacuum cleaners were roughly the same, so that price became the central question. Serious and unbiased testmakers are more careful in trying to identify and evaluate the entire set of relevant characteristics.

It may very well be that CI groups, if they ever grew to powerful positions, would have a hampering and delaying effect on innovation. As they tend to be conservative, to view all improvements as sales promotion techniques, and innovations as a means to entice the consumer to waste, a government-run agency with ample resources could make a substantial impact on change in the marketplace. That it could also become a manipulative influence of Orwellian or Galbraithian type is obvious.

As mentioned earlier, most of the CI testers select the brands to be tested based on market share, amount of advertising and national availability. If it is true that minor brands have less of a chance to be tested than major ones, regardless of their merit, testing agencies might be accused of fostering greater concentration and in effect of discouraging small, regional or new firms. Consumers Union has a policy of attempting to include brands covering 75 to 80 percent of the market sales in any given test. They depend upon feedback from their shoppers and from readers to alert them to meritorious regional brands and outputs of small manufacturers, but they have no perfect system for assuring that the best alternative brands are always included in testing. Consumentenbond claims it strives to locate brands with special characteristics in addition to those with large market shares. Most of the European CI organizations are not adverse to testing a brand overlooked in the original test. Here the labeling and certifying groups could do a magnificent job. And in fact small manufacturers have often used the services of these organizations.

If the small share brand is included, it has more to gain from the ratings than does a large share one. Take the case where the dominant brand has a 50 percent market share and a newcomer has a 5 percent share. If the "major" receives an unfavorable rating and loses 10 percent of his market to the favorably rated "minor," the minor doubles his market share. In the opposite case, where the minor loses 10 percent of his market share to the major, the major's share "rockets" up to 50.5 percent—a nearly imperceptible change. This in part may explain the reluctance of some major manufacturers to become involved with CI programs. They may have more to lose than to gain by attracting publicity.

Misleading and controversial information is a serious complaint in all three CI programs. This has become most evident in the discussions on safety: microwave ovens, aerosol cans, PCBs, additives and preservatives. By labeling inconsequential characteristics, the consumer's attention may be diverted from meaningful matters. There seems little doubt that all three CI techniques tend to hamper poor quality, low price items that may constitute real value to some.

An interesting question is the "halo" effect of a good or bad rating: If X was rated best in 1976 but only acceptable in 1977, do consumers register this shift? If company Y's brand of one product is rated excellent does that company's brand of another product receive any derived benefit? This area is not well researched to date. The Philips studies in Holland suggest that the answer is "no" to the latter question.

A dysfunctional consequence of labeling and certifying programs (as of industrial standardization) is that a minority of consumers (as many as 25 percent in one VDN study) believe that the program actually guarantees that the goods involved are of *high* quality. In our opinion this effect can be countered only by educational measures, preferably including a disclaimer on the label itself in the case of informative labeling.

COST AND BENEFITS

Benefit-cost analysis is a highly current systematic methodology for selecting among resource allocation alternatives. Its chief and commendable merit is that it injects the discipline of economic thinking into the process of weighing the benefits and costs of each alternative. In the present context, benefit-cost analysis suffers from severe limitations. It is next to impossible to assign dollar tags to the benefits (and the dysfunctional impacts) discussed in this chapter without a heavy element of subjectivity. It is equally difficult to define objectively the time period over which such benefits are distributed.

Thus, we doubt that cost-benefit analysis would be particularly useful in assisting a country like Italy (which lacks CI programs) in deciding whether to promote CT, IL or QC. (As it happens, we would suggest a dual system of comparative testing and quality marking in that particular case.) Nor do we think that at the level of deciding on measures to promote the open market system, cost-benefit analysis would of itself be sufficient to indicate the proper resource allocation to antitrust enforcement on the one hand and CI programs on the other.

We do not think it worthwhile to attempt a detailed cost-benefit analysis of CI systems here. The reader interested in such an exercise will be aware that benefits (and dysfunctional impacts) have been summarized in preceding sections of this chapter. Costs are summarized in Table 8-1, with some more recent data in Appendix E. A potent reason for not pursuing this line of thinking at length here is the discouraging experience of cost-benefit studies from two other fields broadly concerned with the dissemination of information, namely, advertising and education. Neither macro nor micro benefit-cost analysis in these areas has really carried the discussion very far. Yet firms do not hesitate to pour billions of dollars into advertising and governments gladly pour billions into education every year. The authors are personally convinced that at the macro level the direct and indirect benefits of CI programs far outweigh the costs and dysfunctional effects of such programs.

PERFORMANCE PLANNING
AND EVALUATION

Performance relative to resource use is also a critical issue at the level of the individual CI program. A professional approach to management is based on the definition of yardsticks—objectives, plans, budgets—against which performance can be evaluated. As noted in the *Handbook*, there was not much use of these or other professional techniques in CI programs before 1970. Objectives tended to be vague, and typically there was no formal plan of any kind. Budgets, when existing, tended to be of the natural kind rather than oriented around functions. Since 1970 the larger CT organizations have adopted several professional techniques. Stiftung Warentest is especially commended for its easily available annual reports, which analyze and evaluate activities and performance in detail.

Performance evaluation involves both effectiveness and efficiency. Effectiveness refers to external performance: getting the right kind of information about the right products (services) at the right time and place to the greatest possible number of consumers. The "right" kind of information includes such factors as comprehensiveness (and/or relevance), reliability, credibility, readability, understandability, use and usefulness as perceived by the audience. Amazingly few CT groups regularly ask either their subscribers or other readers, former subscribers and nonreaders to evaluate their effectiveness. Labeling and certification programs, in descending order, have done even less evaluative research or management performance auditing of their own activities. Although the use of marketing research techniques is fairly well developed with CU and CA it is still surprising that CI programs, purporting to be the consumer's special friend, in general have made such scant use of survey techniques. We are aware that evaluative research is costly. Yet we strongly suspect that the relative neglect of such activity goes far to explain the slow growth (or outright decline) of many programs in years past.

Efficiency is productivity in internal resource use. It is—or should be—a matter of continuing management concern. A typical question is, Do we get as many tests of as many products, brands and characteristics reported as we might for the amount of resources (money, personnel, office space, etc.) we use to produce them? The concern is with outputs (tests, reports, subscribers, etc.) relative to inputs (personnel, laboratory space, advertising dollars, etc.). The relationship between several performance variables and a variety of organizational, strategy and environmental variables of CT programs is examined in Chapter Eight and Appendix C.

A KEY TO IMPACT: CREDIBILITY

Credibility is based on perceived independence and objectivity of the CI program on the one hand and the quality of the information it generates on the other. Determinants of quality are such factors as readability, understandability, relevant products, relevant brands, relevant characteristics, timeliness, comprehensiveness, reliability and publicity of test methods. These factors are discussed elsewhere. In accepting the credibility challenge all consumer information organizations have to meet head on agonizing questions of suitability or fitness in their definitions of products and characteristics, and whether they admit it or not they encounter questions of minimum thresholds of acceptance. Even the labelers, though they deny it vehemently, realize that if many truly inferior products were to carry labels, the consumer might shy away from all labeled products, thereby defeating their purpose.

Perceived independence and objectivity tend to be linked to the perceived sponsorship of CI programs. Some major questions of sponsorship were discussed in Chapters Two and Four. To achieve credibility, the private testing organizations sponsored exclusively by subscribers, such as CU, CA, CB and AC, stoutly refuse to allow any reprinting of their tests or the use by commercial sources of their recommendations. By purchasing their test products on the open market, maintaining a stand-off position from manufacturers and distributors, not receiving grants or aid of any sort from manufacturers, and, of course, carrying no advertisements in their journals, they righteously proclaim the utmost credibility for their test results.

It is easy to understand the preoccupation of these private CT organizations with controlling the use of their ratings. CU has often said that "Credibility is our most important product." Yet in the interest of effectiveness—getting good product information to all consumers—and efficiency—more effectiveness per dollar—much is to be said for using the communication resources of other organizations and media (commercial and nonprofit) to get more exposure for each of the costly tests. Assuredly, allowing commercial use of ratings in any way may open Pandora's box, but it also opens a sizeable purse of additional resources. A middle ground tradeoff between possible loss of perceived credibility and certain gain of exposure is needed, with carefully structured and supervised use of test results. This should be a high priority issue for private testing organizations.

The government testers, while also concerned with credibility, are much less concerned with the use of their test results. Stiftung Warentest's policy of distributing test results to the media in a compact, ready to use format (see Appendix E) has increased its market enormously while controlling the content of the added exposure.

Credibility is hard to come by once lost. In some measures, German *DM* encountered this problem. The U.S. government experiences this problem repeatedly. The Food and Drug Administration's hastily banned products (e.g., cyclamates) have created a skepticism among consumers. The Environmental Protection Agency is undergoing similar problems. An exploratory study on consumer information influence on breakfast cereal preference showed that when exposed to a *CR* test report, consumers chose products rated highly by CU, while a product rated highly by the Department of Agriculture was determined to be mediocre by comparison.[33] The Department of Transportation's unfortunate safety belt interlock system mandated on 1974 cars is yet another example.

By giving information contrary to general knowledge the Swedish VDN occasionally lost some credibility. Their washing advice (tvättrad) on 100 percent white cotton socks carried the legend to use water at 40°C. The home economists were quick to fault the label, pointing out that a much higher temperature is needed for best results. Basically, however, VDN is a good example of high credibility and consumer goodwill emanating from an organization with pluralist sponsorship. Unless quality certifiers attend to complaints of consumers who find marked products not performing adequately, such organizations cannot maintain their reputation. Underwriters' Laboratories in the United States has encountered this problem from time to time.

In 1970, Consumers' Association was reported as saying that the time has come to tell manufacturers what consumers want and "if necessary describe it and give its features and its qualities."[34] If its consumer information is to meet the test of objectivity, certainly an organization's large-scale involvement in the design of the products it tests may raise as grave problems of bias as does any other connection in the marketplace.

In short, maintaining credibility while not "leaning over backward" so far as to sacrifice reasonable external effectiveness and internal efficiency is indeed a major challenge to CI programs.

NOTES

1. *Test* was not available at newsstands at that time.

2. Hans B. Thorelli, "Concentration of Information Power Among Consumers," *Journal of Marketing Research* 8 (November 1971): 427-32.

3. The Dutch study is summarized in J.M.F. Box, "Consumption Standard and Information Behavior" (Paper presented in Workshop II on Cognitive Models of Consumer Decision Processes, January 30-31, 1976, Delft; Technische Hogeschool, 1976; mimeographed). All other studies referred to in the text are summarized in our companion volumes.

4. Thomas Bergsøe Marketing, *Analysis, Design, Evaluation of Informative Labels* (Copenhagen: Dansk Varedeklarations-Naevn, 1973). Abridged English version.

5. R.J. Lenahan, J.A. Thomas, D.A. Taylor, D.L. Call, and D.I. Padberg, "Consumer Reaction to Nutritional Labels on Food Products," *Journal of Consumer Affairs* 7 (Summer 1973): 1-12.

6. Raymond C. Stokes, "Consumerism and the Measurement of Consumer Dissatisfactions" (Paper presented to the American Marketing Association Conference on Attitude Research Bridges the Atlantic, Madrid, February 1973); and George S. Day and William K. Brandt, "Consumer Research and Evaluation of Public Policy: The Case of Truth in Lending," *Journal of Consumer Research* 1 (June 1974): 21-32.

7. James M. Carman, "A Summary of Empirical Research on Unit Pricing," *Journal of Retailing* 48 (Winter 1972-73): 63-72; and Hans R. Isakson and Alex R. Maurizi, "The Consumer Economics of Unit Pricing," *Journal of Marketing Research* 10 (August 1973): 277-85.

8. "The Uptight Consumer—What Is She Up To?" *Progressive Grocer* (November 1975): 41-57, 42.

9. H.R. Isakson and A.R. Maurizi "Consumer Economies of Unit Pricing," *Journal of Marketing Research* 10 (August 1973): 277-85.

10. Federated Department Stores, "Buying Guide Tag Pilot Program," February 1970.

11. Strictly speaking, the NF mark does not represent quality certification. The general significance of the mark is to certify with regard to a given brand of product that that particular brand conforms to whatever AFNOR standards are applicable to it.

12. *Consumer Reports* (March 1972): 154.

13. *Consumer Reports* (June 1972): 364.

14. OECD, *Labelling and Comparative Testing* (1972): 112.

15. This idea was expressed in Eugene Beem and John Ewing, "Business Appraises Consumer Testing Agencies," *Harvard Business Review* 32 (March-April 1954): 113-27, and was also mentioned in a series of articles on CU in *The Washington Post* (April 22-25, 1973).

16. Quoted by Nancy Ross in *The Washington Post* (April 23, 1973): Al.

17. "Consumer Reports: Read, Respected, and Feared," *The National Observer* (February 26, 1968): 5.

18. From an interview with the testing agency, Schweizerisches Institut für Hauswirtschaft, in Zurich. This observation is obviously contrary to that of Procter and Gamble referred to in the text.

19. "Consumer Reports: Read, Respected, and Feared," p. 5.

20. *MBA Magazine* (June 1976): 32.

21. "STP Head Terms Consumers Union Blast at Its Oil Additive 'Completely Distorted,'" *Wall Street Journal* (June 6, 1971).

22. "Consumers Union Puts on Muscle," *Business Week* (December 23, 1967).

23. Beem and Ewing, p. 116.

24. Sylvia Lane, "A Study of Selected Agencies That Evaluate Consumer Goods Qualitatively in the United States" (Ph.D. dissertation, University of Southern California, 1957).

25. Cited by Christina Fulop, *Consumers in the Market* (London: Institute of Economic Affairs, 1967): 26.

26. Stiftung Warentest, *Annual Report* (1966): 10f.

27. George S. Day, "Assessing the Effects of Information Disclosure Requirements," *Journal of Marketing* 40 (April 1976): 42-52.

28. See "Tougher Rules Asked on Radiation Leaks in Microwave Ovens," *Wall Street Journal* (July 23, 1973): 17.

29. Although this list is published annually by the government Consumer Information Center it has not become one of the best sellers of that agency. According to a GSA spokesman, one of the reasons is that for a major part of routine government procurement sophisticated testing has never been deemed necessary.

30. Consumers' Association, *Annual Report 1970-71:* 9.

31. Forbrugerrådet press release, "Hvad forbrugerne kan få ud af Haka/Kirk," June 8, 1971: 5.

32. Philip Kotler, "Marketing During Periods of Shortage," *Journal of Marketing* 38 (July 1974): 20-8, 21.

33. Thomas J. Stanley and Carl A. Johnson, "Consumer Information Influence on Breakfast Cereal Preferences: An Exploratory Study" (School of Business, SUNY, Albany, probably 1975; duplicated).

34. *Campaign Interviews* (December 11, 1970): 29.

Part III

The Ecology of CI Systems

Chapter 6

Theoretical Considerations

THE ECOLOGIC VIEW: A PRIMER

Much of the study of institutions and their policies proceeds with but scant attention to the particular environment in which these institutions and policies operate. Historically, the study of the law has been especially sterile in this regard, but to a great extend the statement is also valid in other areas of behavioral science, such as economics, history and government. Yet it is, of course, crystal clear that neither structure nor function develop in a vacuum.

In recent years a number of hopeful developments in the direction of an environmentalist or *ecologic* view toward the study of organization and policy have occurred.[1] Applied here, the ecologic approach suggests that it is insufficient in a comparative study of consumer information systems (CIS) to analyze the characteristics of such systems without reference to the social, economic, political and technological environment of the country in which any given system is operating. Indeed, were it not for the enormous practical as well as conceptual complexities involved, the authors would have infinitely preferred to steep the entire project in an ecologic mould. The nature of the present chapter is that of a working paper intended to be suggestive of what is involved in the application of an ecologic perspective to CIS, and what this approach might yield in terms of theoretical insights and empirical findings.

This chapter will outline a general ecologic model of CIS and present some hypotheses that may be derived from it. In the next two chapters a preliminary ecologic analysis is made of some of the materials obtained in the course of research. Chapter Seven presents a longitudinal case study of Sweden—in several respects the most controversial country to students of organized consumer information, and a country with whose culture we are conversant. Chapter Eight makes a series of cross-cultural comparisons and observations bearing on several of the hypotheses presented in this chapter.

Before developing the model, it may be useful to review briefly some of the basic notions of ecology as construed here. Our views of some of the underlying theoretical precepts of what we have termed organization ecology are detailed elsewhere.[2] Organizational ecology focuses on the *inter*action between the environed unit (organization, organism, institution, individual, policy, decision) and the environment. Thus it must not be confused with trite environmental determinism of the type espoused by such diverse writers as Marx and Spencer as well as by numerous classic geographers and contemporary starvation doomsday prophets.[3] Even in its postulate as to the basic motivation or objective of human organizations and individuals, modern ecology is quite relativistic. The basic driving force is simply assumed to be survival and growth. Indications are many that such an objective is compatible with a considerable variety of stances in any given environment. In the world environment we witness the simultaneous existence and prosperous growth of countries of such diverse size as Denmark and the United States and of such different economic systems as those of Switzerland and the USSR. Although the argument does not need to be resolved here, we doubt strongly that there exists only a single demonstrable optimal stance in any complex operating environment.

While survival is an overriding goal, it is not of itself sufficient to guide an organization or to formulate strategy. The organization *must* have a more specific mission (set of objectives). It cannot live by its own steam. Every organization serves a clientele—or it dies. No clientele (i.e., no market, no task environment) is willing to keep the organization going merely for its own sake. Beyond survival are such specifics as marketing appliances, promoting religiosity, providing dry-cleaning service, winning votes, and so on. The growth of the organization is directly contingent on the relative success with which it fulfills its mission: i.e., satisfies the demands of its operating environment. As a goal is realized or turns out to be unattainable, we frequently find, as indeed we might expect given the imperative of survival, a displacement or addition of goals rather than a dissolution of the organization. The elementary and important conclusion is that goal formation is unthinkable without interaction with the environment. Equally clear, the environment does not dictate or determine the specific objectives of the organization. The fact that a variety of goals (or goal sets) is possible within a given environment emphasizes the importance of leadership in organizations.

Strategy may be defined as the stance adopted by an organization to cope in its environment. Ecologically, strategy provides the mechanism of harmonizing the resources and objectives of the organization with environmental opportunity at acceptable levels of risk. In starkly simplified language, the environment may be likened to an arena, while strategy would be the play staged by the home team. The interaction strategy of any organization (profit or nonprofit, private or public) is reflected in the "marketing mix"—that is, the peculiar combination the organization makes of such instruments as the product (or service) it provides, the sacrifice (price, budget appropriation, volunteer efforts) it requires from the environment in order to provide the product, the promotional effort it undertakes to alert the environment to its product, and the marketing research it performs to assure that it stays in tune with environmental needs. As they depend on the environment for sustenance, *all* organizations are engaged in marketing, whether or not they choose to recognize this fact explicitly.

Strategy is what makes the elements of the marketing mix work in a coordinated fashion, as a whole rather than as disparate parts. Strategy is a qualitative concept, related to the idea of intermesh and synergy and the German notion of Gestalt. To build a house we need a materials mix of bricks and boards, mortar and nails. But without a strategy for putting them together we would more likely wind up with a big pile of rubble than with a house. Strategy is a scheme or a recipe for applying the means to reach the objectives (ends) in view. The fact that several strategies may coexist in the same general environment is illustrated in the automobile market, where we find the classic strategies of high price–high quality–selective promotion (Rolls Royce) and low price–mass volume–mass promotion (Volkswagen). If Rolls Royce began charging VW prices for its cars it would soon go bankrupt, as would VW if they tried to build Rolls Royce type cars without changing the other elements of their strategy. Not just *any* strategy will succeed.

In contemplating nondeterministic interaction we have found two basic concepts useful. One is *ecologic possibilism*, the other *ecologic probabilism*. To understand ecologic possibilism one may think of capability analysis as practiced by students of military strategy and international relations. In other words, the concern is with the opportunities and limitations existing in any environment, defining, we may say, the set of viable stances with regard to structure and function (organization and strategy) adoptable by the environed unit. If the unit strays outside these possibilities and constraints it is apt to suffer decline or extinction. A corresponding degree of attention must be given to the opportunities (assets) and contraints (liabilities) inherent in the environed unit itself at any given time.[4] The resource configuration of the organization is their basic source. The number, motivations and skills of the leaders and their associate decisionmakers, the way the organization is structured, and the size and composition of its finances are perhaps the most important exponents of resource structure. Thus, the salient elements from an ecologic viewpoint of both the environment and the environed unit are permissive, supportive or restrictive. The neutral element is one that at any given time is of little relevance to interaction or to the pattern of structural coexistence in environment and organization.

Ecologic probabilism, on the other hand, may be looked upon as a "generic term for the relationships better than chance existing between, and due to, an organism and variables in its . . . surroundings."[5] In our view, the words "due to" in this context may refer to no more than the coexistence of the organism (organization, etc.) and its environment. Hence, the words do *not*—in any case, should not—necessarily imply a direct causal relationship. Very much in line with contemporary philosophy of science in general, the ecologic probabilist acknowledges "the indeterminacy in predictions based on 'odds of occurrence.'"[6] It must be admitted that with regard to socioeconomic organizational and political phenomena the ecologist can put forward few propositions to which he can attach empirically based probability estimates of occurrence. In part this is due to the fact that probabilistic models are manifestly better suited to prediction of the behavior of large aggregates than that of any specific constellation of environment and organism or *ecosystem*. As any market analyst knows, macro forecasting (of the economy) is a great deal easier than micro (of a specific industry or, even more, of a given firm). More important, ecologic study of the phenomena referred to is in its infancy. In sum, ecologic possibilism defines the framework of organism-environment interaction, while probabilism emphasizes the relative likelihood of specific types of interaction among variables in the environment and the organism within the framework.

A key issue is whether it is the environmental "facts" or the environment as *perceived* by the actors in the situation that counts in ecologic applications in behavioral science. The answer is: both! Harold and Margaret Sprout rightly emphasize that perceptions of the situation are most relevant in decisionmaking. They cite the British Cabinet's decision to reoccupy the Suez Canal in 1956 as an example. Had the Cabinet known and correctly evaluated all the germane facts, it is unlikely that the decision to invade would have been made.[7] On the other hand, the facts of the situation are most relevant to the outcome of interaction. The would-be Cuban liberators thought they had air cover, but the fact of the matter was that President Kennedy on second thought had decided to withhold air support. Consumers Union abhors any cooperation with manufacturers on the grounds that such collaboration might reduce public faith in the integrity of the organization. Should the fact of the matter perchance be that the environment would not lose its faith in CU, such a misperception might well retard its rate of growth. This is not to deny that in cooperating with producers the organization might change character in ways abhorrent to its founders and current leadership.

That perception of self is as important as of environment must be emphasized. The key to self-perception is evaluation of the resources, opportunities and constraints of the organization. Beyond the perception of environment and of self lies the next challenge: the perception of the results of interaction. This is a test of prognostic ability, with which every market analyst is familiar: Suppose we cut our price, what will competition do? If they match our cut, what will happen to industry sales? What will happen to our sales and profits? If everyone cuts price and industry sales still do not rise appreciably, *what then* should be our next move?

The distinction between anticipated result and actual outcome is simply a projection in time of the difference between perceived and actual facts (states) in the environment. At this stage the question may be asked whether there exists any mechanism that will bring a convergence between perception and reality. This question is too complex for detail discussion. It is clear, however, that to some extent men will learn from experience, even if occasionally it will be the "wrong" thing. In some respects the interaction process is like a continuous feedback mechanism. If the world of the decisionmaker is a dream world he may be in for a rude awakening. Admittedly, some leaders of unusual capability will grab a dream and run with it. While total synchronization is not to be expected—there are always more variables in the environment than we can take full account of, and there will always be chance events beyond our control—we can indeed expect a *rapprochement* between perception and reality to occur *over time*. Individual decisions of a *short-term* nature may be seriously out of whack. In the long term the infinite series of individual decisions will work in the direction of mutual adjustment of environment and organization, although a steady state equilibrium is not attainable (even if desirable to some) in a changing world.

Before concluding this brief outline of the ecologic approach we must add a major reservation. The linkage between organization and environment is frequently difficult to discern, and the difficulty mounts with the growing complexity of either one. Further, the tightness of the linkage will vary considerably from one case to another and from time to time. The relationship may be obscured by chance events, by the existence of "slack" (underutilized resources, resilience, etc.) in some part of the ecosystem,[8] by the existence of a particularly dynamic leader in the organization who for some time may pursue successfully a policy against heavy environmental odds, by time lags in the mutual adjustment process,[9] or by the plethora of interacting variables.[10] While this all adds up to an exciting long-term challenge for ecologists, we must be modest in short-term expectations. Nevertheless, at the very least ecologic models provide a convenient framework for identifying and classifying variables in research on organizations as environmentally sensitive as CIS.

CI SYSTEMS ECOLOGY: AN INTRODUCTION

In order to apply the broad ecologic framework to the study of consumer information organizations it is desirable, first, to develop a model incorporating the classes and species of variables thought relevant and, second, to develop a set of hypotheses based on these variables to express patterns of ecologic interaction. Before doing so it seems helpful to take an intermediary step between the general overview of the ecologic approach in the preceding section and the development of a detailed model in the next section. This intermediary discussion focuses on two sets of variables:

Environmental sets of variables	*Consumer information organization sets of variables*
Macroenvironment	Single CI organizations
Consumers in general	The total CIS in a country
Subscribers to test journals	

The term macroenvironment denotes the set of variables in the broader economic, social, political and technological environment ("culture") assumed to be of relevance to the operations, or even the existence, of CI organizations. Consumers in general constitute the principal task environment ("market") of information organizations (advertisers, producers, other CI organizations and the mass media may constitute other participants in the CI market). A subset of the general consumer population of special interest is represented by the subscribers to the journals of CI organizations. While part of the environment as narrowly construed, the subscribers for some purposes may be regarded as *part of* the organization. Indeed, in Consumers Union, voting subscribers are ipso facto members of the organization. From an ecologic interaction point of view it will nonetheless generally be more pertinent to look upon subscribers as the most crucial part of the environment.[11] This is especially evident in considering subscriber turnover and the fact that the general consumer population is a source of potential subscribers. More importantly, however, a principal objective of the organization is to keep its present subscribers satisfied; CA and CU would have to disband if their subscriber-members abandoned them.

At the center of ecologic interaction is the environed unit, in this case one or several CI organizations. We distinguish between two different levels of analysis. The first level is concerned with interaction between a single CI organization and its environment. In this case it should be kept in mind that in countries with more than one CI organization, those other information organizations constitute a part of the environment that the unit under study could hardly afford to neglect unless they were trivial in size. Though most of our discussion will proceed at the level of individual CI organizations, it would be highly unrealistic to overlook the fact that in countries with several organizations, the total CIS includes all these units. Thus, we have a second level of analysis, in which the total CIS is viewed as a semiorganizational unit interacting with the local environment.

We are postulating ecologic interaction between the environment and the organization (or CIS). While there is *always* some degree of interaction, it is frequently legitimate to assume that the "causal arrow" runs in one direction rather than the other. For example, when we hypothesize that the greater the size of population, the greater the chance of a profitmaking or self-sustaining CI organization we are naturally assuming that population size has an effect on the organization rather than vice versa. On the other hand, if we say that the more critical consumers are of advertising, the more positive they are about CIS it is far less clear that all the action is from the environment (consumers) to the organization. Indeed, it is quite legitimate to assume that many CI organizations stimulate or reinforce critical attitudes toward advertising.

For better or (from an ecologic-analytical viewpoint) often for worse it is also necessary to consider interaction among many variables within each set. A hypothesis illustrating interaction among variables in the general consumer environment is that "the more critical consumers are of advertising, the more left-oriented they tend to be in politics." Interaction among organizational variables is illustrated by the proposition that "the greater the age of the organization, the greater the diversification of its activities." Of special interest is the interaction among variables within the total CIS. By way of illustration, we may postulate that "the more complementary the activities of the individual CI organizations, the closer the coordination of the total CIS in a country."

Speaking broadly, our interest here is confined to the *outcomes* of interaction, whether the interplay is ecologic or within a given set of variables. We are essentially taking a snapshot of the state of each variable at the time of research or at some earlier date for which data exist. It has not been possible to make extensive observations concerning the *process* of interaction. We may make it believable that interaction tends to yield certain results—but will generally have to stop short of that challenging question: exactly *why* does the process yield these results? Although data were collected for at least a three year span for each organization, our field survey was admittedly, in some respects, a fairly static study. We maintain that such cross-sectional research is an excellent device for the rapid gathering of intelligence where some initial hypotheses will be rejected or made more credible and some new ones will be generated. Other researchers will then hopefully be better equipped for the intensive and dynamic studies to follow. A first fling at dynamic analysis is made in the next chapter, a case study of CIS in Sweden 1940-75.[12]

ECOLOGIC MODEL OF CONSUMER INFORMATION SYSTEMS

We are now ready to develop an ecologic model of CI systems and organizations in some detail. The question immediately facing us is: Just how detailed should the model be? We foreswear from the outset the "total" viewpoint of general systems theory. In spite of all the talk and a flood of articles, this type of approach has proven disappointingly unwieldy in practice.[13] There is neither practical need nor theoretical reason to aim for a model including "all" variables that might be relevant in a total explanation. On the other hand, one who wishes to study the context of organizations can hardly afford to confine himself to just one contextual feature.[14] The selection of variables in the model to be presented here is governed by the twin rationale that they seem of theoretical interest in the study of CI organizations or systems and/or that they yielded hypotheses on which we have some evidence in Chapters Seven and Eight or in the companion volumes. In Appendix C we present a more full blown set of propositions for the benefit of readers not averse to some free-ranging speculation.

Figure 6-1 presents a diagrammatic view of our model. An interaction system of four interdependent sets of variables in envisaged. To simplify the representation of interaction between the organization and its environment we have depicted the two as entirely distinct. Actually, the organization is totally immersed in the environment; as we have seen it is frequently difficult to distinguish the borderlines between them.[15] Objectives and performance are in the identical part of the model, as they are defined and measured in similar terms: objectives are in fact anticipated results. It should be noted that performance may include some effects of CI agency operations not foreseen or even intended by management.

Figure 6-1 is aimed at individual CI programs. Little is required, however, to extend the model to the entire CI system of a country. As such a system is in effect a pseudo-organization of the individual CI programs in the nation, the basic model is itself applicable with only marginal modifications. However, we do need to add a set of variables pertaining to the system as a whole:

The Total CI System (CIS)
1. Number of CI organizations
2. Complementarity versus overlap among CI groups
3. Degree of coordination of the system
4. Total budget of CIS

By this time the reader will have observed that several of the "variables" introduced under the various sets in the model are quite encompassing. Indeed, in some cases (such as E4, social and political values) it might be preferable to think in terms of a cluster of variables rather than a single one. Many variables are difficult to measure in practice, in which case we have resorted to qualitative judgment (e.g., S5, extent of marketing research) or to episodic illustration (01, leadership). The problems of operationalization of specific variables are addressed in the context in which they were studied in the *Handbook* and *The Information Seekers*.

The Variables
It would seem that the designation of most variables is self-explanatory. A few of them may warrant some comment before we proceed to state illustrative propositions derived from the model. Among strategy variables, intensity of counseling (S2) ranges all the way

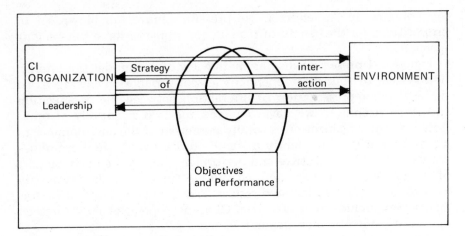

An action system of four interdependent sets of variables is envisaged. A variable is designated by its set and number; thus 02 refers
to the budget of a CI organization.

Most variables are discussed extensively in this book (see Index). The
Handbook and Appendix E are rich in empirical evidence on a case-
by-case basis. *The Information Seekers* generalizes about the audience
of CI programs and their effects on consumers (variables P6–12).
Most empirical generalizations about the other variables are made in
Chapter Eight and Appendix D of this book.

CI Organization (O)

1. Leadership
2. Budget
3. Sponsorship and influence
4. Employee number
5. Resource mix (testing facilities, specialized personnel)
6. Age
7. Diversification of activities

Interaction Strategy (S)

1. Types and diversity of products tested, labeled, marked
2. Intensity of counseling
3. Style and frequency of reports
4. Promotion
5. Marketing research
6. Pricing
7. Distribution
8. Trust and credibility

Figure 6-1.   An Ecologic Model of CI Programs

Environment (E)

1. Size
2. Audience
3. Economic development
4. Social and political values

5. Government share in GNP
6. Pluralism
7. Other CI agencies

Objectives and Performance (P)

Direct outputs:

1. Survival
2. Growth
3. Sales
4. Number of products, brand: covered
5. Number of subscribers

Effects on consumers:

6. Subscriber satisfaction with CI organization
7. Consumer awareness of CI organization, tests
8. Perceived usefulness
9. Use
10. Perceived savings
11. Purchase satisfaction of users, nonusers
12. Attitudes, values

Other effects:

13. On manufacturers
14. On trade
15. On advertising
16. On other CI organizations
17. On public policy

Figure 6-1. Continued

from neutral reporting of objectively measurable characteristics via classification of models and brands into varying degrees of acceptability, to the recommendation of "best buy." It may be noted that an element of counseling is inherent in quality certification, but not necessarily in informative labeling or comparative testing. In S3, style and frequency of reports, "style" refers both to the dimension of scientific reporting and popular generalizations and to the proportion of total contents of the CI magazine devoted to CI, as distinct from editorials, public policy articles and items of general consumer interest. With regard to variable S7, distribution, in the case of comparative test reports one might be interested in sales versus gift copies, in the relative distribution of subscriptions, newsstand and bookstore sales, and direct sales from the CI agency.[16] As of late, reports of some testing agencies are also reprinted by the press by permission or even by other CI journals in the same[17] or other countries.[18] Some test reports have been aired on TV or radio. Distribution is also a vital matter to the purveyors of informative labeling and quality certification programs. Beyond the matter of how many brands of a product use the label or mark are such questions as their market share, what types of stores feature these brands, and to what extent sellers use the labels and brands in advertising and other forms of promotion. S8, trust and credibility, has been included in view of its manifest importance in the CI as well as many other markets (political vote getting, medical service, industrial purchasing).

Turning to environmental factors, E2, audience, clearly stands for an entire cluster of variables, comprising the potential as well as the actual audience ("market") and their characteristics. Among their characteristics our research has established the relevance of demographics (income, education, social status), media habits and buying criteria. From the viewpoint of CI programs some salient aspects of E3, economic development, are size of GNP, complexity of the economy, the diffusion of major appliances ("white goods") and the prevalence of mass media. Of E4, social and political values, local views of advertising, degree of leftism in politics and, we believe, the degree of personalism (as contrasted to humanistic individualism) are all of interest. Another catchall variable is E6, pluralism. This might include the degree of polarization among interested groups (such as consumers and business); the propensity for voluntary organizations; heterogeneity in language, religion, or in ethnic and regional factors; the intensity of political cleavages; and the cooperation of government and interest groups.

Among objectives and performance variables the direct outputs (P1-P5) are most readily and uniquely definable. These variables were extensively treated, and related to organizational and environmental factors in the *Handbook*. Effects on consumers (P6-11), in conjunction with environmental factors, constituted the focus of *The Information Seekers*. P12 stands for consumer attitudes and values other than those elsewhere defined in the schema. If CI programs make consumers more information-minded and more logical in their buying activities, this is presumably a desirable effect on their values; if the counseling element of CI programs were strong enough to make consumers stop thinking for themselves, this would presumably be a dysfunctional side effect. Depending on one's values it would also be a positive or negative outcome if the counseling effect were strong enough to constitute manipulation of consumers. As regards P17, effects on public policy, such effects may be direct in that CI organizations may influence policy and appropriations relating to CI programs. They may also lobby for general consumerist causes. Public policy effects may also be indirect. Thus, for example, the reinforcement of open market competition resulting from CI programs might obviate the need for certain types of public regulation of business.

Sample Propositions
The ecologic model of CI programs and systems will serve as a fruitful generator of propositions for research and analysis. A fairly extensive inventory of such propositions is given in Appendix C. In the present context we will only restate a few propositions for purposes of illustration:

1. Strong leadership (01) may overcome environmental obstacles (e.g., small audience, E2).
2. The larger the environment (E1), the larger the CI organization (02, 04).
3. The greater the government share in GNP (E5), the greater the government influence on CI organization (03).
4. The more promotion (S4), the greater the consumer awareness of CI (P7).
5. Pricing policy (S6) will tend to have relatively little influence on the number of subscribers (P5).
6. The more pluralist the environment (E6), the greater the number of organizations in the CI system (CIS 1).

As it happens, there are varying degrees of evidence in our research in favor of each of these hypotheses. Again, the reader is referred to the *Handbook* and *The Information Seekers*.

The Dynamics of Interaction
It seems proper to end this chapter by returning briefly to the dynamics of ecologic interaction. The formulation of the CI ecosystem model was in essentially static terms. This is reasonably adequate for cross-sectional (in this case, inter-national) research, but insufficient for dynamic analysis. It is important to emphasize that by adding the words *"the rate of change in"* in front of each variable in our static model we in effect transform it into a dynamic one. To illustrate, sample proposition 3 in dynamic format would be: The greater the rate of change in the government share in GNP, the greater the rate

of change in government influence on CI organization. Proposition 4 would sound like this: The greater the rate of change in promotion, the greater the rate of change in consumer awareness. Another example would be: The greater the rate of change in the CI agency budget (02), the greater the rate of change in the number of products and brands covered (P4). This example also suggests three major complications in dynamic analysis: interaction between variables may take place in both directions, there may be time lags between a change in one variable and a corresponding change in the other, and, of course, the "corresponding" change may not reflect a simple linear relationship between the variables. For the sake of simplicity, illustrations of interaction in this chapter have all been limited to two variables at a time. Clearly, however, interaction patterns are often a great deal more complex.

Ecologically influenced writings not unfrequently suggest that firms and other organizations go through a "life cycle" somewhat akin to biological cycles.[19] While this idea for the analysis of organizational evolution was in the back of our minds, we are not really enthralled by it after empirical study of two score CI organizations. We did note a trend toward diversification of activities with increasing age of the organization. Typical activities added over the years were in-house testing facilities, participation in standards work (especially for SMMP), consumer advice bureaus and international contact work (not necessarily in this order). There was also evidence of the "displacement of goals" often attributed to mature organizations by sociologists, such as the recent tendency of CU and CA to become general consumer lobbies rather than "mere" consumer information organizations.[20]

We have attempted in this chapter to develop an ecologic approach to the study and understanding of organizations in general and CI programs and systems in particular. While this approach guided our research for the *Handbook* and *The Information Seekers*, it was not explicitly developed in these companion volumes. In the next two chapters we shall attempt to restate some of our findings in terms of dynamic and cross-sectional ecologic analysis. The reader is reminded that the very origin of CI programs is explained essentially in ecologic terms in Chapter One.

NOTES

1. For an integrative summary of some of these developments, see Harold and Margaret Sprout, *The Ecological Perspective on Human Affairs* (Princeton: Princeton University Press, 1965).

2. Hans B. Thorelli, "Organizational Theory: An Ecological View," in Acad-

emy of Management, *Proceedings*, 27th Annual Meeting, Washington, D.C., December 27-29, 1967 (1968): 66-84.

3. Typical of the latter is Georg Borgström, *The Hungry Planet; the Modern World at the Edge of Famine* (New York: Macmillan, 1966), and, in some respects, the original Club of Rome visions of the future. Equally trite, of course, is the opposite of environmental determinism as illustrated by Galbraith's notion of unilateral manipulation of the (consumer) environment by the "technostructure."

4. This point is not given sufficient emphasis in the literature, including the chapter on possibilism in Sprout.

Our thesis holds even before the emergence of the environed unit. At least one variant of a possible set of *latent* viable resource configurations and strategies must be on hand for the unit to emerge. For instance, the IOCU could hardly have emerged without the prior existence of a number of national organizations, some internationally oriented persons perceiving the benefits to be derived from joint lobbying and mutual exchange of experience, and so on. Incidentally, we refuse to accept the sophistry that it is impossible to speak of an environment until there is also an environed unit.

5. Egon Brunswick, "The Probability Point of View," in M.H. Marx, ed., *Psychological Theory: Contemporary Readings* (New York: Macmillan, 1951): 188.

6. Sprout, p. 199.

7. Sprout, p. 137. On other occasions ignorance about the milieu may be blissful, as witness the statement by many a successful businessman: Had I known about all the difficulties at the time I started I would probably never have gone into business.

8. Indeed, there are reasons to believe that slack would tend to be greater in nonprofit markets—such as those worked by most CI organizations—than in the markets for commercial products and services.

9. Note that the effect of time lags in the interaction process often is obscured by intervening events affecting the cause-effect relationships that otherwise might have been expected.

10. It must be remembered that environmental variables interact with other environmental variables as well as with organizational ones. This observation also applies to organizational variables.

11. There is an analogy here with students in a school, patients in a hospital, consumer cooperatives and many other organizations.

12. We also refer to the dynamic comparison of Consumers Union and Consumers' Research in the U.S. section of the *Handbook*.

13. Ida R. Hoos, "Systems Techniques for Managing Society: A Critique," *Public Administration Review* (March-April 1973): 157-63. See also *Academy of Management Journal* (December 1972): 349-540, special issue on general systems theory; and F.E. Emery, ed., *Systems Thinking* (London: Penguin Modern Management Readings, 1969).

14. D.S. Pugh, D.J. Hickson, C.R. Hinings and C. Turner, "The Context of Organization Structures," *Administrative Science Quarterly* (March 1969): 91-114.

15. Incidentally, the term "structure" in organization theory refers to the or-

ganization, while in economics it typically refers to the environment (market structure). Being transdisciplinary, ecology uses structure in both senses. See Hans B. Thorelli, ed., *Strategy + Structure = Performance* (Bloomington: Indiana University Press, 1977).

16. Whether industry and trade are allowed to buy mass copies is a question that has (we think unduly) worried a number of CI leaders. We do admit to raising our eyebrows, however, upon finding in retail stores dozens of reprints of high-fidelity magazine reviews of various brands all equally (and monophonically) laudatory.

17. As when *DM* reprints reports from STIWA.

18. As when French UFC continuously reprinted reports from Belgian AC.

19. See, e.g., Edith T. Penrose, *The Theory of Growth of the Firm* (Oxford: Blackwell, 1959).

20. The fact that the founders of CU (as opposed to those of CA) had the idea of a general consumer pressure group in mind during the organization's formative years (1936–World War II) would not seem to affect the validity of this observation.

Chapter 7

Dynamic Analysis: The Case of Sweden Since 1940

The evolution of Sweden's consumer information and policy programs is of special interest in view of her rich and in some respects pioneering heritage in this area. The purpose here is to present a longitudinal analysis of that experience, applying an ecologic viewpoint throughout. By contrast, the next chapter is an example of cross-sectional ecologic analysis. Ecologic inferences of great stringence or precision are not to be expected in this exploratory treatment, as indicated in Chapter Six. Some observations relevant to the model outlined there, however, will be made periodically and then summarized in a separate section, including some aspects of the Swedish experience that might be transferable. The reader not already conversant with the principal CI institutions in Sweden prior to 1973 may wish to read the country study in the *Handbook*. Some familiarity with this material is assumed here.

The second half of the chapter surveys in some detail the central consumer policy agencies and their activities as of 1975. In effect, this section represents an update of the Swedish country study in the *Handbook*. A postscript highlights 1976 developments.

Before proceeding to the analysis of ecologic interaction, certain enduring characteristics of the Swedish environment believed to be relevant to the development of the local consumer information system (CIS) are briefly outlined. The subsequent analysis will be divided into three periods of special significance to this development: the World War II years; the era of the affluential, 1948–65; and the Left Twist, 1966 to date.

ENDURING ENVIRONMENTAL CHARACTERISTICS

Sweden is *a small country* where "everyone knows everyone else." It is also a culture bent on airing its problems in the open. Taken together, these facts mean that no important producer could afford to stray very far out of line as regards community standards of product performance, advertising ethics and customer relations without being hit by the boomerang of unfavorable publicity. So it is that until the current "Left Twist" in Swedish politics there was much less of a dichotomy between producer and consumer than in a country like France.

This relative closeness of producer and consumer was reinforced by a phenomenon that most aptly may be labeled as *homogeneity cum pluralism*. Sweden is singularly homogeneous on almost any score: economically, ethnically, culturally—even politically. Homogeneity has not meant uniformity, however. Variety has been ensured by what Swedish political scientists have fondly called a system of pluralist democracy. Every opinion, every interest is represented by an organization. Every cause of significance has its own "folk movement." When a group reaches prominence it will frequently be given semipublic responsibilities by law or government subsidy as well as representation on officially created or sanctioned bodies, such as the former Consumer Council (KR) and the Informative Labeling Institute (VDN). At least until the last few years an extremely important aspect of Swedish pluralism has been interest group representation on the multifarious government investigating committees. If not directly represented on a committee, each interest group has always been given an opportunity to make its opinion known or felt through lobbying and hearings and by formal written statements concerning committee reports and governmental proposals. These statements have been regularly included in the investigating committees' exhaustive published reports or cited in subsequent government proposals.

Another enduring feature is one of the *highest standards of living* in the world. Sweden has been the pacesetter of the affluent society in Europe. While strangely reluctant to admit it, Swedes have a strikingly materialist bent. The taxation and welfare apparatus is monumental by international standards. Through it, redistribution of income and wealth has proceeded to a point where most people have a sense of well-being and security, if not necessarily of excitement.

Hard work, a set of puritanical values, and private enterprise and initiative have been the cornerstones of Swedish economic growth, vastly facilitated by fairly harmonious labor-management relations pluralistically developed. To these observers it is evident that these values are increasingly put to the test under the current Left Twist. With a small domestic market, Swedish industry and trade have been distinctly cosmopolitan in orientation. Some 24 percent of the standard of living is directly derived from international trade. Policies in this area have been among the most liberal in the world. The Swedes are probably the most international-travel-oriented of all peoples; they also get new impulses and experiences as consumers by the extensive use of second homes among all social groups.

While Sweden may have less to boast about as regards *education*, standards in this area are still quite high—especially in the adult education programs, a heritage of the folk movements. Until the Left Twist, education was squarely based on a merit system. This emphasis on merit was reflected in the spirit of objectivity and dispassionate analysis in the civil service. These values have been very much in evidence in past approaches to consumer information in general and in the leadership of the former Consumer Institute (KI) and VDN in particular.

Man as consumer seems everywhere to be self-centered. The Swedes are no exception. The country has a strong consumer cooperative movement, but at least during the period under review its success has been due to skillful management rather than to ideological or idealistic support by members.[1] Even this organization-minded society has seen no spontaneous formation of local groups to articulate matters of common consumer concern. A handful of local consumer committees centrally sponsored by folk movements and interest groups is able to survive only by means of outside injections of ideas and funds. Thus, most of the consumerist impulses have come from a set of dedicated individuals and pressure groups on the national scene and from such blunt environmental influences as wartime shortages. The political parties responded to these signals at an early stage. It is indeed significant to note that until the mid-1960s the development of CI programs in Sweden was a matter substantially removed from partisan controversy.

A final enduring feature of the period remains to be emphasized: the dominant role of the Social Democrat party in Swedish politics. For decades the philosophy of this party was almost indistinguishable from other Social Democrat or Labour parties in Western Europe. The postwar program published by the party in 1944 is of special interest as the most significant Swedish political document in over thirty years. In it the party made unequivocally clear that outside of the nationalized and regulated industries it stood for a liberal system of vigorously competitive private enterprise. The free play of market forces was to be promoted by antimonopoly and consumer information policies.[2] It is only in recent years, when the party moved decidedly to the left of most sister parties elsewhere, that it began to develop a different philosophy of government relations to business—and to the consumer.

THE WORLD WAR II YEARS: GENESIS OF CI

In the late 1930s a few Social Democrat women's guilds made abortive efforts at establishing some kind of consumer forum. The first tangible consumer information measure came in 1940 under the impact of World War II blockades of normal trade channels and shortages of many commodities. It is interesting to note not only that this program, Aktiv Hushållning (AH, Active Home Management), was a government venture but also that its aim went considerably beyond the provision of objective information. There was

> . . . a strong need to influence the direction and development of consumption in order to achieve a balance in the scarcity economy in the interest of the individual as well as the collective. . . . The prime means of doing this was rationing. In parallel with it the authorities by means of an intensive information campaign directed toward individual households tried both to interest them in appropriate planning and to make them prevail on the possibilities of making more effective use of whatever means were available. Those who were not forced by circumstances to restrict their consumption were to be stimulated to voluntary restraint. . . . In this way wartime exigencies became the direct reason for the establishment of consumer information under state auspices in our country.[3]

While AH was a government body, it has a strong advisory council representing half a dozen housewives and home economics groups. Soon enough fresh private initiatives of CI significance were taken. The Swedish Standardization Commission (SIS) appointed a special group for the development of standards for consumer goods. The textile manufacturers group already in the 1940s had considerable success with its industry-sponsored "product declarations," which included the phrase "testing methods standardized by SIS." The labels focused on materials content, weight, tensile strength and degree of shrinkage. At the same time the Cooperative Wholesale Society (KF) launched an informative labeling program on its own. Both of these programs were later to be superseded by VDN.[4]

The founding of Hemmens Forskningsinstitut (HFI, The Home

Economics Reseach Institute) by a few dedicated home economists in 1944 illustrates the role of private initiative in a pluralist environment. KF was persuaded to donate to the women's and home economics organizations a grant for this purpose, a grant that these groups then gave to HFI. At this stage both industry and government were ready to contribute financial resources, thereby insuring HFI survival until its ultimate absorption into KI. While HFI home economics research and generic product tests soon gained strong respect in many circles, it failed to have any direct impact on a broader audience.

ERA OF THE AFFLUENTIAL, 1948-65: PLURALISM IN CI

The stage for the later evolution of CI programs in Sweden was fairly well set by these developments when a government investigating committee submitted a report on "Research on Quality and Consumer Information" in 1949.[5] Incidentally, we used the word "evolution" advisedly. From 1948 to 1968 well over a dozen government investigating committees submitted reports in CI-related areas![6] As might be expected the 1949 report was concerned with both product testing and product labeling, and recommended further public effort in this area. While its proposals were not adopted in detail, the report was the direct precursor of VDN.

The report made two observations of ecologic interest. It recommended that any informative labeling program be carried on in close cooperation with SIS, which should be able to render invaluable support in the development of standard methods of measuring performance (SMMP). On the other hand, the report emphasized, it would be inappropriate to subordinate labeling under standardization, which, after all, had a long tradition of producer orientation. Merely adding consumer representation to standards bodies would not likely suffice. Also SIS—like its sister groups in other countries —was not well suited for information programs among ultimate consumers.

The second observation pertained to the nonexistence of a consumer-sponsored CI organization in Sweden of the CU type. After emphasizing that the formation of such a group must depend on the initiative of related folk movements, "whose interest in the matter we have been unable to establish,"[7] the committee hazarded the guess that Sweden had not witnessed the emergence of a CU-type movement due to the fact that Sweden—as contrasted with the United States—had a strong consumer coop movement.[8] As product testing was a desirable activity, the committee proposed increased support of HFI and a corresponding extension of government influence over the institute.

The year 1951 witnessed the creation of VDN. It is to be seen as a typical product of traditional pluralism, shown by its long list of sponsors, and voluntary cooperation among pressure groups, finalized by government-approved statutes and considerable state financial support. No doubt its success relative to labeling programs elsewhere was in large part ecologically conditioned: a preexisting quality consciousness in industry and highly developed quality control systems at the plant level, coupled with cultural homogeneity and the limited number of producers in a fairly small, though affluent economy. Even so, VDN's success fell far short of a smash hit. Most firms—indeed, most branches of industry—were not represented in the program. The fact of the matter is that despite the growing momentum of Swedish consumerism, industry simply did not feel the pressure to join a program whose immediate commercial merit was at least doubtful. Latter-day developments strongly suggest that this short-term perspective at the level of individual firms and industries is to be viewed as a costly mistake.

AH was absorbed into HFI in 1954. In 1955, when the proportion of the institute budget publicly financed had risen to 85 percent, a Ministry of Commerce report recommended that the state take over the institute and, in that context, that certain organizational changes be made.[9] The institute emerged as a government agency in 1957 with a new name: Konsumentinstitutet (KI).

We have tried to explain, in ecodynamic terms, how comparative testing came into the hands of a government agency in Sweden. It was not simply that Swedes looked more than others to the state. There was already a record of government involvement at the time of the establishment of the institute. No great sense of grassroots consumerism could be prevailed upon for voluntary support. It is barely possible that there might have been such support five years later had the question of comparative testing been raised then. By 1962 consumer expectations, seemingly growing exponentially with affluence and the possession of appliances and other consumer durables, had generated "consumerist" feelings sufficiently strong that they might have found an outlet in a popular movement akin to CU or CA. But already ten years later—in 1967—such an opportunity would have passed. The accelerating radicalization in Swedish politics beginning about that time would surely have preempted anything but a government solution.

One fact of KI policy needs attention here: the fact that it did not give "best buy" evaluations in its reports. The reader may recall the "objectivist" predilection of the classic Swedish civil service, the respect for research and "facts," the home economics research tradition. This background probably explains the recruitment of a scientist as director of the institute. Her personal philosophy that the variety of individual consumer needs and the shortcomings in even the most advanced product testing activity should preclude a government agency making brand recommendations is probably the penultimate explanation of the fact that the institute resisted gradually increasing environmental pressure for such recommendations. Again we note the role of personal leadership in the ecological drama.

The 1955 Ministry of Commerce report also proposed the creation of a government consumer council to articulate the consumer viewpoint before government, industry and trade bodies and to stimulate research into consumer problems. The council also was to coordinate the effort of other organs in the field. Established in 1957, the Consumer Council (KR) was reasonably successful as an articulating agent, modestly successful as a research sponsor and stimulant, and an outright failure as a coordinating body. In this case the pluralist composition of the board proved a weakness not so much because of dissentions between representatives of different interests but because these representatives were all incredibly busy people in their own organizations, and generally willing to give only marginal effort to KR. It did not help that the KR secretariat lacked the kind of leadership evident in KI and VDN.

Ecologically speaking, the most interesting aspect of KR was its failure as a coordinator. It might be presumed that in a small and homogeneous culture it would be relatively easy to bring about a centrally coordinated CIS. We believe that, beyond the lack of KR leadership, at least two factors explain the fairly modest development of a systems approach during the period, although the Swedes were surely ahead of everyone else. First, there is the traditional independence and jealously guarded autonomy of Swedish civil service agencies in general, and second, the specific origins of the agencies composing the Swedish CIS. VDN and SIS were semiprivate bodies, while KI, KR and the State Price and Cartel Office (SPK) were public. KI was an outflow of a scientific and home-economics-oriented tradition, while SPK was the antitrust successor of wartime and postwar price control. KR was a rather amorphous body without prior tradition.

The degree of CIS coordination that did exist was the result of three interacting ecological forces. First, the government by way of amending the SPK and KI charters specifically admonished these two agencies to synchronize their pricing and product testing studies. Second, a greater will toward cooperation developed on the part of VDN, KI and SPK as these bodies found their style, staked their claims and began to establish in what specifics cooperative efforts might have synergistic effects. Third, they were markedly assisted in identifying suitable areas of cooperation by increasingly vocal demands from media and politicians.

What, then, was the evidence of systems planning? VDN, KI and SIS did engage in a considerable amount of teamwork in the development of SMMPs. In addition to the publicly available plans submitted by each agency in their annual budget requests, by the end of the 1960s, VDN and KI, at least, exchanged their detailed work programs. There was also a fair amount of cross-representation on boards and committees between all the agencies. In 1968–72 KI and SPK were finally able to coordinate a few SPK price surveys with the comparative tests of KI. In addition, KI advertised its services and publications in the SPK journal, and vice versa. KI reported new VDN activities and labels in its product testing journal *Råd och Rön*, and featured several articles on SPK as well as the new Central Consumer Complaints Board.[10] There could hardly be any doubt that enlarged cooperation of this kind was desirable. There is also every reason to believe that interorganizational cooperation would have become more intimate but for political developments which in a few years were to change the climate of Swedish consumer policy completely.[11]

THE CURRENT LEFT TWIST: GOVERNMENTALISM IN CI

Until 1968, remarkably little political conflict existed concerning the development of consumer information programs in Sweden. In principle, all democratic parties agreed that there was a need for such information and for public support of such programs. No such unanimity exists concerning the most recent developments in the CI field; this fact may need some explanation.

Since the middle of the 1960s the ideology of the dominant Social Democrat party has undergone a dramatic radicalization, resulting in what Swedes aptly refer to as the Left Twist of the local political scene. After the twenty-five-year acceptance of competition and open markets as prime movers of the economy, the party ideologists are reverting to more traditional socialist ideas of government ownership, regulation and—particularly in the consumer area—stewardship. Chief ideologue is Prime Minister Olof Palme, whose favorite theme is "equalism": freedom is equality in all areas, from after tax income to education. The Left Twist is particularly evident in the mass media, but also pervades other aspects of society. The state radio-TV monopoly is staffed largely with left-wing personnel whose views manage to come through in programming. In addition, the voice of the leading Stockholm daily—formerly liberal—is now that of its socialist majority of journalists. The authors believe, on the basis of a score of visits to Sweden, that an atmosphere has been created in which the bourgeoisie has become too timid, or too intimidated, to voice its views on such matters as the epidemic spread of drugs, the virulent criticism of the United States and the rapidly accelerating government influence on the economy.

This influence is manifested by an array of new measures, such as the creation of a governmental supertrust that controls a dozen large state industries, giving them a virtual carte blanche to expand into any economic activity they please. Other measures include the introduction of case-by-case credit controls, the tax on advertising, the appointment of government members to the management of commercial banks, the socialization of apothecaries, and the creation of state monopolies for most school books and official print. Since 1973 a greatly strengthened Price Control Act provides the mechanism for introducing price controls whenever considered needed. Proposals now being considered would compel the closing of "excess" gas stations, the further governmentalization of the drug industry, government direction of research and development in Swedish industry, and so on. Naturally, these and other extensions of statism have been accompanied by considerable antibusiness, antimarketing and, particularly, antiadvertising fanfare.[12]

The policies of equalism paradoxically create new dichotomies. Traditional peace on the labor market was upset at the beginning of 1971 by a long series of strikes and lockouts affecting salaried employees in no mood to hold back while workers were getting their way on most any score it might please the powerful federation of labor unions to name. Another new dichotomy is that between the greatly increased concentration of power in the hands of central government agencies and the grassroots democracy (närdemokrati) advocated by the intelligentsia. Sweden is also experiencing a polarization in consumer-producer relations unknown until the 1970s.

We have stated elsewhere that, somewhat paradoxically, consumer concern and dissatisfaction are likely to increase rapidly in affluent societies—at least until consumers reach a new level of accommodation with the "realities" of technology and the so-called service trades. It follows that consumer dissatisfaction is a "natural" for politicians in Sweden. Left Twist leaders have been quick to recognize this. In the last few years "manipulation" has been the key word in local agitation. The term is used by everyone to characterize everyone else, but Left Twisters have made business the prime agent of manipulation. "Stamp out poor products"; let the government set minimum product standards is one cry. "Refusal to buy is a negative consumer power—now we want positive power" is another.[13] Equalization may also be applied to consumers: "It is really an outrage that people with high incomes have more votes in the marketplace—in this way a free market only yields misallocation of productive resources."[14] In line with this type of thinking, the secretary of one of the latest in the long row of government investigations of CI suggested in a private communication that if comparative testing reports in practice reach only the educated and affluent elite then maybe such reporting should be abolished. Truly consumer-oriented or not, Social Democrats have certainly found in consumerism a new vehicle to revive good old-fashioned antibusiness agitation. In part they have been quite successful; recent polls suggest that the image of business and businessmen has never been lower than among the current student generation.

Yet it is still true that consumerism fails to be a sufficiently burning issue to sustain collective action at the local level. No such movement has emerged spontaneously. It is also instructive to contemplate the fate of the so-called local consumer committees. Six of these were established in provincial cities in 1967 upon the sponsorship of the national workers and salaried employees federations of unions and associated educational groups, the housewives' organizations and the cooperative women's guild. An enthusiastic representative of the federation of trade unions was in charge of a coordinating secretariat supported by a government grant. Three main purposes of the committees were to handle local consumer complaints, to provide consumer information and advice, and to undertake studies and articulate viewpoints of local consumer concern.

The committees have been but a modest success. After three years "more than 1,000 consumers"[15] had brought their complaints to the committees. Many more had received information and advice. A few locally originated studies of some value had been undertaken. But studies inspired by the central secretariat were apparently of less interest; in a survey of local public services all six committee reports were in large part word-for-word identical, suggesting that they were all variations of a centrally prepared model.[16] And after more than six years of operation, the initiative had not led to the formation of other groups elsewhere.

A recent major enactment of interest in the field, the law establishing a consumer ombudsman (KO) in 1971, was partly an expression of the new left in Swedish politics. The law was substantially unopposed by the liberal parties, which have recently preferred accepting a great many things to running the risk of being labeled reactionary or anticonsumer. Some parts of the law actually represent only a consumer-oriented modernization of legislation on unfair competition dating back to the 1930s. Nevertheless, KO has now been presented as St. George fighting the dragon advertisers, despite the fact that what was probably the most advanced self-policing advertising control machinery in the world antedated the new law by more than a decade. Furthermore, for at least ten years prior to KO there had been a clear-cut trend for advertising to become more informative—that is, to fill its natural and vital role in the total CIS.

The trend from pluralism to polarization is more amply reflected in the establishment of the all-comprehensive State Consumer Board (Konsumentverket, KOV) in 1973.[17] Most consumer protection, education and information activities are now centralized under the keynote "household-centered consumer policy." Instant coordination was to be obtained by the board taking over the functions of not only KR and KI, but also VDN. Socialization of the VDN informative labeling activity signaled the end of commercially independent private initiative in Swedish consumer information. After being taken over by KOV, the whole VDN program is now in the process of liquidation despite emphatic declarations in the underlying investigating committee report and government proposals that increased support for the voluntary labeling system would be a high priority for the new agency. CI ostensibly is to be directed more toward the choice between different products and services than toward the evaluation of different brands of the same product. "Normative needs" as identified by the state should have priority over the "subjective aspirations" of individual consumers. In its role as a go-between for producers and consumers, KOV views as one of its dominant tasks that of influencing producer decisions, otherwise known as producer jawboning (producentpåverkan). This apsect of KOV's work involves as a minimum "analysis of business policy and contacts with firms and public authorities as regards such matters as price, assortment, product development, service, and promotion policies."[18] Additional proposals foresee the board guiding local and regional public bodies for consumer protection.

A vocal group of women socialists have urged the imposition of compulsory testing and, presumably, approval by government experts prior to the introduction of any new product or brand. Others talk about a compulsory government quality authentication scheme under which approved products would be awarded a red or green label depending upon how experts view their quality. Then, before they could meet the test of the market, products would first have to withstand the test of the bureaucrats.

The scene is alive with continued debate, numerous and voluminous investigatory reports, institutional and centralistic proposals and massive amounts of new legislation. Today, with the recent establishment or reorganizations of such agencies as the State Food Administration (Livsmedelsverket, 1972), the State Environment Protection Board (Naturvårdsverket, 1973) and its Product Control Board (Produktkontrollnämnd), and attendant legislation, the central government has taken fresh steps toward regulation and control in all matters concerning the consumer. The Market Court, set up in the days when consumers were considered best protected by keeping the channels of trade free from restrictive business practices, is now primarily handling cases on advertising, marketing tactics and improper contract terms. The State Price and Cartel Office (SPK) has formidable powers under the general Price Control Act not only in administering price freezes, in setting ceiling prices and in requiring obligatory price reporting but also in negotiating with business to influence pricing in a direction favorable to the consumer.

The government has explicitly stated that only if it does not prove possible to safeguard consumer interests by "discussions and cooperation" with producers will "other approaches" be considered. Just exactly what this statement means is difficult to see against the background of events in the last five years. Half a dozen major legislative measures of consumer protection based on "other approaches" were under active consideration in 1975.

ECOSUMMARY

Concluding the dynamic analysis we shall try to pull together some of the points of the foregoing discussion in an ecologic perspective. In so doing, we will emphasize what seems generalizable—in the sense of transferable—and what may be more or less unique given the Swedish environment.

The most important lesson of transferability to be learned from Sweden is that *pluralist CI programs can be made to work.* This is the crucial VDN experience. CI programs can certainly not be a trade association prerogative. But VDN demonstrated unequivocally that it would be false to conclude that they must be run by consumers (or, much less, by government) alone. VDN also demonstrated that *industry generally will tend to do little* by way of sponsoring or participating *in CI programs without environmental pressure.* Labeling is no better than comparative testing in selling itself to either consumers or producers. Voluntary CI programs need more substantial promotion than VDN could afford. That the VDN program was more successful than any other IL program thus far was due to the smallness, homogeneity and quality control consciousness of the country and its industry—features that to some degree are unique.

VDN provided a fascinating case study in ecological adjustment. Having reached at least a temporary plateau in its traditional product labeling activity, and experiencing some hot winds in the fervid Swedish consumerist debate, the agency turned to the labeling of services (a highly complex venture) and to the issuing of buying advice pamphlets to supplement its offering. The abolishment during VDN's last couple of years of independent existence of some of its pluralist working procedures detailed in the *Handbook* may be seen as another "concession" to the times. An unfriendly critic might ask whether in its urge to survive VDN became government-oriented more than consumer-oriented. On the other hand, with recent trends toward polarization in Swedish society, and lacking aggressive industry support, VDN could hardly have expected to survive in its orignal form in either case.

Another transferable observation from the Swedish scene pertains to the importance of leadership in the ecological interaction of CI programs. The presence of strong leadership in KI would seem to explain the maintenance of its tradition of research and objectivity until its absorption in 1973, despite vocal demands that the institute tow a more "activist" line. Conversely, absence of strong leadership is the only factor that can reasonably explain the relative failure of KR in a munificent environment. We believe that a more active and farsighted management of KR might have been able to build the kind of CI system in Sweden that would have weathered the current political storm. Free experimentation yielded many different and interesting forms of CI in Sweden. The organizations involved had just begun to learn in earnest about the *benefits of synergy* in a CIS characterized by a reasonable balance of coordination and decentralized initiative.

The most important thing one may learn from the recent developments in Sweden is that, like many other policy instruments, consumer information is a two-edged sword. Given a continuation of the recent political trend we would predict that *CI will simply become an instrument of government planning.* The CIS will be centrally programmed; buying recommendations based on sociopolitical dogma will be issued; and there will be a rapidly increasing flora of government regulations of contents, performance and other characteristics of products. Testing may remain as a foundation of the CIS, but comparative test reports will decline in relative importance as informative labeling is made obligatory for many categories of products, and as buying advice, cross-product information, and, most likely, seals of government approval are introduced. Government marketing research will be vastly extended—focusing on what consumers "should" want—and the results will be used in the manipulation of industry in the field of product planning and for purges of existing product and model assortments.[19] Reluctant firms may experience difficulty in obtaining credit or may find themselves in competition with state-owned corporations or with other firms more anxious to cooperate with the government. There will be a vast increase in public information programs concerning the rapidly growing number of government products and services. How objective this particular form of consumer information will be remains to be seen.

The history of the Swedish CIS provides a beautiful illustration of the usefulness of a general ecologic perspective in the study of organizational dynamics. In its capacity as a specific observation, the Swedish case also lends some credence to a great number of individual propositions in organization ecology set forth in Appendix C. Among these propositions, the following merit some emphasis here:

1. *The greater the share of government expenditures of GNP, the greater the degree of government influence on the organization* (O-E 5).[a] The great share of state expenditure of GNP in Sweden is reflected not only in the fact that the CI organization (KOV) is a government agency but also in the great government influence on the local CIS as a whole.
2. *The more pluralist the environment, the greater the number of organizations constituting the total CIS (and vice versa)* (CIS-E 1).
3. *Organized business will do something about CI only when it feels direct environmental pressure* (E-E 14). This is an area where business tends to lag rather than lead. Despite the success of VDN by

---

[a]Here and in the following notations the parenthetical identification of propositions refers to Appendix C. The acronym O-P 1 refers to the first proposition under "Organization and Performance"; O-E 4 designates the fourth proposition under "Individual CI Organization and Environment"; and so on.

international standards before its socialization, the background, development and collapse of that organization is a good illustration of the proposition.

4. *The more business-minded a cooperative movement, the less it will do about CI spontaneously* (E-E 15). (The United Kingdom furnishes an even better example.)

5. *The more leftwing the government, the more it will tend to regard CIS an an instrumentality of the state* (E-E 16).

6. *Strong leadership may overcome environmental obstacles* (KI, VDN); *weak leadership may fail even in a munificent environment* (KR) (O-E 2).

7. *The greater the rapidity of change in environmental variables, the greater the rate of change in CI organizations as to philosophy, activities and size* (O-E 9).

CENTRAL CONSUMER AGENCIES IN 1975

Konsumentverket (KOV): General

Established January 1, 1973, the State Consumer Board (KOV) is the key and central organ of Swedish consumer policy. Our overview of the agency will focus on the aspects of its work most relevant from a CI point of view—that is, the transformation of the government consumer journal *Råd och Rön* and the fate of testing and labeling under KOV management. Also included is a fairly detailed description of the Central Consumer Complaints Board (ARN), a KOV subsidiary, as complaints constitute a principal means of consumer information to producers and as ARN—next to *Råd och Rön* —in practice represents the most significant part of KOV's work thus far.

It is difficult to write about KOV activities in the producer-jawboning area at this stage. The reason is a simple one: KOV thus far has been markedly more successful in cutting down on objective consumer information and education of the KI and VDN types than in shaping and implementing producer-jawboning policy and defining the "normative needs" of consumers. While the latter activities seem clearly the melody of the future, the mode of proceeding in the first thirty months has been gradual and experimental. Thus, the theory of producer-directed product information and of means of influencing producer offerings so far is actually ahead of practice.

By way of background it may be helpful to present a diagram depicting current and likely types of public product information policy and how their administration may be divided between KOV and the Consumer Ombudsman (KO).[20] Enabling legislation pertaining to standardized mandatory information in advertising and

KOV			KO	
1	2	3	4	5
Comparative testing	Informative labeling	Standardized mandatory information in advertising	Improper omission of information by producers	Misleading promotional practices

to improper omission of information by producers has been drafted but not yet adopted. In the meantime, the jurisdiction over boxes 3 and 4 on the diagram is somewhat uncertain.

According to the guidelines set by the government KOV has multiple goals:

> to identify the needs of consumers and sponsor research on consumerism;
> to pay special attention to "weak" consumers and their needs;
> to support consumer-oriented activities via municipal and regional authorities;
> to examine and appraise merchandise and services on the market;
> to stimulate the use of informative labeling;
> to advise and influence industry and commerce with regard to the needs and demands of the consumer;
> to initiate and support education programs at all school levels and within educational organizations, to publicize findings of research and tests;
> to cooperate with other responsible institutions in solving consumer problems;
> to be responsible for the activities of the Central Consumer Complaints Board.[21]

With the overall goal of effectuating better use of resources in households, KOV has defined four areas of principal concern: weak consumers, products involving risks for health and safety or large economic risks, the rationalization of work in the household, and national planning with finite resources.

The general director of KOV is Lars Ag, a former left-wing journalist. He works with a board comprising an additional eight members, two from labor unions, two from the cooperatives, one from the State Food Administration, two politicians (one a member of the cooperatives' board), and only one from industry. There are no consumers at large on the board. With a staff of about 210 (180 full time) in 1975, KOV is located on the periphery of Stockholm

Table 7-1. Konsumentverket. Income and Expenditures: Actual 1973-74, Budgeted 1974-75, 1975-76 (In thousands of Swedish crowns. $1 U.S. is approximately 4.4 crowns.)

	1973-74	1974-75	1975-76
Expenditures			
Investigations and producer contacts	9,321	10,146	12,221
Information and education	9,170	7,612	12,239
Product tests on commission	1	1	1
Central Consumer Complaints Board	1,830	2,042	2,517
Grants for outside research	1,584	1,719	2,500
Grants for commercial service in sparsely populated areas	2,100[a]	2,500	2,400
Income			
Informative labeling licenses	278	200	160
Publications	1,422	1,400	1,800
Government appropriation	22,306[b]	22,420[b]	29,918[b]
Total	24,006[c]	24,020	31,878

[a]Figures not available; budgeted figure used.
[b]Composite figure by adding expenditures and subtracting income.
[c]Not counting one million crowns KOV received from the Government Information Office to publicize the new Consumer Sales Act.
Source: *Anslagsframställning för budgetåret 1975-76* (Stockholm: Konsumentverket, 1974-08-30, Dnr 1361/74-15. Mimeographed): 4.

in new, well-equipped quarters, occupying some 7,500-8,000 square meters.

KOV is organized into two research departments—one for foods and housing; one for clothing, travel and recreation—a technical department, an administrative department that also includes the supervision of what is left of the VDN program, a planning section that currently includes the Central Consumer Complaints Board, and an information and education department.[22] The total budget of KOV for 1973-74 was about $5.7 million. Table 7-1 gives the actual figures from 1973-74 and the proposed budgets for 1974-75 and 1975-76.

In no way could the changing character of public consumer policy in Sweden be better illustrated than by the journal KOV inherited from KI. Thus, we felt it important to document the transformation in some detail. The ten issue a year *Råd och Rön* uses a 8 1/4" × 11 3/4" format of thirty-two pages with spectacular color pictures, photographs and drawings, and many different types and styles of print. This magazine gets top marks for truly impressive layout on good quality paper. Articles are usually short, though some issues carry longer presentations devoted to a special theme; for instance, winter sports equipment, packaging. With a special grant an extra issue dealing exclusively with energy questions was published in early 1975 and was distributed in schools and to subscribers.

A subscription to *Råd och Rön* has cost $3 (12 crowns) since 1970; its cost of publication is now most likely three or four times greater. In 1968–69 there were 105,000 subscribers; in 1974–75, 110,000. KOV attributes the increase of 5,000 to the change in journalistic style and marketing measures. To us it is much more relevant to ask why these measures have not resulted in any real growth. (It may be, for instance, that the drastic reduction of test reports largely accounts for the tardy growth in spite of the glamour measures.) Materials from other authorities have not increased significantly, despite the establishment of an editorial committee of representatives from KO, the State Food Administration, SPK and KOV. Press releases in the form of articles are sent to fifty dailies after the publication of each issue. KOV claims that thirty-seven dailies, with a combined circulation of 1,087,000 (in a country of eight million), have *each time* published one or more of these releases. *Råd och Rön* is still not available at newsstands.

The results of comparative tests are rarely seen in *Råd och Rön* as the testing of comparable products under the new organization is no longer considered important. In fact, testing itself is viewed primarily as generating background material for the more basic work aimed at influencing producers. Compared with 1969 when thirteen comparative tests giving information on 120 brands were reported, 1974–75 saw the results of only four tests with thirty-seven brands. Of the four, only one on stoves can be considered a full-blown comparative test of the type produced by KOV's predecessor, KI. The one on cameras was performed by the European Testing Group. Of the twenty-eight brands in that test KOV reported on the twelve that were available on the Swedish market. It appears that the test on detergents was chosen so that KOV could present the advantages of buying the cheapest brand. Of the eleven tested, five were "low-priced" detergents, three "regularly" priced and three sold door to door. The table giving the results, however, showed that one of the regularly priced detergents was almost as inexpensive (8 öre—2 cents—a wash more), was clearly better in washing effect and, furthermore, was less harmful to the environment. The test on child gates was undertaken primarily for reasons of safety.

Other product reports do not seem to be based on systematic tests or comparisons or even to give much of the information collected.[23] Aside from no longer being able to get comparative product information, the reader of *Råd och Rön* is also not getting clearly and objectively written articles on consumer products in general. While drafted with considerable flair, too many articles present misleading information, some so grossly misleading that elementary corrections (but no apology) have to be printed in later issues.[24] An article entitled "Old juice can be dangerous" carried a huge picture of the Del Monte brand beside the one found dangerous, although Del Monte was found not dangerous.[25] The article on vitamins called "Uncertain pills" showed that of twenty-one (not twenty-three as stated) tested, while nine had less than the vitamin content given on the label, twelve had more. There was no discussion of what this might mean for the consumer.[26] The title "Best pocket camera not the most expensive" was misleading, as the best cameras were certainly among the most expensive.[27]

Numerous articles carry negative titles;[28] others do not present data very clearly. In the one on deodorants KOV actually only examined labels, basing the text on Warentest's *test*, while leaving the impression that KOV had tested.[29] KOV only partially tested seven brands of blue jeans, but quoted from labels of two brand leaders, Lee Jeans and Levis, without testing.[30] *Råd och Rön* implied that all child gates were tested, yet only those available in the Stockholm area were selected for testing, according to the full test report.[31]

It is startlingly clear that the writers of articles, and perhaps also the researchers who prepare the working materials, have little or no understanding of market phenomena.[32] The article on shelf space implies that consumers are so influenced by the location of products that they are denied the right to choose their own menu—no attempt at a balanced discussion.[33] One article totally ignores marketing costs. A community committed itself to sell two-thirds of a group of tract houses, with the builder selling the remaining one-third. The higher price for the privately sold houses was considered totally unnecessary despite the increased risks and selling costs. The builder had also included a washing machine, wall-to-wall carpeting and kitchen cabinets.[34] Not atypical of the fuzzy thinking is an article entitled "The role of advertising."[35] Reporting on a study financed by the former Consumer Council, the thesis is presented that society is working to redistribute a certain part of consumption to weaker groups, while the majority of the people value their individual consumption highly. Hence, as advertising appeals to the individual, it is working against society!

With initial emphasis on the so-called "weak" (svag) consumer and his needs, KOV has found it essential to define more closely what is meant by weak. A spokesman included in "weak" not only consumers who have limited financial resources but also those who lacked time or interest in consumer matters. Actually, articles in *Råd och Rön* show KOV's contempt for the average consumer and his tastes and choices: it is dumb that folks like blue jeans that fade;[36] we ought not to use soft drinks;[37] it is stupid to buy fashion clothes that belong in the trashcan;[38] if consumers fix chicken in different ways, it is to hide or camouflage the no taste product;[39] the fact that boys preferred sport bicycles is condemnable;[40] it is to be regretted that white bread is even more popular;[41] families with "normal incomes" should not be able to afford a car in the 25,000 crown class, though this car is the best seller on the market; it is too bad that antiperspirants and deodorants are needed.[42] It appears that KOV is moving fast from its theory of the weak consumer to a theory of the naive consumer.[43] An expression of this was given by the general director when he stated in our interview in April 1975, "We are going to make it more difficult for the consumer to make a mistake."

An editorial states that it is more important to examine what need and use one has of a product group than to give comparisons. The editor promises that comparisons will be made, but not always reported; rather results will be used in counseling.[44] Whatever this may mean, unless comparative tests are made and reported somewhere, it is difficult to see that the results can be used in counseling. This was recognized in the report on brand differentiation which stated that in counseling "a large part" has to do with product differences and best buys.[45] According to the editorial just cited; "Through contacts with readers *Råd och Rön* has not been able to observe that comparative tests are missed. At the same time we know through reader investigations that a great many want to have test results in the journal [sic]." It is stated that until KOV can influence producers under stronger legislation, it will have to content itself with "less important measures, like consumer information."[46] But as an instrument of governmental consumer politics, *Råd och Rön* is no longer of much interest to anyone seeking objective product information.

In addition to the journal, KOV produced the following publications in 1973-74.

six reports from investigations, geared to producers and opinion leaders, printed in 500 to 1,000 copies;

eleven fact sheets with results from investigations and presenting buying advice. They are geared to the general public, are free of charge and are printed in 20,000 to 50,000 copies;

seven small booklets, some revised or reprinted from previous years, geared to the housewife, household consultants and home economics teachers. They cost between 10 and 20 crowns and are printed in 5,000 to 10,000 copies;
one pocketbook on the new Consumer Sales Act.

KOV also produces materials for schools, exhibitions and counseling, and in early 1975 began a bulletin called *Konsumenträtt* (Consumer Law) directed toward policymakers, academicians, consumer leaders and trade organizations. Topics covered in this smörgåsbord of publications range all the way from plastics in the bathroom via maintenance problems in tract houses and a survey of people contacting local consumer agencies to a manual on trustees and authorization. Sometimes these KOV publications, too, leave something to be desired. The large investigation of fast food service (called street kitchens) assumed that consumers want cheaper foods, not large portions. The vacuum cleaner fact sheet equates all cleaners by stressing the fact that the suction pressure was adequate on all brands!

TV programs on consumer questions appear intermittently, but never to present objective product information. Three programs produced by KOV in 1974 dealt with the new Consumer Sales Act. A five-minute program, Du Konsument, is aired Tuesdays and Thursdays at 11:45. In addition, short notices are aired once or twice a day.

In the jawboning area a few contacts with producers have brought about some highly publicized results. KOV could report that an importer of a child gate that was found unsafe agreed to cease importing and selling the gate, and to apprise dealers and retailers to take back stocks, thereby incurring a 160,000 crown loss. A dishwasher of exceedingly poor quality is no longer imported. Of four producer-importers contacted concerning the safety of baby scales, three agreed to KOV suggestions.[47]

Electrolux, which sells its vacuum cleaner door to door, however, refused to agree to require its salesmen to distribute KOV's fact sheet when they made calls. While the sheet deemphasizes characteristics other than suction power (and thus might hurt this firm), Electrolux refused primarily on principal grounds. Stressing the importance of price, the sheet gave no data on the prices of cleaners on the Swedish market. KOV dashed off a memo to the Department of Commerce stating the difficulties encountered in convincing companies to adjust products and marketing to consumer needs. When producers-sellers take the initiative in voluntary cooperation with KOV, it is seldom reported. The large furniture dealer IKEA distributed 100,000 copies of the fact sheet "Buying Furniture with Furniture Facts."

KOV has spent its first two years flexing its muscles vis-à-vis producers, petitioning the government to grant it more powers, and concentrating on criticizing products and practices, on underrating product differences, and on overrating price, suction power or some other single criterion. As a longtime member of the staff of KI and now KOV, one spokesman stated that the whole spirit of KOV was hypocritical, one of suspicion of producers, their products and motives. KOV, she felt, had lost contact with the consumer in his daily life.

KOV was anxious to abolish the thirty-nine state regional home economist consultants and the eight who counsel by telephone from KOV offices in Stockholm. In a demographic study of those who contact KOV for counseling on consumer matters—and there were 40,000 such contacts in 1973–74—it was shown that nearly half were junior salaried employees and only 27 percent were workers or office workers. University-trained persons were overrepresented by a factor of 2.5. One-half were homeowners, compared with 19 percent in the general population, and one-half had incomes over 50,000 crowns a year. This was not true in the case of local counseling in selected towns, where 50 percent were workers and office workers and only 22 percent had incomes of over 50,000. KOV concluded that local counseling reached a considerably larger group of economically and educationally weak consumers. However, parliament in 1975 decided to retain the regional consultants. It also passed a law delegating to local government the management of consumer counseling. Each municipality was encouraged to employ at least one consumer secretary who would disseminate general information, arrange exhibitions, start campaigns and work with the mass media. The whole operation would take on a somewhat political touch, either through special consumer boards or by being directly managed by the local government council. KOV would provide central backup in the form of expert advice, materials and training.

Konsumentverket: Informative Labeling

A grim chapter in the story of objective product information in Sweden under the Left Twist has been the rapid demise of VDN. As of December 1, 1974, twenty-eight food labels, thirty-six general product labels and one service label remained in use. Most of the food labeling had already been transferred to the State Food Administration and the last twenty-eight were to be transferred by the summer of 1975. A comparison of data for 1969 with those for 1974

Table 7-2. VDN. Specifications and Licenses by Product Area, 1969 and 1974

Categories	Number of specifications 1969	1974	Licenses granted 1969	1974
Food products	51	26	254	66
Pet foods	2	2	22	15
Home furnishings	25	8	231	65
Clothing	34	6	279	38
Kitchen equipment and appliances	16	8	45	32
Sporting goods	11	11	43	46
Chemical-technical articles	3	2	22	7
Paper products	2	1	7	1
Total	144	64	903	189

Sources: Data for 1969 from *Handbook*, p. 42. Data for 1974 sent by Dr. Hans Näslund, Konsumentverket, April 16, 1975, and entitled "Tillståndshavare 74-12-01, normer," mimeographed.

in Table 7-2 shows by product categories the number of specifications and licenses granted. As the general director put it in our interviews, "We are scrapping VDN."

According to information available in 1975 only one product, namely rugs, was then under serious study for labeling under a new system (not counting three products from a strictly safety point of view: life jackets, helmets and child gates). As of December 1974, nineteen rug manufacturers were still licensed to use VDN labels. The defunct Teltag labeling scheme of the former Consumer Council in England achieved its greatest success in this area.[48] Actually it was the Textile Research Institute (TEFO) that took the initiative in the rug area in Sweden in 1970. It is remarkable how much the proposed rug label resembles that of Teltag, including the designated area of use. On the other hand, such things as moth resistance, stain resistance, flammability and waterproofness were not deemed "important" enough to incorporate into the label. The proposed KOV label appears in Figure 7-1.[49]

In the twenty-four-page presentation of KOV's proposals for an all-Nordic labeling system for rugs, it was clear that KOV has all the agonizing problems faced by its predecessor VDN, starting with the fact that informative labeling demands massive resource inputs in order to provide a factual, clear and strict system.[50] In a well-written report, two experienced researchers reviewed past VDN experience, accounted for recent research projects, and reflected on legislative proposals and problems involved in labeling and quality certifica-

KONSUMENT   This rug meets the
VERKET   minimum standards
                       adopted by KOV

The same standards apply in other
Scandinavian countries.

Suitable for

    Bedroom

    Living room
    HOTEL ROOM

    Living room in frequent use
    OFFICE

    Hall, stairs, hallways
    RESTAURANTS

    Hall, Stairs, hallways
    PUBLIC FOYERS, STEPS, HALLWAYS

X means not suitable

Important characteristics: (three blacked
circles is best)

Color fastness to light	● ● ●
Rug holds shape	● ● ○
Static electricity	● ○ ○
Resists furniture marks	● ● ●

Installation advice:

    Should be glued

    Ask for pamphlet in the store

Care advice:

    Ask for pamphlet in the store

Name:	Superextra
Type:	Tufted
Material:	100% polyamid on wearing surface
Manufacturer:	The Rug Company, Inc., Central City

Figure 7-1. Projected Rug Labeling

tion. They posed more questions than they answered, including such a burning issue as whether or not a marking scheme should include a grading system of characteristics and performance levels.[51] One small study, financed by KOV, showed that in the furniture area where a label is offered by the Furniture Institute[52] consumer preferences in the information field are varied.[53] The study indicates that consumers felt they knew what they wanted, and, by and large, also felt that they were getting it. Over 50 percent had visited the shop earlier, over 40 percent had visited other shops, and over 70 percent had studied the very detailed catalogues which, incidentally, reproduced the label. Furthermore, one of the two large furniture centers in which the study took place had available KOV's fact sheet, "Buying Furniture with Furniture Facts." Twice as many customers in that store declared that they knew what Furniture Facts stood for as did in the other store—again illustrating the importance of promotion. Even after their prior homework and visits, no less than 24 percent of observed consumers in one store and 30 percent in the other looked at the labels. In a study of the cooperatives' shoe label, consumers ranked their needs for a label. First, they preferred one which gave the materials content; second, care information; and lastly, areas of use. In its enthusiasm for use information KOV interpreted this to mean that consumers had not learned to read labels presenting this aspect.

It appears that KOV is waiting until the government acts on several proposals before it makes any definite commitments itself as regards labeling and related CI schemes. These proposals include the report of the government investigation on informative labeling (headed by KO),[54] and a law on obligatory information in sales promotion when ordained by the government (acting through KOV), as proposed in the last report of the advertising commission.[55] The report on IL proposes an enabling law authorizing the government to establish minimum standards for products involving health and safety, with such products to be marked to indicate that they meet these standards. The law would also enable the government (or, presumably, KOV) to make IL obligatory on any other products when this is "of substantial importance from a consumer viewpoint," with the contents of the labels to be similar to that of the VDN labels. The report noted that these proposals for obligatory marking or labeling were intended as a *supplement* to voluntary labeling of the VDN type.

The advertising commission proposal would enable the government to mandate certain information concerning products or services specified by the government when it is "of substantial importance from a consumer viewpoint that such information be provided and there is no reason due to trade practice agreements with the firms concerned or otherwise to legitimately assume that the information would be provided in any case."[56] The types of information would generally be similar to that on VDN labels. Of special interest are the media of information: the government may ordain that it be given in the form of labels on the products, and/or that it be included in advertising or other promotion measures, and/or that it be provided on consumer request. Again, the government would be authorized to establish minimum standards for products involving health and safety and for their marking.

Aside from questions of health and safety, priorities in the selection of products for labeling suggested by the KOV spokesman were: KOV does not like the product, consumers ask a lot of questions about it, the product costs a great deal, there are a great many complaints concerning the product, there are large quality differences among the brands and models offered, and salesclerks are untrained. KOV compiled a five page list of 400 products and projected that to label these products would require six years and a staff of 130, not counting the administration of the labels in use and revising old labels. This might be a conservative estimate in view of the fact that the VDN label for travel services—admittedly a complex labeling object—required three years of work and 200,000 crowns.

Of interest in the information area is, finally, the provision in the Consumer Sales Act (konsumentköplagen) of 1974 that a seller is responsible for all information that has been given about products sold. This rule applies analogously to earlier links in the chain from producer to consumer. In addition, the act specifies certain rights of consumers that cannot be abrogated by contract, such as the right to restitution of part of the purchase price in case the product has a fault that the seller does not correct within a reasonable period of time.

Allmänna Reklamationsnämnden (ARN, The Central Consumer Complaints Board)

ARN was established in 1968 by the then Consumer Council as a pilot project. Transferred to KOV, it is still considered a pilot study and is managed separately, with its own budget. Only complaints by private persons are handled. Of the total number of complaints, some 80-90 percent are actually settled by the staff, either by counseling, referral or by mediation between the consumer and the seller.

Originally functioning with five divisions, the board now has ten: travel, motor vehicles, textiles and clothing, electrical goods, pleasure boats, shoes, laundry and drycleaning, furs, general, and insurance, the last one added in 1975. The full-time chairman is a lawyer with judging experience. He has six part-time vice-chairmen and a board of sixty-six members, composed of representatives from trade and industry, labor unions, the cooperatives, a housewives organization, and KOV. From six to eight members constitute a division. In principle, business and consumer groups are equally represented. ARN is a vestige of pluralism in current Swedish consumer policy.

In 1973-74 the staff consisted of twenty-three persons, compared with seven in 1968. It has since increased to twenty-seven in 1975, most of these professionally trained. The staff is organized in a manner corresponding to the divisions of the board. As shown in Table 7-1, ARN's budget for 1973-74 was 1.8 million crowns.

Most of the complaints are disposed of quickly. In 1972-73 ARN received 11,900 telephone calls; in 1973-74, 14,900; and in 1974-75, 17,000. The increase in complaints is not viewed as an indication of growing consumer dissatisfaction so much as an index of growing awareness of the board and of the fact that it really *can* help. Calls are taken for two hours in the morning and two in the afternoon, five days a week, a total of fifty-man hours a day in 1973-74.[57] In 1974 ARN had 375 visits from consumers with complaints; the modest number is doubtless influenced by the fact that KOV is inconveniently located.

A formal complaint must be in written form. Table 7-3 gives their number by product/service area for 1972-74. An especially troublesome area has been used automobiles. Out of the 1,083 motor vehicle complaints in 1974, 958 had to do with used automobiles. Fifty percent of the complaints come from the metropolitan areas of Stockholm, Gothenburg and Malmö (accounting for somewhat less than 25 percent of the population). Stockholm alone accounted for 33 percent, though its population is only 13 percent of that of Sweden. (Some concentration of complaints to metropolitan areas is to be expected.)

About one-half of the written complaints are settled by the staff. However, a consumer, no matter how hopeless his claim may appear, has a right to a hearing by the board. About 50 percent of recent settlements involve some form of adjustment for the consumer. This figure continues to follow the pattern not only of past Swedish experience, but also that of other European countries with formal complaint-handling machinery. The board has no enforcement powers. Its decisions are in the form of recommendations.[58] KOV has agreements with some trade associations that their members will abide by the decisions of the board. Among these, the shoe and travel agree-

Table 7-3. Allmänna Reklamationsnämnden. Written Complaints by Product/Service Group, 1972-74

Product/service group	1972	1973	1974
Travel	408	509	706
Motor vehicles	700	858	1,083
Textiles, clothing	566	616	806
Electrical goods	435	479	721
Pleasure boats	51	57	80
Shoes	a	311	732
Laundry and drycleaning	a	388	651
Furs	a	82	332
General[b]	404	458	734
Others[c]		46	128
Total	2,564	3,804	5,973

[a]Prior to 1973 complaints in these areas were handled by the trade associations.
[b]Including such groups as furniture, photographs, handbags, wigs and hair treatment, watches, eyeglasses, toys, baby carriages, moving, books and newspapers.
[c]Real estate and insurance. Real estate questions are not usually handled by ARN. Insurance matters became a separate group in 1975.
Source: *Allmänna reklamationsnämnden: Diarieförda anmälningar—efter vissa varu- och tjänstegrupper, antal,* mimeographed, 6 pgs. (Stockholm: Konsumentverket, 1975-01-17).

ments cover 100 percent of the market; coverage in the motor industry is about 85 percent.

The amount of time required for board decisions varied considerably with the subject matter. For example, in a three-hour period, twelve to fifteen motor vehicle complaints, eighteen travel complaints, but forty shoe complaints, can be handled within the respective divisions. According to the spokesman for ARN, representatives from trade and industry support their trade associations in the board. The board handles matters on a case-by-case basis, and refers to prior decisions, of which meticulous detailed records are kept. It takes an average of four to five months for a complaint to go from registration through the board's decision.

Of the complaints decided in favor of the consumer, 85 percent are followed by trade and industry. The names of those not following the decisions are made public, printed faithfully in *Råd och Rön* and, generally, in several newspapers. The noncomplying traders are placed on a publicly available "blacklist," which is prepared every six months, but mercifully purged every two years.[59] An intriguing development, with the establishment of the Small Claims Courts in 1974, has been the possibility of bringing a claim, regardless of size, provided it has first been heard by ARN. The ARN spokesman was under the impression that it was merely a matter of form, as the courts usually followed the board's decision. The Small Claims Court is open to *all* in cases where the amount of the dispute does not exceed $1,000.[60] ARN has received a good deal of publicity. *Råd och Rön* carried twenty-one articles on its work in the 1971-74 period and the press is fairly interested.

Konsumentombudsmannen (KO)

The Office of the Consumer Ombudsman is headed by a lawyer, appointed by the government originally for three years, currently for six.[62] An aggressive and sublimely self-confident (and incidentally a very peripatetic) man, the personal selection of the prime minister, the present KO is another example of the left outlook in high government circles. He is concerned exclusively with administering two laws: the Marketing Practices Act (Marknadsföringslagen) and the Act Prohibiting Improper Contract Terms (Avtalsvillkorslagen).

Housed in a magnificent building overlooking Stockholm's famed Kungsträdgården, a park in the city center, the KO works with a staff of thirty-three (twenty-seven full time), about half of whom are professionals. The KO's budget was 2,331,000 crowns ($530,000) in 1974-75. By far the largest number of matters brought to his attention are complaints emanating from outside his office. Any member of the public is free to contact the KO. Questions concerning improper contract terms account for 10-15 percent of the total. Table 7-4 gives the number of complaints and their disposal.

Table 7-4. Konsumentombudsmannen. Activities of the Office, 1971-75

	1971	*1972*	*1973*	*1974*	*1975*	*Total*
Complaints from outside the office	2,473	3,688	4,282	4,505	4,242	19,190
On KO's initiative	476	798	541	445	280	2,540
Total	2,949	4,486	4,823	4,950	4,522	21,730
Of this total, number concerning improper contract terms	87	473	612	783	370	2,325
Number of matters concluded	1,860	3,512	4,149	4,649	4,379	18,549
Number of accepted cease and disist orders	23	78	77	35	57	270
Number of matters referred to Market Court	18	34	45	41	22	160
Number of cases referred to the prosecutor	5	4	5	3	—	17

Source: Data obtained from Press Officer Brita Bodén, Konsumentombudsmannen, April 17, 1975, and from *KO* (January 1976):2.

The KO is *not* concerned with individual complaint handling on behalf of consumers. These are routinely referred either to ARN, to KOV or to a home economist consultant. (It is claimed that the KO receives a total of some 20,000 inquiries a year.) His actions are solely concerned with policing marketing practices and improper clauses in contracts and with taking those measures deemed by him to be necessary to eliminate malpractice or to introduce what he considers good practice. Markets subject to complaint run the gamut of consumer products and services, with foods leading the list with approximately 15 percent; and health products and services and charter travel next, with 10 percent each. Cosmetics, books and newspapers, major household appliances, textiles and clothing, toys, sports equipment, and housing account for 5 percent each; and automobiles and hair pieces, 2 percent each.

When a complaint is registered against a seller, his advertisement or a questionable practice, the first action taken is to contact the seller either by telephone or letter. As a rule this leads directly to negotiation, and in a majority of cases these negotiations end with some form of settlement: either the practice is revised or it is discontinued. In all negotiations the burden of proof is reversed: it rests with the seller to show that his data, claims and actions are not misleading or otherwise improper within the meaning of the act. According to a spokesman, 5 percent of complaints are dismissed as having little or no public interest; 15 percent are considered outside of the KO's jurisdiction, and 20–30 percent are dismissed without statement after preliminary investigation. Then, 95 percent of those remaining are concluded by negotiation. There can hardly be any doubt that many firms accept the KO's proposals simply to avoid unfavorable publicity, regardless of the merits of the issue at hand.[62]

In cases where negotiation fails—a mere 5 percent—the KO has the authority to issue cease and desist orders (*förbudsförelägganden*). By issuing a written order to the seller, under penalty of a fine, he can prohibit the seller from continuing to use a particular marketing procedure or a particular standard contract. A fine is usually set between 1,000 and 50,000 crowns depending on the size of the company and the type of offense. The seller is directed to append his written acceptance of the prohibition and to return it to the KO within a specified time limit. Once approved, a cease and desist order has the same effect as an injunction issued by the Market Court (see below). If the order is not accepted, the KO may either drop the matter, which he does in about 5 percent of these cases, or refer the matter to the Market Court. Of those orders that reach the court about 90 percent are upheld.[63]

The KO's most noteworthy activity lies, however, in his trade practices agreements (överenskommelser) with private organizations on what may be called codes of marketing ethics or guidelines governing marketing practices in specific areas. This type of settlement has been reached with the Swedish organization of mail-order firms concerning the methods of marketing products by mail-order catalogues and with the Swedish Travel Bureau Association as to the advertising of charter travel.[64] The Improper Contract Terms Act has provided a basis for negotiations between KO and the State Telecommunications Administration, the Swedish Travel Bureau Association and the Association of Travel Agents, the Swedish Association of Autodealers and Service Shops, the Association of Swedish Laundries, and others. To complement the system, KO has an agreement with distributors of direct mail advertising whereby they submit one copy of all the direct mail advertising material to the KO for his scrutiny. We may note incidentally that while the KO officially disclaims making use of declaratory judgments, it is a fact that he will give advice rather freely to firms consulting his office informally about a proposed advertising or promotion measure.

One of the KO's major strengths lies in his phenomenal ability to catch the public imagination. He is in the news, oftentimes by his activities in bizarre areas such as the use of scantily clad models in advertising or deceptive sales promotion for pornography. No doubt exists that the KO's activities have had considerable success in cleaning up in the field of health care products, mail-order selling and deceptive packaging.

KO publishes a journal called *Konsumentombudsmannen*, aimed primarily at marketing men and lawyers. The journal reports individual cases and trade association agreements, statistics of KO's activities, and usually has an article by the KO himself or his deputy. Circulation is 2,000. Beyond the journal, KO's information activities include a report of his office (3,000 copies of 150 pages), a flyer on his office in many languages, advertisements in telephone directories and materials for exhibitions.[65] *Råd och Rön* has carried occasional articles or notices on KO's work, though none appeared during the period April 1974 to April 1975.

There is a goodly amount of friction between KO and KOV, which has heightened as each agency tries to take the lead in the current crusade to achieve more informative content in advertising and sales promotion. The KO feels that his office should administer any mandatory information law, as it is "just the other side" of regulating misleading advertising. In fact, as of September 1974 he had been successful in negotiating no less than forty-two agreements that included as an integral part the obligation of the seller to include specific information in the marketing of his products.

The Market Court and Freedom of Commerce Ombudsman (NO)

The Market Court (*marknadsdomstolen*, formerly the Freedom of Commerce Board) consists of a permanent chairman, a vice-chairman, one specialist in matters relating to marketing practices and contracts, one specialist in restrictive business practices, three representatives from trade and industry, and three representatives of consumers. The consumer representatives invariably are named by the two big labor organizations (LO for workers, TCO for salaried employees) and the cooperatives (KF).

A court of first and last instance, the Market Court is used in cases arising under the Marketing Practices Act, the Act Prohibiting Improper Contract Terms and the Restrictive Business Practices Act. The first two acts are administered by KO. The Restrictive Business Practices Act of 1953 (with major amendments in 1956) is Sweden's principal antitrust statute. It is administered by the Näringsfrihetsombudsman (NO).

With a 1973–74 budget of 740,000 crowns, the secretariat of the Market Court consists of the chairman and a staff of four lawyers. Between January–June 1973 the court settled twenty-five cases: sixteen under the marketing practices act, four under the improper contract act and five under the restrictive business practices act.

The instances of improper restrictions on the freedom of commerce observed by the NO or brought to his attention as a rule are settled by negotiations between his office and business representatives. Those unresolved are referred to the Market Court. His secretariat, consisting of a staff of about twenty, is financed by a grant of around 1.7 million crowns. He dealt with about 430 matters during 1974, of which only eight had to be referred to the Market Court.[66]

Statens Pris- och Kartellnämnd (SPK)

The State Price and Cartel Office was formed in 1957 to take over some of the remaining, largely investigative, duties of the then dissolved Price Control Board (*priskontrollnämnden*) and the duties of the Monopoly and Cartel Investigation Bureau (*monopolutredningsbyrån*). In 1970 SPK was vested with administrative functions under the Price Control Act when a general price freeze was imposed for a year. In 1973 changes in the act authorized extended use of price controls as a means of stabilizing the economy and broadened SPK's investigative and monitoring activities. In this connection a reorganization took place to provide for more effective supervision of prices.[67]

SPK is principally an instrument in the implementation of national *economic* policy, with special reference to prices and competition. It is not primarily a consumer policy agency. It reports to the Minister of Commerce, but is also in liaison with state industries. In its broad powers of inquiry and control SPK has assembled massive amounts of data from private enterprise. We got the impression that the big and freely expanding government companies might indirectly at least find the data useful in their further penetration into economic life.

The board is composed of nine members: a chairman, a vice-chairman, the general director of SPK, and three members representing private enterprise and three representing the unions and coops. The SPK staff of 225 is organized into a large division for monitoring (or controlling) prices and trade practices and conducting research, a statistical department, an administrative department, an information section and a planning secretariat.[68] SPK's budget for 1974–75 was 15.3 million crowns. The share of the budget allocated to information activities has been declining in recent years. Proposals being considered in 1975 would centralize most of the informational activities directed to the consuming public to KOV.[69]

SPK's price-monitoring scheme is monumental. It includes price freezes, maximum prices, and obligations to give advance notice of price changes, in addition to the vast authority to call in *all* lists of recommended retail prices, and otherwise to investigate continually the movement of *all* prices and margins relating to *all* categories of goods and services.[70]

Every year SPK undertakes some forty major investigations, often of a whole branch of industry. Some are requested by NO, but more often SPK initiates them, inspired by materials collected through price monitoring or through the registration of agreements in restraint of trade or mergers. SPK maintains both a cartel register and a big business register, enabling it to follow trends toward economic concentration. Examples of studies of interest to consumers in 1974 were: pleasure boats and boat motors; automobile repair costs; prices and margins in ready made clothes and shoes, paints and wallpaper, hardware, and furniture; prices for funerals, hairdressers, photographic equipment, radio and TV.

SPK has no publication directed toward consumers. Its popularly written *Prisaktuellt* was discontinued in 1971 with the advent of price supervision and control.[71] SPK does publish a journal, *Pris- och kartellfrågor*, in collaboration with NO and the Market Court, accounting for SPK investigations and reports, NO's activities, and the decisions of the Market Court. There is also a monthly report showing how prices and margins are moving at all stages of distribution from producer to consumer. Press releases are available in a cumulative bulletin. SPK distributes free to firms, press and trade associations its *Prisregler* (Price Rules), containing government rules and regulations under the Price Control Act. A series in looseleaf format called *Marknad och fusioner* (Markets and Mergers) is issued quarterly, giving entries in SPK's cartel register and big business register. Some research reports are available in mimeographed format. Teaching aids and participation in exhibitions play a modest part in SPK's information service.

In 1974–75 some 50,000 crowns were spent on advertising. About 300,000 crowns is said to have been spent on SPK's big campaign to further voluntary unit pricing and to encourage comparison shopping among consumers. This included advertising, exhibitions, posters, and the publication *Priset ska fram, en rapport om klart pris* ("The Price Must Come Forth—A Report on Unit Prices"), printed in 100,000 copies in 1973 and available at a cost of 1 crown. This well-written piece was clearly consumer-oriented.

The traditional pluralism of Sweden, with all partners represented on commissions and boards and in the legislative process, is vanishing fast. It may be replaced by a government pluralism, the pluralism of public bodies and agency heads. Successors to the interplay of interest groups and popular movements, organizations such as KOV, KO, SPK and the State Food Administration are jealously guarding their prerogatives and jockeying for position in the scramble for more power and larger allocations of resources. The strong trend toward state capitalism in economic life seems likely to accelerate such a development. The private business sector is already subject to government manipulation—next in line is the consumer. Indeed, manipulation of producers inevitably entails manipulation of the consumers of the offerings of such producers.

POSTSCRIPT 1976: CONSUMER POLICY CENTRALIZATION; END OF VOLUNTARY CI[72]

The two most significant developments in Swedish consumer policy in 1976 are indicated by the heading. On July 1 KOV and the office of the KO were merged under the name of KOV, with the KO as head of the new agency. ARN remains inside KOV. The new KOV has been given a budget marginally greater than the aggregate of the budgets of its predecessors.[73] The fusion completes centralization of consumer policymaking in Sweden. The Food Administration and other specialist organs will now clearly be in the back seat in this area. The KO emphasizes his keen interest in regional and local consumer agency contacts, but our firm prediction is that these contacts will be confined largely to the execution rather than the formation of policy.

January 1, 1976, also marked the end of voluntary CI programs in Sweden, as the use VDN labels is not permitted on products made after that date. Nor does *Råd och Rön* any longer publish the results of comparative testing in the sense of most CT agencies, except on a purely ad hoc basis. On the other hand, there are as yet few serious cross-product tests of the type long advocated by consumer radicals.

Mandatory and negotiated CI will replace voluntary measures. This is provided for in a new Marketing Act,[74] superseding the Marketing Practices Act of 1970. Negotiated CI (experimented with in the past) will be the result of agreements between KO and individual firms or trade associations. Should a firm resist negotiated CI, the law authorizes the KO to mandate information of the type (labels, advertisements, salesman communication, etc.) he deems suitable in "less important" cases. In important cases—and when a party refuses to accept his own mandates—the KO (or organizations of consumers or other third parties) may request that the Market Court mandate the information. There is no appeal from the decision of the court.[75]

One of the authors had the privilege of participating in a day-long group interview with the KO in May 1976. The KO interpreted the law as encompassing, in principle, such far-reaching measures as mandatory comparative data about other brands or even information about deficiencies in a firm's own brand, if the KO deems this desirable. He did stress that in his view the emphasis on protection rather than information would remain the cornerstone in Swedish consumer policy. He does not believe that CI and education will ever place consumers in the position of equal partners (much less governors) of the marketplace.

The provisions of the new Marketing Act concerning improper trade practices are similar to prior law. Of great principal significance are the new rules about what the Swedes call "product control." The Market Court (KO in simpler cases) may prohibit the sale of a product endangering persons or property. But the law goes further than product safety: the same kind of cease and desist order may be issued "if the product is obviously unfit for its main purpose." In our mind, this provision opens the way for government censorship in the marketplace. According to the KO, however, he will only be after grossly unsuitable products; he has no interest in direct regulation of individual goods.

Whether or not this view will prevail will undoubtedly be determined by the extent to which radicals will continue to influence policy. Certainly they are coming up with new proposals. The Minister of Commerce in 1976 appointed a government investigating committee to study the desirability of giving KOV extensive powers to subpoena data about internal marketing plans and personnel training and marketing research, as well as product planning and development activities in firms. The presumed advantage here would be to enable KOV to affect and regulate the marketing and product policies of business *in advance* of their taking effect.[76]

In the directives to the investigating committee, advance information on the durability of new products or models is given as one specific example of information KOV might wish to require. Durability has become a new rallying point for the radical interest. In the more vulgar propaganda, business is accused of planned obsolescence. At a more sophisticated level, the costs and nuisance of repair and service are emphasized as well as the positive resource conservation effect of more durable products. A lively discussion is taking place about mandatory guarantees concerning minimum durability. We are referring to these developments because we believe the area of product durability is one in which Sweden again may be serving as a pacesetter.

The Cabinet Secretariat for Futurology Studies is also populated by radicals. One of their proposals is that the government decide on a continuous basis what products (and, presumably, brands) may be produced. It should also prescribe minimum acceptable durability for all consumer durables. A firm should not be allowed to make such a product (or brand) unless it can demonstrate that when the product is worn out it can be repaired and that after the repair the product again will function more or less like new! Product development in general should be transferred progressively to government agencies. Should this happen, Sweden would indeed have reached the millenium of socialist consumer radicals: freedom from choice!

This is written just before the Fall 1976 elections. Should the liberal parties take over the government after over forty years of Social Democrat rule there may well be a gradual shift toward education-information, voluntarism, pluralism and decentralization, measures aimed at promoting self-reliant consumers and open markets. But we would not bet either on a change in government or on a fast or marked change in policy should a succession in power take place. After all, history amply demonstrates that once a matter has been placed in the custody of government it is not easy to return it to citizens.

NOTES

1. A well-known consumerist journalist, Brita Åkerman, is quoted as writing: "The cooperative movement is today no longer an instrument for an active consumer policy. This billionaire company has a core of soft, conservative, conventionally commercial thinking patterns." *Sweden Now* (July-August 1970): 40f.

2. *Arbetarrörelsens efterkrigsprogram* (Stockholm, 1944): sections 24 and 26.

3. Edith Anrep, *Från AH och HFI 1940–56 till KI* (Undated monograph): 3.

4. We have been told that a KF board resolution from the 1950s directed the use of VDN labels on all products for which norms existed. However, in practice KF division chiefs did not always follow this rule, and there was little KF enthusiasm for labeling its so-called B assortment of food stuffs until the recent passage of a food-labeling law.

5. *Kvalitetsforskning och konsumentupplysning* (SOU 1949: 18).

6. For an extensive listing of such reports see *Konsumentupplysning—principer och riktlinjer* (SOU 1968: 58): 220. There have been about ten additional reports of importance in the area since 1968.

7. An interesting statement in view of the fact that both coops and unions had representatives on the committee. Presumably, this was a roundabout way of saying that these organizations were not overly interested.

8. This observation was probably off the mark. First, Sweden had not yet reached the degree of affluence and consequent consumer consciousness characteristic of the United States. Nor, on the other hand, were producers of consumer goods perceived by large segments of the public as perpetrating the kind of abuses that were one powerful impetus to the founding of CU. Second, the writers believe that the modest development of consumer coops in the U.S. is due to an overwhelmingly simple cause: there has been but modest need—indeed, room—for such a movement in the American climate of intense competition.

9. *PM angående konsumtionsvaruforskning och konsumentupplysning* (Stockholm: Handelsdepartment, 1955).

10. Number of *Råd och Rön* pages allocated to the work of related agencies:

	1968	1969	1970	1971	1972	1973	1974
VDN	29	4	19	22	15	6	1
SPK	6	7	7	17	10	15	5
Central Consumer Complaints Board (ARN)	25	40	34	8	5	4	4
Total *Råd och Rön* pages	384	416	384	440	316	328	320

It should be noted that twenty pages of the VDN material in 1968 were published in the form of three inserts; these pages are not included in the *Råd och Rön* total page count for the year. In 1968–70 many ARN cases were reported individually, later in summary form. We are grateful to Ms. Maria Skagersjö for 1970–74 data.

11. From a systems point of view another interesting development at the end of the 1960s can be mentioned. Several large supermarkets and department stores established so-called consumer corners, in which shoppers could consult *Råd och Rön* and SPK surveys, as well as numerous other educational guides and brochures published by public and private agencies. Pioneered by the consumer coops (KF), occasionally such corners were staffed by a home economist specializing in consumer information. Still in existence, the corners represent a fairly successful illustration of private consumer policy.

12. According to a report by Björn Tarras Wahlberg cited in *Sverige Nytt* (no. 15, April 15, 1975), trade and industry were subjected to 285 new laws concerning their affairs in 1974, one every thirty hours. While ownership of Swedish industry formally is over 90 percent private, enterprise itself is being rapidly "socialized."

13. Lillemor Erlander, semiofficial consumer voice of the federation of trade unions, in a radio program on consumer power, August 5, 1969.

14. Olle Svenning, editorial writer in the Social Democrat Stockholm evening paper in the radio program referred to in note 13.

15. "Sweden—Local Consumer Committees," *International Consumer* 1970:7): 15–18, 15.

16. Mineographed report on public services (January 29, 1969) by Lillemor Erlander. It was a bit peculiar to see the central secretariat draw policy conclusions on the basis of this "local" material.

17. The official translation is The National Swedish Board for Consumer Policies.

18. Translated from the suggested organization chart of the State Consumer Board, a chart appearing in the Progress Report of the Royal Commission on Consumer Policy, "Synpunkter på den framtida konsumentpolitiken" (Stockholm: Handelsdepartment, H. 1969: 5. Mimeographed.) The final report of the commission, *Konsumentpolitik—riktlinjer och organisation* (SOU 1971:37), stated that "the information activity should primarily be directed at questions of greater significance rather than questions of choice of model or brand." Yet this choice is a critical means of expressing personality, needs and preferences at the individual level. The statement is another example of the new collectivism of the Left Twist.

19. In the words of another observer: "But newer Swedish thinking, although not yet quite in the laws, goes even further [than producer jawboning]. When a direct purging of the product markets is carried out it is clear that some consumers will feel their rights impinged upon. In defense of the actions it is argued that in certain cases the consumers do not know where their best interests lie." Johnny K. Johansson, "The Theory and Practice of Swedish Consumer Policy" (Urbana: Faculty Working Papers, College of Commerce, University of Illinois, 1973; mimeographed): 3. This is an excellent piece of writing, published in somewhat revised form in *The Journal of Consumer Affairs* 10 (Summer 1976):19–32.

20. The authors are grateful to Professor Karl Erik Wärneryd of Stockholm for the idea of this diagram.

21. Konsumentverket, *The National Swedish Board for Consumer Policies.* English flyer. Undated. Where information received in interviews differs from documents dated earlier than April 1975, the data obtained in visits and interviews during that month are used in the text in this section.

22. The deployment of the staff of 169 accounted for in the appropriations request submitted on August 30, 1974 was as follows:

Administration and planning	41
Food and housing	30
Clothing, travel and recreation	27
Technical	15
Information and education	33
Central Consumer Complaints Board	23

Konsumentverket, *Anslagsframställning för budgetåret 1975-76* (Stockholm, 1974) Bilagor: 140, 187.

23. For instance, a report on deodorants stated that of the forty-one firms asked to give total ingredients of their products, thirty-two answered completely. Yet the information was not given in the article. Of the 133 brands purchased by KOV, only eleven were selected for a table giving type, weight, price and label text. *Råd och Rön* No 5 (1974): 18-19 (*Råd och Rön* articles will hereafter be cited in the form 5:1974:18-19). In 9:1974:24-26, the article on nine vitamin preparations quoted the State Food Administration analysis of strength of vitamins compared with the label. The article in 10:1974:25-27 on kitchen fans may have been based on systematic tests, but no brand information was given. Interestingly, the State Environmental Protection Board tested twenty coffeemakers, to be reported in the State Food Administration's journal, *Vår Föda.* Although only one on the consumer market was found to be dangerous, *Råd och Rön* ran an article entitled "Poisonous Coffeemakers" (1:1975:13).

24. In an article on film in 6:1974:24-26, eight mistakes were made. These were corrected in the usual journalistic manner—namely, small box and miniature print—in 7:1974:23. In a reference to a publication by a private publishing firm, KOV asserted, without checking, that three pamphlets available from the government at 10 crowns each were copied by the company and sold for 575 crowns (5:1974:31). Later KOV stated that *Råd och Rön* unfortunately did not have available all the material when the notice was written (7:1974:29).

25. 5:1974:20.

26. 9:1974:24-27.

27. 1:1975:24.

28. Examples are: zippers are so poor these days (3:1975:10); the lousy soft drinks (6:1974:15); wall-to-wall carpet in kitchen is not less hygienic (tests showed it was just as good as tile) (3:1975:31). In an article entitled "Must eyeglasses be so expensive" the author states that the reason is "small lots and monopoly," and then goes on to decide that there are too many importers and wholesalers (7:1974:12-13). In 2:1974 a title claimed "Deep frozen foods—a

product which can disappear," implying that here was yet another unnecessary gimmick. Later, in 4:1974:22, a squib appeared stating that no existing method could keep the original characteristics of a food product as well as deep freeze. As KOV subsidizes stores in outlying areas by enabling them to buy deep freezers, it is clear that negative reporting has consequences even for KOV.

29. 5:1974:18-19.

30. 5:1974:24-25.

31. KOV, *Barngrinder* (Stockholm, 1974):7.

32. It may be that they refuse to exercise their abilities for reasons of prejudice. In a typical downgrading of marketing per se, one article on kitchens (9:1974:12-13) complained that the technical people know all about kitchens, but that they are not the ones who sell the product; those are the advertising people, "sadly enough." In KOV the technical people know about the investigations, but the journalists write up the reports—sadly enough. It is not easy for self-styled consumer advocates to see that they may follow the same patterns they criticize in others.

The whole question of brand differentiation is cavalierly claimed to be revealed in a one page article called "Brand mystique," with no attempt made to present any data from the vast amount of research on this extremely complicated subject. It appears to be assumed that the sole reason for differentiation is to fool the consumer, to increase costs to him, to eliminate competition in the marketplace or perhaps simply to confound the investigators at KOV (9:1974:11). The title "The larger the store, the larger the markup" is not a consumer-oriented article at all (9:1974:27). Actually the article should say the larger the store the cheaper the price to the consumer, as it explains how the larger stores, by larger orders and lower overhead, can make more money in the highly competitive radio-TV trade. In 2:1975:3, *Råd och Rön* makes statements not backed up by the investigation: "the more expensive a vacuum cleaner is the more often it breaks down," "the more expensive a vacuum cleaner, the more expensive are the costs of repairs," and a title posing the question "Expensive vacuum cleaner less durable?" Actually, of 900 interviews, one-third of the currently owned vacuum cleaners had been repaired; and of those repaired, "the more expensive had been repaired more often." No data were collected (or at least reported) on the age of the vacuum cleaners, on whether they were repaired under warranty, on satisfaction with the performance of the cleaner, or on whether cheap cleaners were thrown away or traded in when in need of repair, etc. One got the impression that cheap cleaners lasted longer.

33. 7:1974:4-6.

34. 7:1974:28-29.

35. 2:1975:31.

36. 5:1974:24-25 and 3:1975:8-9.

37. 6:1974:15-17.

38. 7:1974:8-9.

39. 7:1974:16-17.

40. 7:1974:32.

41. 8:1974:16-17.

42. 1:1975:12, and 5:1974:18–19.

43. We believe that the word *naive* best expresses the view of the consumer held by KOV and associated consumer radicals. Johansson uses "the paradigm of the ignorant consumer" in this context alternately with "naive." However, this expression suggests that the remedial policy is information, while the KOV philosophy of course is protection and direction. As Johannson cogently puts it, in an increasing number of cases the idea is to have "the consumer protected from himself/herself as it were" (*Journal of Consumer Affairs*: 28).

43. 5:1974:18–19.

44. 10:1974:3

45. KOV, *Märkesdifferentiering—ett konsumentproblem* (Stockholm, 1974): 9–12.

46. 9:1974:11.

47. 7:1974:18–19.

48. See *Handbook*, p. 176, and discussion there.

49. 9:1974:10.

50. Konsumentverket, *Nordisk klassning av textila golvbeläggningar. Förslag* (1974-09-25). See also "Sveriges Grossistförbund med yttrande över förslag till nordisk klassning av textila golvbeläggningar" (Dnr 1247/73–59; Remiss 1974-09-25; dated Stockholm 1974-12-13; mimeographed).

51. Ursula Wallberg and Marianne Wangemann, "PM angående märkning" (1975-02-20; mimeographed). This is an internal working document of KOV. A thorough and scholarly treatment of informative labeling is Hans Näslund, "Tre studier av konsumtionsprocessens måluppfyllnadsgrad och varudeklarationssystemet" (Lund: Institute for Business Administration, Lund University, 1973; mimeographed). Dr. Näslund comes out as a strong advocate of type-of-use-oriented labeling. All three authors are employees of KOV.

52. The Furniture Institute, established in 1973, is financed partly by the industry and partly by the government. "Furniture Facts" is a new system of labeling minimum standards in the areas of use, safety, durability and performance. No attempt is made to give outside measurements, materials content, upholstery or care instructions. "Furniture Facts" does use a three scale grading system: minimum standard, high standard and extra high standard. Fakta från Konsumentverket, *Att köpa möbler med Möbelfakta* 3 (April 1974). The basis for labeling rests on the functional research and standard testing methods adopted by the Furniture Institute in cooperation with KOV.

53. Claes-Robert Julander, *Utvärdering av Möbelfakta*. An English paper on the study by the same author, "Evaluation of Consumer Information," was presented to the Second Workshop on Consumer Action Research, Wissenschaftszentrum Berlin, in April 1975, and is published in the proceedings from the workshop. *Proceedings of the Second Workshop on Consumer Action Research, April 9–12, 1975* (Berlin: Wissenschaftszentrum, 1975).

54. See *Varudeklaration—ett medel i konsumentpolitiken* (Stockholm, SOU: 1973:20)

55. See *Reklam V: Information i reklamen* (Stockholm, SOU: 1974:23). English summary.

56. *Reklam V*, p. 9 (Section 1 of draft law).

57. Sweden has an ingenious system of telephone queuing so that a person can leave a message with the operator to call a number when it is vacant.

58. The Swedish word "yttrande" has recently been changed to "beslut." An *yttrande* is a pronouncement or recommendation, a *beslut* is a decision.

59. One instance at least appeared unfair. A consumer with a complaint against a coat manufacturer wanted money to repair the coat herself. The manufacturer wanted to refund the purchase price, insisting on the return of the coat, claiming that it was bad business to have faulty merchandise in the hands of a consumer. The board decided in favor of the consumer. The manufacturer refused to pay, and was placed on the blacklist.

60. The local courts of first instance (*tingsrätten*) are empowered to hear the cases in greatly simplified procedures. The filing fee is 25 crowns. An extra amount, 30 crowns, may be assessed where travel and collection expenses are required. If a lawyer is used, his fee is limited to a maximum of 60 crowns ($13). In some cases fees to witnesses may be necessary. The losing party is responsible for all costs. The Legal Aid Act (Rättshjälpslagen) may cover a part of the costs depending on a consumer's income. Appeal to the Circuit Court and finally to the Supreme Court is possible from the Small Claims Court.

61. Sven Heurgren, the present—and first—KO, gives detailed information on the activities of his office in "Konsumentombudsmannens verksamhet," *Svensk Jurist Tidning* 1974:561-77. The Ministry of Commerce issued an English paper entitled "Institutional means for implementing consumer policy in Sweden," dated 1973-10-04 (mimeographed).

The institution of "ombudsman" has a history dating at least as far back as the constitution of 1809. As constitutional officers, the two original ombudsmen, one to handle complaints against the military and one to handle complaints against the bureaucracy, maintain a position independent of both government and parliament. A point frequently missed by non-Scandinavian observers is that ombudsmen safeguard the interests of the citizenry at large; they are not a glorified "legal aid" to individual citizens. They sue on behalf of their office to rid society of a reprehensible activity, procedure or practice. Simply by using the name, ombudsman, the KO (and earlier, NO) office achieved instant status.

62. See, e.g., Federation of Swedish Industries, *KO 72-En undersökning av KOs verksamhet under 1972* (Stockholm, 1974). For a rather critical review of KO activities under the improper contract terms act see James E. Sheldon, "Consumer Protection and Standard Contracts: The Swedish Experiment in Administrative Control," *American Journal of Comparative Law* 22 (Winter 1974): 17-70.

63. These referrals are costly in terms of KO's budget. It is estimated that roughly 200,000 crowns are spent on Market Court cases—almost 9 percent of the total budget.

64. Agreements in specific matters apply to such diverse areas as weekend sales advertisements, price marking of sale goods, renewal of subscriptions, exchange goods, advertising of gasoline prices, hairdressing advertising, restaurant advertising on prices, placing of candy and chewing gum at checkout counters, and marketing of school photographs.

65. Konsumentombudsmannen, *Angående anslag för budgetåret 1975/76* (Dnr A 62/74, dated 1974-08-29, Bilagna 3a).

66. "Näringsfrihetsombudsmannens verksamhet 1974," *Pris- och kartellfrågor* 2(1975):72-73.

67. *Svensk författningssamling* 1973:609, June 5, 1973.

68. SPK, *Styrelse- och personalförteckning*, 1974-06-19.

68. Handelsdepartement, *Bakgrundsmaterial—Konsumentpolitik* (1974-04-26; mimeographed):46.

70. On January 1, 1975, price freezes were set for a number of goods, including meats, dairy products, diapers, refrigerators and freezers, dishwashers, washing machines and dryers, electric stoves and ovens, hooded stove fans, a number of building materials, and paper products. Maximum prices applied to gasoline, motor oil and heating oil. Obligation to give notice of price changes affected about 3,500 firms and trade associations and included such products as flour, bread, paints and wallpaper. "Om prisstopp och andra prisregleringar," *Pris- och kartellfrågor* 2 (1975): 39. On the strength of legislation SPK can order businessmen to furnish data "necessary to promote public knowledge of pricing and trade practices." Statens pris- och kartellnämnd, *Fakta om SPK* (Stockholm, SPK, 1974).

71. See *Handbook*, p. 379.

72. We have deliberately not rewritten prior parts of the chapter, drafted in Spring 1975.

73. *Regeringens proposition med förslag till organisation av och anslag för det nya konsumentverket* (1975/76:159).

74. *Marknadsföringslag 15 dec. 1975* (SFS 1975:1418).

75. At the same time the Consumer Sales Act has been amended so that goods sold are considered "faulty" in the sense of the act if the seller has neglected to give information mandated by the Market Court.

76. Interestingly, the KO in private conversation emphsized that in no sense had he inspired this investigation. He seemed to share our evaluation that the Ministry of Commerce was somewhat disappointed with the first three years of KOV activity, and that the ministry may have felt that results might have been more outstanding had KOV had greater powers to demand inside information from business.

Two random observations from the KO interview will be added here. The KO attaches considerable importance to the code of the International Chamber of Commerce concerning advertising practices. He also volunteered the proposition that the institution of consumer ombudsman seems appropriate primarily in a small, homogeneous country where it is comparatively easy to keep track of everyone. This is very much in line with our ecologic model.

Chapter 8

Cross-Cultural Ecology of CI Systems

PANORAMA OF CI PROGRAMS IN THE NORTH ATLANTIC COMMUNITY

From the dynamic analysis of the CI system in a single country setting we turn our attention to the cross-cultural comparison of CI programs and systems in the North Atlantic community.[1] The first section provides an overview of all such programs in fourteen community nations plus Yugoslavia. Against this background, CI programs, the role of their leadership and the nature of their clientele are analyzed in an ecologic perspective. The other sections of the chapter are devoted to the international experience of joint tests and the related question of transferability of CI technology from one nation to another.

A grand summary view of CI systems in the North Atlantic community is presented in Table 8-1.[2] The data reflect the situation in 1969, and are based on extensive field research in 1970. The reader may well ask why the table is not based on more recent data. A bit paradoxically, the answer is that consumer information about many CI organizations could be a lot better; at times one would also wish that the data given out for public relations purposes were less misleading. Ample experience has demonstrated to us that on-the-spot interviewing and examination of files is indispensable to veracity and comparability of data. Even so, the data for many organizations (and, therefore, countries) are highly approximate, although there is little doubt that the table in the main gives a fair picture of the total situation in 1969.

Table 8-1. CI Programs in North Atlantic Community of Nations in 1969 (budget figures based on 1969 dollars and exchange rates)

country[2]	Sponsorship and number of brands tested, labeled or certified[1]					Country totals (in thousands)	
	consumers[3]	business[4]	government	pluralist[5] private	pluralist[5] government	CT subscribers[6]	budgets (dollars)
Austria	CT 845				CT 402, QC 240	22	300
Belgium[7]	CT 129+					190	500
Canada[10]	CT 78					23	25
Denmark			CT 95	IL 180	IL 54	40(53)	686
Finland	CT 163		CT 20		CT 30	4(13)	115
France[8]				QC 747	QC 250	10	480
Germany	CT 701		CT 940, IL 13		QC+IL	67(190)	2,107
Netherlands	QC 715	CT 800			na	260	1,065
Norway[9]		QC 70	CT 189			156	878
Spain						20	20
Sweden				QC 697	IL 868	105	1,334
Switzerland[2]	CT 180		CT 120			20	217
United Kingdom	CT 1,274		IL 77			562	4,008
United States[10]	CT 1,420+		CT 200		QC 251	1,560+	9,520+
Yugoslavia						2(40)	53
GRAND TOTALS[11]						3,021	21,308

CT = Comparative testing   IL = Informative labeling   QC = Quality certification

1. Numbers for CT are total brands in tests reported in 1969 only; often older tests would still be valid. Some products and brands may overlap between organizations in a country as well as internationally; a test reported by A and reprinted by B will be counted twice.
IL and QC data given represent the cumulative number of licenses in force in 1969, unless otherwise indicated. The number of brands would generally be considerably larger, although in most cases no exact data are available.
Brand and license data refer to products only; several of the European CI organizations engage in the testing, labeling or certification of services as well.

2. Only nationwide organizations are included. Regional organizations in Switzerland reported—or reprinted—tests comprising perhaps sixty brands on a total budget likely not in excess of $25,000.

3. The term 'consumers' is used rather than 'members' in that outside the Anglo-Saxon countries and the Netherlands the subscribers to comparative test reports generally do not elect the governing body of the organization publishing the reports.

4. Programs limited to a single trade or group of products (such as appliances) are not included. Many such programs are sponsored by trade associations.

5. Pluralist sponsorship may be private, involving, e.g., consumer organization plus business sponsors. It is listed as governmental in every case where government influence in terms of representation or financing was appreciable and yet not so dominant that the program could be regarded simply as a government organ.

6. When newsstand sales were great relative to number of subscribers, total circulation is stated within parentheses.

7. Occasionally a CI program is a mere sideline activity of a group whose prime interest is elsewhere, such as the Belgian family organization (QC). In such cases a rough estimate has been made of the funds going to the CI part of the organization. The Belgian CT totals include two consumer-sponsored organizations.

8. Data about the French CT organization OR.GE.CO. are excluded, as data given by its president are in stark conflict with what all other French public and private bodies in the consumer field as well as our research team could observe about OR.GE.CO. activities.

9. The figure for Varefakta, the Norwegian IL body, refers to brands for which labels were in force, rather than to licenses.

10. The U.S. subscriber figure includes 20,000 Canadian subscribers to *Consumer Reports* not separately accounted for under Canada. U.S. data do not include Consumers' Research, a CT organization from which we have been unable to acquire this type of information. The circulation of that organization in 1975 was some 96,000 copies.

11. The grand total for CT subscribers does not include newsstand sales, which may add 5–10 percent to circulation in 1969.

In view of the above it would have been too resource-demanding an exercise to attempt a systematic update of our 1969 information. For more recent data from selected organizations and countries the reader is referred to Appendix E (and, for Sweden, to Chapter Seven).

A first striking observation in Table 8-1 is that comparative testing (CT) programs exist in all fifteen countries but Spain. Informative labeling (IL) is running a poor second, confined essentially to half a dozen countries in the northwest corner of Europe. After 1969 the U.K. abandoned its Teltag labeling program, while France embarked on one. The Swedish IL program in 1976 was fading fast from view. Quality certification (QC) also existed in half a dozen nations, spread along the East Atlantic border from Germany and the Netherlands to Spain, with the focus of interest in France.[3]

Again, looking at overall data we find that the total number of subscribers to comparative testing reports in the fifteen countries was a little over three million (in 1975, over 4.5 million). It is an established fact that each copy of these reports is read by a greater number of persons than are popular magazines, the readership being perhaps two to six times the number of subscribers.[4] A hip-shot estimate places the total population of the fifteen countries at 500 million, which would mean a readership of about 2–4 percent (3–5 percent in 1975). It may be more meaningful to relate subscribers to the number of households. Again, a free estimate would be 150 million, implying a subscriber rate of 2 percent as an overall average (1975: 3 percent). However, the rate differs strongly between nations. Norway is setting the pace with a subscriber rate of 20 percent of all households (1976), while in France the rate in 1969 was well below one in every thousand households, though it has since risen dramatically.

Budgetwise, our estimate is that a little over $20 million was spent on all CI programs in the fifteen nations. It may be instructive to relate this figure to some others. We may, for instance, state with some confidence that the total amount of product-oriented advertising in these countries was well over $20 billion, in itself a sum 1,000 times larger than the total spent on CI programs. While there is no reason to equate CI and advertising (as indicated in Chapter Four), it is clear beyond doubt that CI programs could have used greater sums to advantage. One might say, for instance, that $100 million would have been a much more reasonable figure. One hundred million dollars certainly does not seem exaggerated when one learns that the promotion budget of the International Woolmark Secretariat in 1969 amounted to some $25 million globally.[5]

Several columns in Table 8-1 are devoted to sponsorship information. It must be emphasized that sponsorship is an elusive concept. Representation on boards may or may not be indicative of actual influence. The same thing is true of financial contributions. In either case, influence is a matter of degree. For instance, the Danish CT organization (Forbrugerrådet) listed as consumer sponsored actually receives major government contributions, but vehemently asserts its independence. Some programs are actually conducted by second or third order organizations. This is the case with one of the Swiss CT and the Dutch QC organization, for example. It is also interesting to note that IL programs uniformly are pluralist or government sponsored. Nevertheless, the table probably does do justice to the amazing diversity in sponsorship among CI programs.

To complete our panorama we shall briefly examine the relative size of CT, IL and QC organizations. Table 8-2 gives baseline data for the largest, median and smallest organization of each type. We see a tremendous difference in size between the median and largest CT organizations on the one hand and corresponding IL and QC organizations on the other. In 1975 this difference seems even more accentuated, even if not all data are on hand. The smallest organizations of each type are of little interest due to their limited practical impact. It might be said that the table is misleading insofar as it mixes CT, IL and QC organizations from different countries. Yet in only one country (France) out of the ten in which a CT organization co-existed with either an IL or a QC organization (or both) was the non-CT program larger in terms of budget and personnel than the CT agency.[6] Reasons for the discrepancy in size are discussed in Chapter Four.

ECOLOGY OF COMPARATIVE TESTING PROGRAMS

With this background overview in mind we may now proceed to the comparative ecologic analysis. In this section we are confining the discussion to CT organizations, which are numerous enough to permit generalizations with some confidence.

Size

Table 8-3 presents the cumulative number of tests reported by the largest CT organization in each of ten countries in the 1967-69 period. Table 8-4 shows the number of brands for which tests were reported in the year 1969. In both tables the organizations are listed according to size of budget (i.e., income) in 1969. Looking

Table 8-2. Budget and Personnel of the Largest, Median and Smallest CT, IL and QC Organizations in the North Atlantic Community in 1969 (budget figures are in terms of thousands of dollars and exchange rates in 1969)

Program Type	Largest		Median		Smallest	
	budget	personnel[a]	budget	personnel	budget	personnel
Comparative testing	9,520	309	954	85	25	2
Informative labeling	308	22	60	6	21	3
Quality certification	240	25	57	5	20	2

[a]Permanent personnel only

Table 8-3. Cumulative Number of Tests Reported by Product Categories in 1967, 1968 and 1969 and Size of Permanent Personnel in 1969 (CT organizations are listed in the order of size of budget in 1969; for each country only the largest CT program is included)

Products (services) tested	CU[a] U.S.	CA England	STIWA Germany	KI Sweden	CB Netherlands	FR Norway	SHR Denmark	AC Belgium	VKI Austria	UFC France
Textiles[b]	12	7	12	1	6	3	—	—	12	—
Foods	16	13	30	6	9	4	4	20	15	4
Major household appliances	20	16	23	15	13	11	21	14	1	5
Minor household appliances	19	21	16	1	9	4	3	10	2	7
Household utensils and supplies	37	37	22	12	19	3	10	12	8	3
TV and audio	27	7	8	1	12	4	—	10	2	3
Hygiene products, medicine, cosmetics	5	13	7	—	6	1	—	3	6	—
Sports, recreational, educational and travel	39	32	26	4	28	11	—	14	6	4
Cars	29	12	8	—	—	9	—	—	—	1
Services	7	29	21	—	11	5	—	5	8	—
Total Products	211	187	173	40	113	55	38	93	60	27
Personnel	309	256	86	85	55	57	59	32	45	6

[a] See List of Abbreviations in Appendix A.
[b] For itemization of product categories see Appendix B.

Table 8-4. Number of Brands for Which Tests Were Reported in the Year 1969 by Product Categories*

Products tested	CU U.S.	CA England	STIWA Germany	KI Sweden	CB Netherlands	FR Norway	SHR Denmark	AC Belgium	VKI Austria	UFC France
Textiles	47	223	21	—	121	7	—	—	125	—
Foods	173	146	210	21	66	—	9	83	77	18
Major household appliances	154	101	101	27	85	37	68	82	14	30
Minor household appliances	110	112	83	—	72	34	—	73	—	46
Household utensils and supplies	397	294	159	39	94	—	18	78	58	24
TV and audio	169	75	57	16	52	—	—	50	—	16
Hygiene products, medicine, cosmetics	18	71	59	—	94	—	—	23	125	—
Sports, recreational, educational and travel	265	226	246	17	117	87	—	73	3	22
Cars	87	26	4	—	—	19	—	—	—	7
Total brands[a]	1,420	1,274	940	120	701	184	95	462	402	163

*Notes from Table 8-3 apply.

[a]Brands here is equal to "separately tested product units." Thus if a small and a large model of General Electric refrigerators were tested, this would count as two "brands." Note that services are not included in Table 8-4, as names of service establishments often were not given in test reports.

at the grand totals of products and brands tested, it is obvious that the greater the income, the greater the number of products and brands covered tends to be[7] (proposition O-P 1).[a] It is equally clear that there are several exceptions to the rule. These variances can generally be explained by particular circumstances. The low totals of the Scandinavian organizations in both tables is likely due both to the multipurpose nature of these groups and to a tendency to over-scientification in testing activities.[8] The Scandinavian agencies also evidenced high concentration on major appliances, which are notoriously cumbersome and expensive to test. The high score of modest-sized VKI should be viewed against its focus on repetitive tests (pantyhose three times, cigarettes four times during the period) and its fairly simple tests of wines and other alcoholic beverages. The VKI achievement is nonetheless a significant one.[9]

Another indicator of organization size is number of permanent employees, also given in Table 8-3. We may note first that there is a high correlation between size of income and number of permanent personnel.[10] It seems reasonable to assume that the larger the personnel the greater the diversity of products tested (O-S 4). Superficially, the proposition seems only vaguely supported. However, it must be borne in mind that the product category data in Table 8-3 represent a gross summary of activity. With a more stringent view, one might say that for a product category to "count" in a measure of diversity at least two tests of products in that category must be reported for each of the years 1967-69. The covariation between personnel and diversity of product tests now becomes more clear-cut.[11] Given this more stringent definition it seems only natural that diversity and total number of tests are even more clearly related.[12]

Subscribers

Perhaps the most interesting variable of all (and not least from a size point of view) is the number of subscribers to CT journals. In our ecologic model subscriber characteristics are listed as an element of the environment. For present purposes, the *number* of subscribers more legitimately may be viewed as an indicator of performance of the organization. The focus of the analysis is to try to "explain" the number of subscribers in terms of organizational, strategy and environmental variables.

---

[a]Here and in the following notations the parenthetical identification of propositions refers to Appendix C. The acronym O-P 1 refers to the first proposition under "Organization and Performance"; O-E 4 designates the fourth proposition under "Individual CI Organization and Environment"; and so on.

Table 8-5 is an ecologic correlation matrix of such variables with subscribers and other performance indicators. Again, the reader is cautioned concerning the interaction of causal arrows and the existence of extensive intercorrelation among the "independent" variables. The classification of variables into ecologic categories—admittedly, in part a question of taste—is based on Chapter Six and the associated Appendix C. The coefficients of correlation are based on eleven observations, including the ten CT programs in Tables 8-3 and 8-4 plus Swiss SIH, and their environments. The limited number of observations precluded extensive use of multiple regression analysis; some exploratory equations based on such analysis appear in Appendix D.

Before examining the subscriber variable in some detail we may make a few observations on the interaction of the four categories of ecologic variables. Organization variables correlate moderately with the strategy variables used in the study. Organization size correlates strongly with performance. This is to be expected, as our performance variables are expressed in terms of output size rather than in quality or productivity of activities. There is substantial correlation with most of the environmental variables included in the matrix.[13] The covariation is especially strong with GNP. Incidentally, although a case might be made for the importance of GNP per capita, it turns out that GNP itself uniformly is the stronger variable.[14]

Strategy variables relate strongly with performance. It may seem strange that their correlation with the environmental variables is weak (except between price and GNP). It must be kept in mind, however, that TV, autos and GNP are variables with a distinct macroenvironmental flair. Strategy tends to be focused on a specific market, a microenvironment. If we permit ourselves to let subscribers change categorization for a moment, reverting to their environmental role as clientele of the organization, we note a moderately strong relationship between the strategy variables included and the number of subscribers. Finally, for reasons analogous to those applicable to strategy, performance variables relate only modestly to the macroenvironmental ones.

Returning to subscribers, there is a high correlation of their number with personnel and an even higher one with income (the largest coefficient on the matrix). Among strategy variables we note the high correlation with subscription price, against the background of which the strong relationship between subscribers and income should constitute no surprise. In effect, it seems that "nothing succeeds like success": a higher price yields an income that permits both

Table 8-5. Ecologic Correlation Matrix

	Org. variables		Strategy variables			Performance variables			Environment variables			
	INCOME	PERSNL	PRICE	DIVPRO	PAGES	SUBSCR	3YTEST	BRANDS	TV	AUTOS	GNPPC	GNP
Income		.902	.803	.607	.610	.989	.809	.786	.636	.787	.740	.965
Personnel			.690	.702	.769	.897	.839	.864	.745	.599	.551	.779
Price				.698	.550	.832	.797	.772	.500	.474	.460	.807
Diversity of products					.610	.632	.870	.871	.512	.077	.145	.481
Total pages						.626	.722	.419	.242	-.131	-.220	.183
Subscribers							.801	.784	.636	.747	.701	.938
Three-year test total								.983	.668	.346	.341	.742
Total brands 1969									.646	.292	.248	.699
TV households, percent										.507	.497	.506
Auto households, percent											.948	.821
GNP per capita												.764

Definition of Variables in Ecologic Correlation Matrix: (variables listed in the order of Table 8-5; data pertain to 1969 except as noted)

INCOME   = income in 1969 dollars and with exchange rates applied
PERSNL   = number of permanent employees
PRICE   = CT journal subscription rate in 1969 dollars
DIVPRO   = number of different product categories (as specified in Tables 8-3 and 8-4) for which at least two comparative tests were reported by a CT organization in each of the three years 1967, 1968 and 1969
PAGES   = total number of pages of a CT journal for the year 1969 (a gross measure; no consideration of content, size of page, size of print)
SUBSCR   = number of subscribers
3YTEST   = total number of products tested in the three years 1967-69
BRANDS   = separately tested product units. If a small and a large model of General Electric refrigerators were tested this would count as two "brands." Note that services are excluded here.
TV   = percent of all households in a country with at least one television set
AUTOS   = percent of all households in a country with at least one automobile
GNPPC   = gross national product per capita in 1969 dollars
GNP   = gross national product in 1969 dollars

a good product (high quality test reports) and aggressive promotion to garner new subscribers. These new subscribers, in turn, yield increased income with which additional personnel may be hired to further improve and promote the product. The strong positive relationship between price and number of subscribers is evidence of our previously stated conviction that within surprisingly wide limits the elasticity (sensitivity) of demand for test journals with reference to price is low (S-P 1).[15] This observation, in turn, has its natural origin in the nature of their prime clientele: the affluent Information Seekers.

The covariation of subscribers with other performance variables is fairly strong. While doubtless there is some cross-action, it would seem that increasing the number of products and brands tested is one good recipe for increasing the rolls of subscribers. That environmental affluence has something to do with the prosperity of CT organizations is suggested by the remarkably strong correlation of subscribers with GNP (E-P 8) and the moderate one with the rate of ownership of TV sets and automobiles. It is sometimes claimed that interest in CI programs is a direct outgrowth of the "white goods revolution," symbolized by the arrival and popularization of home appliances, autos and TV (E-P 13, cf. O-E 3 and E-P 6). Although we do not doubt that this is a factor, it is—as we pointed out in Chapter One—only one determinant among many. Among the supplementary correlations displayed in Table 8–6 we find those of subscribers with the proportion of vacuum cleaner and refrigerator households. They are unimpressive. So were correlations of subscribers (as well as income and personnel) with the density of telephones, toasters, portable transistor radios and sewing machines.[16]

Aggregate population would appear to be a highly important agent of environmental interaction with CI programs in this set of affluent countries.

Education is an environmental factor that may legitimately be assumed to relate strongly with the number of subscribers. We did not obtain comparable data for primary and secondary school training in all eleven countries. Table 8–6 suggests close to zero (or even mildly negative) correlation with the number of college graduates per hundred persons (E-P 10). Similarly, the number of subscribers was found to vary only mildly in tune with the percentage of grownups taking adult education courses. As subscribers themselves have much more than average education, these results suggest to us that CT programs in a number of countries have a considerable unexploited market potential.

We have hypothesized that the mechanization and consequent

Table 8-6. Supplementary Correlations

	Subscribers	*Income*	*Personnel*
Vacuum cleaner households, percent	.382	.392	.402
Refrigerator households, percent	-.073	.017	-.118
Population	.909	.941	n.a.
College graduates per thousand persons	-.056	-.081	-.207
Retail stores per thousand persons	-.150	-.231	-.231
Imports as percent of GNP	-.541	-.625	-.595
Advertising expense per capita	.500	.584	.420
Total advertising expense	.916	.954	.756

"anonymization" of distribution would generate a greater felt need for CI programs (E-P 7). To the extent that a greater density of retail stores indicates a low degree of mechanization of distribution, the table has at least circumstantial evidence in favor of the proposition.

A high level of imports as a percentage of GNP might be expected to cause brand proliferation and lacunas of information. Thus the number of subscribers would vary positively with the share of imports (E-P 11). The evidence about the proposition is negative. (Obviously, the United States, with enormous brand proliferation but a small import quotient, is one of the "exceptions" to the proposition.) The hypothesis that the greater the extent of advertising the greater the number of subscribers (E-P 9) is supported. Indeed, the simple correlation between subscribers and total advertising expense is the strongest in the column. The per capita measure of advertising correlates less strongly.

The analysis of the interrelations of subscribers with environmental factors would be incomplete without any consideration of consumer-policy-oriented variables. We found it difficult indeed to quantify the breadth and depth of consumer protection measures, the extent of consumer education, etc. On the other hand, the authors do purport to have some of the expertise needed to evaluate the strength of antitrust policy and the intensity of consumerist debate in different cultures. Our rankings of eleven countries on these variables in 1970 appear in Table 8-7 with the rankings of subscribers. The Kendall coefficient of concordance is W = .76 (at the

Table 8-7. Rankings of Strength of Antitrust Policy, Intensity of Consumerism Debate and Number of Subscribers in 1970

		Antitrust	Consumerism debate	Subscribers
CU	–United States	1	2	1
CA	–United Kingdom	4	7	2
CB	–Netherlands	7	6	3
AC	–Belgium	10	11	4
FR	–Norway	5	4	5
KI	–Sweden	3	1	6
STIWA	–Germany	2	5	7
SHR	–Denmark	6	3	8
VKI	–Austria	9	9	9
SIH	–Switzerland	11	8	10
UFC	–France	8	10	11

.01 significance level), which is substantial. Nonetheless, there are some significant deviations from our expectations (E-P 12). In England, CA was created long before consumerism became a real issue. In Belgium the great enthusiasm and administrative skill of AC leadership pulled that organization way ahead of the general consumer policy climate. In Sweden and Denmark the somewhat "official" nature of the journals may in part explain the subscriber "lag." As regards Germany, it must be remembered that Warentest at this time was only four years old.

The Role of Leadership

The role of leadership in the success or failure of human ventures has always held great fascination. For a long time, the "great man" school even held sway over the entire discipline of history. Leadership *is* clearly an important factor, and it is recognized as such among the organization variables in our ecologic model (01). Worrisome it is, however, that we really have surprisingly few hard facts about what constitutes leadership. Clearly, this is not the place to resolve this great issue. We shall have to be content with an operational definition—a definition, furthermore, that avoids two tempting tautologies. We must not define leadership simply as ability to cope with the environment. Also, we must not equate strong leadership with success (such as increasing the number of subscribers). And we must recognize that environments and organizations both change over time—what was a strong leader yesterday may be a weak one today.

Our definition of leader encompasses the personal energizer—sometimes a truly charismatic type—as well as the entrepreneur. The energizer has the ability to select and to motivate capable associates and to fuse the group into an entity (Gestalt) capable of accomplishing far more than a mere assemblage of the same individuals. The entrepreneur is endowed with uncanny facility in selecting operational goals and strategies that will ensure progress toward the attainment of ultimate objectives as well as the survival of the organization itself. While skilled primarily in one of these areas, leaders must be reasonably well endowed in the other one as well, or have the ability —or good fortune—to select the right kind of associates to compensate for their own weakness.

In our mind, Dr. Colston E. Warne of CU and Dr. Louis Darms, the founder of AC in Belgium, represent the energizers. Mr. Gilbert Castelain, the indefatigable man behind the scenes in AC and in the 1970–74 AC-UFC combination; Miss Anna Fransen of Dutch CB; Dr. Roland Hüttenrauch of Warentest; and the late Walter Sandbach, executive director of CU in 1965–74, equally well represent the entrepreneurs.

Operationally, a strong leader may be defined as an influential one. He may either put his personal stamp on "his" organization, or he may extend the influence of the organization in its environment (or both). The first type of leader may not (or no longer) be in tune with the environment. This would appear to be the case with Mr. Frederick J. Schlink, president of Consumers' Research of the U.S.—the world's oldest consumer testing organization—since its inception in 1929. The extended influence type of leadership is illustrated by all the persons named in the last paragraph.

From the viewpoint of leadership-environment interaction it seems relevant to classify environments into munificent and inhospitable ones. Clearly, the task of leadership is "easier" in a munificent environment, whether the need for the services of the organization is manifest or latent. It is harder—indeed, sometimes foolhardy—to "row upstream" in an inhospitable environment. The resistance may be due to a lack of perceived need for the services of the organization, to open hostility to it, to consumer lethargy, to producer indifference or animosity, or to competition. Interestingly, the question of whether the leadership is ahead of its environment or vice versa is quite analogous to the discussion of the relations between producers and consumers in the marketplace in the discussion of consumer sovereignty in Chapter Two. Kaiser brought out his excellent little Henry J. in 1950, long before American consumers were ready for compact cars, while a decade later there were numerous complaints to the effect that Detroit had been too slow to respond to the demand for such cars.

Again, it must be emphasized that our views in this area are but

Table 8-8. CI Program Leadership and Environment

		Environment	
		Munificent	*Inhospitable*
Leadership	Strong	CU–USA after 1950 VDN–Sweden 1951–73 UFC–France 1970–74	CU before 1950 UNC–Italy before 1973 QF–France before 1948
	Weak	Teltag–UK UFC before 1970	FNAC–Spain Switzerland

impressionistic. They are based on a small sample. Further, a field study of leadership in action is a full-blown research project in itself. Finally, the practice of leadership is often a group rather than an individual exercise, as evidenced in the recent experiences of CU, CA and AC. Yet it seems important to reflect on the matter; without reference to leadership or lack thereof it seems difficult to explain some of the relative successes and failures of CI programs in different types of environments.

After all these indispensable preliminaries and reservations, we present the matrix in Table 8-8. Probably the most brilliant illustration of leadership in the CI field is Dr. Warne. The CU experience well illustrates the proposition that strong leadership may overcome environmental obstacles (O-E 2). The relative turbulence of the first fifteen to twenty years of CU's history was probably due to Warne pioneering an idea whose time had not yet quite come. He was ahead of a fairly inhospitable environment.[17] During the last fifteen to twenty-five years, he and CU have been able to reap the fruits of that uphill battle. Where UFC leadership had failed to capture more than a few thousand subscribers before 1970, M. Castelain, in transplanting his strategies and managerial techniques from Belgium, replicated an outstanding performance in France. The proposition is also exemplified by Miss Fransen of CB, and by Dr. Hüttenrauch, who moved Warentest from catastrophe to greatness in a few years. Another example was Sweden's VDN, whose Mr. Henry Kirstein deserved the name Mr. Informative Labeling. On the other hand, UNC in Italy and QF in France (under M.F. Aubry before 1968) provide instances of strong leadership failing in the face of inhospitable environments. UNC had to contend with fundamental indifference among Italian consumers, QF with lack of indispensable cooperation on the part of French industry as well as with distrust or competition from consumer and standardization groups.

CI programs have also had their share of weak leadership. The failure of the Teltag program in England was definitely in part due to lack of aggressive leadership. Although the French environment before 1970 certainly was less munificent than in recent years, it appears that UFC at that time did not really have the right kind of leadership. One hundred thousand members by 1970 would have been a more reasonable UFC membership figure than a few thousand. The Spanish federation of consumer groups was a paper tiger with weak leadership in an inhospitable environment. The problem in Switzerland was the inability of any leader or leadership group to bring about a reasonable measure of concerted effort among overly fragmentized CI programs and consumer groups.

Ecolore

Considering the current modest development of the ecologic approach in the behavioral sciences and the dearth of truly comparative data about cultural differences between nations,[18] the additional reflections in this subsection are definitely tentative; one might say they are in the realm of ecolore. We shall speculate about the applicability of the life cycle concept in the CI field. Several attempts have been made to bring the life cycle apparatus of biological ecology to bear on the study of product markets,[19] firms,[20] organizations[21] and social movements.[22] Confining our discussion to the circle of advanced countries under study, we might first inquire as to the changing nature of environmental needs of CI of different types over the product market life cycle. Taking the tape recorder as an example, it would seem that the need in the introductory phase of the cycle is for education, for the kind of detailed technical information and evaluation typically provided in comparative test reports. In the phase of rapid growth, some of the educational requirements of the marketplace have already been taken care of, and consumers representing the "mass" market are ready to buy. CT programs now need supplementation with informative labeling. (It should also be noted that IL programs more than CT demand a certain degree of standardization among the brands offered, to make possible shorthand descriptions and comparisons of the type that will fit within the space of a label.) In the maturity phase of the cycle the product often takes on characteristics similar to those of a standard commodity. The need for supplementation with further simplified information in the form of quality certification marks now seems apparent. In contradistinction to some other observers we are definitely *not* saying that CT programs are now superfluous—product technology and cost as well as consumer demands are constantly changing even in seemingly stable or mature markets. We are simply talking about matters of emphasis.

Next, one may consider the applicability of the life cycle notion to CI programs themselves. Organization sociologists contend that a proliferation (or succession) of goals of an organization tends to take place over time.[23] Such a tendency is observable among a number of CI organizations, such as CU (consumerist action programs, consumer education, research funding, etc.), CA (consumerist action, ergonomics, etc.), and VDN (buying guides). More detailed study might well indicate that this is a generalizable proposition. On the other hand, it does not apply cross-sectionally. Different CI programs *started out* with such great differences in number and mix of goals that no significant correlation was observable in our sample between age and diversification of activities.

At least one attempt has been made to apply the life cycle concept to consumerism in general.[24] This is a venture fraught with danger. To make such a discussion meaningful, consumerism as a social movement may have to be separated from the institutional forms that may develop (unless the purpose is to apply the life cycle to the institutionalization process itself). This is no different from studying Christianity as a religion, as distinct from all the churches in which it is institutionalized. Kotler talks about four stages of a social movement: crusading, popular movement, managerial and bureaucratic (the last two stages clearly assume that institutionalization has taken place). But this model is not easy to apply. Looking back to Chapter Seven it would seem that Sweden has reached, if not the bureaucratic, at least the managerial stage. Yet consumerism was never a popular movement in the country. In the United States there is certainly a lot of crusading, but do we have a popular movement? There are millions of members in consumer groups, but they are typically middle class intellectuals. Thus, there is a popular movement if the term stands for a movement embracing a common theme and a lot of adherents; but there is no such movement if the word "popular" implies a reasonably proportionate representation among all social groups. The problem here may well be that the concept of social or popular movements is even more amorphous than the concept of the life cycle that we started with.

The Information Seekers

The large square represented by Figure 8-1 is the total population of any North Atlantic community nation. Within that population the prime clientele (market)—actual or potential—of CI programs is

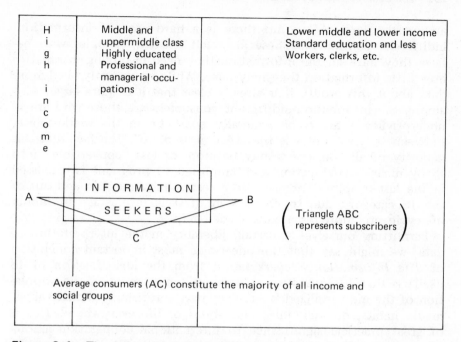

Figure 8-1. The Information Seekers, Average Consumers and Test Journal Subscribers: Demographic Characteristics

depicted by the rectangle marked off as the Information Seekers (IS). This group of consumers is distinct from the majority of "average consumers" (AC) in at least four important respects:

1. IS are more conscious about information than AC. IS will rank availability of information as a much more important buying criterion than will AC.
2. IS are knowledgeable about more information sources than AC.
3. IS consult a greater diversity of information sources than AC.
4. IS consult more systematic and complex sources of information than AC.

The existence of the Information Seeker elite among consumers is strongly indicated (indeed, we believe, demonstrated) in the *Information Seekers* volume and the research cited there, and is supported by other sources drawn to our attention.[25] Too, there is no rigid border between IS and AC—the categorization is, in part, a matter of arbitrary definition. Yet just as it is abundantly clear that there is indeed an IS elite in these countries, it is also clear that among the large AC group there is a hard core of information-indifferent consumers. These are "self-satisfied" people, who believe they have all the information they need in buying—no matter how little information they may have. While we urgently need more data about this group, it is already clear that it is quite large. Also among the information-indifferent consumers are those who are so underprivileged as to be generally apathetic in the marketplace. Between the two poles is the great mass of AC. The fact that this majority of all consumers may be more or less "convertible" into IS by means of education and simplified CI programs is discussed in the last chapter. There is also a certain movement in and out of the IS category due to changes in lifestyle, age, stage in family life cycle, etc. More research is needed here.

Permitting ourselves a certain liberality in the interpretation of data, we might say that the one single most important conclusion of *The Information Seekers* (apart from the identification of IS itself) is that IS constitute a *cosmopolitan* segment of the population of the industrialized West. They have surprisingly similar values, media habits, demographics and styles of life everywhere. This is of great practical significance to international cooperation among CI programs, to cross-national CI programs (the Woolmark may be taken as an isolated example) and, obviously, to the marketing efforts of multinational companies. Conversely, AC evidence much greater cross-country differences; they, in effect, much more than IS, represent the embodiment of local cultural values and idiosyncracies.

How large is the IS group? We can only speculate that the proportion of the population constituting the IS will vary with extent of middle class and middle class values, educational standards, certain historical traditions, intensity of consumerism generaly, and so on. Our Norwegian data suggest that in rare instances one might find one or more IS in as much as 20 percent of a nation's households. A wild guess would be that the corresponding figure for the United States might be around 15 percent and in Germany 10–12 percent. Going South in Europe one would generally expect smaller numbers; in Italy and Spain the figure is surely less than 5 percent.

Subscribers to testing magazines, while not comprising all of the IS species, constitute the most readily specifiable embodiment of it. The general relationship between the two groups is indicated by Figure 8-1. There is a great deal of commonality between the subscriber triangle and the IS rectangle, although not all subscribers are IS (they may subscribe by routine rather than interest; their subscription may be a gift without much interest to the receiver, etc.), and not all IS are subscribers (one can get product information by other means than CT programs, one may borrow test reports, etc.). The IS group is everywhere larger than the subscriber group. Just how much larger varies a great deal. Norway—with a subscriber rate of about 20 percent of all households—may be the only country about which one can say with total confidence that subscriber households comprise the majority of IS households. Contrast this with France, where in 1969 the subscriber rate was well below one in every thousand households, while the proportion of IS households even then may well have been a hundred times larger.[26] In the United States subscriber households would appear to represent between one-fourth and one-third of IS households. Thus it seems that market potential is almost everywhere considerably greater than "realized market" for comparative testing journals.

Subscribers—and IS—have *much* higher income, education and occupational status than AC. A typical subscriber is a professional person at the upper middle income level with at least a four year college degree.[27] The subscriber also possesses a significantly larger assortment of consumer durables than AC. Recent Dutch data indicate that one aspect of the cosmopolitan character of subscribers is their greater geographic mobility within their countries.[28] These data also agree with our German-American findings with regard to media habits: subscribers are readers, while AC are viewers of TV.[29] At least in Germany and the United States, subscribers are more often traditional liberals than ultraconsumerists. For instance, they tend to be rather positive about the business system in general, even though they are quite critical of misleading advertising and other market malpractices. Hence they are typically in favor of governmental action in the consumer policy area.[30] In the area of values the Dutch researchers found a further manifestation of a more cosmopolitan orientation among subscribers, who more than AC were interested in international problems and policies (Middle East, Watergate, energy crisis).

In their attitudes to, and use of, product information subscribers conform to our definition of IS: availability of information to them is a more important buying criterion than to AC; they are knowledgeable about more information sources; they consult a greater diversity of information sources in purchasing a major durable;[31] and they consult more systematic and complex sources of information (such as test reports).

Subscribers perceive themselves as more planful in their activities than do AC. Even though many AC apparently think they are well-informed, subscribers think that they are better at getting value for money than average persons much more often than do AC. A high concentration of subscribers designate themselves as opinion leaders; the percentage of AC doing so is very much lower. On the other hand, German and American subscribers do not perceive themselves as active innovators: they disclaim that they are among the first in their circle of friends to adopt a new product, tending to prefer to see how other people like new brands before trying them. We see no incompatibility at all in being an opinion leader but not necessarily an innovator. It may be added that a Norwegian study confirms the characterization of subscribers as opinion leaders at a high level of statistical significance and also suggests that Norwegian subscribers more often than AC are innovators, though this relationship was not statistically significant.[32]

Although focusing on the subscribers to CT journals, it is strongly believed that this section has defined the clientele of all existing CI programs fairly well. It is true that we would expect that with proper resources and strategy IL and QC programs would reach broader audiences than do test reports. However, we maintain that thus far no IL or QC program has had the resource endowment necessary to go beyond the IS elite, or to help convert more AC into IS. One might also pose the question whether CT programs have found their clientele among these sophisticates only because they constitute an easy target. We believe the answer is in the negative. Indeed, in most nations the CT programs have not done too well even in reaching this "easy" target! Further, CU and CA have done fairly systematic marketing research as to what consumers want to have tested —although it must be admitted that most of this research has been directed at subscribers or former subscribers. Nevertheless, comparing CU's original goals (including the emancipation of the workingman-consumer) and the philosophy of its board (a bit more consumer-activist-oriented than its members), it would seem that at least the world's largest CT organization has been pushed toward the present more limiting reality with regard to clientele by inhospitable forces in the environment beyond that clientele. In effect, CU might say, "we tried and we were rebuffed." Be that as it may, most CI programs could do a lot more marketing research than at present— and not least beyond the circle of already loyal adherents. Further, they might well engage in more experimentation with different media and different formats of communicating their information. An even greater challenge is to partake in educational activity that will convert more consumers into Information Seekers.

A final observation: the opinion leader role of subscribers—and of IS in general—is of tremendous significance to the viability of an open market system. In effect, these persons serve as educators of

AC and, in some respects, as their proxy purchasing agents. There is also evidence that among the Information Seekers are found the vigilantes of the marketplace, the people who will take on the often thankless task of blowing the whistle, of filing a complaint, of battling public and private bureaucracy in the perennial struggle to ensure consumer sovereignty.[33]

INTERNATION TRANSFER OF CI TECHNOLOGY AND EXPERIENCE

Internation transferability of CI programs will be discussed in the context of the North Atlantic Community. The members of this circle of nations evidence somewhat similar degrees of economic development and reasonably similar market systems, and share a fairly similar cultural heritage. A cardinal commonality in the community is represented by the Information Seekers. Indeed, our main thesis here is that, *in the main*, CI technology and experience is freely transferable among community nations.

Empirically, there is solid evidence of the success of intracommunity transfer of all three main types of CI programs. CA was patterned largely on the model of CU, from which CA also received an initial grant. As stated in the *Handbook* in 1969, a rather small part of the total activities and budget of the Consumers' Association of Canada (CAC) was devoted to comparative testing. This was the year before the agreement between CAC and CU of mutual cooperation in the sponsorship and dissemination of tests and test reports in Canada. This agreement would seem to be highly successful in that by April 1972 there were 77,000 members of CAC (of which 63,000 were also subscribers to *Consumer Reports*). In effect, CAC membership quadrupled in three years. During the same period, the somewhat similar arrangement between AC and UFC was an even more smashing success, with subscribers to the French journal climbing from at the most 10,000 in 1969 to some 105,000 in 1972 (with a total circulation of some 300,000 copies). This story is detailed in Appendix E.

In the labeling area Sweden's VDN served as both stimulus and model in the foundation of Norwegian VK and Danish DVN. The Dutch labeling foundation was patterned on the Swedish scheme, which also served as a major source of inspiration for the ill-fated British Teltag program. Qualité-France, the pioneer quality certification organization, in some respects served as a model for Qualité-Belgique, and did so even more in the establishment of Spanish Calitax.

Transferability is also one of several questions facing cooperative efforts simultaneously involving CI programs in a broad range of countries. Recent activity in the area of joint testing was discussed in Chapter Four. Of course, technology transfer can also take place semispontaneously, involving little by way of formal cooperation. The wave of dishwasher tests around the continent in 1966–69 may be cited as one of several examples of the international diffusion of innovations in the CI area. It also illustrates the importance of SMMP; all tests were based on a then newly developed German DIN standard.

Of course, transferability is a relative thing. Not every technique or every experience is transferable in identical form and with identical impact in all environments. (Indeed, this would call the entire ecologic view as developed here into question.) We have, for instance, warned against indiscriminate transfer of CI programs from the industrially advanced to the underdeveloped countries. But often even very insightful leaders may be unduly pessimistic about the transferability of international experience into their own milieu. Only a few months before the conclusion of the AC-UFC agreement and the explosive growth of both the UFC and the INC journals, M. André Romieu, the grand old man of French consumerism and a leading influence in UFC since its founding, explained to us the lack of growth of that organization as due to Frenchmen feeling more strongly than Northern Europeans that "I work hard to get my money, and I certainly don't want to have to work to spend it." If there were such a deep-rooted national characteristic, it could hardly be subject to change overnight! On the other hand, in a country where producers are unable or unwilling to act in response to consumerism on any other basis than under governmental duress, one can hardly expect that the introduction of a voluntary informative labeling system of the VDN type or a quality certification scheme of the Qualité-France type would meet with unqualified success.

Again, sometimes only a particular feature may be nontransferable. To us it seems likely, for instance, that the heavy Latin emphasis on what we have termed personalismo would limit the usefulness of "best buy" and other directive recommendations in comparative testing programs in Southern Europe and Latin America. We may well be wrong, of course. Sometimes legal or institutional conditions place obstacles in the way of transferability. The cozy rule in a few European countries that, in the absence of a specific request to discontinue, a magazine subscription is automatically renewed could not be used by an American CT program. In the area of sponsorship it may seem just as natural to look to consumer groups in one country as it does to look to the government in another, and so on.

The fact remains that a large part of CI technology *is* transferable, at least among the advanced countries. This is clearly true for testing methods, and it is often true for product characteristics and standards as well. Indeed, the International Standards Organization has demonstrated that in industrial products, components and materials standards of tests and goods can frequently be developed with global applicability. In sum: there is plenty of room for intensified transfer of CI technology and experience as well as for extended multinational cooperation in the field.

NOTES

1. Simple resource limitations confined our research to the circle of nations around the North Atlantic. Outside that community vigorous programs exist in such developed nations as Australia, Japan, and New Zealand; in some parts of India; and in Israel and Singapore. In other LDCs and in the part of the world dominated by Soviet imperialism progress has been slower.

2. Iceland, Ireland and Luxembourg are not included, although each of these nations has at least one CI program. Although Italy had a rather vigorous consumer association, it lacked a formal CI program during the period of our initial research. See Appendix E, under BEUC.

3. The quality certification programs operated by standardization groups in several countries reach consumer products only to a very modest extent thus far and are not included in the table.

4. These reports are also saved by the average subscriber for long periods of time, much like the National Geographic in the United States.

5. Figure obtained by the authors from the secretariat in London.

6. The Schweizerische Institut für Hauswirtschaft (SIH) while principally a QC organization also evidenced features of a CT program and thus was excluded from the above comparison. SIH was considerably larger than the pure CT groups in Switzerland. In 1975 the situation in France had turned around dramatically, with both the INC and the UFC far outranking the Qualité-France.

7. The simple correlation coefficient between budget and products tested is .809 and between products and brands is a high .983.

8. It may be noted further that the average number of brands tested per product was appreciably lower for the Scandinavian organizations than for the others.

9. Given income, personnel and test data, one might be tempted to undertake a comparative productivity analysis. Such a study would, however, be fraught with great difficulties. To name but three examples: the importance of CT activities in the mix of objectives of different organizations varied greatly, as did the mix and difficulty of products tested, the tendency to use in-house or contracted testing facilities. We might add that there also appeared to be ap-

preciable differences in the quality and thoroughness of tests performed, a subject not pursued in any detail in our inquiry.

10. The simple correlation coefficient is .902.

11. The simple correlation coefficient is .702.

12. The simple correlation coefficient is .870. For data on the correlation between income and personnel on the one hand and certain environmental variables on the other the reader is referred to Table 8-6.

13. It will be seen that several other environmental variables gave disappointing results.

14. For this reason, no further mention will be made of GNP per capita. That variable most likely would be highly significant if the analysis were couched in relative terms, focusing, e.g., on the number of subscribers per 100 households.

15. Hans B. Thorelli, "Consumer Information Programmes," *International Consumer* 13 (Autumn 1972): 15-21, 19. CU apparently went beyond the limit in the 1973-75 period. When the subscription rate was increased from $8 to $11 per year, the previously rapidly growing number of subscribers stagnated and then fell back some 10 percent. However, this incident must be viewed against the background of simultaneously occurring "stagflation." In 1976 the circulation of *CR* is again the highest ever.

16. We are not excluding the possibility that the aggregate relationship of appliances, cars, TV, etc., with subscribers might prove substantial in a multiple regression analysis with sufficient number of observations.

17. Cf. historical note in *Handbook*, p. 438-47.

18. In working on *The Information Seekers* the author team was shocked to discover the lack of literature attempting systematic comparison of the U.S. and German cultures, for example.

19. Early attempts here include Arch Patton, "Top Management's Stake in the Product Life Cycle," *Management Review* 48 (June 1959): 9-14 and 67-79; and Hans B. Thorelli, "Marketing Strategy over the Market Life Cycle," *Bulletin of the Bureau of Market Research* (Pretoria: University of South Africa, Fall 1967).

20. Edith T. Penrose, *The Theory of Growth of the Firm* (New York: Wiley, 1959).

21. E.g., Philip Selznick, *Leadership in Administration* (Evanston, Ill.: Row, Peterson, 1957). Eric Rhenman in his *Organization Theory for Long-Range Planning* (New York: Wiley, 1973) is one of several scholars warning against indiscriminate attempts at applying the life cycle idea to the study of organizations.

22. Philip Kotler, "The Elements of Social Action," *American Behavioral Scientist* 14 (May–June 1971): 691-718.

23. Peter M. Blau and W. Richard Scott, *Formal Organizations* (San Francisco: Chandler Publishing Co., 1962): 230.

24. Ira Kaufman, "Consumerism: An International Growth Movement" (Mimeographed manuscript, Manchester Business School, Manchester, England undated).

25. Johan Arndt, *Consumer Search Behavior—An Exploratory Study of Decision Processes among Newly-Married Home Buyers* (Oslo. Universitetsfor-

laget, 1972); Per Furnes et al., "Opinionslederskap og innovatörstatus i relasjon til lesning av Forbrukerrapporten" (Bergen: Norwegian School of Economics and Business Administration, 1971; mimeographed seminar report); W. Fred van Raaij and Gery M. van Veldhoven, "Membership of the Dutch Consumenten-bond: An Investigation" (Paper at First Workshop on Consumer Action Research, International Institute of Management, Berlin, 1974; summarizes the more complete report in Dutch); Ronald H. Rotenberg, "The Role and Importance of Non-Commercial Sources of Consumer Information as an Input in the Consumer Decision Making Process," (Doctoral dissertation, Pennsylvania State University, 1974). Rotenberg studied test journal subscribers and average consumers in Canada.

26. The proportion of subscriber to IS households in France is currently very much higher.

27. Van Raaij and van Veldhoven found that gainfully employed housewives tended to be subscribers more often than home-oriented housewives, but Furnes et al. found no such difference between the categories of women.

28. Van Raaij and van Veldhoven, p. 5.

29. On the other hand, there is relatively little difference as regards listening to the radio. AC therefore as often as (or sometimes more often than) subscribers reported having heard consumer programs—including comparative test reports on electric hobby machines—on the radio in a Norwegian study. Terje Assum, "Om utnytting av service-tiltak som tilbys forbrukerne" (Olso: Statistisk Sentralbyrå, 1970; mimeographed): ch. 7, pp. 5–6.

30. In the Netherlands, too, subscribers had a "more liberal-conservative political orientation than . . . socialist-radical orientation" (Van Raaij and van Veldhoven, p. 3).

31. For instance, in considering nine different information sources for auto and durables purchases American subscribers rated five sources as "very important" or "important" more often than did AC. AC rated only one source, "personal observation," as important more often than did subscribers on both purchases. On remaining sources results were mixed.

In our German data 42.5 percent of subscribers visited several (more than two) stores for their durable goods purchase; the corresponding figure for AC was 24.3 percent. Helmut Becker, "Consumer Information and the Image of Advertising in Germany with Significant Comparisons to America" (DBA dissertation, Indiana University, 1971): 164.

32. Furnes et al., p. 19. The Norwegian evidence on innovator status was based on only one interview question.

33. Central Statistical Bureau of Norway, Rapport fra kontoret for intervjuundersökelser Nr. 8, *Undersökelse om Forbrukerrapporten, vareundersökelser og reklamasjoner 1969* (Oslo: Statistisk Sentralbyrå, 1970): 45. Complaints to the Consumer Council of Norway are made much more often by persons with high education, high occupational status and high income than by persons who do not have these characteristics. As this is true in one of the most homogeneous cultures in the world, one must *a fortiori* be expected to find analogous conditions elsewhere. An American study of consumer dissatisfaction showed that an almost incredible one-half of upset consumers (in households

with a telephone) who did take complaint action were readers of *Consumer Reports*. The demographics of the group were typical of Information Seekers. Rex H. Warland, R.O. Herrmann and J. Willits, "Dissatisfied Consumers: Who Gets Upset and Who Takes Action," *Journal of Consumer Affairs* 9 (Winter 1975): 148-63. A Canadian study that did not inquire as to test journal subscription also showed that the average complainer is a well-educated, affluent, managerial-professional person. J.P. Liefeld, F.H.C. Edgecombe and Linda Wolfe, "Demographic Characteristics of Canadian Consumer Complainers," *Journal of Consumer Affairs* 9 (Summer 1975): 73-80.

Part IV

CI Systems of the Future

Chapter 9

Surging CI Systems

Informed consumers are protected consumers—more than
that, they are liberated consumers.

BY WAY OF INTRODUCTION

This chapter is concerned with strategic planning for the
consumer information systems of the future. This is a vital
area of consumer policy, private and public. It also happens to be a
vital part of any realistic policy aimed at retaining and improving an
open market economy in an era of product complexity and proliferation and consequent consumer information gap.

Planning in general involves two principal elements: forecasting
the future and providing for it. *Strategic* planning is concerned with
the longer range, with overall considerations and with the principal
means (strategies) by which objectives at hand may be realized. Applying our ecologic view, the forecasting element of strategic planning
is the futurology of the environment—the first part of this chapter—
while providing for the future is the programmatics of the organization, constituting the second part of the chapter. As organizations
interact with their environment, it is clear that no irontight distinction can be made between futurology and programmatics; certainly,
this chapter is the result of many "feedback loops" between the two.
Our time horizon may be anywhere from five years to the end of this
century.

Strategic plans aim at the realization of the main objectives of an
organization or system of organizations. Objectives in large part are
derivatives of the environment in which the organization finds itself,
but they also reflect the values of the planners. This is true even in
our armchair exercise. The reader is again put on guard with regard

to the values of the authors. We tried to declare them in introducing the book. In capsule form we have restated them in the epigraph of this chapter.

FUTUROLOGY

The view of the future environment relevant to CIS to emerge here is based in large part upon analytical material from our own research or derived from other sources. In several instances we are projecting and evaluating trends already at work. However, many pieces of the puzzle are necessarily based on mere assumptions, whose credibility must be left to the reader to evaluate. At least we have tried to make them explicit.

Environmental Trends and CI
Aspiration Levels

Open Market Economy. This book is focused on industrialized countries with open market societies. In communist economies the consumer has a hard time making his voice heard, as indicated by our discussion of consumer sovereignty (Chapter Two). Few, if any, of the less developed countries (LDCs) have well-behaved open market systems, and the situation of consumers in these nations, too, is quite different.

There can be little doubt that there is a global leftward trend in the sense of increased government coordination and regulation of the economy.[1] It may also be that Sweden—currently perhaps the most affluent country in the world—will turn into a kind of postindustrial Yugoslavia as a consequence of further increased government management of the economy and of the trade unions' likely emergence as the largest owners of industry. We seriously doubt, however, that such a precedent would be widely followed. One seems fairly safe in predicting that most industrial nations will continue to be based on open market systems, albeit with local modifications. That, in any case, is a critical assumption underlying this chapter.

Economic progress will continue in these nations. Contrary to the "zero growth" gospel, they will not voluntarily lower their growth rates under the influence of environmental pessimism or some introverted flight from things material. True, resource constraints may force a slower rate of growth, which may also result from a decline of the old work ethic. At the same time Mr. Jones is still interested in a higher standard of living (forever a major part of *his* definition of quality of life)—and for all we know, he stands to get it. While one may doubt that the quest for material progress will diminish in an absolute sense, it is clear that it will decline in importance relative to other elements constituting the quality of life, such as cultural pursuits, the return to nature and "doing your thing" in other ways than by conspicuous consumption.

Consumers, Values and Lifestyles. Increasing affluence and growing emphasis on self-actualization and personalismo will be followed by greater differentiation in lifestyles. Differences in consumption patterns will remain an important means of expressing individualization. The psychosocial characteristics of products will not diminish in significance relative to the functional ones as a greater part of all spending becomes discretionary. Individualization will stimulate the revival of specialty stores, while consumers bent on instant gratification will accept whatever brand happens to be available in scrambled merchandising types of outlets.

Work will continue to decline in importance in terms of both time and qualitative significance in the life of average consumers (less so in the case of the Information Seekers): "Don't live to work—work to live!" For many the slack in time and interest will be taken up by artful hedonism as a way of life. Everyone will place an increasing premium on time—we shall have more and more "harried consumers."

Even those of us with a conservationist or nonmaterialist bent will come to realize the importance of good CI systems precisely as means of resource conservation (the right purchase for the right purpose) and of minimizing input of personal time on those purchases that even the most frugal nonmaterialist must make. Indeed, in this sense CI programs are countermaterialist. Generally, CI should grow in importance with the urge to control the environment coupled with preservation of consumer freedom of choice.

The conservation urge and a healthy recollection of the stagflation problems of the midseventies will mean that the greater price sensitivity often observed in that recession period is likely to become a long-term characteristic of many markets. Such sensitivity will also result from increasing cross-elasticities of demand with respect to price as the product spectrum continues to be filled in by new product developments. Thus, increasing affluence will not mean that price will be dethroned as the single most important buying criterion.

The great majority of adult women will work outside the home, most of them full time. This will lead to a redefinition of male and female roles, of which we have seen only the beginning in a handful of advanced countries. A major consequence will be more joint decisionmaking in areas of family consumption and buying and more independence in buying for personal needs.

More Information Seekers, Higher CI Aspiration Levels. The proportion of Information Seekers (IS) in a society is closely related to levels of education and income. Barring war and other catastrophic events we may confidently predict growth in general education as well as in income. Possibly of even greater significance will be the emergence of consumer education as a major social influence. This influence is likely to be greatest in the growing number of states and localities in which consumer education will become an integral part of the public school curriculum. But many aspects of "consumer civics" will also be broadcast on a scale hitherto unknown by consumer advice bureaus, voluntary consumer groups, business and its trade associations, government agencies, and the media. Nor should it ever be forgotten that a vital ingredient in CI systems themselves is consumer education—about functions performed, properties of component materials and other relevant characteristics to keep in mind in considering the acquisition of the products about which information is disseminated.

The intensification of consumer education in our view will have major effects. The single most important effect will be greatly enhanced information consciousness as more citizens become aware of what intelligent decisionmaking is all about. Where the average consumer in the past blithely reported that he had all the information needed when he bought his car or refrigerator, his ambition for solid data will be much greater in future. In response to these new demands the quality of *all* product information sources will improve.

We believe that with growing affluence consumer aspirations as regards product performance (functional and psychosocial) tend to outrun the capability of business to meet them. What will be the effect of education in this area? One may assume that better educated average consumers will be quite a bit harder to satisfy than their counterparts of the past—a powerful lever for consumerism and a strong incentive to business to improve the quality of products. As far as the IS are concerned, our guess is that the effect of better consumer education will be somewhat the opposite, that is, the injection of a certain "sobering realism" in their expectations of the open market system.

Consumer education will swell the ranks of IS. But a dramatic influx into this group is bound to occur even in the absence of new educational programs, as growing cadres of women find employment outside the home and acquire what for many of them will be a new type of independence as decisionmakers in the marketplace. We wish to make perfectly clear that significant numbers of homemakers are IS. However, it does seem very likely that the proportion of IS among women employed elsewhere is appreciably greater.

Among other effects of consumer education we should finally mention an increased awareness of the cost (in money, time and nervous energy) of both producing and searching for information. This should increase the viability of self-supporting CI programs and may also create more appreciation for simplified and easily available CI varieties.[2]

Marketplace Changes. From our point of view the most critical aspect of the emerging marketplace is the continuing proliferation of products and brands and the ascending complexity of the average product. The open spaces in the "product spectrum" will be filled increasingly with new types and variants.

In a number of mature markets the intense competition between brands will periodically make the offerings of all producers increasingly similar. In such situations it may be true for some time that differences between units of the same brand become more significant than differences between units representing different brands. Basing their reports on single units, comparative testing organizations in these instances should become much more concerned with quality control in producer establishments. Some critics have argued that in cases of interbrand similarity CI programs are of little interest. We fundamentally disagree, and on two grounds. First, consumers are well served by being informed of such similarity, which is often as difficult and time-consuming to establish as are interbrand differences. The dissemination of such information will focus consumer attention on price, which is important to him as well as to a viable market system.[3] It will also bring to the fore service, easy availability, psychosocial characteristics and other features of the offering not generally equalized between brands of the same product. Second, widespread consumer awareness of interbrand similarity, coupled with the urge toward individualization in lifestyles, will serve as a powerful incentive to sellers to improve and distinguish their products. Few complex products—the automobile, for example—ever get "frozen" in a "standard commodity" stage; they go through cycles of homogenization and heterogenization. Sometimes the standard item and the highly differentiated one will exist side by side, as the Volkswagen and the Land Rover. All the better for consumers.

Product proliferation will mean much greater interproduct competition, cases where different products may meet the same need. This will increase the importance of interproduct and cross-functional tests. The larger role of product and service systems (apartment comes with appliances and common laundry facility; hi-fi system comes with tuner, turntable, amplifier and speakers) will present yet another challenge to CI programs.

Labor costs as well as consumer time constraints will place a premium on uninterrupted product performance. Some products will be redesigned to facilitate service and maintenance, others will be built in modules which simply can be replaced in case of breakdown. Specialized product service establishments may well have a comeback. *Pre-sales service* will be an important new concept, comprising product information, and information on warranty and on what the customer may expect in terms of after sales service, as well as access to owner's manuals and assembly instructions *before* purchase. Improved production quality control will be another major ingredient in pre-sales service.

Improved quality control will also be a natural consequence of manufacturer desire to minimize service problems. This in turn will stimulate competition in extending warranty terms. Again, quality control in manufacturing will be promoted by such laws as the U.K. Trade Descriptions Act and the U.S. Warranties and FTC Improvements Act. Not least will intensified quality control be stimulated by sellers joining voluntary IL and QC programs, a feature of which is that the manufacturer guarantees that his product lives up to the underlying claims.

The prime characteristic of postindustrial society is that the service trades are outgrowing physical production. To meet the demands of the times, CI programs will have to come to grips with how to evaluate services, the local and personal nature of many of these trades notwithstanding. A similar challenge is confronting us in the rapidly growing area of institutionalized or "collectivized" consumption, such as in the health, postal, transportation and public utilities areas. There is a great need for CI in these "managed markets," a need presently poorly met. When, as is often the case, these services are provided by government or under close government regulation, it is especially important that CI programs be conducted by *independent* organizations.

Developments in retailing may actually be rather favorable from a consumer information viewpoint. In the vital food area the trend in leading countries is clearly toward the extremes of *hypermarchés* (superstores of 150,000 square feet or more) and neighborhood convenience stores. A large part of the superstore assortment will be small appliances, housewares and other nongrocery items. By and large, the convenience store will carry strictly routine items for which the need for CI (beyond conventional packaged goods labels) is fairly limited. A major function of the superstore, on the other hand, is precisely to permit choice based on *in-store* comparative shopping. This is vastly facilitated by the large sales volume, which permits the store to carry a great number of brands of individual food as well as nonfood items and to make use of such devices as unit pricing, open dating, consumer corners, etc., at surprisingly low marginal cost. The resurgence of small delicatessen stores in food retailing is symptomatic of a general trend toward specialty stores catering to special needs in all areas. In these stores it will be a true delight to witness the comeback of personal selling, but based now less on satisfying neighborhood social needs than on providing consumer information and advice. In the more progressive of these stores, the old-fashioned salesclerk will be transformed into a customer consultant.

Even in countries where consumerism has already come of age—as in Scandinavia and the United States—there will most certainly be additional government regulation of markets and marketing. For example, there will be new restrictions on output and/or consumption and/ or number of brands or models of certain products, and minimum standards of performance will be prescribed for others, notably as regards health and safety. Such considerations may also make CI obligatory for the products involved. Mandatory information requirements are also likely in markets where the position of buyers is particularly weak, such as the funeral industry.[4]

By far the single most important measure the United States could take in the interest of consumers at this time would be to make metrication mandatory within a short transition period. As long as consumers have to multiply or divide with such factors as 8, 12 and 16 before prices can be compared Americans have a grotesque obstacle course in comparative shopping. Tardy producers also use the archaic measurement system as an invisible—but tangible—barrier against imports. In many countries governments will promote or mandate unit pricing, and a drastic reduction in the number and types of package and container sizes, in the interest of resource conservation, consumer information and promotion of competition. Legislation aimed at truth in packaging, in lending and in other marketing activities will be enacted in additional countries. Advertising regulations are briefly discussed in the next section. The total range of likely public policy measures of relevance to consumers is too vast to discuss here; we have given a number of illustrations of special interest in the consumer information context.

Consumerism. "Consumers' liberation" will gain full recognition as a movement of urgency similar to women's liberation and ethnic group liberation (black, Algerian, migrant foreign workers, etc.) in the civilized part of the world. The ultimate driving force will remain the frustration gap between consumer aspirations and the capabilities of the economy to satisfy them as well as the consumer information gap characteristic of affluent economies. There is no more reason to think that consumerism will "go away" than that women's lib or labor unions will disappear. Sweden and the United States are likely to remain the precursor nations for the foreseeable future, though there is reason to believe that their approaches to consumer policy will grow increasingly dissimilar (Chapter Seven).

What will consumerists demand? Just as in the case of other social movements, the easiest and yet most pungent answer is "more." Some probable demands have already been touched upon. A likely new development is pressure for more active and direct consumer participation in business and government decisionmaking. There is no need to speculate about the implications of such demands here, as that would carry us way beyond CI programs. Lest we be misunderstood, let us emphasize our belief that at least outside Sweden the mainstream of consumerism is perfectly compatible with—indeed but a contemporary expression of—classic ideas of liberalism and pluralist democracy.

Future of Commercial, Personal and Independent Information Sources

In Chapter Four we discussed the nature and interaction problems of commercial, personal and independent product information sources in some detail. Having found that a projection of that discussion would be unduly repetitive, we shall approach the future of these information sources from a different viewpoint. It is well known that "knowledge is power." The approach here will be to examine the product information system as a system of power, as we think this will be helpful to an understanding of what is likely to happen to its different parts (subsystems). Our thoughts in this area have been stimulated by Gerhard Scherhorn, the prominent German economist and social scientist.[5]

The current product information system is dominated by sellers. Maynes estimates that producers in the United States spent $64 billion (i.e., milliards) on advertising, sales promotion and personal selling in 1970.[6] Total expenses of the two leading independent CI programs were around $12 million; that is, less than one-five-thousandth as much. Many reservations surround these data, but they do give a perspective. It is impossible to place a dollar tag on the cost of personal (consumer-to-consumer) information; if it were we are fairly certain that the impression of producer dominance would remain. Estimates have been made suggesting that the average American gets 100–200 or more seller information "cues" a day; it may be doubted that he has as many as half a dozen product-oriented conversations with other consumers in the same time.

The fact that business dominates the product information system certainly does not of itself mean that consumers are helpless victims of manipulation. As discussed in Chapter Two, the recipients of these communications are neither slaves nor automatons. Further, it must be remembered that business is *not* a unified technostructure. A major part of all commercially originated messages is actually in the nature of counterinformation—that is, information transmitted by firm B to counteract the competitive inroads of firm A. We have also emphasized that a sizeable share of all advertising and sales promotion has a base in solid facts. This is not just a matter of social responsibility; for a firm in business for the long haul credibility is crucial.

Yet dominating the product information flow does convey an undeniable strategic advantage. Over the years many a seller has made questionable use of the concentration of information power in his hands. Our own research and other studies reported in *The Information Seekers* show that consumers around the North Atlantic consider misleading advertising their most serious complaint about business. There are other ways in which power over information channels may be—and frequently is being—abused. One is withholding relevant information, a sin of omission learned to near perfection by the funeral industry in many countries, but also practiced by many firms in other trades.[7] Another ploy is to make comparison more difficult—the dozens of toothpaste sizes put out by U.S. manufacturers are no accident. On the other hand it is sheer nonsense (one of the authors had to listen to it) when the chairman of the Procter and Gamble Executive Committee declares at President Ford's Inflation Summit Conference in Detroit in 1974 that this is all done on consumer demand. A more subtle, and therefore insidious tactic is the interweaving of self-serving sales arguments with factual information that is especially common in personal and "professional" selling, whether it is an appliance salesman or your dentist speaking.

Power may also be used to the good. To provide high quality information and to facilitate its use by the consumer is indeed a positive competitive strategy, and one of differential advantage to any firm that has no reason to be embarrassed about its offerings. Voluntary unit pricing has been mentioned as but one example. What is the likely future of superior information as a competitive strategy? We think it is bright indeed. Growing numbers of Information Seekers will enlarge the audience. CI programs will make business more product information conscious and will indeed both set some examples and provide opportunities for a superior information strategy (reprinting a label as part of an ad, for example). Finally, we predict that progressive management will come to the realization that improved consumer information is in league with the long-term survival of the open market system—that is, of private enterprise itself. Self-regulation (and/ or community policing) of misleading advertising and related abuse of information will finally "trickle down" to the local level, where nowadays the preponderance of such malpractices occur.[8]

Clearly we would be on our way to vastly improved reliability of commercial information sources if we were even more serious about the idea that advertisers (employers) and their agencies in effect should be liable for the veracity of functional claims made in advertising, promotion and personal selling (Chapter Four). It is true that this would likely lead many advertisers to make fewer claims, but the consumer is probably better off learning about a few valid claims than a lot of doubtful ones. Some claims might be made in more relativistic terms—a healthy change. We would also introduce a stronger incentive for firms contemplating a superior information strategy. Similarly, we could expect to get a more clear-cut distinction between the objective and the subjective components of information. Generally, this would also be in the interest of consumers.

The analysis of environmental trends suggested that certain institutional trends in business, such as the arrival of the superstore and the revival of specialty stores, are likely to improve the quality of information from commercial sources. Indeed, the success of the catalogue discount store in the United States and a few European countries in large part is likely due to the poverty of salesclerk information in most general stores as well as to the urge of consumers for better information.

No one could seriously question the legitimacy of advertising and sales promotion in an open market economy. Nor is there much doubt that advertising in various forms will remain the most important single source of product information in such economies. This generalization seems fairly obvious if we check back with Table I-1 in the Introduction and keep environmental trends in mind. Personal experience—be it our own or that of our friends—seems likely to continue its relative demise, assuming that the pace of change and proliferation will remain brisk. It is important to note, however, that rising standards of education will make everyone both more information conscious and more capable of evaluating data, regardless of source.

The future of CI programs will be bright. Their core audience of Information Seekers will grow. Their natural advantage—saving the consumer time in comparative shopping—will be increasingly important. The need for greater transparency in the marketplace will be recognized in ever wider circles. As average consumers become more information-minded, and as IS become more harried, simplified, point-of-purchase-oriented CI programs will be especially vital. If CI programs can be given a local anchorage (see next section), they may even supersede commercial and personal information sources as the most important element in the product information system at the community level as regards such vital matters as the local prices and availability of offerings, the after sales service of various dealers, etc.

We think the media will become more interested in product information. There will be market overviews (based on producer specifications) and independent product reviews in the daily press. Additional hobby magazines will appear, publishing market overviews and perhaps even comparative tests of their own. In affluent countries where the daily and/or specialized press fails to seize this kind of opportunity to serve consumers, CI groups will themselves fill the void. *Handyman Which?*, *Holiday Which?* and *Money Which?*, published by CA, and specialty issues produced by several continental CT programs, demonstrate that this is not idle talk.[9]

The last paragraph illustrates the gradual and informal, even subconscious, emergence of a product information *systems* approach. We shall have more to say about a deliberate systems view in this area. For the moment we only wish to emphasize the need for anchoring such systems in various parts of their operating environment—most notably in consumer education. Naturally, education should also be integrated with the total product information system.[10]

Technology Assessment, Computerized
CI Utility, Localized CI

We need only think of the role of TV advertising in countries in which sellers are free to use this medium to realize that technology impacts the product information system, just as it permeates most aspects of modern life. The makings of a technological revolution in this area are already on hand; the problems in harnessing these technical advancements are primarily economic and institutional. Pending the fusion of these forces, the scenario here will be impressionistic and suggestive rather than specifically prognostic.

The pressure of time will make buying from the home increasingly attractive. Home buying will be greatly facilitated by such developments as the picture phone and by two-way cable TV. Sales presentations may also be made on videocassettes, which the potential customer can play back through his own TV set. It may soon be economically feasible for individual households to be linked to large central computer facilities by means of input-output terminals attached to their telephone or TV. As most of these developments have built-in feedback capability, they also provide new opportunities for the consumer to "talk back" to sellers in market surveys, product tests, satisfaction studies, and so on. Furthermore, and this is of special interest here, all of this communications technology has tremendous potential for the creation of new types of CI programs. Even more important, however, from a CI point of view, is the capability of large computers to store, and instantly retrieve, astronomical quantities of data.

We predict that the next breakthrough in CI programs will be the computerized CI utility. Independently of each other, this grand vision was conceived by Consumers' Association of Canada (CAC) and Sweden's VDN in 1968. CU sponsored some exploratory work shortly thereafter. Large-scale data banks in several respects similar to the anticipated computerized CI utility are illustrated by the inventory control system of the U.S. Air Force, keeping track of hundreds of thousands of different parts on well over a hundred bases literally around the globe on an instant retrieval basis; the REAL-TRON nationwide computer register of homes for sale to which hundreds of brokers subscribe; and the computerized files of legal and medical cases and symptoms at the disposal of lawyers and doctors. The World Trade Center in New York has a computerized system managing tens of thousands of trade inquiries every year. Closer to CI is the activity of a couple of firms that for a fee will give any consumer a computer printout of the automobile's actual cost to the dealer for the basic car plus any accessories specified by the consumer.[11] That this information conveys a substantial advantage in bargaining for your new car is clear.

A pilot module of a computerized CI utility based on a VDN experiment was developed at Indiana University in 1971 under the direction of one of the authors. This embryonic Consumer Enquirer Program, which takes the form of a dialog between a prospective buyer of a tape recorder and the computer, is admittedly a primitive creation—something of a Rube Goldberg contraption—yet it does demonstrate the technical feasibility of computerized CI banks. In hopes that the reader would like to tinker with it in his basement, the program (since somewhat refined by other students) is reproduced as Appendix F.

We confidently predict a bright future for a properly conceived computerized CI utility as a supplement to existing programs due to some powerful inherent advantages. The greatest of these is the dialog feature, which literally makes possible information—and advice, if so desired—tailored to the personal needs and preferences of the individual consumer. The dialog possibility might be a special attraction to average consumers. Even our primitive program demonstrates two other important advantages. It incorporates basic consumer education about tape recorders, not merely brand comparisons. The consumer who already has sufficient background knowledge can simply bypass the educational program routines. The program also carries data about local availability of various brands of tape recorders and corresponding service facilities in Bloomington, Indiana, thus combining education and product information with highly desirable local data. Pending the everyday availability of the communications devices discussed earlier, access to a CI utility might be arranged by calling an intermediary operator at a time-sharing terminal from any telephone.

Obviously there are also certain weaknesses in the idea. At present there is no easy way for the computer to arrange an actual viewing of the product. The logic of computers is also to focus on one characteristic (buying criterion) of the offering after another in staccato fashion, leading the prospect down an orderly decision path. However, in this way the consumer may lose sight of the forest for the trees. Like so many other phenomena, a product has Gestalt—that is, it may appear different when viewed as a whole than in the impression gained by examination characteristic by characteristic. Care must also be taken to achieve a distinct separation between factual information and buying recommendations. (This problem is certainly solvable, though the experimental program reproduced in the appendix is deficient on this point.) This is especially important in view of the naive respect in which many hold computers and of the fact that the CI utility could be expected to reach great numbers of consumers who might not themselves spontaneously see the distinction between data and advice.

One may wonder why we do not already have a computerized CI utility system. There are at least two good reasons. First, no data bank can be any better than the information that is fed into it. Even assuming the willingness of testing, labeling and certifying programs to cooperate, it is a formidable effort to prepare all their information in a format suitable to the computer, not to speak of attendant programming of educational and dialog routines for all products involved. It is also a fact that for hundreds of products the requisite data do not yet exist. Here one would have to make do with market overviews based on manufacturer catalogs pending neutral testing data. One might assume that individual producers would be anxious to be included, but if the data have to be submitted in a standardized format to facilitate easy comparison, this cannot always be taken for granted. It will also be a very big—and costly—job to keep the information up to date. There would be some scale economies, in that product information would have national—sometimes even international—validity. Yet it is self-evident that to be successful a CI utility system would have to be extensively decentralized, so that in any given community it would include local availability, price, service and perhaps even complaint data. In sum, there is clearly a king-sized organizational challenge in prospect in bringing all relevant interests and groups to bear.

Second, the economics of this kind of venture are still highly uncertain. The CAC speaks of a nonprofit, nongovernmental venture[12] (which philsophically has our own preference), while E. Scott Maynes talks in terms of either user (subscriber?) or local government financing.[13] The main point in favor of the latter alternative would be the public goods (externality) nature of the information provided by the utility. As we would be speaking about taxes, the question arises how they would be paid. Assuming that the data bank at least from a consumer viewpoint would be a partial substitute for advertising, a local advertising or volume-of-business tax might be one alternative. Incidentally, advertising might gradually shift its focus in the direction of visualization of the product, emphasis on supplementary (e.g., psychosocial) characteristics and, of course, changes in models, price, availability and other important characteristics of local offerings.

It may be added that Maynes is member of a team that has received a major grant from the National Science Foundation to undertake exploratory research and development work for a local product information system. The CAC envisaged that such a utility would also incorporate not only all local commercial services but also data about all public services (educational opportunities, job vacancies, library hours and facilities, babysitting, transportation schedules, etc.).[14] Other important approaches to local CI systems are the German Verbraucherzentrale described in the *Handbook* as well as the more recent Consumer Advice Centres pioneered and still largely serviced by CA. These seventy-odd centers focus on the consumer of products and commercial services, while the 670 older British Citizens' Advice Bureaux are more directed to the consumer of public and welfare services.[15] Ideally, of course, community advice centers of the German and British types would be the local bodies administering the CI utility discussed earlier.

PROGRAMMATICS

Having thus attempted to forecast the operating environment, we turn now to the policy conclusions and recommendations part of our exercise in strategic planning for CI systems.

Attending to the Information Seeker

We know that the preponderance of the Information Seekers are highly educated, middle class professional-managerial people (Chapter Eight). As they are a good deal more information conscious than average consumers, IS in practice tend to be the direct beneficiaries of CI programs. In a country like Sweden where the CI programs of the past were mainly financed by taxes this was bound to raise a political issue. In the spirit of nivelation (achieving equality by leveling downward) characteristic of socialism in its more extreme forms, Swedish consumer radicals have demanded, and achieved, the cancelation of local comparative testing and informative labeling programs (Chapter Seven). If the reader feels that this policy smacks of book burning, the reader is right. However, the policy is logical if the ultimate objective is to do away with the open market system—the aim of the radical fringe in that country. For those of us who have faith in the merits of consumer sovereignty and open markets there is a need to reemphasize the increasing urgency of public as well as private policies aimed at fortifying the Information Seekers, increasing their numbers and stimulating information consciousness among consumers in general.

In open market democracies the Information Seekers are the shock troops in the perennial struggle to maintain and increase consumer sovereignty. We know that the IS, more than average consumers, will

1. personally enforce consumer rights;
2. personally exercise consumer responsibilities;
3. keep suppliers on their toes by pinpointing poor service, deficiencies in products, out-of-stock conditions, misleading advertising and other malpractices;
4. voluntarily finance CI programs;
5. disseminate information and advice to fellow consumers; and

6. serve as proxy purchasing agents for many less information conscious and planful consumers.

The IS do perform the role of St. George; they are the vigilantes of the marketplace. Indeed, IS themselves constitute a public good in more than one sense! It has been said that we have spent the last hundred years perfecting producer institutions, but that unlike the firm, the average consumer has no purchasing agent, quality control system or expertise on hand to enforce sellers' contractual obligations. There is much truth in this notion. Due to the diseconomies of scale involved we can never hope that the average household will reach similar degrees of professionalism. Nor could (or, we think, should) public policy ever be expected to do this job in full. Consumer education will be an important assist. So, it will be seen from the above, are the Information Seekers. They, more than others, are indeed professional consumers.[16]

Someone may object to the pacesetter role of the IS, feeling it undesirable that average consumers (AC) pick up middle class values and tastes that they can ill afford or that are out of touch with their styles of life. There is actually little ground for this objection. Individualization of demand is stronger among IS than among AC. At the same time, it is probably true that on balance IS are more concerned with the functional features of products than AC. Important, too, is the fact that many AC in effect are IS when it comes to certain products of special interest to them. Finally, even if on occasion IS might be considered as exercising undue influence in the marketplace we would consider this a state of affairs vastly preferable to the only alternative mankind has seemed able to come up with thus far: the committee of wise persons who know better than the consumer himself what is good for him.[17]

In the end, it seems to us, the question is, Should we deprive *all* consumers of the right to be informed just because only a minority make use of it? It is analogous to the question, Should we abolish national parks because only 15 percent of the population visit them? The answer is "no." We do not want equality where in practice it essentially means a leveling down. What we want is equality of opportunity with focus on *mobility*: everyone must be free to become an Information Seeker. An indispensable part of this upward thrust is a comprehensive set of policies aimed at the emancipation of underprivileged consumers. Average consumers are most readily helped along the way by consumer education and simplified CI programs.

CI programs indirectly benefit everyone, and in important ways. The fact that such programs benefit IS most directly is no reason why public moneys should not be used to support consumer information systems. Indeed, as a matter of principle rather than of practical importance we should recognize the public service performed by IS by making subscriptions to comparative testing journals—and contributions to CI programs—deductible for income tax purposes. It behooves business and political leaders concerned with the long-term survival of the open market system to seek the cooperation of IS. The typical Information Seeker is also a friend of the open market in principle—but if it fails in practice the allegiance of these sophisticates is apt to turn into distrust.

The Challenge of Underprivileged Consumers

We now turn briefly to the problems of underprivileged consumers. It is our plan to deal with them at length in a forthcoming book on our field study of consumer problems and consumer behavior in a less developed country (Thailand). In that context we shall compare underprivileged consumers in the industrially developed countries with those in the LDCs. It is fashionable to point to similarities here; there will also be reason to point to major differences.

The reader may wonder why there is no special section on average consumers (AC) following that on the IS. The reason is our conviction that if we look after the interests of the IS we are in effect looking after AC as well, as IS are the vigilantes of the marketplace. It is ture that AC will be more interested in simplified, point-of-purchase aspects of CI than will IS. As we have seen, however, IS also need simplified CI as they do not have the time to read specialty literature about everything they buy. We also expect that obligatory consumer education will do much to "upgrade" AC to Information Seekers.

The discussion here is confined to noncoping consumers in the affluent countries: that is, essentially, the nations around the North Atlantic, Australia, New Zealand and Japan. The terms underprivileged and noncoping will be used interchangeably. Clearly, they are relative and reflect nonconformity with middle class values of economic striving and rationality-seeking behavior in the marketplace. Inasmuch as these are majority values and inasmuch as both the majority and the underprivileged minority consider the position of the noncoping consumer a major social issue, we feel the use of these terms is legitimate.

In focus are primarily spatially concentrated pockets of such consumers as the black ghetto in Amsterdam, the Arab quarters in Paris, the rural population in Southern Italy and many of the ethnic enclaves in large American metropolitan centers. No affluent nation is without underprivileged consumers. Indeed, they constitute a major concern of public consumer policy in wealthy, homogeneous Sweden. We are talking about a relative phenomenon, just as our definitions of poverty tend to reflect time and circumstance.

An integrated approach is needed, an approach making concerted use of a variety of consumer policy measures dovetailed to the special needs of the clientele. It would take us too far to develop this theme in detail here. The major shift in focus is indicated by the shift in policy priorities required. For IS they would seem to be (1) information, (2) education and (3) protection; for AC, education, information, protection. For underprivileged consumers (UC), on the other hand, the priorities would rather be education, protection, information.[18] We shall not go into protective measures here. Although the object of consumer education in large part might be similar for UC as for other consumers, the media must be different. The training should be more practical, less conceptual. Material should be presented in "case" or "story" form whenever possible, and comic books, films, discussion groups, live demonstrations used as widely as possible. The noncoping consumer's need for personal contact and for concrete advice rather than anonymous and abstract data should be recognized by neighborhood consumer advice centers, combining education, advice and information. These centers should be grounded in neighborhood associations, religious groups and so on. As regards point-of-purchase information, a quality certification scheme would be most important. Peace Corps type volunteers might well be induced to work as salesclerks–consumer consultants in neighborhood stores. Consumer cooperatives should be encouraged not only as a self-help economic institution but also as one providing entrepreneurial experience in everyday economics and operation of the marketplace.

Great emphasis should be placed on the value of shopping around and of brand comparison. Multibrand display centers in underprivileged neighborhoods are a crying need. Public transport—incredibly important to the underprivileged—should be equipped with consumer education posters, notably reminders that shopping around is a good idea.

Two guideposts are especially important. First, that the aim of consumer policy for the underprivileged is emancipation, not permanent stratification. It is help to self-help and circulation, not paternalism and permanent dependence. It is to instill self-confidence and self-respect in lieu of fatalism and resignation. Second, here more than ever it is true that a pluralist effort is called for. Neighborhood associations, volunteer groups, schools, coops, merchants, manufacturers, transportation companies, advice and display centers, foundation officials, welfare agencies, labor unions, credit institutions, religious congregations, and government agencies all have to learn to act in concert for the common good. It is abundantly clear that none of these bodies can go it alone. The American experience also suggests that some spirited, essentially voluntary and yet disciplined cooperation is needed.

What Business Can Do

The number of transactions between sellers and individual consumers in the affluent democracies of the world may well exceed one billion per day. It appears that in a clear majority of these transactions consumers are at least fairly well satisfied. To say that the open market system is a failure seems to us grossly unfair. Yet we are singling out business, among all consumer policymaking groups, for separate discussion here as there is so much more than it can do that is either yet undone or done to much less than perfection. Much of this can be accomplished by voluntary action, in the spirit of free societies. It must also be admitted that not until the last few years has business received any strong signals from its operating environment that it needed to view its activities from a CI perspective. A further reason for such a discussion is a conviction that individual firms in the future may secure an important differential advantage by adopting superior information as a competitive strategy.[19] Finally, it seems clear that business in general stands to gain by being proactive rather than merely reactive in dealing with the modern consumer and his needs, aspirations and problems. Again, the interest is centered on CI and related areas of consumer policy. No one denies that business also faces important tasks in the consumer education and product safety areas. With regard to some CI-related measures, business could well take action single-handedly, whether at the firm or trade association level. In other cases it would seem more natural, or statesmanlike, to proceed in cooperation with other groups.

Beginning with the former type of measure, *pre-sales service* has been mentioned as an important growth area in discussing environmental trends at the beginning of this chapter. To the component elements of service mentioned there we may add giving the manufacturer's name and country of origin on products even when this is not required. The consumer certainly has a right to these identifying data (even in the case of private brands).

Business should make *advertising and sales promotion more informative*. An excellent way of making ads and mail-order catalogues more informative is to use material from CI programs to the extent that this is permissible. Let the package inform, not deceive. Facilitate comparability by *sensible* and fair comparative advertising, by unit pricing, by providing an assortment that offers real choice (a major weakness of U.S. retailing outside of supermarkets), and by participating in fairs, collective displays and multibrand outlets. Most retailers could vastly improve sales training to *upgrade clerks into consumer consultants*, and large retailers should make much broader use of consumer corners for advice, information and educational materials. In providing consumer education materials business should scrupulously avoid promotion. Trade associations would do consumers a service by combining educational materials (about canoes and canoe trips as instruments of recreation, say) with market overviews of the offerings of member manufacturers. Department stores should not make consumers feel that the first service that is dropped in a recession is the information desk (as did L.S. Ayres in Indianapolis in 1974).

Owner's manuals and assembly instructions could be markedly improved. *Warranties* could be made more specific and yet more understandable. Other manufacturers might take a cue from the automobile industry in which competition in more generous warranty terms has become an important strategy of winning customer confidence and allegiance.

Business should also learn to look upon *market communications as a genuinely two-way information flow system*. In the past the emphasis on outbound communication (advertising and sales promotion) has been one-sided indeed. Marketing research, when existing, is not only given a budget that typically is totally trivial next to advertising; it is also generally confined to issues of interest to the producer, i.e., questions that may or may not be of consumer relevance. Certainly conventional marketing research has next to nothing to do with a consumer satisfaction audit. Yet, ten or twenty years from now such audits may be as commonplace as employee satisfaction surveys are today among progressive companies. Most businesses do get some unrequested information from consumers in the form of complaints. It is characteristic of today's situation that very rarely is such information used as input to quality control and product planning managers. Typically, complaints handling is a function existing in splendid isolation.[20]

This brings us to some of the things business could do *in cooperation with others, notably consumers.* In the past decade or two of consumerism we have witnessed a kind of "fighting on the barricades" in most affluent countries. We firmly believe the time has now come when both business and consumer groups are ready to sit down for problem-solving of mutual interest, just as management and labor have learned to do after an initial period of mutual suspicion. As part of this process consumer affairs management must be given much more weight in corporate affairs.[21] Also, through this channel, and/or by means of consumer sounding boards, panels and surveys, consumer inputs may be of value to product planning, advertising and other aspects of marketing strategy.

Whether in the interest of long-term survival of the open market system or as a matter of social responsibility or as an element of a superior competitive information strategy, it behooves business to do what it can to *promote voluntary CI programs* together with consumers and perhaps other interested parties such as independent experts and government. The same thing applies to SMMP development at national and international levels. Whatever the effect on the individual firms, American business would do consumers a tremendous favor by hastening the conversion to the metric system, and by loyally using that splendid opportunity for package size standardization.

There are several *CI-related causes at the community level* inviting business cooperation, such as local business-consumer review boards for misleading advertising and other malpractices. Pending computerized CI banks as discussed earlier, business could help materially by publishing community catalogs of model and brand availability, service capabilities, etc., of local dealers, preferably in cooperation with consumer groups or community organizations. (Telephone catalog directories are of course inadequate in this regard.) We have also discussed things that should be done for underprivileged consumers. Constructive business initiatives should be more common in this context.

Business may select not to engage in the kinds of CI and consumer policies illustrated here, or to do so only in a perfunctory way. If so, we have to put aside our programmatics and go back to prognostics. The scenario then most likely will be quite different. It will most likely involve obligatory information requirements, counterinformation programs, mandated corrective information, an advertising tax to finance government CI programs, etc.—all these measures adopted in an atmosphere of animosity toward business. Some of these things may come anyway, but then more likely in less severe form, and with business-proposed amendments incorporated with due respect for a legitimate viewpoint.

Further away on the horizon of that type of scenario are such prospects of questionable merit in an open market system as censorship of new products, mandated economy models, and such detailed controls and regulations at every step of managerial activity that we shall have to accept zero growth whether we want it or not.

Lest we be misunderstood we take it for granted that, like consumers, producers have some rights in an open market system. Their most important right is to produce and market what they think will meet the demand, with a minimum of government interference. This right is entirely parallel with—it may indeed be a prerequisite to—the consumer right to free choice. Of course, the right, to be valid, must not be exercised in such a way as to upset other consumer rights such as the rights to be informed and to be safe. A business must also have the right to choose what customers it wishes to deal with, as long as the exercise of the right does not interfere with the open market system. Like consumers, business has the right to be heard (never questioned in the United States, this right is no longer taken as seriously as it should be in Sweden); but, when heard, business should, as Americans are wont to say, "Tell it like it is."

A reward of more straightforward product information will be fewer complaints. But better CI will also increase consumer satisfaction. In the long run, consumer satisfaction is the single most important determinant of business survival, both at the firm and at the system level.[22]

CI International

Internationalization of CI Programs. In the past, next to nothing has been done in the direction of true internationalization of CI programs.[23] As far as we know the Woolmark is the only "global" consumer products symbol in existence! Yet the world is becoming increasingly interdependent, and we now know that in the Information Seekers the affluent democracies have in common a highly cosmopolitan clientele. It should be eminently feasible to conduct joint testing for many more products than is currently the case—gaining both common economies and division of labor.

The greatest promise for multinational CI programs is in the IL area. A label format could be standardized for the entire universe, as long as a firm using the label would only have to indicate the performance of its brand on the characteristics identified on the label. Theoretically, QC programs could be made universal even more readily. However, in this case one runs into the problem that national member groups might wish to establish different minimum thresholds (Italian men want their suits to be cool, Swedish men want them to be warm—both groups with good reason). Even so, the mark itself could well be standardized internationally.

The lack of suitable SMMP is a key bottleneck hampering more aggressive development of CI programs of all kinds. National and international CI groups should exercise relentless pressure on national and international standards bodies to press development in this area at a dramatically accelerated pace. But CI programs must also be willing to give more of their own expertise and other resources to the job. A majority of them have actually been seriously remiss in this respect.

International Organization of CI Programs. The International Organization of Consumers Unions needs drastic revitalization in terms of quality of personnel, monetary resources and active support of members. Perhaps IOCU should also invite IL and QC organizations with adequate consumer representation to join on an adjunct basis. A golden opportunity to create an international umbrella organization for all types of CI programs exists at this time, when international interest in IL and QC programs is experiencing a lull likely to be temporary. In the fragile field of international relations a unified organization would surely do a better job than three splinter groups. For IOCU to become effective—which it currently is not—influence on the policies of the organization must more faithfully reflect the contributions by member groups than in the past. Also, non-CI consumer lobbies should be excluded from full membership. If not, IOCU is likely to evidence the same inexorable trend toward ineffectuality as the United Nations in recent years (see Appendix E).

Should it prove impossible to reorganize the IOCU along the lines suggested, our best advice is that the members interested in an effective grouping form a separate organization. This is really no more remarkable than the creation of the OECD at the level of international economic policy.

Functions of IOCU (or its Successor). The most important task of a revitalized IOCU is the internationalization of CI. International CI programs may have seemed utopian in the fifties and sixties, which may explain past IOCU neglect in this area. The time to launch a passionate effort behind this idea is now here, before the proliferation and institutionalization of national programs renders the realization of international ones utopian in a different sense. Although IOCU directly and through the International Standards Steering Committee for Consumer Affairs (ISCA) has traditionally taken an interest in the development of international SMMP, this task should also be pushed with much more vigor.

Most of the classic activities of IOCU as a member service organization and an international stimulant should be pursued with greater determination. These activities are detailed in the *Handbook*. We are thinking especially of the clearinghouse and experience exchange function with regard to national tests and testing methods. But IOCU should be much more of a management service body. For example, it should develop model functional budget and financial statement formats for CI programs as well as model management audit procedures. Carefully pretested questionnaires to subscribers for program evaluation and to obtain subscriber suggestions for products and services to test, and their experience record of product durability, service and operating costs should be on tap. Procedures for testing the psychosocial characteristics, for taste tests, etc., should also be developed, as well as a directory of suitable computer programs and statistical techniques for data analysis. The modest manual of survey research techniques published by IOCU a few years ago represents an isolated step in what should be an ongoing activity.

IOCU should also take part in CI-related issues of international economic and development policy. The creation of invisible trade barriers by artificially contrived national standards and chauvinist restrictions on the use of national labels or quality marks are examples of practices that must be aggressively resisted. At the same time, IOCU should contribute to procedures whereby the compliance of international brands with performance indicated on local labels or by quality marks may be assured. On the other hand, IOCU should avoid the pretense of being a "lobby for consumers of the world." The resources are simply too limited, and the interests of consumers too diversified. We also referred earlier to credibility problems. At least as long as assistance to less developed countries must come from internally generated funds, IOCU should maintain a low profile here, recognizing that the priorities of consumer policy in these nations are consumer protection and education rather than CI. The challenges in the CI and CI-related areas are numerous enough to keep IOCU's hands full. We are confident that when the time has come, national consumer lobbies will form their own international organization.

Wanted: Decentralized Pluralist CI Systems

This concluding section is addressed not only to members, students and leaders of CI programs but also to consumer policymakers in business, government, media, education and other circles representing vital aspects of the environment in which CI systems operate and to which, therefore, such systems should be related.

CI Program Development. As this is a policy-oriented work, it has been natural to interweave recommendations for future action throughout. To minimize repetition, only four guideposts to strategic planning in the CI area will be introduced. Such planning will benefit from

1. adopting an ecologic perspective;
2. viewing CI as part of consumer policy;
3. viewing CI as part of a pluralist marketing communications system; and
4. taking into account a tenfold operating challenge.

The ecologic perspective introduced in Chapter Six and developed in Chapter Eight and Appendixes C and D provides a key to strategic planning. The message is simply stated: to attain desirable performance (P), organizational resources (O) must be matched up with environmental opportunities (E) by means of appropriate strategy (S).[24] This is easier said than done to be sure, but in the parts of the book just referred to there are a good deal of conceptual and empirical data that provide a fair indication of how P, O, E and S variables are related.

It is also important to view CI as part of consumer policy, a notion introduced in Chapter One and detailed in Chapter Two, and a recurring theme throughout the book. The numerous tradeoff and reinforcement opportunities between education, information and protection should be especially considered. So, it will be reemphasized, should the tradeoffs and reinforcements between different types of CI programs and different groups of consumer policymakers.

Related areas of private and public consumer policy include the following:

Antitrust and competition policy
Standardization
Advertising
Sales training
Consumer education
Product safety
Complaints handling and redress mechanisms
Environmental protection

In the past, few CI programs have looked upon themselves as integral links in a product information network. At least we may say that if this was commonly done it left scanty manifestation in objectives and strategy. However, to do this must again be a major guidepost in strategic planning. Figure 9-1 gives a highly simplified integrated view of a pluralist market communications system. Here CT represents all varieties of CI; manufacturers represent distributors as well; and underprivileged consumers, governmental agencies, educational institutions, etc., are excluded for reasons of practicality. Even so, the figure points to several lacunas in current systems and to other opportunities for improvement and cooperation, all of which have been discussed elsewhere in the book.

The last guidepost in strategic program planning to be emphasized here involves the consideration of operating problems. We have tried to summarize them in a tenfold challenge.

1. The Challenge of Takeoff

Consumers do not flock around a new CI program automatically. Leadership, substantial promotion and a "critical mass" of initial financing, experience shows, are indispensable ingredients to takeoff, with little room for tradeoffs between these variables. Too many CI programs have floundered around for years (see *Handbook*) when one of these prerequisites to real growth was not at hand.

2. The Challenge of the Audience

CI programs need to do a lot more "consumer testing" via marketing research. CI programs must focus on IS as their prime clientele. Summary reports may be directed to average consumers (AC) through the lighter media they commonly use. IL are used both by IS and by many AC. QC programs are used by everyone; they have a natural focus among underprivileged consumers. Local data banks would initially be used by IS but have the potential of permeating the entire social structure (just like the trade pages in telephone directories).

There should be a great deal more two-way communication with the audience than at present, as suggested by Figure 9-1. CI programs should realize that the manufacturers whose products are being tested, labeled or certified are inevitably a highly relevant part of their audience, as are the media.

CI organizations owe it to consumers to provide much better CI about themselves and their operations. Detailed annual reports—such as that of Stiftung Warentest—should be available, and financial statements (as well as internal planning) should be based on functional rather than natural accounting principles.

3. The Challenge of Relevance

Relevance is related to the selection of products, brands and characteristics to be tested, labeled or certified. Other determinants are the timeliness, availability and understandability of CI. Here again is an area calling for extensive use of marketing research and consumer advisory panels.

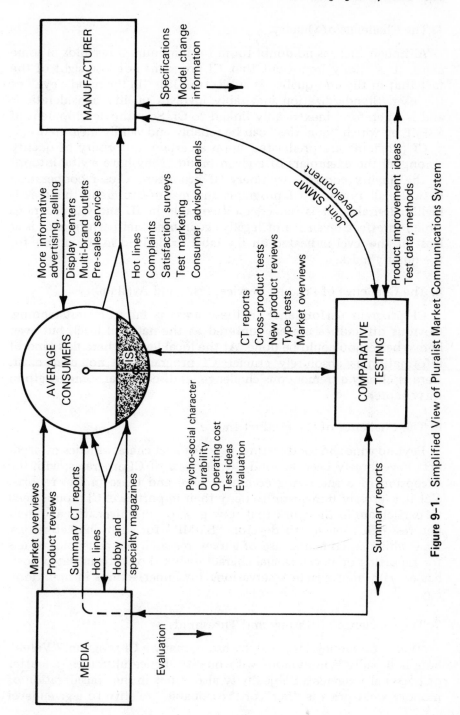

Figure 9-1. Simplified View of Pluralist Market Communications System

4. The Challenge of Quality

Although there is no doubt room for minimum thresholds in some areas, it is vitally important that CI programs not lose sight of the fact that in the end quality is subjective. It is "in the mind's eye" of the user. Standardization inevitably involves quality considerations and is, therefore, inextricably linked to CI. So is the development of SMMP by which "qualities" can be reliably and validly measured.

CI programs are predicated upon a certain uniformity of quality among all the exemplars of a given brand. They have a vital interest in the quality control machinery of producers. Closer cooperation between all types of CI programs and manufacturers in this area is highly desirable. It is indeed indispensable in IL and QC programs which in effect (even if not legally) guarantee that performance is at least at the level indicated on the label or defined in the norms for the quality mark.

5. The Challenge of Product Service, Price and Availability

CI program performance in these areas is far from outstanding. Obvious difficulties are encountered at the national level, but even here a better job could be done. At the local level—where this kind of information is absolutely crucial—CI programs do not even exist. Here is clearly a tremendous challenge, as discussed at some length in this chapter.

6. The Challenge of the Product Image

Beyond wine and food tasting, psychosocial characteristics of products have largely been beyond the purview of CI programs, with the exception of a snickering comment here and there in test reports. Yet it is grossly unrealistic to deny their importance. CI groups need to participate in the work that now goes on in universities and market research agencies to develop "SMMP" for such characteristics. Meanwhile experimental use of survey research and consumer panels for reporting on psychosocial characteristics should be initiated posthaste, with appropriate reservations for imperfections in methodology.

7. The Challenge of Ratings and Thresholds

"Value for money" is a watchword in many a CI program. "Value" here is broadly synonymous with quality, hence ultimately a matter of personal judgment. Subjectivity also enters in the consideration of money: what price is "fair" or "reasonable" relative to a given level of value? Should we avoid this issue by check rating only the best brands, regardless of price? Or should we forget about recommendations altogether, even though this goes against the manifest desire of a vast majority of the CI audience everywhere? These challenging questions relate primarily to CT programs.

Labelers face the difficult issue of whether to require a certain minimum level of performance before permitting a brand to be labeled. If it is decided to impose such requirements, experience suggests that many producers will stay away from voluntary IL programs for philosophical or tactical reasons. On the other hand, if a gadget that is called a vacuum cleaner by its maker turns out to have zero suction power, *is* it then a vacuum cleaner?

Certification programs by definition involve minimum threshold requirements. The meaningfulness of the program is closely related to the level of the threshold. If too high, too few brands can qualify. If too low, everyone qualifies and the mark adds not CI but noise to the marketplace. Again, whose needs do we have in mind in defining our threshold—those of the AC, the IS or of underprivileged consumers? Should we perhaps have two or three colors for our mark, permitting the use of different thresholds?

8. The Challenge of Product Systems

A hi-fi system consists of components that may be acquired separately or as a prepackaged system. The water, the detergent, the washing machine and the textile fiber constitute another system. CI focused on only one component of product systems may be missing the boat.

As the product spectrum fills up, we get more and more competition between different products that can fill the same or closely similar functions. Cross-product testing, on the border between consumer education and conventional CI, will have to be given more attention in CI programs.

9. The Challenge of Services

In postindustrial society, services employ more people than does manufacturing. As services grow increasingly important, the complex challenge of providing adequate CI about them must be met. A modest but reasonably promising beginning has been made to handle services within the frame of CT, IL and QC programs. Local CI banks offer special promise in this area, at least as long as there are no nationwide quality standards (or little effort to enforce them).

A most underdeveloped field is the evaluation of government services. That performance here leaves something to be desired in most countries is clear. Yet the evaluation of a state employment bureau is hardly more complex than the evaluation of automobile repair service. There is clearly much to be said in favor of nongovernmental groups as testers of public services.

10. Credibility

The importance of credibility was amply evidenced in the field research reported in *The Information Seekers*. It was also discussed at the end of Chapter Five. Nature of sponsorship, independence in CI agency decisionmaking, and public availability of test methods and procedures are some ingredients. We think there is also need to emphasize the requirement of plain objectivity. This has always been self-evident to CI program leaders as far as physical characteristics of products are concerned. It has not been equally obvious as testers have ventured to evaluate (or comment on) psychosocial, ergonomic and environmental impact characteristics. Yet it is crystal clear to these writers that objectivity requirements should be equally stringent for all characteristics.

We have also pointed out the long-term credibility risks inherent in CI organizations doing CI work in the spirit of objectivity with one hand while they attempt to lobby for consumers in the spirit of advocacy with the other—as if there were not enough challenge still to be met in the CI area itself! If CI executives feel a need for variety in their work, we would suggest a modest amount of diversification into the production of consumer education materials (and maybe lobbying for education programs). CI and consumer education are functionally closely intertwined. In addition, they will have the satisfaction of seeing their audience of IS grow with rising standards of consumer education.

Systems Development. The need for viewing CI programs as parts or extensions of consumer policy, marketing communications, education and other social systems has been emphasized. But as indicated in the last part of Chapter Four there is also need to think of all CI programs existing in a given culture as constituting a CI system (CIS). The opportunities for synergy and reinforcement are great—as are the somewhat opposite needs of independence and experimentation. We are convinced that in a pluralist, decentralized system the benefits of both competition and cooperation can be obtained without incurring an overdose of either.

As our collective term "the testmakers" implies, all CI programs are based on tests. Cooperation is obviously called for in the arduous process of developing SMMP. Testing itself (not to speak of ratings) is a less than perfected science—as evidenced by the dramatically different results different testers have reached for identical products. It is much less obvious, however, that tests for all programs should be carried out by a single consumer agency. Even less obvious to us would be joint administration of CT and IL as a single program—although the Kompass summaries of Warentest reports might well serve as an important input in a labeling program.

Excessive variety of similar programs must be avoided at all costs— or we will end up with noise and frustration instead of information and satisfaction. The dozen or more product quality certification schemes of the U.S. Department of Agriculture—where Grade A may mean top quality in one scheme and "barely edible" in another—provide probably the most abhorrent example of all time. Note that a unified format in no way would prevent decentralized administration of these schemes by different bodies.

Many other opportunities of systems thinking have been identified here. A truly significant opportunity for synergy is the use of a joint format (decentralized administration is again possible) for IL and QC. This would solve the dilemma of whether or not to use minimum thresholds in labeling, as that function would be handled by the appearance of the quality mark in a corner of the label only when a given threshold had been exceeded. Such an arrangement would also render irrelevant the doubtful criticism of certification schemes that they might remove the incentive to producers to strive for higher quality than the minimum threshold. There are also obvious opportunities for synergy between classic CI programs (especially of the CT variety) and emerging local community CI utilities.

Experience indicates that maintaining the delicate balance between competition and cooperation advocated here calls for a decentralized, pluralist system. But there is an even more compelling ground to opt for such a system rather than a centralized, monolithic one: at least at the present state of the art virtually all CI programs involve varying degrees of subjectivity.[25] This is a key reason to prefer voluntary programs to mandatory, to prefer nongovernmental programs to governmental when possible, and to prefer decentralized administration even in cultures where the government simply has to do everything.

Consumers' Liberation. There can be no doubt about it: "The idea of the autonomous and responsible individual is at the very core of Western Civilization."[26] For democracy to survive in the long run, this idea applies in all areas of life: in politics, in our personal relations and in the marketplace. The prime object of consumer policy is to foster self-reliance and to implement consumer rights in an open market. The principal vehicles of consumers' liberation are education and information. There is also a role for protective measures of various kinds. But new protective measures should not be adopted lightly or without serious reflection on undesirable side effects that typically attend them. Although some protective measures (antitrust, for example) aim at keeping markets open, most protective measures constrict the area of consumer choice.[27]

Consumers' liberation calls for equality of opportunity in decision-making—decisionmaking in meeting individual and family needs that develop spontaneously or in pluralist interaction, and are satisfied in the same manner.[28] Authoritarians—left wing or right wing—contemptuously speak of "contrived needs." Probably some of our needs are in this category. But better a few contrived needs than a multitude of *ordained needs*, needs specified for us by the "Besser-Wissers" (the folks who know better than you do yourself what is good for you). After all, we trust individuals with the choice of mate, career, employer and neighborhood in which to live. Why should we second guess them when they choose products and brands?

Thus, the rationale of CI programs is simple. It is the liberation of the citizen in his role of consumer. That role is a major one, whatever our interests or stations in life. CI is in and of itself an instrument to enrich the quality of life. It helps us free time and resources for other concerns than purely material ones. It helps us save on material resources for society as a whole. It has virtually nothing to do with inculcating or reinforcing materialism as such.

It is incompatible with the idea of a free society to prevent anyone from spending his money foolishly, but it is quite within the scope of this ideal to assist people in spending their money less ignorantly. The costs of doing this are miniscule relative to the costs of everyday commercial information.

In the end it may well be that the principal effect of such programs is analogous to that of the Sherman Antitrust Act of the United States, whose mere "omnibrooding presence" affects the very ambient of business, even though the specific effects of antitrust have proven hard to measure concretely. Antitrust is an instrument of perfecting the open market system. Let it not be forgotten that in a free society the market itself is the greatest comparative testing agency of them all!

We have argued the need for integration of CI programs into an overall consumer information system. To the extent that the parts of the system reinforce each other and the wastes of overlap are avoided, this will be all to the good. However, care should be taken to decentralize the units of the system and to encourage different sponsorship of the parts—and for two reasons. First, the field is still in need of free-wheeling experimentation and innovation. Second—and most importantly—only by decentralization and differentiation in sponsorship can we guard against the ever-present possibilities of abuse.

After all, knowledge is power. A monopoly on information would be worse than one on a product. Hidden informers would be worse than hidden persuaders, and we do not want our testmakers to become our tastemakers. Freedom of consumer information is quite as important as freedom of the press.

NOTES

1. Hans B. Thorelli, "The Globe Is Twisting Left," *Business Horizons* (February 1975): 53–56.

2. The reader will note that the discussion is based squarely on the prognosis that education in general and especially consumer education will play an ever-increasing role in the future. We think this is a pretty safe prediction. Should it be false, much of this chapter would have to be rewritten in a scenario based on consumer protection and immensely intensified government regulation of markets instead of the education-information approach that we (perhaps wishfully) believe will prevail.

3. What we are referring to appears to be the main part of what Scherhorn calls counterinformation. See Gerhard Scherhorn and Klaus Wieken, "On the Effect of Counter Information on Consumers," in B. Strumpel, J.N. Morgan and E. Zahn, eds., *Human Behavior in Economic Affairs: Essays in Honor of George Katona* (Amsterdam: Elsevier, 1972): 421–31. Even more striking than this research was the general lowering of German gasoline prices after the publication of Warentest's report on the similarity of brands (Chapter Five).

4. Indeed, at the time of writing (July 1976) one of the authors is testifying in favor of a proposed FTC Trade Regulation Rule proposing mandatory information in the funeral trade.

5. See especially Gerhard Scherhorn, *Gesucht: der mündige Verbraucher* (Düsseldorf: Droste, 1974).

6. E. Scott Maynes, *Decision-Making for Consumers: An Introduction to Consumer Economics* (New York: Macmillan, 1976): 323.

7. A straw in the wind was the May 1976 ruling by the U.S. Supreme Court that the advertising of prices on prescription drugs constitutes an element of the constitutional right to free speech not to be restricted by state and local government ordinances inspired by druggists associations.

8. It may be objected that competition will eradicate such abuses over time. This may be, but consumers will not have the patience to wait in an era where such a premium is placed on time.

9. The emergence of new specialized product information sources—possibly

as an integral part of marketing channels—is predicted by A. Thomas Hollingsworth, "Applying Organization Theory to Marketing Channels," *Journal of Retailing* 49 (Summer 1973): 51–64.

10. Maynes represents a commendable effort in this direction.

11. "Broker Discounts on Cars Stir Dealer Controversy," *New York Times* (December 26, 1971): 1.

12. Consumers' Association of Canada, *A Community Information Network* (mimeographed; Ottawa, 1969).

13. E. Scott Maynes, "The Local Consumer Information System: An Institution-to-be?" in *Proceedings of the Second Workshop on Consumer Action Research, April 9–12, 1975* (Berlin: Wissenschaftszentrum, 1975).

A distinction in financing might be made between setup costs and operating costs of the system. Government might take a greater part of the former, users and business of the latter.

14. Consumers' Association of Canada, pp. 45–46; and Gail Stewart and Cathy Starrs, "The Community Information Network Proposal," *Canadian Consumer* (January-February 1972): 17–21.

15. Michael Tilleard and Gillian Clegg, "Consumer Advisory Services," *Aslib Proceedings* 28 (February 1976): 56–68. The authors are both with the Advice Centre Servicing Unit of Consumers' Association.

16. Naturally, this does not necessarily mean that IS are obsessed with materialism.

17. In the background is the classic question of Rome: "Who is to guard the guardians?"

We are not inveighing against propaganda against smoking, or for better nutrition by government agencies, nor even against mandatory requirements for an "economy version" of products and services of great social significance in instances where market forces seem to fall seriously short of providing this kind of alternative.

18. For LDC consumers our Thai research suggests these priorities: (1) protection, (2) education and (3) information.

19. In a study of 3,400 business executives it was found that no less than 62 percent at least somewhat agreed with the statement that "marketers should make a sincere effort to point out the failings and limitations of their products as well as their strengths." Stephen A. Greyser and Steven Diamond, "Consumerism and Advertising: A U.S. Management Perspective," *Advertising Quarterly* (Spring 1976): 5–9.

20. Claes Fornell, *Consumer Input for Marketing Decisions: A Study of Corporate Departments for Consumer Affairs* (New York: Praeger, 1976).

21. Fornell studied 305 U.S. consumer affairs departments and found that most of them were confined to complaints handling and public relations. Whether consumer affairs management worthy of the name should be in a separate department or part of the marketing function is a question that we need not face here.

22. Hans B. Thorelli, ed., *Strategy + Structure = Performance* (Bloomington: Indiana University Press, 1977), introductory editorial essay.

23. The agreement between CIPQ member groups to recognize the quality marks of fellow members in other countries has been of close to zero practical

significance, as the dispersion of products using these marks across national borders has been infinitesimal.

24. Analogous reasoning may be applied to business firms and other organizations; see note 22.

25. See Chapter Three, subsection on voluntary versus obligatory programs.

26. Newton P. Stallknecht, "Philosophy and Civilization," in Marjorie Grene, ed., *The Anatomy of Knowledge* (London: Routledge and Kegan Paul, 1969).

27. Boulding points to another risk: "There must be a point . . . at which the protection of the buyer is carried too far. Then the attempt to correct sins of commission leads to the producer's failure to do anything at all, simply because the cost of uncertainty and honest mistakes are unbearable. . . . If we had a law that anybody who drilled a dry oil well would be shot, very few wells would be drilled. . . . [I]t may be that the epitaph of our society will read: 'Died of extreme accountability.'" Kenneth E. Boulding, "Doers and Stoppers," *Technology Review* (MIT, October-November 1975): 8.

28. Contrast with this the views of E. Dahlström, a typical Swedish social science radical: "The crucial controversial issue in research on human needs may be tied to a distinction between human needs in an *objective meaning* (ideal regarding needs) and social needs in a subjective meaning (want regarding needs). Needs in the *subjective meaning* is what is the common research object of behavioral science; what people choose to have or support, the desires and wants they express. Happiness, satisfaction and subjective adjustment refer to this subjective side. Needs in an objective sense imply ethical and political considerations and presumptions." This is undiluted buncombe. Far from being objective, needs thus defined express the subjective values of a governing elite (or of behavioral scientists who would like to be a part of it). This is simply the gospel of authoritarianism given to us sotto voce. People who define "objective" needs in this way are not trying to liberate the consumer; they are out to *standardize the consumer*, i.e., deprive him of the characteristics which make him a free agent.

Quote from Edmund Dahlström, "Social Science and Social Rationality" (Paper presented at the Eighth World Congress of the International Sociological Association, Toronto, August 18-24, 1974).

Appendixes

List of Organizations and Abbreviations

TERMS USED FREQUENTLY

AC   Average consumers (as contrasted to IS)
CI   Consumer information issued by an independent CT,
          IL or QC organization interested in a broad spectrum
          of consumer products
CIS   Consumer information system—that is, the number,
          size, diversity of and interaction between the CI and
          CI-related organizations in a country
CR   *Consumer Reports*, published by CU
CT   Comparative testing
IL   Informative labeling
IS   Information Seekers
LDC   Less developed countries
QC   Quality certification
SMMP   Standard Methods of Measuring Performance, stan-
          dardized testing and measurement techniques
test   Published by STIWA

ORGANIZATIONS

AC   Association des Consommateurs (Belgium), also known
          as Verbruikersunie
AFNOR   Association Française de Normalisation (France)
AGt   Ausschuss Gebrauchstauglichkeit (Germany)

AGV	Arbeitsgemeinschaft der Verbraucherverbände (Germany)
ANSI	American National Standards Institute
ARN	Allmänna Reklamationsnämnden (Sweden)
BEUC	Bureau Europeén des Unions de Consommateurs
CALITAX	La Fundación Española Calitax (Spain)
CA	Consumers' Association (U.K.)
CAC	Consumers' Association of Canada (Canada)
CB	Consumentenbond (The Netherlands)
CIPQ	Centre International de Promotion de la Qualité et d'Information aux Consummateurs
CU	Consumers Union (U.S.)
DM	*Deutsche Mark* (Germany)
DVN	Dansk Varedeklarations-Naevn (Denmark)
FR	Forbrukerrådet (Norway)
FRC	Fédération Romande des Consommatrices (Switzerland)
FRD	Forbrugerrådet (Denmark)
IEC	International Electrotechnical Commission
ILC	The International Labelling Centre
ILEC	Institut de Liasons et Etudes des Industries de Consommation (France)
INC	Institut National de la Consommation (France)
IOCU	International Organization of Consumers Unions
ISO	International Standards Organization
IVHA	Stichting Institut voor Huishoudtechnisch Advies (The Netherlands)
KI	Statens Institut för Konsumentfrågor (Sweden)
KO	Konsumentombudsmannen (Sweden)
KOV	Konsumentverket (Sweden)
NO	Näringsfrihetsombudsmannen (Sweden)
OR.GE.CO.	Organisation Générale des Consommateurs (France)
QF	Qualité-France (France)
RAL	RAL, Ausschuss für Lieferbedingungen und Gütesicherung (Germany)
SHR	Statens Husholdningsråd (Denmark)
SIH	Schwiezerisches Institut für Hauswirtschaft (Switzerland)
SKB	Schweizerischer Konsumentenbund (Switzerland)
SKS	Stiftung für Konsumentenschutz (Switzerland)
SPK	Statens Pris- och Kartellnämnd (Sweden)
STIWA	Stiftung Warentest (Germany)
UFC	Union Fédérale des Consommateurs (France)

UFIDEC	Union Féminine pour l'Information et la Défense du Consommateur (Belgium), also known as Vrouwenverbond voor Informatie en Verdediging van de Consument
UNC	Unione Nazionale Consumatori (Italy)
VDN	Varudeklarationsnämnden (Sweden)
VK	Varefakta-Komiteen (Norway)
VKI	Verein für Konsumenteninformation (Austria)
VW	Vergelijkend Warenonderzoek (The Netherlands)

Product Categories Used in Statistics of Comparative Testing Journals

Textiles, including blankets, carpets, clothing, curtains, footwear, mattresses, paper pants

Foods, including wines, soft drinks

Major household appliances

air conditioners	kitchen ventilators
carpet sweepers, electric	lawnmowers, electric and gas
dishwashers	refrigerators
dryers	rotisseries
foodmixers, table model	sewing machines
freezers	stoves
furnaces	tractors, suburban
grills, electric	vacuum cleaners
heaters, hot water	washing machines
ironing machines	waxing machines

Minor household appliances

beaters, electric	floorwashers
blankets, electric	garbage disposals
blenders	hair clippers
Christmas tree lights	hair dryers
cigarette-making machines	hearing aids
coffee grinders	heating pads
deep fryers, electric	humidifiers, room
fires, heaters, electric	irons

Minor household appliances continued

knitting machines, hand
kettles, electric
knives, electric
massagers, electric
mattresses, electric
mixers, hand
potato peelers, electric
razors, electric

toothbrushes, electric
toasters
transformers, miniature
vacuum cleaners, hand
water heaters, over-the-sink
waffle irons
window ventilators

Household utensils and supplies

antifreeze
baby carriages
bathroom disinfectants
bathroom scales
bottled gas
car wax
children's car seats
chrome protectors
cleaning powders and detergents
curtain rods
fire extinguishers
fire guards
fuels
furniture
gasoline
gloves, household
insecticide

ironing
knives
light bulbs
linoleum floor
motor oil
paint
playpens
potato peelers
pots and pans
pressure cookers
shelving
shopping carts
tools
wallpaper
water softener
window blinds
windshield wipers

TV and audio

high-fidelity equipment
loudspeakers
pianos
record players
radios, including car

stereo equipment
tape recorders
transistor radios
TV
tuners

Hygiene products, medicine, cosmetics and toiletries

aspirin
cigarettes
deodorants
diapers
facial tissues
hairspray

heated rollers
nipples
razor blades
shampoo
soap
sunglasses

Hygiene products, medicine, cosmetics and toiletries continued
toilet paper
toothpaste
vitamins

Sports, recreational, educational and travel goods

ballpoint pens
barbeque grills
batteries
bicycles
binoculars
boats
cameras
camping equipment
crash helmets
drills, electric
encyclopedias
fertilizers
film
film projectors
film viewers
fog lights
garden equipment
golf balls and clubs
hedge clippers

hobby machines
knives, pocket
lawnmowers, hand
life jackets
magnetic tapes
mopeds
outboard motors
records
safety belts
sleeping bags
slide projectors
suitcases
tennis balls
tents
thermos bottles
tires
toys
typewriters
wheelbarrows

Cars only (Automobile accessories not elsewhere classified appear under sports, recreational, educational and travel goods).

Services
book clubs
financial service reporting
prefab housing
travel

Appendix C

Further Theorizing on the Ecology of
CI Programs

The purpose here, as indicated in Chapter Six, is to develop the model of CI program ecology in *somewhat* further detail than that deemed of interest to the average reader of the balance of the book. We are saying "somewhat" greater detail, as the possibilities of developing this kind of open systems model are really unlimited. When you take the ecologic view, it is literally true that "everything relates to everything else." Thus two limits are arbitrarily placed on the discussion. First, we shall proceed along any given path only long enough to enable the reader to go further in the same direction if desired. Second, we shall confine ourselves to a selection of variables and propositions with which we have had some practical experience. Not all of the variables may be important; however, they all seem relevant and are at least potentially measurable, directly or by proxy.

For a convenient starting point, Figure 6-1 from Chapter Six without the diagram is reproduced as Figure C-1, which also incorporates the Total CI System (CIS) and a few new variables commented on below. It will be remembered that the O variables characterizing individual CI organizations may also be applied to CIS as a whole. Also, from the viewpoint of the individual CI program the total CIS in effect constitutes part of the operating environment, although the program is part of the system.

There is little need here to add to the sets of CI organization, strategy, performance and total system variables. As a species of O3, "degree of financial self-sustenance" may be regarded as a significant measure of the room for independence from program

CI Organization (O)

1. Leadership
2. Budget
3. Sponsorship
   influence
   self-sustenance
4. Employee number

5. Resource mix
   testing facilities
   specialized personnel
6. Age
7. Diversification of activities
8. Activity focus
   testing, labeling, marking, other
9. Producer cooperation

Interaction Strategy (S)

1. Types and diversity of products
   tested, labeled, marked
2. Intensity of counseling
3. Style and frequency of reports
4. Promotion

5. Consumer orientation
   marketing research
6. Pricing
7. Distribution
8. Trust and credibility

Environment (E)

1. Size
   extent of middle class
   aggregate population
2. Audience
   subscribers
   users of other CI sources
3. Economic development
   timing of "white goods"
   revolution
   mechanization of distribution
   GNP, GNP per capita
4. Social and political values
   personalismo
   self-satisfaction as buyer
   traditionalism
   faith in open markets
   views of advertising
   faith in experts

5. Government share in GNP
6. Pluralism
7. Other CI agencies
8. Extent of consumer policy
   consumer education
   consumer protection
   consumerism debate
   antitrust policy
9. Characteristics of good and brands
   proliferation
   expensiveness
   complexity
   standardization
   necessity vs luxury
   orientation to style and fashion
   diffusion of autos, major appliances
10. Extent of advertising
11. Imports in percent of GNP
12. Education
    number of college graduates
    years obligatory schooling

Objectives and Performance (P)

Direct outputs:

1. Survival
2. Growth
3. Sales
4. Number of products, brands
   covered
5. Number of subscribers

Effects on consumers:

6. Subscriber satisfaction with CI
   organization
7. Consumer awareness of CI organization,
   tests
8. Perceived usefulness
9. Use
10. Perceived savings
11. Purchase satisfaction of users,
    nonusers
12. Attitudes, values

Figure C-1.   Ecologic Model of CI Programs and Systems

Other effects:

13. On manufacturers
14. On trade
15. On advertising
16. On other CI organization
17. On public policy

Total CI System (CIS)

1. Number of CI organizations
2. Complementarity vs overlap among CI groups
3. Degree of coordination of the system
4. Total budget of CIS

Figure C-1. Continued

sponsors. Different types of CI organizations do have some inherent differences, as demonstrated in Chapters Three and Four. Hence it might be worthwhile to add a variable 08 designating principal activity of the CI program organization: testing, labeling, certifying or activities other than the CI program itself. Our comparative studies in Chapter Eight and in *The Information Seekers* were all based on testing organizations, due to the relative paucity of independent labeling and certification programs. In the strategy area, variable S5, marketing research, might itself be seen as a species of a genus that might be labeled "degree of consumer orientation."

Due to the vastness and richness of the environment, there are, however, a number of amendments to make in this area. An important species under E1, size and characteristics of the population at large, is the extent of a middle class. In *The Information Seekers* we studied "average consumers," confining ourselves to samples of the adult population in Germany and the United States. The "audience" (E2) was identified operationally as subscribers to testing magazines. For the CI system as a whole this is clearly too restricted a view. There are other users of test reports than subscribers, and there may be users of informative labels and quality marks, etc. To the aspects of E3, economic development, identified as salient in Chapter Six, one should add at least "timing of the major appliance (white goods) revolution" and the "degree of mechanization of distribution." Major appliances are an integral part of the middle class style of life, and they are complex and expensive enough to bring information needs to the fore. Mechanization of distribution in practice has meant an increase of the functional distance between buyer and seller, thus inhibiting information flow (see Chapter One).

To Chapter Six variables under the heading E4, social and political values, should be added at least the following:

Self-satisfaction with role as buyer
Traditionalism
Faith in open markets
Views of advertising
Faith in experts

In most cases the reasons for including these factors are presumably self-evident. Some degree of faith in private enterprise is a likely prerequisite for the credibility and success of any voluntary labeling or certification program. Within E7, other CI agencies, we include advertising insofar as it serves as an information medium.

Two new "conglomerate variables" should be added: E8, extent of consumer education and protection, and E9, characteristics of goods and brands in the marketplace. For reasons developed in Chapter Two, education and protection are interactive with information in consumer policy. With regard to goods and brands we are interested in their proliferation and also in such inherent product characteristics as expensiveness, degree of standardization in design, role of style and fashion, degree of complexity, and necessity versus luxury. (Presumably such characteristics have something to do with the felt need for CI on any given product.)

Hybrid Variables. Sometimes hybrid variables are of greater interest than the "basic" variables of which they are composed. For instance, in analyzing the total CIS in a country, the amount of money spent per capita on the CIS may prove more meaningful than CIS 4, the total budget of CIS, or E1, the total population of the country. In examining the performance of testing programs, the percentage of subscriber households of total households is sometimes more useful in international comparisons than P5, the absolute number of subscribers. Again, one would assume that the standard of living of a country has something to do with the development of CI. An oft-used summary measure here is GNP per capita, derived by combining items from E3 and E1.

Interaction Possibilities. It would appear that the possibilities of interaction even within the limited configuration of variables included in our model are well nigh boundless. To illustrate, there may be interaction between the sets, such as between a pair of variables in the organization and the environment, or in strategy and performance. There may be interaction inside a set, such as between economic development and the size of the CI audience in the environment. Further, in accord with general systems theory, we must typically expect simultaneous or sequential interaction between a great number of variables, rather than simple-minded pairwise reactions. A large group of variables from different sets acting and reacting upon each other may constitute a "change cluster." It was argued in Chapter One that such a cluster of changing variables in the environment would seem to explain the emergence of CI programs (indeed, consumerism in general) in highly industrialized nations. In Chapter Eight an attempt was made to apply multivariate statistical analysis to a volley of variables derived from the model, although the base of hard data was narrow and the problems of measurement formidable.

In Chapter Six we pointed to the well-known problem in ecologic analysis of determining the direction of the causal arrow. (Does a broad assortment of products tested [S1] help explain a large audience [E2], or vice versa?) Only in a minority of cases would the direction of causation seem obvious (e.g., greater economic development [E3] presumably contributes to a larger CI audience [E2], but the reverse might not be expected). The trouble is actually even worse: causation in many instances is a two-way street. It may also be circular, spiraling (up or down) or be similar to the movement of a pendulum. For purposes of the present research project the ambition has been the low key one of merely postulating and, when feasible, demonstrating interaction.

Notwithstanding the methodological problems indicated, and other ones, we are persuaded of the basic soundness of the ecologic approach. It is a tool for increased understanding and a stimulant in the direction of conceptual clarity. We have found it invaluable for comparative analysis across types, sizes and philosophies of CI programs and across cultures and national borders. Above all, our model has rendered indispensable service as a generator of hypotheses concerning likely patterns of interaction.

Hypotheses—Introduction. Theoretically our model could indeed generate a number of hypotheses that would be virtually out of bounds for all practical research purposes, as each variable could be related to every other variable in combinations of two, three, four and so on. To illustrate a three variable proposition: if the CI audience (E2) is significant and growing, and attitudes to advertising are critical (E4), advertising will tend to become more informative (P15). And to illustrate a four variable proposition:

if the audience (E2) is small relative to the total well-educated middle class (E1), more promotion (S4) will be likely to yield an increase in the number of subscribers (P5). Several other multivariable propositions are discussed in Chapter Eight. To keep our discussion within bounds, it will be confined to propositions that involve only two variables *and* for which we have at least some qualitative or tangential evidence. To minimize tedium we are also avoiding repetition of the type "the more refrigerators, the greater the audience" and "the more TV sets, the greater the audience." The reader is asked to keep in mind that most propositions are surrounded by that great classic proviso: other circumstances being equal. Most propositions are stated in a static form. It should be borne in mind that they generally may be restated in a dynamic mode by adding the words, "the greater the rate of change in," in front of each variable.

A personal evaluation has been made of the direction (positive or negative) and strength of the evidence obtained regarding each hypothesis. The evidence is frequently quantitative (in relatively few cases statistically significant). Often it is qualitative, as in the case of "strong leadership may overcome environmental obstacles." The evaluation is expressed by a scale of symbols as follows:

+ + strong positive evidence
 + some positive evidence
 0 no or mixed evidence
 − some negative evidence
− − strong negative evidence

Parentheses around a symbol indicate that the evidence obtained was indirect. To avoid repetition the reader is referred to the core of this volume and our other writings for supportive evidence.

We will first introduce propositions illustrating the interaction between variables belonging to different sets (O-E, S-P, etc.) and then some which reflect intraset relationships (O-O, E-E, etc.). We shall forsake trying to indicate in which direction causation may flow most strongly between any two variables.

INDIVIDUAL CI ORGANIZATION (O) AND ENVIRONMENT (E)

1. The greater the size of the middle class (E1), the larger the CI organization (O2, O4).   +
2. Strong leadership (O1) may overcome environmental ob-

stacles (e.g., small audience, E2); weak leadership may fail
even in a munificent environment. ++

3. The earlier the "white goods revolution" (E3), the older the
CI organization (O6). +

4. The greater the size of the population (E1), the greater the
chance of a profitmaking or self-sustaining CI organization
(O3). +

5. The greater the government share in GNP (E5), the greater
the government influence on the CI organization (O3)
and the smaller the degree of self-sustenance of the organization (O3). +

6. The greater the GNP per capita (E3), the greater the age of
the organization (O6). (Will likely not hold true after Arab
oil embargo!) +

7. Producers (E4) will more readily support labeling than comparative testing programs (O8). ++

8. The greater the GNP (E3), the more CI programs can be
self-sustaining or earn a surplus (O3). +

9. The greater the rapidity of change in environmental variables
generally, the greater the rate of change in CI organizations as to philosophy, activities and size. +

10. CI programs sponsored by business alone (O3) enjoy less
credibility among the public (E1) than others. ++

11. Regardless of sponsorship (O3), product test reports will
tend to have similar clienteles (E2). ++

THE TOTAL CI SYSTEM (CIS)
AND ENVIRONMENT (E)

1. The more pluralist the environment (E6), the greater the number of CI organizations (CIS 1). +

2. The greater the middle class (E1), the more diversity of CI
organizations (O7). +

3. The greater the government share in GNP (E5), the greater the
degree of coordination of the CI system (CIS 3). +

4. The greater the GNP (E3), the greater the total CIS budget
(CIS 4). (+)

ORGANIZATION (O) AND STRATEGY (S)

1. The more specialized the testing facilities (O5), the fewer types
of products will be tested (S1). 0

2. The greater the degree of government influence (O3), the lower the price of test reports (S6). (Cost would likely be higher.) ++
3. The greater the budget (O2), the more marketing research (S5). +
4. The greater the number of employees (O4), the greater the diversity in types of products tested, labeled or marked (S1). ++
5. Private organizations more than public ones (03) will feel free to recommend best buys (S2). 0
6. CI programs sponsored by business alone (O3) must place greater emphasis on credibility (S8). 0

ORGANIZATION (O) AND PERFORMANCE (P)

1. The greater the budget (O2), the greater the number of products and brands covered (P4). ++
2. The greater the number of employees (O4), the greater the number of subscribers (P5). ++
3. The greater the budget (O2), the greater the impact on manufacturers (P13). (+)
4. The greater the degree of cooperation with producers (O9), the more subscribers. –

STRATEGY (S) AND PERFORMANCE (P)

1. High price of test reports (S6) is not incompatible with a large number of subscribers (P5). ++
2. Price *change* (S6) will have only short-term effect on the number of subscribers (P5). +
3. The more intense counseling (S2), the greater the perceived usefulness of CI (P8). +
4. The greater the diversity of products tested, labeled or marked (S1), the greater subscriber satisfaction (P6). (+)
5. Promotion (S4) has a very great effect on sales of CI programs (P3). ++
6. Greater consumer orientation (S5) yields greater subscriber satisfaction (P6). 0
7. The greater the number of channels of distribution (S7), the greater consumer awareness of the CI organization (P7). +

ENVIRONMENT (E) AND PERFORMANCE (P)

1. The larger the middle class (E1), the greater the number of subscribers (P5).   +
2. The more critical the views of advertising (E4), the greater the number of subscribers (P5).   0
3. The greater the faith in experts (E4), the greater the sales of test reports (P3).   0
4. The greater the self-satisfaction with role as a buyer (E4), the greater traditionalism (E4) and the more *personalismo* (E4), the fewer subscribers (P5).   +
5. The greater the extent of consumer education (E8), the greater the number of subscribers (P5).   +
6. The simpler, the cheaper, the more standardized the product environment (E9), the fewer subscribers (P5).   0
7. The greater the mechanization of distribution (E7), the more subscribers (P5).   (+)
8. The greater the GNP (E3), the more subscribers (P5).   ++
9. The greater the extent of advertising (E10), the more subscribers (P5).   ++
10. The greater the percentage of college graduates (E12), the more subscribers (P5).   −
11. The greater the share of imports of GNP (E11), the more subscribers (P5).   − −
12. The stronger the antitrust policy (E8) and the more intense the public debate on consumerism (E8), the more subscribers (P5).   ++
13. The greater the difffusion of TV and autos (E3), the more subcribers (P5).   +
14. The larger the population (E1), the more subscribers (P5).   ++

INTRAORGANIZATION (O-O)

1. The older the organization (O6), the greater the diversification of activities (O7).   +
2. The larger the organization (O2, O4), the greater the diversification of activities (O7).   0
3. The greater the nongovernmental influence (O3), the closer the CI organization tends to be to self-sustenance or profitability (O3).   +

4. The older the organization (O6), the greater its formal engagement in international activities (O7).   (+)
5. Countries where sponsorship of CI programs (O3) is more differentiated will have greater diversity of CI organizations (O7).   ++

INTRASTRATEGY (S-S)

1. Beyond a certain threshold necessary for minimum effectiveness, promotion (S4) and distribution (S7) may substitute for each other to a fair extent.   +
2. Within wide limits, pricing (S6) is less important than style and frequency of reports (S3) and the types and diversity of products tested (S1).   +

Note: As every marketing man knows, the various elements of strategy (fairly well specified by S1–S8) must be well integrated for the strategy as a whole to be successful. In other words, the strategy must have synergy (be more than a random collection of S1–S8 ingredients); it must have *Gestalt.* As suggested by our first proposition, the various elements can be both complements to and substitutes for each other to a fairly great extent. Perhaps it is not such a great wonder that neither marketing nor organization theory nor, certainly, economics thus far has done a very good job of specifying in any detail just what strategies are well- (or poorly) suited for particular markets or task environments. This is indeed an area in crying need of solid research.

INTRAENVIRONMENT (E-E)

The environment is vast. It does not make much sense here to attempt to trace all intraenvironmental linkages that might be of relevance to improved understanding of CI organizations and their operations. Some linkages were observed in Chapters One and Six through Nine. We have chosen instead to present in some detail propositions concerning the CI clientele, the Information Seekers. Most propositions are derived from *The Information Seekers,* in which subscribers to testing magazines served as representatives for the aggregate of this cosmopolitan consumer elite. In the propositions their characteristics are contrasted to those of average consumers.

1. Subscribers (subs) have higher education, higher income and higher social status than do average consumers (AC).   ++

2. Subs perceive themselves as more planful than do AC. +
3. Subs identify themselves as opinion leaders more often than do AC. +
4. Subs identify themselves as early adopters less often than do AC. +
5. Subs are less favorable to advertising than AC. (+)
6. Subs media habits differ from those of AC. ++
7. Subs are more concerned with the availability of information as a buying criterion than are AC. ++
8. Subs are less concerned with the availability of credit than AC. +
9. Subs who used their test reports in buying are more satisfied with their purchases than AC. ++
10. Subs have stronger "consumer activist" attitudes than AC. ++
11. Subs seek redress for complaints about products and practices more often than AC. ++
12. Subs are more skeptical of business in general than AC. 0
13. Subs form a more or less cosmopolitan group, while AC from different countries express greater intercultural differences. ++
14. Organized business will do something about CI only when it feels direct environmental pressure. (Note: this proposition is not directed toward information programs of individual firms.) +
15. The more business-minded a cooperative movement, the less it will do about CI spontaneously. +
16. The more left wing the government, the more it will tend to regard the CIS as an instrumentality of the state. +

With Chapter Six, this appendix represents an effort to project an ecologic theory of all organizations to the study of CI programs and systems. For a brief statement of the general theory the reader is referred to Hans B. Thorelli, ed., *Strategy + Structure = Performance* (Bloomington: Indiana University Press, 1977).

Appendix D

Ancillary Ecologic Data Analysis

This review of data may be viewed as a low profile extension of Chapter Eight. The data are presented without much pretense. They are confined to comparative testing (CT) programs, of which there were a sufficient number (eleven, as in Chapter Eight) to permit some statistical analysis.

SELF-SUSTENANCE, GOVERNMENT INFLUENCE AND PRODUCER COOPERATION

Among CT program variables of interest are the degrees of self-sustenance, government influence and cooperation with producers. The degree of self-sustenance was taken to be the percentage of total income generated by the organization itself through sales of test reports or other services.

Government influence may be exerted in innumerable—and often subtle—ways and is therefore extremely difficult to pinpoint. We had to make do with reasonably observable variables. A government influence index was constructed, composed of four parts:

1. Governmentally appointed majority of the board (whatever the origin of the appointees). This variable only takes the values of 0 or 1.
2. Program accepting ad hoc grants from the government. This variable also takes the values of 0 or 1.
3. Direct government representation—for each full 10 percent of

board members who are government employees *and* appointed by the government or by its agencies[1] add one index unit. This variable can take any value from 0 to 10.

4. Part of the regular 1969 budget financed by government—for each full 10 percent thus financed add one index unit. This variable also takes any value from 0 to 10.

Maximum government influence is a score of 22. Our observations ranged from a score of 0 government influence in the cases of AC and CA to 13 for SHR, 12 for KI and 11 for Warentest.[2]

In considering producer cooperation among CT organizations, it must be remembered that none of the programs in the sample was producer-sponsored or dependent on financial contributions from business. Our index was designed to incorporate eleven variables:

1. Producer representation on the board
2. Producers consulted on what models to test
3. Producers consulted on what characteristics to test
4. Producers consulted on testing methods
5. Producers consulted on defective test units
6. Producers given a chance to react to advance copy of test report
7. CT journal publishes producer statements re: product deficiencies rectified and/or new models released after publication of original test report
8. Organization doing contract testing for producers
9. Organization working with producers in the development of testing methods and/or in standardization bodies
10. Organization checking quality control procedures of producers
11. Organization using trade association laboratories

Individual variables only take the values of 0 to 1. Maximum score is 11. Several organizations gave ambiguous information concerning items 5 through 7. In these cases, we had to rely on judgement. Unlike labeling and certifying organizations, no CT agency was found engaged in inspection of quality control procedures. Producer cooperation scores ranged from a low of 3 for UFC to a high of 9 for KI and 8 for Warentest.

Table D-1 presents the simple correlation coefficients between each of the three indicators specified here, and between each of them, price and number of subscribers. As might be expected (government influence being in part defined in terms of its financial

Table D-1. Further Ecologic Correlations

	Self-sustenance	*Government influence*	*Producer cooperation*
Government influence	-.777		
Producer cooperation	-.514	.726	
Price	.724	-.605	-.367
Subscribers	.564	-.413	-.270

contributions to CT programs), self-sustenance is inversely related to government influence (0-0 3). Indeed, this is the largest coefficient in the matrix. The correlation between self-sustenance and price is also high, although the direction of the causal arrow is less clear. Quality of tests and reports might be an intervening variable, although no attempt was made to gauge the quality of CT journals. It may also be a simple reflection of the fact that many CT organizations had not discovered (or made use of) the relative insensitivity of demand to price. Those who had not had to look to other sources than journal sales to supplement their income. In this context we observe the substantial negative correlation between price and government influence. Doubtless, this is caused in large part either by government mandating a low price as a condition for subsidizing a CT program or by a feeling by CT program administrators relying on government support that they might lose it were they to raise journal price substantially. We may note, incidentally, that it is highly questionable whether a drastic lowering of price would really attract large new groups of subscribers (see the Information Seekers section of Chapter Eight).

None of the indicators at the head of the table columns display any marked correlation with subscribers. We may, however, note the strong correlation between government influence and producer cooperation. Organizations with strong governmental backing—notably Warentest, SHR and KI—have displayed a more cooperative attitude to producers than others. This seems to be due to both a feeling among the government-backed organizations that their credibility would not be questioned by consumers, and to their view of themselves as bodies performing an information function in the public interest rather than in the spirit of consumerism. By contrast, there is an ideological resistance to intensive cooperation with producers among several organizations deriving their support exclusively from consumers, e.g., CA, CU, AC, UFC. Generally, the credibility discussion in Chapters Five and Nine would seem relevant here.

EXPLORATORY REGRESSIONS

Applying the gross rule of thumb that multiple regression analysis calls for at least five observations per independent variable, our N = 11 provides a rationale for presenting a few regression equations with two explanatory variables each. The first two equations pertain to variables well known from Chapter Eight; for simple correlation coefficients the reader is referred to Table 8-5. With regard to all the regressions presented, it is true that when subjected to the "F test," all coefficients of multiple determination (R^2) were found to be different from zero at levels of significance of .05 or better. The levels of significance of all partial regression coefficients in two-tailed t-tests is .001 or better.

Equation (D.1) related the number of CT program subscribers (in thousands) to one organization variable (personnel) and one strategy variable (price, i.e., annual subscription rate in cents):

$$\text{SUBSCRIBERS} = -410 + 2.91 \, (\text{PERSONNEL}) + 1.39 \, (\text{PRICE})$$
$$R^2 = .892 \qquad\qquad (14.8) \qquad\qquad\qquad (6.36) \qquad\qquad (D.1)$$

The two independent variables proved the strongest combination in a set also comprising such variables as diversity of products tested, degree of self-sustenance and number of brands tested in 1969. The strong simple correlations between subscribers on one hand and personnel and price on the other were discussed in Chapter Eight.

Equation (D.2) also relates the aggregate number of tests in the years 1967, 1968 and 1969 (3YTEST, another performance variable) to one organization variable (personnel again) and one strategy variable (diversity in product categories tested, DIVPRO):

$$\text{3YTEST} = 7.11 + .279 \, (\text{PERSONNEL}) + 14.6 \, (\text{DIVPRO})$$
$$R^2 = .860 \qquad (5.85) \qquad\qquad\qquad (8.89) \qquad\qquad (D.2)$$

The two independent variables proved the strongest combination in a set also comprising such variables as price, total number of pages of the test journal in 1969 and degree of producer cooperation. Again, the relationships demonstrated are not surprising. It seems but natural that an organization doing many tests finds itself covering a broad range of products while one doing few tests covers a narrow one. We may note, too, that a couple of the narrow range testers (e.g., KI, SHR) focused on major appliances, adequate testing of which represents a major resource commitment.

Our last equation introduces a new dependent variable into the discussion: the aggregate budget of *all* CI programs in each of the eleven nations in 1969. The actual size of this CI systems organization variable appears in the last columns of Table 8–1. Equation (D.3) relates the total CIS budget (in tens of thousands of dollars) to the environmental variables population (in hundreds of thousands of persons) and ownership of TV sets (in percent of households):

$$\text{TOTAL CIS BUDGET} = -411 + .431 \text{ (POPULATION)} + 5.71 \text{ (TV)}$$
$$R^2 = .942 \qquad\qquad (68.4) \qquad\qquad\qquad (5.22) \qquad (D.3)$$

These two independent variables proved the strongest combination in a set also comprising such other environmental factors as the relative extent of automobile ownership and the percentage of women using facial beauty aids. It was satisfying to discover that population and TV ownership yielded a higher R^2 for the total CIS budget than for the income of the largest CT program in individual countries. In effect, this means that in nations such as France, where the size of the largest CT program was modest relative to the size of the country, the *relatively* greater income of other CI programs took up at least some of the "slack."

NOTES

1. University professors—on CT program boards in many countries—were not considered government employees is view of their presumed independence of mind, nor were the quasi-public syndicalist groups in Austria considered government agencies.

2. Obviously resource allocation reflects the government's view of the consumer information programs in all countries where the agencies are public or where the private groups receive subsidies. During the period of our initial field studies, 1970–72, even the government-financed agencies, such as SHR in Denmark, FR in Norway, KI in Sweden and STIWA in Germany, were clear on one point: they assiduously avoided influence by the government on their policies and were largely (though nowhere entirely) successful at this. It was greatly feared by some that the INC in France would not be able to produce comparative tests as political pressure would be so severe as to preclude the publication of any worthwhile findings. These fears have proven unfounded. It is interesting to note that IOCU history is replete with heated debates as to whether this or that organization was subject to undue influence by government as well as business.

Appendix E

CI Programs in the North Atlantic Community: A Selective Update

The purpose of this appendix is to update selected materials appearing in the *Consumer Information Handbook: Europe and North America*, published by Praeger in 1974. Most of the data presented there were gathered in 1970–72, with statistics primarily from 1969. Our own interest focused on consumer product information agencies, but attention was also given to bodies dealing with other aspects of consumer affairs and protection.

Here no attempt is made to cover all countries (or all agencies within a country) dealt with in the *Handbook*. Rather, we have selected those countries in which we have had close contact, or those where developments or changes have been dramatic or especially noteworthy. Even so, we could not go into the same depth as the *Handbook*, and hence the reader is cautioned of inadvertencies and inadequacies. Our remarks as to developments in the U.S., superficial as they are, will only indicate a trend in the momentum of the vast consumer movement. Sweden has been singled out for special treatment in Chapter Seven.

The test report statistics here are from the years 1974–75 or 1975. Appendix B gives the product categories used. Brands denote the number of different models tested, not the number of makes. For instance, the Vega and the Monza are two brands though they are both produced by Chevrolet.

The countries selected are presented in the following order: Belgium, England, France, Germany, the Netherlands, Norway and the United States. Also presented are the three multinational consumer groups: IOCU, BEUC and Nordiska Ämbetsmannakommittén för

Konsumentfrågor. The International Labelling Centre (ILC) became defunct in 1974–75, and the Centre International de Promotion de la Qualité (CIPQ) has been semidormant for the last few years. Because of the interest other international organizations have taken in the consumer area in the 1970s, a few are commented on here: OECD, the Council of Europe, EEC.

Standards bodies continued their modest activities in the consumer product area in much the same vein as before. The only new departure of interest here is the accelerated development of consumer product safety standards. This has been stimulated by such bodies as the Consumer Products Safety Commission of the United States, although traditional standards groups have taken an active part in this new effort. Some of this work has generated international cooperation; for example, with regard to cigarette lighters.

BELGIUM

From 1969 to 1975 one Belgian consumer organization, Association des Consommateurs (AC), more than doubled its number of subscriptions from 102,000 to 240,000, while the other, Union Féminine pour l'Information et la Défense du Consommateur (UFIDEC), grew from 85,000 to 100,000. Both have continued under the longtime management of faithful directors. The quality certifying organization, though changing name to L'Institut du Contrôle de la Qualité et d'Etiquetage Informatif, may even have slipped further from view. The Conseil de la Consommation continues its interest in informative labeling. Radio-Télévision Belge continues with TV consumer programs that are participated in by the two consumer groups and others. A women's group within the cooperatives has established a special telephone service, d'Infor-Femmes, which two half days a week gives out information to twenty to thirty callers per session based on studies and tests. The commercial practices law of 1970 deals with the description of goods, certain sales techniques and advertising, and prohibits pyramid selling, door-to-door selling and the mailing of unsolicited goods. For the first time, in spring 1975, a Belgian court recognized the right of an association to sue on behalf of its members. The development of great interest on the Belgian scene in the product information area is that of the Association des Consommateurs.

Association Des Consommateurs (AC)
Giant strides have been made by this organization as indicated by its March 1975 subscriber roll of 243,213. Management remains in

the same hands as in 1969. The journal *Test Achats* appears in French and Flemmish with subscribers about evenly divided between the two editions. It has maintained the same format and size, appearing eleven times a year, with an occasional special number of summaries of tests.

In October 1970 AC launched a new quarterly publication available to *Test Achats* subscribers only, *Test Budget*, similar in many ways to CA's *Money Which?*, though *Test Budget* is a separate journal of forty pages. In March 1975, 65,689 subscribed. In May 1974 *Test Droits* appeared, covering issues of consumer law. Also quarterly and forty pages, it had 13,022 subscribers in March 1975. Some 27 percent of AC's subscribers take *Budget*, some 5 percent *Droit* and 11 percent take all three publications.

Below are the schedules of charges for the three publications:

	1974	1975
Test Achats	250BF[a]	300BF
Test Achats + Test Budget	430	480
Test Achats + Test Droits	450	500
Test Achats + Test Budget + Test Droits	600	600

Reductions are made if subscription is taken for three years.

Beginning in 1972 AC has issued a number of consumer guides of about 150 pages each. Their titles to date: small savings, family planning, hi-fi, credit, slimming, nourishment.

AC's budget for 1975 should have been in excess of 75 million BF, using AC subscriber figures and subscription charges as indications of income. According to internal accounts, within the seven month period July 1, 1974–January 31, 1975 AC received 30 million BF and spent 28 million BF. If these months are typical it would indicate a year's expenditure somewhere in excess of 50 million BF.

Staff has almost doubled since 1970, from thirty-two to sixty. Most of the increase is due to the addition of the new journals. The electrotechnical laboratory, Euro-Labo, has now been spun off and is independently budgeted, though still managed by AC's director. The number of tests performed in this lab has grown from seven in 1971 with a total of twenty participating groups representing half a dozen countries to eighteen in 1974 with forty participants. In other areas cosmopolitan AC works with seventeen different laboratories: eight in Belgium, three in France, two each in U.K., Germany and

[a]The rate of exchange in 1976 was Belgian francs 40 to U.S. $1.

Holland. Having rented space since it was formed, AC had plans to move into its own quarters in 1976.

The number of product tests reported in 1974 was forty-two, compared with twenty-nine in 1969. The number of brands has increased even more dramatically: from 462 to 858. The number of tests are distributed among the categories as shown in Table E–1.

AC remains very much a first class subscriber service; it is in no way a lobbying group. Membership in the government Conseil de Consommation is of little consequence. For three or four years the two professors who act as president and treasurer of the association collected data from AC subscribers on buying intentions. In the spring of 1975 AC was embroiled in two legal matters, one involving an article on mercury in fish, the other, the dispensing of ethical drugs without prescriptions.

The big news in 1969 was the accord between AC and Union Fédérale de la Consommation (UFC, now named Union Fédérale des Consommateurs) in France. As detailed in the *Handbook*, the agreement to combine testing and publication between the two organizations occurred at a time when AC had 100,000 subscribers and UFC less than 10,000. Under the brilliant leadership and massive promotional effort of AC, UFC grew rapidly to 200,000 subscribers by the end of 1973! At that time UFC's board, anxious to resume pre-1969 activities—legal advice, local consumer association work, lobbying— changed its bylaws so that one-third of the board would be selected from local consumer groups. While a committee of eight, four from AC and four from UFC, had ostensibly directed the efforts of the two organizations, AC's director had managed the operation fairly independently (some French observers would say autocratically). Fearing a shift from subscription generating and maintaining activities, AC wanted some changes in the arrangements. Several attempts at agreement, including some manifestly ill-conceived ones, coupled with UFC's very poor management of the sizeable sums flowing in as subscriptions soared to 300,000, came to a head in the fall of 1974. At that time several board members resigned at the UFC General Assembly meeting when the last draft AC-UFC accord was not accepted.

Differences between the two organizations were finally ironed out with the aid of BEUC and the Dutch Consumentenbond. As of 1975 the two organizations are again separate and independent. UFC has agreed to pay back debts (reportedly £140,000 for 1973 and £60,000 for 1974) and to pay in advance for any future testing carried out by AC.

The collapse of the collaboration between AC and UFC was perhaps less a source of amazement than the fact that a semimerger had

Table E-1. Association des Consommateurs. Comparative Test Reports in *Test Achats* **1969 and 1974**

| | Number of Tests | | Number of Brands[a] | |
	1969	1974	1969	1974
Textiles	—	3	—	38
Foods	5	11	83	271
Major household appliances	5	6	82	57
Minor household appliances	4	4	73	52
Household utensils and supplies	4	3	78	37
TV and audio	3	6	50	116
Hygiene, medical, cosmetics and toiletries	2	2	23	71
Sports, recreational, educational and travel goods	6	7	73	216
Cars	—	—	—	—
Services	4	b	—	—
Totals	33	42	462	858

[a]Services not included
[b]Not available
Note: See Appendix B for product categories.

been effectuated and lasted for a solid five years. Here were two very different organizations, one a subscriber service, the other for all practical purposes a second order consumer group with lobbying a prime concern. UFC had been in the testing field only incidentally, though jealously guarding their prerogatives in the area. In neither group was there a groundswell of consumer activists.

ENGLAND

Through energy crises, rampant inflation, devaluation, postal increases, unemployment, labor disturbances and all the other economic tribulations affecting Britain, the big private consumer organization Consumers' Association has remained a staunch consumer voice in England. With the demise of the Consumer Council in 1971, CA, its council and senior staff were called on to represent the consumer in government circles and especially the British consumer in EEC matters. In late 1973 the Office of Fair Trading, under a director general, was set up with wide powers and a large staff to inquire into virtually any trade practice affecting consumers. An independent Consumer

Protection Advisory Committee was appointed to examine his proposals and recommend new laws to strengthen the position of the consumer in the marketplace. In 1974 a Department of Prices and Consumer Protection with ministerial rank was set up as one of three new departments created from the former Department of Trade and Industry. In 1975 an independent National Consumers' Council was appointed to see that the consumer voice is loudly heard and ostensibly to establish consumers as the fourth estate, along with the industry, labor and the government. The British Standards Institution has set up a Consumer Standards Advisory Committee to replace the Women's Advisory Committee.

Consumers' Association (CA)

By February 1975 CA had increased its subscribers to *Which?* to 700,000 and its budget to £2.7 million. Subscription and budget figures appear in Tables E-2 and E-3. Voting membership, however, has not grown appreciably since it was generally opened to subscribers in 1968; at that time 1,300 were voting members, in 1975, 2,000.

Which? appears monthly. *Money Which?*, *Motoring Which?* and *Handyman Which?* appear quarterly as bound-in supplements, except for the *Money Which?* issue in March, which is devoted exclusively to tax saving, and the *Motoring Which?* issue in July, which is presented as a buying guide. *Holiday Which?*, a superlative addition introduced in February 1973, is a totally separate publication appearing quarterly with sixty-four pages an issue. Almost one-third of CA subscribers take four of the *Which?* periodicals, not counting *Holiday Which?* The fact that *Holiday Which?* had not met with appreciable success compared with the other publications has undoubtedly been in large part due to Britain's austere economic situation with the recession in travel the most severe since World War II.

The majority of existing subscribers paid in 1973–74 at a rate held constant since 1965, £1.50.[b] Subscribers from 1970 to September 1974 paid £2.50. Subsequent subscribers pay £3.75. The *Annual Report* of 1973–74 promised "that present members will be asked to bring their own subscriptions more closely into line."

Staff at CA has increased from 306 in 1970 to 391 in 1974, including temporary and part-time staff and accounting for 26 percent of the expenditures. CA's laboratory at Harpenden, a suburb of London, which was barely on stream in 1970 now has a staff of forty-two permanent (of which twenty-five are professionals) and twelve to fifteen regular part-time employees. With 15,250 square feet of laboratory

[b]The rate of exchange in 1976 was £1 to U.S. $1.75.

Table E-2. Consumers' Association. Subscription Statistics 1970 and 1975

	March 31, 1970	*February 28, 1975*
Which? (monthly)	610,000	703,982
Money Which? (quarterly)	366,000	553,517
Motoring Which? (quarterly)	195,000	388,779
Handyman Which? (quarterly)	a	428,542
Holiday Which? (quarterly)	b	43,619

[a]Began publication November 1971
[b]Began publication February 1973

Table E-3. Consumers' Association. Income and Expenditures 1970 and 1974 (in thousands of pounds)

	1970	*1974*
Income		
Sales and subscriptions	1,595	2,547
Interest on investments		88
Sundry[a]		118
Total	1,595	2,753
Expenditures		
Research	420	643
Which? printing and dispatch	303	558
Publications	119	165
Subscription administration	150	205
Promotion	416	631
Cost of premises	83	105
Administration costs	127	233
Information and representation	32	153
Taxation	—	18
Total	1,650	2,711

[a]This includes £24,734 from sales of research to the media, £46,560 from sales of research to European consumer organizations and £27,569 from consultancy contract for the Department of Prices and Consumer Protection.
Note: For the years ending March 31

space and equipment valued at £80,000, CA now performs two-thirds of their own tests, some 110–120 projects a year at an estimated £180,000 of work. The laboratory does some testing for other institutions, such as the test for the Institute of Consumer Ergonomics on alarm systems for the elderly sponsored by the National Corporation for the Care of Old People. But 90 percent of all their work is for CA. The laboratory is not involved in editorial policy. CA is a leading partner in the European Testing Group which jointly conducts tests for the benefit of those organizations participating in a specific test (see Chapter Four).

Table E-4 gives the data on test results appearing in the twelve issues of *Which?* publications, not including *Holiday Which?*, from May 1974 to April 1975, with figures for 1969 for comparison. As is amply clear, the number of tests has decreased considerably, though the number of brands has remained about the same. It may be hypothesized that having a captive laboratory with the attendant initial drain on fiscal resources and time constraints to complete projects may be an important factor. Then, too, CA, like Consumers Union, has devoted considerable resources in staff and money to nontesting matters.

CA continues with its discussion of value for money and used the "best buy" format in seven test reports (two in *Handyman Which?*) and "joint best buys" in seven reports (one in *Handyman Which?*). With the addition of the lab facility, CA has instituted a "What's New" column, appearing monthly, updating information of past reports and a quick look at new products.

The Consumer Publications Paperback Series continues with some seventeen new titles since 1970 (seven remaining). A TV correspondence course sponsored by the Open University in 1975 used CA's

Table E-4. Consumers' Association. Comparative Test Reports in *Which?*, *Motoring Which?*, *Money Which?* and *Handyman Which?* 1969 and 1974-75

	Number of tests		Number of brands[b]	
	1969	1974-75[a]	1969	1974-75
Textiles	7	4	223	181
Foods	13	1	146	39
Major household appliances	16	16	101	117
Minor household appliances	21	6	112	72
Household utensils and supplies	37	16	294	262
TV and audio	7	8	75	159
Hygiene products, medicine, cosmetics and toiletries	13	1	71	56
Sports, recreational, education and travel goods	32	16	226	337
Cars	12	8	26	27
Services	29	6[c]	—	—
Totals	187	82	1274	1250

[a]For the calendar year 1969; the twelve issues appearing May 1974-April 1975
[b]Services not included
[c]*Holiday Which?* is not included
Note: See Appendix B for product categories.

"Coping with Disablement" as a textbook. A series by CA entitled "Wise Buying," and published by Longman's, is part of CA's recently undertaken school projects. In collaboration with the Office of Fair Trading, the British Standards Institution and the Inner London Education Authority, CA has prepared an education kit for schools.

CA's survey unit continues with monthly readership surveys and its more detailed questionnaires on specified subject matter; product liability, reliability and servicing of electrical appliances, satisfaction with gas servicing, and footwear were the subjects of some recent surveys. The subscription-based, £5 a year, Advice and Complaints Service is in an experimental stage. The Advice Centre Servicing Unit, however, has trained the staff of some fifty advice centers and mobile units administered by local governmental authorities. CA has developed the materials used by the centers and even employs the staff for three such centers. The unit serves as a hotline for the local operations. The Special Projects Unit has a contract with a London paper to write a consumer page every month. Thames and BBC TV occasionally order programs on such matters as hygiene, common market, price surveys, credit, cosmetics, strength of beer, water in chicken. This unit also supplies radio tapes, and a lawyer with CA appears with a disc jockey once a week.

Members of CA's senior staff meet as a Consumer Campaign Committee once a fortnight to prepare position papers on broader questions affecting consumers: enforcement of legislation, advertising and labeling, metrication, credit. CA is invariably called upon to give evidence to various commissions investigating consumer matters.

CA's European Unit operates under a consultancy agreement with the new Department of Prices and Consumer Protection to examine especially the common agricultural and harmonization policies of the EEC. This unit, with four full-time staffers, performs research in such areas as food labeling, hygiene of poultry, sizing and unit pricing, antibiotics in foods, and testing of imported and domestic E-marks for safety in electrical products.

Acting as secretariat, CA participates in the newly formed Consumers' Co-ordinating Group which represents more than a dozen British organizations interested in consumer matters. Meeting six times a year to examine background papers on topical consumer issues, they include such bodies as the Coop Union, Trading Standards, the National Federation of Consumer Groups and various women's associations.

With Britain's entry into the common market CA became a full-fledged member of the Bureau Européen des Unions de Consommateurs (BEUC). CA's deputy director is the part-time director of BEUC.

Department of Prices and Consumer Protection

The department has responsibility for consumer affairs, including consumer protection and safety, consumer credit, standards, and weights and measures. It supervises the work of the Price Commission and deals with prices in the shops including food and food subsidies (The Prices Act of 1974). It has the responsibility of the Office of Fair Trading (OFT), which is concerned with monopolies, mergers and restrictive trade practices and consumer affairs, and for the Metrication Board. Figure E-1 attempts to depict the areas of concern of relevance here. The staff serving under the permanent secretary numbers around 300.

The divisions dealing with consumer protection are Fair Trading; Standards, Weights and Measures; and Consumer Credit. Fair Trading is responsible for general competition policy, consumer protection (other than weights and measures and consumer credit) and product safety, the latter taken over from the Home Office. It also deals with questions on pyramid selling, real estate agents, auctions, door-to-door selling, stamp trading, privacy and product liability. Though this division is concerned with much the same areas as the Office of Fair Trading (below), divisional directives are political and administrative rather than statutory.

Fair Trading also handles a number of EEC matters (rules of competition, harmonization of laws on unfair competition, EEC program and directives on consumer protection) and other international matters such as the OECD Committee on Consumer Policy. It serves as the secretariat to the Consumer Protection Advisory Committee (below) and as liaison with the new National Consumers' Council (below). It also promotes the work of the now 600 Citizens' Advice Bureaux and fifty local advice centers. The division is much involved with preparation of proposed new legislation, such as the Sale of Services Act, corresponding to the Sale of Goods (Implied Terms) Act of 1973.

The Standards, Weights and Measures Division supervises the work of the eighty to one hundred local Trading Standards Departments (formerly Weights and Measures authorities), and handles matters such as price marking, unit pricing, packaging. Consumer Credit was in 1975 writing instructions and regulations to make the Consumer Credit Act of 1974 effective. Among other things the law specifies that all credit-granting entities are to be licensed, probably entailing as many as 100,000 licenses.

The Office of Fair Trading (OFT).   The OFT is a statutory agency headed by a director general appointed by the Secretary of State for

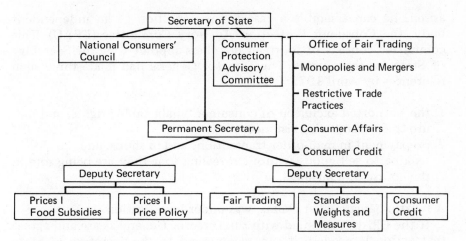

Figure E-1. Department of Prices and Consumer Protection: Partial Organization

five years. As shown in Figure E-1 it is organized into four major divisions: monopolies and mergers, restrictive trade practices, consumer affairs, and consumer credit. The OFT had a staff of 196 on December 31, 1974, with Consumer Affairs accounting for some forty.

The Fair Trading Act (Eliz II, 1973, c 41) required the Director General "to keep under review the carrying on of commercial activities" relating to the supply of goods and services to consumers in the U.K. and to collect information with respect to such activities where they may adversely affect economic and other interests of such consumers. Information reaches the OFT from a variety of sources, Citizens' Advice Bureaux, local authority consumer advice centers, consumer organizations, Trading Standards Departments, and through the OFT's own information-gathering activities. The OFT does not handle individual complaints, but does collect statistics and analyze by type of goods and services and by trading practice complaints received by other groups. Some 160,000 consumer complaints were catalogued by April 1975.

In consumer matters the Director General has three broad powers: to make proposals to the Consumer Protection Advisory Committee, to promote voluntary codes of practice in the trades, and to obtain agreements with individual traders or companies who violate civil or criminal law in a manner detrimental to consumers.

If the Director General feels that a pattern of unfair trading has arisen, he can assemble a case for presentation to an independent body, the Consumer Protection Advisory Committee (CPAC). This committee consists of fourteen members appointed by the Secretary of State for three years. The Director General had made three such references by April 1975:

1. the purported exclusion of consumer "inalienable" rights, and failure to explain their existence;
2. prepayment in mail-order transactions and in shops; and
3. seeking to sell goods without revealing that they are being sold in the course of a business.

A fourth, bargain offer claims, was under investigation.

If the CPAC is satisfied with the Director General's case and agrees that action is needed, it can recommend to the Secretary of State that a draft order to deal with the unfair practice be laid before Parliament for approval. The committee's report on the first reference was presented to Parliament at the end of 1974. If approval is given and the order is made, Trading Standards Departments may prosecute offenders at court.

The OFT has achieved success in persuading two trade associations to prepare and disseminate codes of practice. The Association of Manufacturers of Domestic Electrical Appliances, which includes all U.K. manufacturers, adopted a code of practice on servicing (AMDEA Code); the Association of British Travel Agents, which includes most agencies, adopted a code (ABTA Code). The Electricity Council, a nationalized industry, has a code on servicing. OFT is currently working in three areas: automobiles, both new and used; footwear; and radio and television.

Of especial interest in this connection is the Code of Advertising Practice (CAP Code), first adopted in 1962. The Advertising Standards Authority, an independent body set up and paid for by the advertising industry, is to ensure that its system of self-regulation works in the public interest. It is a remarkable document of clarity and forthrightness. In his first annual report, the Director General assured the Secretary of State that he will take a keen interest in this field to see whether the system can prove itself satisfactory and effective.

OFT has the details of 12,000 convictions imposed on traders during the past five years. Of the thirty-seven companies investigated, three have been asked to give written assurances that they will refrain from persisting in the detrimental course of conduct. One has done so. If a company breeches an agreement, the matter is referred to the Restrictive Practices Court. The office maintains a special central register of convictions under consumer legislation. During 1974,

3,221 convictions were entered in the register, amounting to almost £200,000 in penalties.

An information division of the OFT has prepared leaflets for general distribution, a handbook describing how the law protects consumers, sets of posters, a teaching packet, arranged interviews and tapes for the broadcast media. While OFT plans to continue to prepare printed materials, a spokesman indicated that "written information is of limited value," and that more emphasis would be placed on oral information.

National Consumers' Council (NCC)

The NCC, set up in early 1975, is a nonstatutory body with a projected membership of fifteen appointed by the Secretary of State. As described in a White Paper (Cmnd 5726) published in September 1974 it will:

1. make representations of the consumer view to central and local government, to the director general of Fair Trading, to industry, and to any other quarter where a consumer voice ought to be needed;
2. be available to be consulted by those, including the government, seeking a consumer view on policies and proposals;
3. represent the consumer on appropriate government and other bodies, including international organizations;
4. review the present arrangements for consumer representation in the nationalized organizations.

It will not deal directly with individual consumer complaints.

The selection of Michael Young as NCC's first chairman indicates the Labour government's seriousness of purpose. As founder and first chairman of CA and its president since 1965, and as the first chairman of the Social Science Research Council, Young has been energetic, insightful and inventive. In a statement accepting the appointment in early 1975 he stressed two examples of the sort of work he hopes the new council will do: pressing the case for price restraint, for which income restraint is a necessity; and getting the poorer consumers of social and other services treated with more respect.

NCC's budget is reported to be around £300,000 annually, though specially requested projects will probably be funded separately. NCC was not yet in operation at the time of writing.

FRANCE

By 1975 consumers in France had available two outstanding comparative testing journals: *Que Choisir?*, published by a private consumer organization; and *50 Millions de Consommateurs*, published by the government, each claiming around 300,000 circulation. Even assuming some overlap of circulation to these two magazines, a respectable 3-4 percent of French households have sought objective product information and have been willing to pay for it. A reported 745 local or regional consumer groups were in operation. The informative labeling organization, founded in late 1970, had achieved some success at a time when the Swedish, English and Dutch labeling organizations had either been abandoned outright or left to expire.

Yet another labor union–sponsored consumer group appeared on the scene, though it may be no more than an offshoot of the union itself. The government continued to grant subsidies to some private groups. In 1975 these amounted to half a million francs. The Laboratoire coopératif d'analyses et de recherches changed its name to Laboratoire coopératif pour l'information, la protection et la representation des consommateurs. Its test review, *Labo-Coop*, reported 115,000 circulation in 1973.

New legislation, the Loi d'Orientation du Commerce et de l'Artisanat of December 27, 1973, called familiarly le loi Royer after the minister who was instrumental in its passing, Jean Royer, contained a new provision of far-reaching importance. It allows all duly registered associations whose declared aim is to defend consumer interests to seek redress by civil action in any court for practices that directly or indirectly damage the collective interests of consumers. In 1974, two organizations sued a manufacturer of meat pies on behalf of consumers for misrepresenting the quality of his merchandise and for misleading advertising. In a historic decision they were awarded a symbolic 1 franc.

Le loi Royer also strengthened the regulations concerning false or misleading information or presentation. Those who disseminate information may also be liable. Further, advertisers may be required to justify claims. Courts are empowered to enjoin the continued use of certain advertising and to require amending statements. New legislation exists on door-to-door selling. Prepackaged foods, with notable exceptions, are required to be labeled with net weight or volume, all ingredients and additives, and expirary date for perishable products.

Private Organizations

Union Fédérale des Consommateurs (UFC). With less than 10,000 subscribers in 1970, UFC's journal, *Que Choisir?*, could boast 300,000 subscribers in November 1974. As discussed earlier, this explosive development was directly due to the cooperation with Association des

Consommateurs initiated in 1969. This arrangement collapsed in the fall of 1974 (see above under Belgium). The French journals are no longer edited and printed in Brussels. It is claimed that UFC plans to gradually build up its own testing organization. It will surely buy tests from AC and participate in the European Testing Group tests during the next few years, however.

New bylaws adopted in 1973 prescribed that one-third of the board would be representatives from some thirty local consumer groups affiliated with UFC. *Le Monde* stated on December 14, 1974, that these locals had some 3,500 members. The lasting effect of seven members resigning when a new AC-UFC proposal was stoutly rejected by UFC's General Assembly is not known. It was reported that these "Paris Seven" founded a new organization called Association Française des Consommateurs.

UFC is no longer a member of the big government Institut National de la Consommation. Claiming that this organization was not independent of government and objecting both to business representation on the board and the fact that INC entered the testing field, UFC withdrew in 1972. Together with some ten other organizations in 1972, UFC formed or rather regrouped under the name Comité de Coordination des Organisations de Consommateurs (CCOC) with the secretariat at the offices of the Fédération Nationale des Cooperatives de Consommation. The aim of CCOC, according to the IOCU Directory, is "concerted agreement for activities in the field of consumer protection."

Assuming UFC averaged 200,000 subscribers in 1973–74, with subscriptions costs at 46 F each, the budget should be a whopping 9.2 million F.[c] UFC also received a 100,000 F subsidy from the government. Even if massive amounts were spent on promotion it is difficult to understand how UFC built up its big debts to AC.

During the more than five years of the AC-UFC accord, *Que Choisir?* and *Test Achats*, the Belgian journal, were almost identical, using the same layout, pictures, tables, discussions. Not infrequently, however, more tests items were used in one country (seventeen pressure cookers in *QC?* and fifteen in *TA*; thirty-nine cartridges with stylus in *TA* and thirty-seven in *QC?*) than in the other, presumably in response to local market conditions. Interestingly, *TA* stated that pressure cookers had not become a usual household item but needed to be tested, while *QC?* stated that they had become usual and therefore needed testing. Especially noteworthy are the different conclusions reached by *TA* and *QC?* on the same test results. Both magazines

[c]The rate of exchange in 1976 was French francs 4.76 to U.S. $1.

have phono cartridge Jelco MC 14E listed with exactly the same results, but *QC?* does not list it in its recommendations and *TA* lists it first. In 1969, *QC?* published nineteen tests; in 1974, forty-two. The reader is referred to the Table 11.1 in the *Handbook* for the 1969 classification, and to Table E–1.

It is not known whether subscribers were aware of what has been dubbed by British observers as the "Franco-Belgian War." The only interruption in publication occurred with the January 1975 issue, when UFC announced to subscribers that *QC?* was securing necessary "independent financing." *QC?* is available only on subscription.

UFC also has launched *Que Choisir Budget?*, which was very different from *Test Achats Budget*, presumably due to major differences in Belgian and French financial markets. Here the only savings, aside from management, accrued in the general layout and the long-term arrangements with the printers.

The phenomenal success of AC-UFC's promotional activities indicate that Information Seekers do exist and are reachable in France, and that they will support a publication geared to their need for product information.

Organisation Générale des Consommateurs (OR.GE.CO.).   Established in 1959 by four syndicalist labor unions, OR.GE.CO. continues to exist with headquarters at a new address. It received a 42,000 F subsidy from the government in 1975. It is still represented in BEUC.

F.O. Consommateurs. A new organization, formed under the auspices of the powerful trade union Force Ouvrière, was created in 1974 for reasons that remain obscure despite a three page interview with a high official of both organizations appearing in *50 Millions de Consommateurs* in May 1975. Called F.O. Consommateurs, it could claim an instant membership of 950,000. Supposedly each member pays 1–2 F. It is difficult to be enthusiastic as to the future of this paper dragon in the cause of the consumer. Force Ouvrière had been the leading partner in OR.GE.CO. There is no indication that matters will change appreciably.

Public Organizations

Institut National de la Consommation (INC). Under the able direction of Henry Estingoy, INC has enjoyed continued growth and increased prestige. New statutes have reinforced the stability and multipurposefulness of this government agency in its effort to provide consumer information and coordination of information concerning consumers and consumer groups. INC is charged with weighing opinions and needs of all partners in the marketplace. Its board in 1975 included four senior staff. The authority of the director relative to the board has increased dramatically, undoubtedly in recognition of the success of INC in its work. Professional personnel concerned with publication matters numbered over fifty.

The budget of INC in 1975 was probably at least 20 million francs, with about one-half generated by the sale of publications. Government grants have grown from 3.5 million francs in 1970 to over 9 million in 1975.

INC's major publication aimed at the general public, *50 Millions de Consommateurs*, reached over 300,000 in circulation, with subscribers accounting for about 60 percent. In 1974 a subscription cost 25 F for twelve issues; in 1975, 35 F. Single copies were available at newsstands for 2.50 F.

50 is a highly noteworthy addition to the consumer information field. Its appearance and layout are totally professional, its style readable, its presentation both concise and comprehendable without sacrificing thoroughness and accuracy. A "What's new" (*produits nouveaux*) section allows INC to examine individual products of special interest as they appear on the market but prior to its usual detailed study of many brands. Almost one-third of the fifty-two page journal is devoted to comparative tests. During 1974–75 the journal was much concerned with high-rise rental complexes and generally matters relating to housing. The coverage of consumer questions and affairs has ranged broadly over the entire field including such matters as dental care, medical problems, pollution, repairs, services, mail order, food products, public services, packaging, court system and moving. Interviews by INC with prominent spokesmen from both political and organization life have appeared regularly during 1974–75.

Consommateurs Actualité is still aimed at experts in consumer affairs, though its format since the beginning of 1975 has shifted considerably, making it appealing to an interested layman. Now released twenty-two times a year at 80 F a subscription and 5 F a copy, *CA* is a sixteen page, tightly written, small print, three column presentation of topical matters in consumer news at home and abroad, as well as long-range research projects and analyses wherever performed. Specific columns appearing regularly: environment, energy, health, daily life, legal and economic communications, foods, and other products.

INC issues consumer guides (pocketbooks) dealing with such subjects as stoves, watches, housing, automobiles, savings, vacations and insurance that sell for 9.50 F and are available at bookstores. Avail-

Table E-5. Institut National de la Consommation. Comparative Test Reports in *50 Millions de Consommateurs* **1974**

	Number of tests[a]	Number of brands[b]
Textiles	4	70
Foods	7	130
Major household appliances	3	46
Minor household appliances	—	—
Household utensils and supplies	1	12
TV and audio	2	25
Hygiene products, medicines, cosmetics and toiletries	4	97
Sports, recreational, educational and travel goods	2	23
Cars	—	—
Services	1	—
Totals	24	403

[a]For the calendar year 1974; twelve issues January 1974–January 1975 (November 1974 issue not on hand, substituting January 1975)
[b]Services not included

able from INC are some fifty *Notes d'information* at 2 F to orient the consumer briefly on a variety of subjects such as credit, furnished apartments, textile fibers, used cars, door-to-door selling and mail order.

INC regularly broadcast two TV programs in 1975, "6 minutes pour vous défendre" each Saturday night at 6:39 and "D'accord, pas D'accord" each Tuesday, Thursday and Saturday night at 8:30.

Following the prescriptions of its statute, INC has indeed become a center for tests. By 1975 INC had published ninety-four comparative tests, averaging about two a month. As shown in Table E-5, twenty-four were reported in 1974, covering some 403 brands. INC has had no problem in reaching conclusions based on the comparative tests of brands. Price is invariably a consideration. After testing fashion watches INC concluded that they were less a question of consumption than they were of wastage (*gaspillage*). INC will test additional models if manufacturers complain. Some studies are presented comparing prices of brands in different kinds of shops.

In the January 1975 issue of *50*, INC included a four page questionnaire to learn more about subscribers, their views of *50*, and their wants and needs, actions and attitudes.

Association Française pour l'Etiquetage d'Information (AFEI). As the Swedish VDN, the avowed leader in the informative labeling area in 1970, quietly slips from sight, AFEI, founded in 1970 by INC and the Conseil National de Patronat Français (CNPF, the Confederation of French Industry) and headquartered at INC, has managed to demonstrate its seriousness by adopting norms and by selling a number of them to industry. In a country where industry has traditionally been slow in recognizing consumers as worthy of consideration, the accomplishments are striking. Table E-6 gives data on the schemes in operation as of April 1974. Some ten additional norms had been adopted (detergents, insecticides, deodorant, sheets, refrigerators, freezers, black and white TV, shampoo and toilet paper), and some six products were under study (salad oil, chocolate, canned goods, shoes, baby products and carpeting). According to reports, the carpeting and rug labels are expected to cover 85 percent of the French production during 1976.

If an AFEI-labeled product conforms to standards set by AFNOR (Association Française de Normalisation, the French standardization group), and many products are required to do so by law, the label will carry this information. It will also show where the product falls on a scale depicting the AFNOR standard minimum and the maximum quality available in the market.

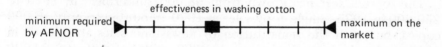

Perhaps following the recommendations of the authors, AFEI has issued a eight by four inch booklet of all labels so that the consumer may compare labels even before visiting any store. The first issue of over 100 pages appeared in January 1974.

Table E-6. Association Française pour l'Etiquetage d'Information. Labeling Statistics, April 24, 1974

Product	Number of manufacturers	Number of brands	Number of models or varieties	Market covered
Washing machines	12	13	49	c 80%
Vacuum cleaners	7	7	21	c 60%
Gas stoves	3	3	18	
Sleeping bags	1	1	4	
Food products	4	26	96	
Total	24	50	188	

Source: Information obtained by letter from the director, M.R. Ement, AFEI, September 3, 1974.

AFEI followed up the thirty-eight consumer complaints—a modest number indeed—in 1973.

GERMANY

Unlike England, France, Belgium and the Netherlands, Germany has no private national consumer organization that publishes reports on product tests. The Arbeitsgemeinschaft der Verbraucherverbände (AGV, the Council of Consumer Associations) remains a second order organization, composed in 1975 of some thirty-two organizations and 50 percent financed by the government. Local consumers centers (Verbraucherzentrale, VZ) specializing in counseling have grown both in number and in importance. They are government financed. *DM*, which in 1970 still commanded the attention of the Information Seeker, has stagnated in circulation. Stiftung Warentest's *test*, on the other hand, has quadrupled its circulation. While RAL's quality certification program has continued, its informative labeling schemes are in abeyance.

Stiftung Warentest (STIWA)

The journal *test* has grown from 68,000 subscribers in 1970 to 250,000 in 1975. Single copy sales in 1970 amounted to only 16,000 copies, but with the reinstitution of newsstand sales abandoned in 1967, such sales soared to about 225,000, with an additional 20,000 still sold directly from STIWA. Schools, press, TV and radio, and other such institutions accounted for 28,500 gratis copies. All total STIWA printed some 545,000 copies a month. The cost of a subscription in 1975 was DM 24, DM 2.50 a copy.

In 1973 STIWA published its first yearbook. Unlike CU which includes the last report on products tested regardless of date, STIWA's yearbook is limited to product tests reported during the year. The yearbook is not included in the annual subscription. It sold for DM 7.50 in 1975.

STIWA's budget jumped from DM 4.6 million in 1969 to DM 14.4 million in 1974, with over one-half covered by the sales of publications.[d] The director anticipated a government grant of DM 7.7 million for 1975, and stated that STIWA was now close to 60 percent self-financing. With a staff of some ninety, only a slight increase since 1969, STIWA is now being subject to government personnel rules, especially as they pertain to pay scales.

[d]The rate of exchange in 1976 was DM 2.56 to U.S. $1.

STIWA has continued its practice of preparing special summary reports for the press. This has paid enormous dividends. Some 300 newspapers and magazines reprinted STIWA's handouts in forty million copies a month in 1975. STIWA's coverage in the mass media, both on TV and in newspapers, has undoubtedly been the prime reason for the growth in circulation, as STIWA allots less than 5 percent of its budget to promotion.

Test is a sixty page monthly with a four page cardboard insert, easily removable, containing a summary of the test reports appearing in that issue. When cut apart these synopses (called "test kompass") can be saved in a standard card file for ready reference. Three-fourths of the magazine is devoted to tests. In the issue examined (April 1975), five product and two service tests were reported. In addition *test* gave two market overviews, one on prices and one on warranties. The director indicated that such overviews would as a rule include buying advice and cover such matters as care and maintenance. General consumer articles, now less than 10 percent of the journal, will gradually take a growing share of the page content in the future.

Table E-7 gives the data on the product tests reported in 1975 and reproduced in the yearbook. Note that service tests are not included. Data from 1969 are included for comparison. While best buys are not listed as such, STIWA invariably gives an overall judgment of its test results. With resale price maintenance outlawed in Germany, price reporting in the test results has generally been the price suggested by the manufacturer. AGV has done an occasional price survey for STIWA, and the local consumer groups (VZ) have published compilations of the price range in the locality of the products tested by STIWA, although with what regularity is not known.

Reproduction of STIWA tests are not disallowed. *DM*'s presentation of the tests are nowhere near as thorough, and in fact in April 1975 a suit pending against *DM* attacked *DM*'s cavalier treatment of the data including additional evaluative comments by *DM*. The two big German mail-order firms, Quelle and Neckermann, have included on some of their product labels the fact that STIWA rated the product "gut."

STIWA continues to serve on standards committees and to be an active participant in international contexts. It is a council member of IOCU, and since 1974 has been an associate member of BEUC. While continuing as a leading partner in the European Testing Group, STIWA's position and the requirements of German law as to STIWA's responsibility for utmost rigor in all test reporting make for some hesitance in expanded use of the system. STIWA is pleased that other organizations reprint its tests.

Table E-7.   Stiftung Warentest. Comparative Test Reports in *test*, 1975

| | Number of tests | | Number of brands[a] | |
	1969	1975	1969	1975
Textiles	2	6	21	102
Foods	12	6	210	98
Major household appliances	9	8	101	123
Minor household appliances	5	6	83	128
Household utensils and supplies	8	5	159	95
TV and audio	4	8	57	171
Hygiene products, medicines, cosmetics and toiletries	4	2	59	65
Sports, recreational, educational and travel goods	14	23[b]	246	447[b]
Cars	4	—	4	—
Services	11	na	—	—
Totals	73	64[a]	940	1,229

[a]Services not included
[b]Car accessories accounted for seven tests and 138 brands

DM

While subscriptions to *DM* have doubled since 1969 from 20,000 to 40,000, newsstand sales have plummeted from a steady 100,000 to around 30–40,000 in mid-1975. The print order figure of 115,000 given by management includes some 35,000 copies that are included in the materials available to reading circle members.

The monthly *DM* sells at DM 3 an issue, DM 36 on subscription. Consumer-oriented articles account for about one-half of the content; advertisements, 30–35 percent; test reports, around 5 percent. Almost all of the tests are taken from STIWA's publication, with a lag of some months. The test reports are shortened and edited, with an embellishment not regarded favorably by STIWA. *DM* contrives its own quality index, the makeup of which is not explained.

With advertising revenue supplying one half of *DM*'s total, the magazine is returning a modest profit according to the managing editor. With all of the publicity surrounding STIWA's monthly release of test results, it is clear that *DM*'s role in supplying consumer product information has decreased during the 1970s. Yet by reprinting the test results *DM* does reinforce a modicum of objective information in the marketplace. The articles are generally examples of sophisticated consumer journalism.

RAL

In 1973 RAL became an association independent of DNA, the German standards organization. Since then its budget is derived in about equal proportions from the government, quality seal organizations and the sale of publications. The organizations issuing quality seals are now members of RAL, and in principle the letters RAL appear on all such marks (of which a great variety exist). The conditions of approval and continued use of quality marks remain essentially the same as before 1973. RAL-approved marks are registered by the German Patent Office.

As detailed in the *Handbook*, RAL was also the pioneer in the creation of an informative labeling system (RAL-TESTAT). Although endorsed by the Ministry of Commerce, the labeling program in the last few years has been in abeyance. Political, business and consumer organizations as well as various governmental bodies have been unable to reach agreement on whether the RAL-TESTAT or some other labeling system should be officially adopted by the Federal Republic and whether the system should be voluntary or obligatory. It is well-known that industry favors a voluntary system without minimum quality thresholds.

THE NETHERLANDS

Consumers in the Netherlands continue to support the big private organization, Consumentenbond (CB), which had grown to 470,000 members in 1975, or about 10 percent of the Dutch households. New on the scene is the CB- and industry-sponsored Stichting Consumentenklachten, handling consumer complaints. The labeling organization, Stichting voor Informatieve Etikettering, founded in 1964, expired quietly in April 1975. The meager resources, provided almost totally by subsidies through the Ministry for Economic Affairs, were never sufficient to engender the needed interest.

Consumentenbond (CB)

CB remains a very accessible organization. All subscribers are automatically members. Policies are openly debated at the annual meeting, and at the April 1975 meeting a group of activists made themselves loudly heard. Financial data are presented in Table E-8 with figures for 1970 for comparison. Staff had increased from seventy-one, including sixteen part time, to 119, with thirty part time. Some organi-

Table E-8.   Consumentenbond. Income and Expenditures 1970 and 1974 (in thousands of florins)

	1970	1974
Income		
Subscriptions		
Consumentengids	3,352	6,948
Consumenten Reisgids	a	290
Publications and informative circulars	48	99
Interest/investments	101	371
Reimbursements by Ministry of Economic Affairs[b]		58
Payment for VW testing		264
Diverse	226[b]	27[c]
Reserves		348
Expenditures		
Board meetings	19	39
General personnel and office costs	362	1,176
Membership registration	292	598
Publications		
Consumentengids	891	2,673
Consumenten Reisgids	a	369
Testing and research	1,617	1,811
Membership service and legal assistance	279	984
Public relations, advertising	208	356
Renovations and alterations		33
Diverse	362	247[d]
New posts[e]		119
Excess	147	
Total	3,727	8,405

[a]Not published until 1973

[b]For price surveys

[c]Included both years the sale of test products; in 1970 included both of the two posts listed immediately above

[d]Df 143,000 for membership in other organizations: i.a., BEUC, Df 31,000; IOCU, Df 45,000; VW, Df 12,500; Consumentenklachten, Df 36,000; local groups received Df 8,000 and court cases cost Df 52,000

[e]Includes costs for changes in membership administration, Df 101,000; management consulting fees, Df 13,000; contribution to an Indian consumer group, Df 5,000

zational changes have been made to reflect the increased importance of reporting financial matters and of providing legal assistance to members. For example, the legal assistance staff has grown from nine to twenty-five. A section of four handle financial reporting.

The *Consumentengids* (*CG*, Consumers Guide) has grown from 440 pages a year in 1970 to 568 in 1974. Still primarily a comparative testing journal, *CG* has broadened its reporting in related areas such as advertising, mail order, safety, energy, water and noise. A decided interest is taken in the question of the durability of products. Reports tend to be shorter; tests are repeated more often, though *CG* does not use the update format found in CU's *Consumer Reports* and CA's *Which?* In 1970 *CG* cost Df 12; in 1975, Df 19.[e]

In 1973 CB launched a separate *Consumenten Reisgids* (Consumer Travel Guide) available to members only. In January 1975 its subscription cost was raised from Df 10 to Df 14. At the end of 1973 subscriptions numbered 19,000; in 1974, 37,500; in 1975, 41,000. It is still a long way from breaking even. *Reisgids* appears quarterly in the same format as *CG*, with fifty-six pages an issue, carrying nine to thirteen articles on various recreation spots, with tables for comparison on facilities and estimated prices. In the four issues examined from 1974–75, three articles were from CA's *Holiday Which?*, one from the Austrian Verein für Konsumenteninformation's *Konsument* and one was an European Testing Group (ETG) project.

CB's laboratory is still small, even primitive when compared to those of CU, CA, KOV (Sweden) and VKI (Austria). Almost all tests are performed in outside labs. CB is a leading partner in the ETG, and continues to manage the tests ordered by Stichting Vergelijkend Warenonderzoek (VW).

The director of CB states that in the area of household and audio-visual equipment the quality of products has greatly improved during the past five years, and differences between brands have grown smaller. Based on survey research on subscribers, it appears, however, that readers still feel a need for detailed comparisons.

Table E–9 gives data on test reports and number of brands during the 1974–75 year, with 1969 information for comparison. While the number of tests has decreased, the number of brands has increased. CB no longer reports automobile tests. The Royal Netherlands Touring Association (ANWB) performed five CB-reported tests on auto accessories in 1974–75. Dutch and EEC regulations and directives on foods have undoubtedly influenced CB in discontinuing food tests. CB continues the practice of grading characteristics using symbols, but invariably gives conclusions as to the brand, or more likely, the brands that performed best.

Many of the thirteen services tests are in the financial area: insurance, investments, credit. CB has no plans to publish a separate journal on these matters as it is felt that there is an international market for money in Holland. Even if CB were to do so, the director stressed it would continue publishing financial articles in *CG*.

Of the tests appearing in 1974–75, ten were performed with at

[e]The rate of exchange in 1976 was Df 2.70 to U.S. $1.

Table E-9. Consumentenbond. Comparative Test Reports in *Consumenten-gids* 1969 and 1974-75

	Number of Tests		Number of Brands[b]	
	1969	1974-75[a]	1969	1974-75
Textiles	6	6	121	85
Foods	9	—	66	—
Major household appliances	13	3	85	52
Minor household appliances	9	5	72	57
Household utensils and supplies	19	9	94	178
TV and audio	12	6	52	173
Hygiene products, medicines, cosmetics and toiletries	6	—	94	—
Sports, recreational, educational and travel goods	28	23	117	358
Cars	—	—	—	—
Services	11	13		
Totals	113	65	701	903

[a]For the calendar year 1969; twelve issues May 1974-May 1975 (October issue out of print, substituting May 1975)
[b]Services not included

least one other consumer organization, often with two or more. CB's usual partners were Association des Consommateurs (AC, Belgium) and CA, though Stiftung Warentest (STIWA, Germany) participated in three, and Forbrukerrådet (Norway) in one. Seven tests were reprinted from VW directly; and VW participated with AC and STIWA in a test. ANWB participated in a STIWA-AC test. Altogether twenty-two of the fifty-two product tests were jointly executed.

CB does a brisk business in the sale of single copies of *CG*. For a nominal fee, members can obtain written information, called *koopwijzer* (buying advice), on almost any consumer product tested. These mimeographed circulars often combine a number of products performing similar work, such as the one on table and hand mixers, liquifiers and juicers. Between 10-12,000 copies of *CG* and *koopwijzer* are distributed a month. Telephone service is heavily used as an information channel: 35,000-40,000 calls a month![1]

To commemorate membership rolls reaching 400,000, CB in 1973 distributed 20,000 free sets of ten standard consumer contract conditions to pressure consumer products industries to review and standardize their sale contracts. Terms included warranties, delivery time, repairs, payment and an obligation of manufacturers to sell a product conforming to advertising claims. CB was refused permission to advertise the campaign on TV, but the TV news picked up the story as well as the daily press. Shops were allowed to reprint if no changes were made. CB has not sought any feedback on use by consumers.

Local groups have not grown appreciably in number. At the end of 1974 only seven existed, averaging eighteen members each. These are involved with local authorities on local policy questions: shopping centers, urban renewal, open markets. They do some research for CB on local levels: price comparisons, public transportation, day care centers.

Stichting Consumentenklachten, founded by CB together with industry to provide the format to solve consumer complaints, is open to all. In 1975 four arbitration committees were in operation: dry cleaning, laundry, travel tours and camping. These committees hear about 2,000 complaints a year. By the end of 1974 the board had handed down 4,628 binding decisions, amounting to Df 400,000 in damages. In about one-third of the instances the consumer got the redress he sought. Decisions of the board are enforceable at civil law, as all members of the respective trade associations are bound by contract with CB. Any consumer may file a complaint, accompanied by Df 25 which is refundable if the consumer wins. CB expects to receive a government grant to enable the board to expand its activities. The Stichting provides one of the still rare examples of direct cooperation by member-based consumer groups with business.

CB has devoted considerable resources to legal assistance. Beyond legal advice, CB in a growing number of cases has been preparing cases and arguing them in the lowest court (Holland has no small claims court). At any one time some twenty to thirty cases are being prepared or pending in the courts. Cases run the gamut of consumer problems: housebuying, insurance, misleading advertising, malfunctioning products, services of doctors, painters.

CB continues to pressure the government for legislation. In 1975, foremost on CB's list in order of importance were: minimum requirements for safety, minimum requirements for information on many products and services, standard contract clauses and mandatory disclosure of interest rates. CB also continues to press for unit pricing, coupled with a standardization of product quantity.

According to the director, CB's requests to present TV programs on the government channel have been refused, ostensibly on the grounds that the subject matter involved is not cultural enough and has no spiritual value to offer the public. As one of the broadcasting corporations presents monthly TV consumer programs, the government's decision is more likely politically motivated. Many of CB's articles are picked up by the press, especially on such matters as ecology. Incidentally, tirades against multinational firms are noticeably absent from the Dutch consumer movement.

Since 1971, several studies by outsiders have been made on CB subscribers involving demographics, preferences in testing, buying intentions, attitudes toward information, and perceptions of subscribers versus average consumers. In 1975 CB established its own survey unit.

Other Developments

As mentioned earlier, Stichting voor Informatieve Etikettering was liquidated on April 25, 1975, never having received any support from industry, not even a token grant. IVHA continues to issue its quality marks, and under a new director has announced that specifications will be made public.

Konsumenten Kontakt is Stichting Consumenten Contact Orgaan in new format. It reprints studies in its publication, *Koopkracht*, which has some 23,000 subscribers and appears eleven times a year. Still acting as a clearing house operation, it is financed primarily by memberships and a government grant. The Stichting Vergelijkend Warenonderzoek functions solely to channel government money into comparative testing. In 1975 VW received about Df 1,200,000 compared with Df 550,000 in 1970.

NORWAY

This will not be a "full" country story, as we have not been able to revisit Norway. The reader will recall from the *Handbook* that Norway had the greatest number of subscribers relative to households in the world to a comparative testing journal (published by the state Consumer Council). The Norwegians can still claim this distinction. In June 1975, 235,000 subscribed, up from 169,000 in 1969. Our report will focus on informative labeling, as the Norwegian picture here is more diverse than elsewhere and hence a matter of principal interest.

The 1968 law on mandatory labeling of consumer goods in instances where the government deems improved CI a matter of impelling urgency is administered by the Ministry of Consumer and Administrative Affairs. The Varefakta-Komiteen (VK), the mixed private-public body administering the voluntary labeling program of long standing, serves as an advisory body to the ministry with regard to mandatory labeling. Thus far only two product areas have been subjected to this obligation, namely packaged food products and textile goods, both in 1975. The 1974 report of the Royal Commission on Advertising, an investigation patterned on the Swedish one discussed in Chapter Seven, proposed that the 1968 legislation be replaced by a new law concerning mandatory information in marketing, broadening the government's powers to prescribe labeling to direct the inclusion of mandated information content in advertising and other forms of sales promotion.

In the *Handbook* we were interested to see whether the mere possibility of mandatory labels would in itself stimulate the VK voluntary IL program. We may now say that in the 1970–75 period this was not the case. On the other hand, we are not aware that mandated labeling has been used as a threat to coax industries into "voluntary" action. This in itself is fairly remarkable in a nation governed by the most left-wing Social Democratic party in Europe during most of the period. However, the 1968 law had a secondary, dysfunctional effect. Thus we read in the 1975 annual report of VK that its "new duties" (presumably mainly its advisory work on mandatory labeling) "had reduced our capacity for work on voluntary labeling."

In the voluntary area Norway since 1970 presents the only case of a program comprising a straight information label (so-called A-declarations) and a label embodying minimum standards for specific properties of the product (B-declarations). Use of either label is voluntary. However, for any given product VK decides whether type A or type B shall be applicable. This decision is not left to individual producers.

Due to the introduction of A and B type labels, statistics concerning labeling activities before and after 1970 are not comparable. It is, however, clear that in the aggregate the VK program has evidenced moderate growth. The total number of product label schemes available was sixty-four in 1970 and seventy-three in 1975. Of the 1975 total, twenty-nine represented "holdover" norms from 1970 or earlier, while there were forty-four A and B schemes. The number of companies making use of the voluntary labels decreased from 115 in 1970 to eighty-seven in 1975. On the other hand, the number of brands (including models) increased from 549 to 584.

UNITED STATES

The United States has witnessed an avalanche of consumer proposals, hearings, litigation, research, conferences, complaints, bills and legislation on the national, state and local levels. The several states have public consumer protection agencies and/or private better business bureaus; small claims courts have started to flourish, along with hotlines in newspapers and TV and radio consumer programs. As in many areas of public policy in the United States, the diversity is staggering. In legislation the federal government is most visible, and while no clear systems plan is emerging, new laws abound, especially dealing with product safety, labeling and warranties.

As a trial balloon one may regard the proposal by the Department of Commerce (National Bureau of Standards) for an economywide voluntary IL program.[2] It took both the FTC and the business, consumer and academic communities by surprise. Unfortunately, it was not well thought through, and the chances that the proposal will be acted on seem slim. It may well be, however, that it will help stimulate enough interest to generate more viable proposals from industry circles or consumer groups, from the Department of Commerce itself, from other government agencies or from Capitol Hill.

Consumer advocacy defined broadly has taken on new meaning and intensity. The groups spawned by Ralph Nader and his followers have been active in an increasingly wide spectrum of public affairs issues. Local interest groups affiliated with university student bodies have not been reticent in gathering materials and presenting evidence to press and public bodies, stressing consumer concerns in regulated monopolies and professional services such as doctors, dentists, lawyers and funeral parlors.

In general business seems to be playing a more positive role in consumer affairs in the U.S. than in most other countries. It is not unusual to find among the larger firms truly effective consumer affairs directors. As a rule, however, consumer affairs personnel still have very limited influence on corporate policy.[3] A great number of firms have established effective complaints-handling machinery. One of the authors chaired a national conference on complaints-handling systems sponsored by the Office of Consumer Affairs in 1974, a conference attended by over 200 representatives of business. In this area the appliance manufacturers' success has been the paradigm for several other industry groups. Quite a few eyebrows were raised when the U.S. Chamber of Commerce launched directly into long-range thinking on some consumer matters. In 1975 it produced the first model state small claims court statute, including the idea of a consumer ombudsman associated with each court. Even some previously "unreformed" merchants at the grassroots level are gradually relinquishing their cherished position of haughty disregard for the consumer. Still, progressive business leaders will readily agree with consumers that much remains to be done.

Consumers Union with over two million and Consumers' Research with 100,000 subscribers remain the two best known independent all-purpose product information sources. In early 1976 a new group, The Washington Center for the Study of Services, with initial support from the U.S. Office of Consumer Affairs, Consumers Union and a private foundation, launched *Consumers' Checkbook*, a quarterly journal devoted exclusively to the examination of local services in Washington, D.C. The first issue dealt with health care, with reports planned on banks, automobile servicing, employment agencies, plumbers and appliance repair shops. It is hoped that from this prototype similar efforts will be made in other localities. Most consumer journals in the past have found the service area troublesome to report due to its "local" interest.

Comparative advertising, encouraged by FTC, has produced mixed results. The information content of advertisements on television has not been greatly increased, if at all, with or without comparative ads. No doubt for a successful comparative advertisement, large layouts as well as outlays would be necessary. For instance, General Motors has run two page ads in the *New York Times*, comparing eight of GM's cars with fifteen foreign cars in price, gas mileage, maintenance schedules and engine guarantees.[4] Imperceptibly, advertising may be taking on a more reasonable role by weeding out blatantly misleading statements and innuendoes and misrepresentations, by depuffing. Still, there seems to be no effort expended on examining the credibility of the media used. The media itself have been slow indeed to assume any responsibility for the ads they broadcast.

Consumers Union (CU)

In its fortieth year in 1976, CU has a circulation of 2.3 million, with subscriptions accounting for about 95 percent of the total. A subscription cost $11 a year in 1976, up from $8 in 1970; single copies $1, up from 60 cents. In 1974–75 CU ran a deficit of $3 million, and with reserves amounting to $1.7 million the financial situation was far from satisfactory. Some part of the deficit (exactly what part is a matter of controversy within the organization) is due to expansion of consumer activist programs of the non-self-supporting variety. Cost of paper, printing, test products, postage and staff outdistanced income. Stringent economies, including a reduced staff, were deemed essential. By contrast (and, we would deem, necessarily), income procurement (advertising) rose by $1.5 million between 1970 and 1975. Financial data appear in Table E–10.

Among new activities, CU is proud of its consumer reports for TV started in 1974. These short two to three minute capsule presentations of materials prepared by CU itself are usually aired during newscasts. Broadcast by some sixty local TV stations, they reached an estimated potential audience of twenty million in 1975. The expense for this activity is now approaching $500,000. Income from these

Table E-10.   Consumers Union. Income and Expenditures 1969–70 and 1974–75 (in thousands)

	1969-70	1974-75
Income		
Subscriptions, newsstand sales	9,345	15,787
Interest	175	229
Grant, Consumer Product Safety Commission		140
Loss on sale of U.S. government obligations		(92)
Expenditures		
Preparation and publication of material	3,995	8,345
Income procurement	3,238	4,837
Servicing of subscriptions	971	2,155
General and administration	449	845
Maintenance and depreciation	251	483
Printing and mailing expense	562	1,143
Consumer affairs, including grants and contributions	263	592[a]
Ballots and questionnaires	154	152
Washington and west coast offices		152
Consumer reports for TV		411
Excess (deficit)	(363)	(3,051)
Total expenditure	9,883	19,115

[a]Grants were $320,236 in 1973–74; $211,377 in 1974–75

Source: *Consumer Reports* (October 1975): 635.

programs is not reported separately; it is unlikely that this public service activity will ever be a break-even proposition.

CU has also opened a small office on the west coast as it is felt that issues often surface there sooner than elsewhere, making California "a bellwether for the rest of the country."[5] CU also bought the land needed for a new automobile testing facility. As a new public service CU contracted with the U.S. Consumer Product Safety Commission to develop a safety standard for power lawnmowers, now completed. Paperbound consumer interest publications and special teaching tools for schools are both still integral parts of CU's publishing effort.

Reporting the results of comparative product tests remains the heart of CU. So important is this concern in terms of allocation of CU's resources of time as well as money, its staff and board that consumerist zealot Ralph Nader resigned from CU's board October 1, 1975, stating that he could put his ten days a year to better use in the cause of the consumer. It is no secret that Nader's presence on

Table E-11. Consumers Union. Comparative Test Reports in *Consumer Reports* 1969 and 1975

	Number of Tests		Number of Brands[a]	
	1969	*1975*	*1969*	*1975*
Textiles	2	3	47	63
Foods	5	5	173	175
Major household appliances	8	6	154	91
Minor household appliances	5	6	110	171
Household utensils and supplies	17	14	397	337
TV and audio	10	9	169	150
Hygiene products, medicines, cosmetics and toiletries	1	4	18	114
Sports, recreational, educational and travel goods	13	13	265[b]	455[b]
Cars	9	11	87[b]	66[b]
Services	4	1	—	—
Totals	74	72	1420	1622

[a]Services not included

[b]Includes one recapped comparative buying guide of forty-eight brands in 1969 and thirty brands in 1975

the board had been an unsettling influence on CU. Currently over half of *Consumer Reports (CR)* is devoted to test results. Some of the general consumer articles come close to being service tests—for instance, the four part series on banking services. *CR* continues its "Once Over" column, now supplemented with "Follow-Up," "Update" and "Docket" columns, the latter taking up matters of litigation on behalf of consumers.

Product test reports published in 1975 numbered seventy-two, about the same as in 1969. The test involved over 1,600 brands, a 15 percent increase since 1969. As mentioned elsewhere, comparative service testing has met such problems that CU, like many other groups, has opted to present the questions of servicing in broad gauge consumer guidance or educational articles.

Consumers' Research

Consumers' Research, Inc., reported a circulation of slightly more than 100,000 in 1974. The income of Consumers' Research was probably in the $900,000–1,000,000 range. Its journal, renamed *Consumers' Research*, reported fifty-three tests in 1975, up from forty-two in 1969. Figures are given in Table E-12. Almost one-half of the forty-four page journal is devoted to tests. About 20 percent are consumer articles, some giving results of reports of others: for instance,

Table E-12.   Consumers' Research, Inc. Comparative Test Reports in *Consumers' Research* 1969 and 1975

| | Number of Tests | | Number of Brands | |
	1969	1975	1969	1975
Textiles	1	2	21	46
Foods	—	1	—	10
Major household appliances	1	3	6	24
Minor household appliances	4	8	34	65
Household utensils and supplies	9	11	79	164
TV and audio	5	4	76	52
Hygiene products, medicines, cosmetics and toiletries	1	3	28	97
Sports, recreational, educational and travel goods	15	16	197	168
Cars	6	5	29	13
Services	—	—	—	—
Totals	42	53	470	539

the Veterans Administration release of information on hearing aids by brands, and the trade association report on specifications of air conditioners. About 10 percent present notes on what is happening on consumer fronts. A subscription cost $9 in 1975, up from $8 in 1969; single copies cost $1, up from 60 cents. The 224 page annual handbook, published in lieu of the October issue, is available separately for $2.95.

The reasons for the relative stagnation of Consumers' Research were analyzed in the *Handbook*. There is hardly any doubt that with more market-oriented management the organization would find considerable room for expansion.

INTERNATIONAL ORGANIZATIONS

International Organization of Consumers Unions (IOCU)

By the beginning of 1975 IOCU had a membership of ninety-five organizations from some fifty countries; thirty-four were full members (associates) and sixty-one corresponding members. Ostensibly the distinguishing feature of associate members is that they are independent in action and policy irrespective of any government subsidies; in practice the difference lies primarily in the payment of dues. An associate member pays a percentage of its annual gross income, but in no case less than $50 a year. The actual percentage in any one year is decided by IOCU's council, based on the adopted budget. In

1969 this was 0.75 percent. Corresponding members must pay at least $25. There is considerable movement between these membership classes. Resignations occur with some frequency. For instance, Institut National de la Consommation of France joined and resigned within two years. Many of the organizations are exceedingly small, struggling in such unhospitable environments as Greece, Guyana, Indonesia, Iran, Poland and Sri Lanka. That the developing countries are being heard (or courted) is evidenced by the 1975 election of the Consumer Guidance Society of India (Bombay) and the Consumers' Association of Penang to IOCU's council.

IOCU's regular budget reached $190,000 in 1975, up from $100,000 in 1970. An extra $40,000 was specifically allocated for the South East Asia project recently undertaken. About 60 percent of the budget is financed by Consumers Union and Consumers' Association equally. In April of 1975 IOCU's staff numbered five permanent and five part time, but the executive secretary indicated that the regular staff would be reduced to four and the part time staff eliminated by summer 1975. In June 1975 one of the IOCU's publications—*International Consumer*—the excellent medium used to acquaint members and subscribers with other consumer organizations and national consumer policies around the world—was suspended. Both of these moves were economy measures.

Continuing publications are: the *IOCU Newsletter* (ten times a year, print order 600); *Consumer Review* (bi-monthly, print order 500), containing currently four main sections—i.e., technical developments, legislation, consumer education and contents of consumer organizations' publications; and *Consumers Directory* (every other year). Projects in 1974 included: "Consumer Education for Consumer Protection," "Joint Testing," "Survey Work," and "Multinationals and the Consumer Interest." The theme for the 1975 IOCU Congress in Sydney was the cost of living.

The only new initiative of note has been the creation in 1974 of a regional consumer office, the Consumer Centre for Asia and the Pacific, with headquarters (a director and a secretary) set up in Singapore (now in Penang). IOCU issued four times a year the *Asia/Pacific Consumer* (print order 600), edited in the CCAP and produced in the IOCU headquarters in The Hague.

From its inception in 1960 to 1968 IOCU was exclusively—or at least primarily—an organization promoting the dissemination of product information based on comparative tests. While this is still a published goal, IOCU has taken on a "political" flavor, first clearly seen in the 1972 conference in Stockholm with its emphasis on broad consumer and environmental issues and its criticism of multinational corporations. With this broadening of scope and its aid to the formation of consumer groups in the Third and Fourth World, IOCU may soon be faced with the UN dilemma: small and nonrepresentative organizations demanding equal voice and influence and, due to the sheer numbers of such groups, eventually control.

Bureau Européen des Unions de Consommateurs (BEUC)

This group currently consists of eleven member organizations from six EEC nations. All ordinary members are nongovernmental. Stiftung Warentest joined as an associate member in 1974. The Unione Nazionale Consumatori of Italy has been suspended since May 1974. As explained by an inside observer, its secretary general was put in prison for "corruption and extortion" and the Italian organization expressed itself "unrepentant" for taking money from industry.

BEUC's sole present objective is to represent the views of consumers to the EEC authorities. It is headquartered in Brussels, with Association des Consommateurs' director as president, and CA's deputy director as part-time director. The Division of Protection and Information of Consumers of the Commission gave BEUC two million Belgian francs in 1974 to carry out investigations into misleading advertising, exclusion clauses in contracts, home accidents, toy safety, door-to-door selling and clinical thermometers. The study of misleading advertising undertaken jointly by Arbeitsgemeinschaft der Verbraucherverbände and Consumers' Association received wide specialist press coverage, favorable in the U.K. and critical in Germany (workmanship of the German phase of the study left much to be desired). Two investigations in 1975 paid for by the commission are consumer education and after sales service; the latter is also a European Testing Group project.

Nordiska Ämbetsmannakommittén för Konsumentfrågor

The Inter-Scandinavian Committee on Consumer Matters established in 1958 was reorganized in 1974 and integrated into the Nordic Council. Called the Nordic Co-operation Committee on Consumer Questions, it is composed of three government-appointed members from among the bureaucracies within each of the five countries (Denmark, Finland, Iceland, Norway and Sweden). The committee is active in four broad areas: coordination of investigations, including the testing of products and services and standards work; informative labeling of various types; consumer education; and advertising and marketing practices.

Organisation for Economic Co-operation and Development (OECD)

A Committee on Consumer Policy was set up by the twenty-three OECD members in 1969 to examine the status of consumer policies in member states. Its mandate has been extended to 1977. The reports of members on activities in their respective states are published annually. The reports tend to be rather bureaucratic in style, and it is fair to say that they frequently exaggerate the extent of consumer policy activity in individual countries. Further, the government agencies reporting frequently neglect to account for considerable efforts on the part of consumer groups as well as business organizations.

A number of working party reports had been issued by 1975, normally in mimeographed form: consumer policy in OECD countries (1972); labeling and comparative testing (1972); consumer protection against toxicity of cosmetics and household products (1974); and compulsory labeling of prepackaged consumer products (1974). A principal focus has been in the field of labeling; a report on package standardization, unit pricing and misleading packaging was due in late 1975. A group was preparing a report on energy consumption labeling of appliances. This phase of OECD work may be approaching a conclusion. Product safety work continues with reference to toys, inflammability of products, general household chemicals and, following a lead by the U.S. Product Safety Commission, the reporting of household-product-related accidents. New areas of concern are consumer credit and undesirable marketing practices.

It is impossible to evaluate the success of OECD's attempts at assisting its members to develop common principles and guidelines for consumer policies. Two-thirds of the member states are highly developed industralized countries; nine are the members of the EEC; the European members also belong to the Council of Europe. Participation in the working parties of itself undoubtedly has an integrative influence, at least on the representatives.

The Council of Europe

The council, established in 1949 with headquarters in Strasbourg, was composed of some eighteen countries in 1975. The question of consumer protection was included in the 1967–68 work program as a new activity, and two groups were set up. The first report, Consumer Protection (May 30, 1969), was prepared by a working party on "Education and Information" and included a relatively superficial survey of methods employed in each of ten countries to convey information to consumers. The second report dealt with misleading advertising and appeared in March 1972. Resolutions were subsequently adopted by the minister's deputies on both consumer education in schools and misleading advertising. Working parties have dealt with consumer education for adults, door-to-door selling and improper contract clauses. In March 1975 the council prepared a draft convention on product liability in regard to personal injury and death. After sales service is the topic of a new working group; this seems to be the hottest subject matter in 1975–76 in a number of multination bodies.

In May 1973 the council drew up a consumer protection charter stressing the need for some international standardization in the field of consumer policy, defining consumer rights in a form substantially adopted two years later by the EEC and reported below.

European Economic Community (EEC)

The Special Service for Questions of Consumer Interest established in 1968 within the commission bureaucracy has since been renamed several times, and in 1975 was known as the Protection and Information of Consumers Division within the Department of Environment and Consumer Protection. The commission in September 1973 set up a Consumer Advisory Committee that for all practical purposes has the same membership and the same purpose as did the Comité de Contact dissolved in February 1972. It meets five times a year, and presents working papers on such topics as credit, product liability and advertising. Operative since December 1974, the committee by April 1975 had been consulted on such matters as energy policy, agricultural prices and consumer credit. It has twenty-five members: six from trade unions, three from the cooperatives, three from family organizations, three from BEUC and ten "experts" appointed by the commission.

The Council of Ministers adopted a preliminary program for a consumer protection and information policy in April 1975 that is very similar to that adopted by the Council of Europe in May 1973. According to releases from the commission this program established the framework of a genuine consumer policy and constitutes a consumer charter based on five fundamental rights:

1. the right to protection of health and safety;
2. the right to protection of economic interests;
3. the right of redress;
4. the right to information and education; and
5. the right of representation.

The commission planned to prepare by the end of 1975 the following measures as first steps in implementing the five rights:

1. a proposal for a directive on door-to-door selling and one on labeling of foodstuffs;
2. labeling regulations for certain categories of products other than foodstuffs;
3. a proposal for a directive relating to unit pricing on packaged products; and
4. a proposal for a directive on the harmonization of general conditions of consumer credit, including those relating to installment buying.

The commission has declared that it will also encourage cooperation between bodies carrying out comparative tests. It is not clear whether this will include financial support.

NOTES

1. Consumentenbond, *Annual Report* (The Hague: 1974): 16.
2. *Federal Register* 41 (May 25, 1976): 21389-91.
3. Claes Fornell, *Consumer Input for Marketing Decisions: A Study of Corporate Departments for Consumer Affairs* (New York: Praeger, 1976).
4. *New York Times* (February 10, 1976): 18-19.
5. *Consumer Reports* (October 1975): 634.

Consumer Enquirer Program.
Experimental Module for a
Computerized Consumer Information
Utility Language: FORTRAN.
Equipment: Control Data 660

```
WAIT DISK
20        PRINT"THE CONSUMER ENQUIRER - AN EXPERIMENTAL PROGRAM"
22            PRINT"DEVELOPED UNDER THE DIRECTION OF DR.HANS B. THORELLI"
24            PRINT"BY PETER W. MICHNA, RESEARCH ASSOCIATE. BASIC IDEAS "
26            PRINT"FOR THE PROGRAM OBTAINED FROM THE SWEDISH INSTITUTE "
28            PRINT"FOR INFORMATIVE LABELING (VDN)."
30            PRINT
32            PRINT"THE FOLLOWING RECOMMENDATIONS ARE ONLY SUGGESTIVE,"
34            PRINT"RESPONSIBILITY FOR THE FINAL DECISION MUST REST "
36            PRINT"WITH THE USER ALONE."
38            PRINT
39            PRINT"THIS PARTICULAR PROGRAM ONLY PROVIDES INFORMATION"
40            PRINT"ABOUT TAPE RECORDERS."
43            PRINT
44            PRINT"WOULD YOU LIKE 1. INDIVIDUALIZED BUYING ADVICE, OR"
45            PRINT"2. TECHNICAL DATA ABOUT DIFFERENT BRANDS WHICH YOU"
50            PRINT"HAVE IN MIND? PRESS 1, OR 2,"
70            INPUT A1
80            IF A1=2 GO TO 5000
97            PRINT
98            GO TO 100
99            LET R1=1
100           PRINT"WHICH OF THE FOLLOWING CHARACTERISTICS OF TAPE"
110           PRINT"RECORDERS DO YOU WANT TO CONSIDER?"
120           PRINT"1. MONO - ONE CHANNEL ONLY."
130           PRINT"2. STEREO - TWO CHANNELS."
140           PRINT"3. CASSETTE RECORDER."
150           PRINT"4. TAPE - REEL TO REEL RECORDER."
160           IFR1=1 GO TO 199
169           PRINT
170       PRINT"NOTE THAT IF YOU REQUIRE MORE THAN ONE HR. CONTINUOUS"
180           PRINT"RECORDING TIME , THEN YOU MUST USE REELS. BUT CASSETTES"
190           PRINT"ARE MORE COMPACT AND CAN BE CHANGED FASTER"
199           PRINT
200           PRINT"CHOOSE BETWEEN 1 AND 2, THEN 3 AND 4, TYPE THE TWO"
210           PRINT"NUMBERS YOU SELECT SEPARATED BY A COMMA."
```

```
220        INPUT A2,B2
240        IF A2=1 GO TO 270
250        LET B=10
260        GO TO 280
270        LET B=5
280        IF B2=3 GO TO 310
290        LET A=10000
300        GO TO 320
310        LET A=1
320        IF R1=1 GO TO 1150
329        PRINT
330        PRINT"WILL YOU MAINLY RECORD SPEECH, THAT IS THE RECORDER"
340        PRINT"WILL BE USED AS AN ACOUSTICAL NOTEBOOK 1=YES,2=NO."
350        INPUT A1
360        IF A1=2 GO TO 410
369        PRINT
370        PRINT"IF YOU SPECIFICALLY REQUIRE A DICTAPHONE, ENQUIRE"
380        PRINT"SEPARATELY UNDER THIS CATEGORY, OTHERWISE NOTE THAT"
390        PRINT"MOST RECORDERS ARE SUITABLE FOR BOTH SPEECH AND"
400        PRINT"MUSIC -- PLEASE CONTINUE."
410        GO TO 430
420        LET R2=1
429        PRINT
430        PRINT"WILL YOU BE USING AN EXTERNAL AMPLIFIER PERMANENTLY"
440        PRINT"(IE YOU REQUIRE A TAPE DECK ONLY), OR DO YOU WANT A"
450        PRINT"UNIT WITH AN INTEGRAL AMPLIFIER(IE A COMPLETE UNIT)"
460        PRINT"PRESS 1 FOR THE TAPE DECK, AND 2 FOR THE REGULAR UNIT
480        INPUT A3
490        IF A3=1 GO TO 520
500        LET G1=4000
510        GO TO 530
520        LET G1=4001
530        IF R2=1 GO TO 1150
540        GO TO 569
550        LET R3=1
560        GO TO 609
569        PRINT
570        PRINT"MOST PORTABLE RECORDERS ARE BATTERY POWERED, ALTHOUGH
580        PRINT"CERTAIN MODELS CAN BE ATTACHED TO THE MAINS (AC)"
590        PRINT"LARGER, NON-PORTABLE MODELS ARE USUALLY MAINS (AC)."
600        PRINT"POWERED ONLY."
609        PRINT
610        PRINT"TYPE THE NUMBER OF THE FEATURE YOU DESIRE, 1-BATTERY"
620   PRINT"OPERATED ONLY, OT 2. BATTERY/AC OPERATED, OR"
630        PRINT"3. MAINS (AC) ONLY OPEROTYON."
640        INPUT A4
650        IF A4=1 GO TO 690
660        IF A4=2 GO TO 710
670        LET C1=50
680        GO TO 720
690        LET C1=100
700        GO TO 720
710        LET C1=40000
720        IF R3=1 GO TO 1150
730        GO TO 749
740        LET R4=1
749        PRINT
750        PRINT"DO YOU REQUIRE SOUND REPRODUCTION OF QUALITY 1.NORMAL
760        PRINT"OR 2. HIGH, OR 3. PROFESSIONAL? TYPE 1,2,OR 3."
765        INPUT A5
770        IF A5=1 GO TO 810
```

```
780     IF A5=2 GO TO 830
790     LET D1=700
800     GO TO840
810     LET D1=300
820     GO TO 840
830     LET D1=500
840     IF R4=1 GO TO 1150
850     GO TO 870
860     LET R5=1
870     IF G1=4001 GO TO 1010
879     PRINT
880     PRINT"DO YOU NEED SOUND SUFFICIENT FOR: 1. A COUPLE OF"
890     PRINT"PEOPLE SITTING FAIRLY NEAR BY (1-2 WATTS), OR"
900     PRINT"2. A MEDIUM SIZED ROOM (2-20 WATTS), OR 3. A LARGE"
910     PRINT"ROOM (20 WATTS PLUS)? PRESS 1,2, OR 3."
920     INPUT A6
930     IF A6=1 GO TO 970
940     IF A6=2 GO TO 990
950     LET E1=2001
960     GO TO 1000
970     LET E1=2000
980     GO TO 1000
990     LET E1=2003
1000    IF R5=1 GO TO 1150
1010    GO TO 1029
1020    LET R6=1
1029    PRINT
1030    PRINT"HOW MUCH ARE YOU INTENDING TO SPEND ON THE TAPE"
1040    PRINT"RECORDER? 1. $20-$100, 2. $100-$200, 3. ABOVE $200"
1050    PRINT"PRESS 1,2, OR 3."
1060    INPUT A7
1070    IF A7=1 GO TO 1110
1080    IF A7=2 GO TO 1130
1090    LET F1=3001
1100    GO TO 1140
1110    LET F1=3000
1120    GO TO1140
1130    LET F1=3003
1140    IF R6=1 GO TO 1150
1150    LET T=A+B+C1+D1+E1+F1+G1
1160    GO TO 2000
1169    PRINT
1170    PRINT"DO YOU WISH TO CHANGE ANY INPUTS? 1=YES,2=NO."
1180    INPUT A8
1190    IF A8=2 GO TO 8000
1199    PRINT
1210    IF A=1 GO TO 1240
1220    PRINT "1.TAPE - REEL TO REEL RECORDER."
1230    GO TO 1250
1240    PRINT"2. CASSETTE"
1250    IF B=5 GO TO 1280
1260    PRINT"3. STEREO"
1270    GO TO 1290
1280    PRINT "4. MONO"
1290    IF G1=4000 GO TO 1320
1300    PRINT"5. TAPE DECK ONLY - NO INTEGRAL AMPLIFIER."
1310    GO TO 1330
1320    PRINT"6. REGULAR MODEL WITH INTERNAL AMPLIFIER."
1330    IF C1=50 GO TO 1370
1340    IF C1=100 GO TO 1390
1350    PRINT"7. BATTERY/AC POWERED,"
```

```
1360        GO TO 1410
1370        PRINT"8. MAINS (AC) POWERED ONLY."
1380        GO TO 1410
1390        PRINT"9. BATTERY POWERED ONLY."
1410        IF D1=300 GO TO 1450
1420        IF D1=500 GO TO 1470
1430        PRINT"10. PROFESSIONAL SOUND QUALITY."
1440        GO TO 1480
1450        PRINT"11. SOUND QUALITY NORMAL."
1460        GO TO 1480
1470        PRINT"12. SOUND QUALITY HIGH."
1480        IF G1=4001 GO TO 1560
1490        IF E1=2003 GO TO 1550
1500        IF E1=2000 GO TO 1530
1510        PRINT"13. VOLUME SUFFICIENT FOR A LARGE ROOM."
1520        GO TO 1560
1530        PRINT"14. VOLUME O.K. FOR LISTENERS SITTING NEAR BY."
1540        GO TO 1560
1550        PRINT"15. VOLUME SUFFICIENT FOR A MEDIUM SIZED ROOM."
1560        IF F1=3000 GO TO 1600
1570        IF F1=3003 GO TO 1620
1580        PRINT"16. PRICE RANGE ABOVE $200."
1590        GO TO 1630
1600        PRINT"17. PRICE RANGE $20-$100."
1610        GO TO 1630
1620        PRINT"18. PRICE RANGE $100-$200."
1629        PRINT
1630        PRINT"TYPE THE NUMBER OF THE CHARACTER LISTED ABOVE"
1640        PRINT"THAT YOU WISH TO CHANGE (CHOOSE ONE ONLY)."
1650        INPUT W
1660        IF W=2 GO TO 99
1670        IF W=1 GO TO 99
1680        IF W=4 GO TO 99
1690        IF W=3 GO TO 99
1700        IF W=5 GO TO 420
1710        IF W=6 GO TO 420
1720        IF W=8 GO TO 550
1730        IF W=9 GO TO 550
1740        IF W=7 GO TO 550
1750        IF W=11 GO TO 740
1760        IF W=12 GO TO 740
1770        IF W=10 GO TO 640
1780        IF W=14 GO TO 860
1790        IF W=15 GO TO 860
1800        IF W=13 GO TO 860
1810        IF W=16 GO TO 1020
1820        IF W=17 GO TO 1020
1830        IF W=18 GO TO 1020
2000        IF T=9406 GO TO 3000
2010        IF T=9407 GO TO 3020
2020        IF T=49310 GO TO 3040
2030        IF T=49311 GO TO 3060
2040        IF T=19405 GO TO 3080
2050        IF T=59310 GO TO 3100
2060        IF T=19762 GO TO 3120
2070        IF T=19566 GO TO 3140
2500        PRINT"THERE IS NO TAPE RECORDER WITH THE CHARACTERISTICS"
2510        PRINT"SPECIFIED THUS FAR."
2520        GO TO 1169
3000        PRINT"WE RECOMMEND THE AIWA CASSETTE RECORER AT $40."
3010        GO TO 3500
```

```
3020      PRINT"WE RECOMMEND THE YORK KP-55 CASSETTE PLAYER AT $40."
3030      GO TO 3500
3040      PRINT"WE RECOMMEND THE CRAIG STEREO CASSETTE PLAYER AT $60"
3050      GO TO 3500
3060      PRINT"WE RECOMMEND THE PANASONIC CASSETTE RECORDER ST $40."
3070      GO TO 3500
3080      PRINT"WE RECOMMEND THE AIWA PORTABLE 3/1/4 REEL RECORDER."
3090      GO TO 3500
3100      PRINT"WE RECOMMEND THE WOLLENSAK REEL RECORDER AT $90."
3110      GO TO 3500
3120      PRINT"WE RECOMMEND THE SONY/SUPERSCOPE RECORDER AT $400."
3130      GO TO 3500
3140      PRINT"WE RECOMMEND THE ROBERTS STEREO RECORDER AT $180."
3500      PRINT
3510      PRINT"WOULD YOU LIKE DETAILED TECHNICAL INFORMATION CONCERNING"
3530      PRINT"PRESS 1 FOR TECHNICAL DATA, 2 FOR CHANGE, AND 3 NEITHER."
3560      INPUT B4
3570      IF B4=1 GO TO 4000
3580      IF B4=2 GO TO 1199
3590      PRINT
3600      PRINT"WOULD YOU LIKE DEALER INFORMATION? 1=YES,2=NO."
3610      INPUT B5
3620      IF B5=1 GO TO 3680
3630      PRINT
3640      PRINT"WE HOPE THE INFORMATION WILL BE OF SOME USE TO YOU."
3650      PRINT"IN ANY EVENT WE ENJOYED THE DIALOG"
3655      PRINT
3658      PRINT"FOR PRINTED MATTER CONCERNING TAPE RECORDERS, YOU"
3660      PRINT"MIGHT CONSULT CONSUMER REPORTS"
3670      GO TO 9999
3680      PRINT
3690      PRINT"WHERE WOULD YOU WANT TO BUY YOUR RECORDER, 1.BLOOMINGTON"
3700      PRINT"OR 2. ELSEWHERE? TYPE 1 OR 2."
3710      INPUT B6
3720      IF B6=2 GO TO 3840
3725      IF B6=1 GO TO 3740
3740      PRINT
3750      PRINT"THE FOLLOWING DEALERS CARRY THE INDICATED BRANDS AND"
3760      PRINT"OFFER A MINIMUM OF SERVICE COMPETENCE."
3770      PRINT"LEFFERSONS, 405 S.WALNUT; PANASONIC,AMPEX, SONY"
3790      PRINT"THE MUSIC CENTER, 104 E. KIRKWOOD; SONY, WOLLENSAK,"
3800      PRINT"MAGNAVOX, CRAIG."
3810      PRINT"STANSIFIERS, 1805 S.WALNUT; SONY MAGNAVOX, BSR,"
3820      PRINT"PANASONIC, AIWA, ROBERTS."
3830      GO TO 3630
3840      PRINT
3850      PRINT"PLEASE CONSULT YOUR YELLOW PAGES."
3860      GO TO 3630
4000      LET Z6=1
4010      IF T=9406 GO TO 6050
4020      IF T=9407 GO TO 6000
4030      IF T=49310 GO TO 6280
4040      IF T=49311 GO TO 6130
4050      IF T=19405 GO TO 6210
4060      IF T=59310 GO TO 6320
4070      IF T=19762 GO TO 6470
4080      IF T=19566 GO TO 6390
5000      PRINT
5010      PRINT"WE CAN PROVIDE TECHNICAL INFORMATION ABOUT THE"
5020      PRINT"FOLLOWING MODELS."
5030      PRINT"1. YORK KP-55 MONO CASSETTE PLAYER AT $20."
```

```
5040       PRINT"2. AIWA MONO CASSETTE RECORDER AT $40."
5050       PRINT"3. PANASONIC MONO CASSETTE RECORDER AT $40."
5060       PRINT"4. AIWA MONO PORTABLE TAPE RECORDER AT $40."
5070       PRINT"5. CRAIG STEREO CASSETTE PLAYER AT$60."
5080       PRINT"6. WOLLENSAK MONO TAPE RECORDER AT $90."
5090       PRINT"7. ROBERTS STEREO TAPE RECORDER AT $180."
5100       PRINT"8. SONY/SUPERSCOPE STEREO TAPE RECORDER AT $400."
5500       PRINT
5510       PRINT"TYPE THE NUMBER OF ONE OF THE MODELS LISTED EARLIER"
5520       PRINT"THAT YOU HAVE IN MIND. IF NONE, TYPE ZERO."
5530       INPUT B7
5540       IF B7=1 GO TO 6000
5550       IF B7=2 GO TO 6050
5560       IF B7=3 GO TO 6130
5570       IF B7=4 GO TO 6210
5580       IF B7=5 GO TO 6280
5590       IF B7=6 GO TO 6320
5600       IF B7=7 GO TO 6390
5610       IF B7=8 GO TO 6470
5620       GO TO 9000
5990       GO TO 9000
6000       PRINT
6010       PRINT"THE YORK KP-55 CASSETTE PLAYER HAS KEYBOARD CONTROLS,"
6020       PRINT"OPERATES ON 4 "C" BATTERIES, AND COMES WITH AN"
6030       PRINT"EARPHONE, WT. 3 LBS."
6040       GO TO 7000
6050       PRINT
6060       PRINT"THE AIWA CASSETTE RECORDER FEATURES: POP-UP CASSETTE"
6070       PRINT"LOADING, SEPERAT RECORD LEVEL AND PLAYBACK VOLUME"
6080       PRINT"CONTROLS,PUSHBUTTON OPERATION WITH FAST FORWARD"
6090       PRINT" AND REWIND, RECORD LEVEL/BATTERY CONDITION METER,"
6100       PRINT"OPERATES ON 4 C BATTERIES, AND COMES WITH AN"
6110       PRINT"START-STOP MIKE PLUS EARPHONES, WT. 5LBS."
6120       GO TO 7000
6130       PRINT
6140       PRINT"THE PANASONIC MONO CASSETTE RECORDER FEATURES:"
6150       PRINT"PUSHBUTTON CONTROLS, POP-UP CASSETTE EJECTION,"
6160       PRINT"FAST FORWARD/REWIND, AUTOMATIC LEVEL CONTROL FOR"
6170       PRINT"DISTORTION FREE RECORDING, 80-8,000 HZ,MIKE AND"
6180       PRINT"AUX. INPUTS, MONITOR OUTPUT, REMOTE STOP/START MIKE"
6190       PRINT"PLAYS ON 4 C BATTERIES, OR 117VAC, WT. 3LBS."
6200       GO TO 7000
6210       PRINT
6220       PRINT"THE AIWA MONO TAPE RECORDER FEATURES: PUSHBUTTON"
6230       PRINT"OPERATION, USES 4 C BATTERIES, TWO SPEEDS; 3 3/4"
6240       PRINT"AND 1 7/8 IPS, 2 1/2 INCH SPEAKER, RECORD LEVEL/BATT."
6250       PRINT"CONDITION METER, CAPSTAN DRIVE,START-STOP MIKE, 9LBS."
6270       GO TO 7000
6280       PRINT
6290       PRINT"THE CRAIG STEREO CASSETTE PLAYER FEATURES: KEYBOARD"
6300       PRINT"CONTROLS, DIGITAL COUNTER, 117VAC, 50-12,000 HZ."
6310       GO TO 7000
6320       PRINT
6330       PRINT"THE WOLLENSAK MONO TAPE RECORDER FEATURES: AUTOMATIC"
6340       PRINT"LEVEL CONTROL FOR PERFECT RECORDINGS, PUSHBUTTON"
6350       PRINT"OPERATION, DIGITAL COUNTER,RECORDING LEVEL/BATTERY"
6360       PRINT"CONDITION METER, TWO SPEEDS; 3 3/4 AND 1 7/8 IPS,"
6370       PRINT"5 INCH REEL TAPE, BATT/AC, STOP-START MIKE , 9LBS."
6380       GO TO 7000
6390       PRINT
6400       PRINT"THE ROBERTS STEREO TAPE RECORDER FEATURES: TWO BUILT-"
```

```
6410        PRINT"IN SPEAKERS, DIGITAL COUNTER, TWO SPEEDS;3 3/4 AND"
6420        PRINT"7 1/2 IPS, AUTOMATIC SHUTOFF, 20 WATTS PEAK POWER,"
6430        PRINT"40-15,000 HZ, 2 MIKE& RADIO INPUTS, PREAMP"
6440        PRINT"EXT. SPEAKERS, AND STEREO H/PHONE OUTPUT, 7 INCH REEL"
6450        PRINT"117VAC, WT 25LBS."
6460        GO TO 7000
6470        PRINT
6480        PRINT"THE SONY/SUPERSCOPE STEREO TAPE RECORDER FEATURES:"
6490        PRINT"AUTOMATIC REVERSING AT END OF TAPE, SERVO CONTROL"
6500        PRINT"MOTOR, DUAL CAPSTAN DRIVE, NON-MAGNETIZING HEADS,"
6510        PRINT"RETRACTING PINCH ROLLER, NOISE SURPRESSER SWITCH,"
6520        PRINT"DIGITAL COUNTER, TWO 20 WATT SPEAKERS, LEVEL METERS,"
6530        PRINT"THREE SPEEDS; 7 1/2 ANS 3 3/4 AND 1 7/8 IPS,"
6540        PRINT"40-20,000 HZ, 7 INCH REELS, 115VAC, WT 53LBS."
7000        IF Z6=1 GO TO 7080
7010        PRINT
7020        PRINT"WOULD YOU LIKE 1. TO BEGIN AGAIN, 2. TECHNICAL DATA"
7030        PRINT"ABOUT OTHER BRANDS, OR 3. NEITHER. PRESS 1,2, OR 3."
7040        INPUT B8
7050        IF B8=1 GO TO 97
7060        IF B8=2 GO TO 5500
7070        GO TO 3590
7080        PRINT
7090        PRINT"WOULD YOU LIKE 1. TO CHANGE SOME INPUTS, 2. TECHNICAL"
7100        PRINT"DATA ABOUT OTHER BRANDS, OR NEITHER. PRESS 1, 2, OR 3."
7110        INPUT C5
7120        IF C5=1 GO TO 1199
7130        IF C5=2 GO TO 5500
7140        GO TO 3590
8000        PRINT
8010        PRINT"IS THERE ANY PARTICULAR MODEL THAT YOU WOULD LIKE TO"
8020        PRINT"HAVE INFORMATION ABOUT. 1=YES,2=NO."
8030        INPUT C6
8040        IF C6=1 GO TO 5000
8050        GO TO 3600
9000        PRINT
9010        PRINT"WOULD YOU LIKE INDIVIDUALIZED BUYING INFORMATION,"
9015        PRINT"PRESS 1 FOR YES, AND 2 FOR NO."
9020        INPUT C7
9030     IF C7=1 GO TO 97
9040        GO TO 3590
9999        END

READY.
logout.
CP TIME      2.746
PP TIME      68.077
 04/24/72  LOGGED OUT AT 21.16.59.,
```

Appendix G

Condemner Reports*

BERATING THE RATINGS DEPT.

This article is dedicated to the proposition that all things are *not* created equal—not by to-day's manufacturers, anyway. But the American Consumer has an ally in his never-ending battle with poor craftsmanship, shoddy merchandise and Giant Economy Size Packages that are never more than half full...mainly, the Impartial Test Panels. Those dedicated experts who break down a product before they break down and tell us all about it in magazines like....

CONDEMNER REPORTS

OCTOBER 1969 / MANUFACTURERS HATE US SO WE GET / NO ADVERTISING / 50 CENTS

Razors and Blades
Use-Tested by a special 500-Man CR Panel

Styptic Pencils
Use-Tested by the same 500-Man CR Panel right after the Razors and Blades tests

Electric Hot Plates
Almost all models had poor insulation and none had adequate, heat-resistant handles

Burn Ointments
An unscheduled report necessitated by the tests of those %&$#@¢!! Electric Hot Plates

Mixers and Blenders
Our special 26-Man Team tests most brands

The New Long Ties
A special CR Report shows why men who use mixers and blenders should not wear them

Fire Extinguishers
None of the Fire Extinguisher Units that we tested could adequately control a fire

New Construction
CR examines new building construction as it searches for a new home after making those %&$#@¢#!! Fire Extinguisher tests

WRITER: DICK DE BARTOLO   PHOTOGRAPHY: BY IRVING SCHILD   41

LETTERS
FROM
CR's READERS

Ground Meat Contains Ground

I truly enjoyed your recent article, "Most Hot Dogs Aren't Fit For Dogs" (CONDEMNER REPORTS, July 1969). I was shocked by what you found in the hot dogs you tested. I buy hamburger meat from my butcher for 89¢ a pound, and thanks to your article, I've now started examining it. I've found what looks like bone chips, sawdust, hair, and even dirt. What can I do about it?
BROOKLYN, N.Y.   P.U.

Use a lot of ketchup and relish.

Price Puzzle

Which is actually cheaper, an 8 oz. tube of toothpaste for 59¢, a 10 oz. tube for 69¢, a 12 oz. tube for 79¢ or a full pound tube for $1.00?

Please do not send us any jokes or riddles. CR is not a humor magazine.

Executive Type Writes

In your August issue, you published the results of tests made on several portable typewriters, and our brand was one of the machines included in the report. You claimed you found a defect in our machine which you felt was a serious drawback, and therefore rated it "Unacceptable." As president of the Underglass Typewriter Company, I wish to point out that the sample you tested was obviously not typical of the machines we produce here at Underglass. I certainly hope that you will give us another chance and test a more typical example of our Model 7 Portable Typewriter—one that ten of our top engineers are building by hand especially for CR right now.
DAYTON, OHIO   CHARLES ELITE, JR.
                PRESIDENT
                UNDERGLASS CORP.

Mr. Elite's letter, which was obviously typed on one of his company's machines, only served to point out that the glaring defect we found in the Model 7 Portable is present in other models as well. As you can plainly see by the excerpt we have reproduced below, the "period" looks funny.

especially for CR
right now.
          Charles Elite, Jr.
          Pres. Underglass Corp.

Once Is Enough

New Toy, Not Recommended For Kids . . .

Sally Suicide, the new doll that can 'take her own life 12 ways,' has earned CR's NOT-ACCEPTABLE—ICKY POO rating at press time. This new entry from Marx Bros. Toys doesn't live up to its promise, as our disappointed panel will attest: the rope Sally Suicide is supposed to hang herself with broke on the first attempt, the drugs supplied are hardly enough to induce nausea let alone suicide, and the seven story doll house that she's supposed to jump from isn't high enough for anything more than two broken legs!

If the performance of this doll could only live up to its potential, Marx Bros. would have a winner here.

Sally Suicide: "Disappointing"

Thank You, Kind Readers

CR is certainly proud of its readers who take the time to sit down and write us about differences of opinion based on their own findings. It helps us get a better picture of things to watch for when we test new products in the future. Last month we didn't think to check out the "waterproof" casing on the new Brenner Electro Toothbrush, believing in this day and age that a "waterproof" label means just that. To our surprise, many readers found out differently, and a lot of credit must be given them for interrupting their week of mourning to write us.

Brenner Electric Toothbrush: "Not waterproof"

A Note From The Checkmate Toaster Company

Gentlemen:

Thank you for your invitation to have our latest Checkmate tested by your panel of impartial judges. However, we could not get our latest model, the Mock III, out of production in time for last month's deadline, and it would be a waste to have sent you the Mock II since it is being called back.

We trust that you will include a run-down of our new model this issue. A sample of the Checkmate Mock III is enclosed.

Thank you,

William Burns
President
Checkmate Corp.

Ed. Note: As per Mr. Burns' request, a complete rundown of the Checkmate Mock III is included in this issue.

Fowoll-up

An up-dating of previous up-to-date reports

During the past few years, CR has informed its readers to be aware of the "water content" percentage listed on the labels of packaged hams.

Many meat packing houses are injecting water into the hams, raising the weight considerably. The consumer is then paying 'ham' rates for water.

The problem has been faced by town officials of two different locations.

Mayor Heinz Wipfler of Wagsville, North Carolina, is getting back at the meat packers by injecting 'ham' into the local water supply, while Mayor Eric Wessel of Chipneil, Arizona, has upped the water tax from $23 a year to $3000, making the cost of water in the area more expensive than ham, thereby discouraging the practice.

Mayor Eric Wessel

Mayor Heinz Wipfler

CR salutes both of these men with their constructive solutions to the problem.

THE PURPOSES OF CONDEMNER REPORTS are to provide consumers with information and counsel, the publishers with money, and the manufacturers with ulcers.

PRODUCTS TESTED by the Condemner Reports' staff are determined by the needs of the staff since they are paid low salaries and depend on free testing samples in order to live.

SUBSCRIPTION RATES are low considering how much you'll save in one year's time by taking our advice and not falling for false bargains and deceptive pricing. Rates: $6.00 for one year, $15.00 for two years, $25.00 for three years.

A Change In Ratings

No one is perfect. While we come close to perfection here at CR, we too can slip once in a while. And when we do, well, you can bet your boots we'll own up to it and do what's necessary to rectify things even if it means changing a rating.

This is the case with the 1969 Corvex II which was originally listed as "NOT ACCEPTABLE — AWFUL" in the new car review 3 months ago. We now change this rating to "ACCEPTABLE— FANTASTIC".

Shown above: Staff member, pleased at test results, rates new Corvex II highly.

Our Thanks

CR wishes to thank all those who sent us congratulations on our 33rd year of publication. Special thanks go to General Motors Corporation who gave every member of our staff a beautiful new Corvex II.

Shown above: Staff member stands proudly before congratulatory gift, the Corvex II.

Work Under way

Next Month in Condemner Reports:

The Bomb

Which is most powerful, has more fallout, can be launched quicker, etc. Test panel composed of all the nuclear nations.

"Are The Funeral People Really Out To Cheat You?"

Three CR staff members posed as "Dearly Departeds" and were given a complete funeral, including burial. CR is digging up the facts for a complete report.

In Later Months:

"The Birth Control Pill —Does It Work ?"

Tests still going underway due to panelists refusal to stop for a while so tabulations can be recorded. Since CR announcement for this report we have received 1,289,876 requests to participate.

1969 Calendars

Which is the handiest, easiest to read, and best buy for 1969— The full report will be ready by late November.

Sewing Machines

There are 84 models of sewing machines to choose from, and of these, 10 are the leading sellers, representing over 70% of the total sale. However, CR found that although these models are very easy to operate, they are extremely difficult to test. Instead, CR chose 10 models more difficult to operate but easier to test, and, to make things even less complicated, will review only 5 of those 10. And always with the interests and needs of *you*, the consumer, in mind.

CR's Test

While it is true that women are by far the greatest users of home sewing machines, it is the *men* who are mostly employed as professional tailors in both big and small busi-nesses. For this reason; CR used 5 male panelists to test the 5 models chosen, but each was given typical female sewing problems: dresses, skirts, blouses, culottes, aprons, etc.

Test Results

After exhaustive tests where the male panelists had to literally "live" female wear, CR found that of the 5 machines tested, 4 operated normally, one acted strangely. This was a better percentage than the panelists of whom 3 acted normally, 2 strangely.

Shock

In any test of this sort, shock potential is always a consideration. Of the 5 machines, CR found all to be insulated against shock. However, each of the panelists were shocked at the ridiculous prices asked for the machines by their respective manufacturers, and 2 of the panelist's wives were shocked when their husbands ran off with each other.

RATINGS OF SEWING MACHINES

ACCEPTABLE – GOOD

SINGA SONGALA List price marked at $457.85, but CR shopper was able to purchase it for $29.95 at a discount store. This machine offered forward and reverse stitching only, but after being dropped by clumsy panelist, it was found that it could also sew zig-zag.

PFARFF SONGARA List priced marked at $29.95, but CR shopper purchased it for $247.95 at fancy uptown store before being fired. We found this imported imitation of the *Singa Songa* to be identical in every way except for case, motor, controls, performance and other secondary considerations.

ACCEPTABLE – NOT SO GOOD

ZOLTAN ZANDAR This was a deluxe machine with automatic button-holer, trimming device, pattern tracer, embroidery control and watermelon de-pitter. The performance of all special functions was flawless, but only when used simultaneously. For normal mending, it wasn't worth a darn. (CR rates that last gag **UNACCEPTABLE**).

ACCEPTABLE – PRETTY BAD

GIVALT 100 List price $9.00. Obviously an economy model with no chrome, no frills, and no extras. It featured only a plain, black case housing 3 needles, a spool of thread and a stereo recording of a well-operating sewing machine.

NOT ACCEPTABLE – ROTTEN

CHECKMATE MOCK III No price given. This machine would not sew forward or in reverse or at all. It had one adjustment labeled "light-dark" which might refer to the color of the material to be sewed. But then again, it might not. While there was no shock danger, the machine did heat up considerably after a few minutes and "popped up" the material inserted for sewing.

SCOTCH WHISKEY

In response to the unusual amount of inquiries (from CR panelists), we herewith disclose our findings from a recent test conducted on CR's tax deductible testing yacht, *Shnopps II*. It was the first test scoring 100% attendance of the CR panel, many bringing secretaries with them to take notes. The yacht was anchored 3 miles off the New Jersey shore to avoid Coast Guard restrictions as well as suspicious wives. A case each of the 8 generally accepted "top" scotches, 6 "second rung" brands, and 3 "swill" labels were employed along with a case of the 3 leading anti-freezes.

THE TEST

Testing started precisely at 9 AM like any normal work day. When panelist could not make the distinction between scotch and the anti-freeze, he was excused from further testing.

Results were pouring in as fast as scotch pouring out. By 11 AM more than 45% of the scotches had been tested and more than 33% of the panel were in love with their secretaries.

By 3 PM 70% of the scotch was drunk as were 80% of the panel, and the owner of a small runabout had performed 34 marriages as a qualified sea captain. (CR tests Divorces in Sept. Issue.)

By 5 PM all 20 cases of scotch and anti-freeze had been consumed, and many things were said to the boss that wouldn't have been under normal conditions. (CR tests New Jobs, P. 51)

RATINGS OF SCOTCH WHISKEYS

TEST RESULTS The top 5 choices, as recorded by the panel, are as follows:

ACCEPTABLE – ZOWIE

JOHNNY WALKUP Xsellent flavour . . . colorful animalz

PRESSEDTONE SSmmooooooothhh . . . handy cans stead of bopples

SIT CHIVAS Vary lite . . . plescent . . . I love you . . . marry me . . . doll

ACCEPTABLE – YESH INDEED

BAT 69 Nishe flavour . . . nishe shmell . . . nishe girl? Too bad . . .

HAIG ROAD Oky, not grate, but oky . . . know what I mean . . . It's oky, but not grate . . . no need to get mad, bushter . . . sho it's not oky . . . you right, I wrong . . . who carsh anyhow? Ish free . . .

STRETCH SOCKS
for men

Stretch socks can help stretch your budget. They are not only longer wearing, but because some models have a great deal of stretchability, you can put both feet into one sock, thus making a pair last even longer.

CR's test

In CR's rather grueling tests, the socks were soaked for one week in a solution of milk and butter to determine their stain resistance.

Then, as a 'mud' substitute, a mixture of flour and eggs in thick, gooey consistency was poured into the testing vat.

Finally, to simulate the effect of hot machine drying or high temperature summer wear, the socks were then placed in an oven pre-heated to 400 degrees and left for 30 minutes.

Test Results

None of the socks tested held up under CR's rugged test conditions stated above, but several pair not only smelled tempting, but tasted delicious! (Recipe available on request.)

As for our less exciting and more mundane tests of actual *wearing*, CR found only two models worth our highly coveted rating, the *left* sock of the Outerwoven 898 and the *right* sock of the Ban-Lard 989. CR suggests you buy a pair of both and throw out the right and left sock respectively.

RATINGS
ACCEPTABLE—EXCELLENT

OUTERWOVEN 898. As stated above (Test Results), the left sock of this pair was superior to any sock tested, including the right one from the same manufacturer. When purchasing, explain to salesman that you dance as if you had "two left feet" and see if he won't sell you the socks accordingly.

BAN-LARD The "two left feet" ploy will obviously not work on the superior *right* sock of this manufacturer. CR suggests you buy BOTH brands, break up the pairs as stipulated, and giving the worthless matchings to friends.

ACCEPTABLE—POOR

JERKY THOROBRED These stretch socks contained far too much stretch; one panelist pulled it up so high he didn't have to wear pants.

NOT ACCEPTABLE—ECCH

BURLYTON These socks were not color fast. The colored ones came out white after only 3 washings. The white ones came out clear after only one washing.

MANLY These socks had a severe tendency to shrink. This could be circumvented by washing while wearing, but this may prove difficult for those using automatic washers. One panelist approved of their long wear without washing, but we didn't want to get close to him for further comment.

HAND-HUGGERS This brand of socks was the worst tested. They did not stretch at all. However, they were very warm because they were made of leather and were fur lined with individual places for each toe. CR strongly advised against summer wear.

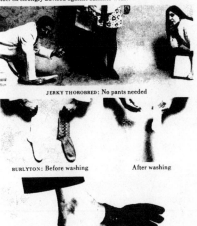

JERKY THOROBRED: No pants needed

BURLYTON: Before washing   After washing

HAND HUGGERS: Not recommended for summer wear

Magazines

Because of the increasing number of magazines available and the decreasing amount of time average consumers can allot to reading periodicals, CR has decided to rate magazines so as to weed out the extraneous from the superfluous.

RATINGS

Top choices, as recorded by panel, are as follows:

COMEDY MAGAZINES—ACCEPTABLE

TIME This weekly shows how to be very funny at everyone else's expense. Cute phrases are used to condemn books, blast plays, pan movies, wreck lives, undermine governments, etc.

SERIOUS MAGAZINES—ACCEPTABLE

MAD This hard-hitting, never-crack-a-smile periodical will appeal to those who like their reading matter straight and to the point with no humor, frivolity or satire to interfere with the somber content.

EDUCATIONAL MAGAZINES—ACCEPTABLE

READER'S DIGEST This very informative monthly enabled our test reader to give l erself a heart transplant: find God; hum her headaches away; and learn to live with and love a sadist—just in the first 10 pages alone!

SPECIAL MAGAZINES—UNACCEPTABLE

CONDEMNER'S REPORT An un-biased panel of readers who had never encountered this periodical before, thought the magazine to be a "comedy" entry at first reading due to the ridiculous procedure of purchasing new products only to wreck them with insane testing devices. Several were offended by the magazine's policy of advising people on how to spend their "hard-earned money". All told, CR has no choice but to award an **UNACCEPTABLE** rating to *Condemner's Report*.

Selected Bibliography

Adolfsson, H., and F. Folkebo. *VDN66—en undersökning av konsumenters användning av VDN varufakta vid ett butiksbesök.* Stockholm. State Consumer Council, 1966.

Albinsson, Göran; S. Tengelin; and K-E Wärneryd. *Reklam och konsument-upplysning.* Stockholm: Studieförbundet Näringsliv och Samhälle, 1965.

Almond, Gabriel, and Sidney Verba. *The Civic Culture: Political Attitudes and Democracy in Five Nations,* Princeton: Princeton University Press, 1965.

Arndt, Johan. *Consumer Search Behavior—An Exploratory Study of Decision Processes among Newly-Married Home Buyers.* Oslo: Universitetsforlaget, 1972.

Bauer, Raymond A., and Stephen A. Greyser. *Advertising in America: The Consumer View.* Boston: Harvard University, Division of Research, Graduate School of Business Administration, 1968.

Beem, Eugene, and John Ewing. "Business Appraises Consumer Testing Agencies," *Harvard Business Review* 32 (March–April 1954): 113-27.

Biervert, Bernd. *Wirtschaftspolitische, sozialpolitische und sozial-pädagogische Aspekte einer verstärkten Verbraucheraufklärung.* Köln: Krupinski, 1972.

Bodmer-Lenzin, Walter. *Die Stunde des Verbrauchers—Neue Wege und Formen der Aktivierung des Konsumenten.* Wien: ECON-Verlag, 1965.

Bower, Robert T. *Television and the Public.* New York: Holt, Rinehart and Winston, 1973.

Box, J.M.F. *Consumption Standard and Information Behavior.* Paper presented at Workshop II on Cognitive Models of Consumer Decision Processes, January 30–31, 1976, Delft, Technische Hogeschool, 1976. Mimeographed.

Brainerd, J.G., ed. *The Ultimate Consumer: A Study in Economic Illiteracy.* Annals of the American Academy of Political and Social Science, vol. 173, May 1934.

Braunschweig, Christa von. *Der Konsument und seine Vertretung—Eine Studie über Verbraucherverbände.* Heidelberg: Quelle & Meyer, 1965.

Cox, Donald M., ed. *Risk Taking and Information Handling in Consumer Behavior.* Boston: Harvard University, Division of Research, Graduate School of Business Administration, 1967.

Day, George S. "Assessing the Effects of Information Disclosure Requirements." *Journal of Marketing* 40 (April 1976): 42-52.

———. "Full Disclosure of Comparative Performance Information to Consumers: Problems and Prospects." *Journal of Contemporary Business* 4 (1975:1): 53-68.

Downs, Anthony. "A Theory of Consumer Efficiency." *Journal of Retailing* (Spring 1961): 6-12.

Doyère, Josée. *Le combat des consommateurs.* Paris: CERF, 1975.

European Association of Advertising Agencies. *Public Attitudes Toward Advertising.* Document 677. Brussels, March 3, 1973.

Fornell, Claes. *Consumer Input for Marketing Decisions: A Study of Corporate Departments for Consumer Affairs.* New York: Praeger, 1976.

Fulop, Christina. *Consumers in the Market.* London: The Institute of Economic Affairs, 1967.

Grubben, B.H.G.M.; J.H. Hörchner; and T. de Vries. *Consument en Voorlichting.* Wageningen: Landbouwhogeschool, 1974.

Hennell, Olof. *Företagens reaktioner på konsumentpolitiken. Med sju praktikfall.* Stockholm: Rabén & Sjögren, 1976.

———. *Konsumtion och sådant. Socialpsykologiska och psykologiska aspekter på konsumtion och marknadsförande.* Stockholm: Bonniers, 1973.

Hughes, George D., and M.L. Ray., eds. *Buyer/Consumer Information Processing.* Chapel Hill: University of North Carolina Press, 1974.

Hüttenrauch, Roland. "Probleme um Qualität und Preis beim Warentest." *Markenartikel* 9 (1973): 434-44.

Institut National de la Consommation. "Consommateurs et commerçants—un sondage de L'INC." *Consommateurs Actualité* 36 (December 1971): 3-18.

International Organization of Consumers Unions. *Consumers Directory 1973-74* (issued approximately every other year). The Hague, 1973.

Johansson, Johnny K. "The Theory and Practice of Swedish Consumer Policy." *The Journal of Consumer Affairs* 10 (Summer 1976): 19-32.

Katona, George; Burkhard Strumpel; and Ernest Zahn. *Aspirations and Affluence—Comparative Studies in the United States and Western Europe.* New York: McGraw-Hill, 1971.

Kuhlmann, Eberhard. *Das Informationsverhalten der Konsumenten.* Freiburg: Rombach, 1970.

Labrousse, J. *L'information des consommateurs.* Paris: Institut Français d'Opinion Publique, 1968.

Lane, Sylvia. "A Study of Selected Agencies that Evaluate Consumer Goods Qualitatively in the United States." Ph.D. dissertation, University of Southern California, 1957.

Leaper, William Joseph. *Implications for Business of the New Trade Descriptions Law.* London: Business Books, 1968.

Liefeld, J.P.; F.H.C. Edgecombe; and Linda Wolfe. "Demographic Characteristics of Canadian Consumer Complainers." *Journal of Consumer Affairs* 9 (Summer 1975): 73-80.

Linder, Staffan B. *The Harried Leisure Class.* New York: Columbia University Press, 1970.

Lundvall, Leif, ed. *Konsumenten och samhället, Rapporter från ett forskarseminarium.* Stockholm: Rabén & Sjögren, 1969.

Marcus-Steiff, Joachim. "Information et défense des consommateurs." *Communications* 17 (1971): 119-30.

Maynes, E. Scott. *Decision-Making for Consumers: An Introduction to Consumer Economics.* New York: Macmillan, 1976.

Meiners, Dieter. *Ordnungspolitische Probleme des Warentests.* Berlin: Duncker & Humblot, 1968.

Meyer-Dohm, Peter. *Sozialökonomische Aspekte der Konsumfreiheit.* Freiburg: Verlag Rombach, 1965.

Meynaud, Jean. *Les consommateurs et le pouvoir.* Lausanne: Etudes de science politique 8, 1964.

Mitchell, Jeremy. "The Consumer Movement and Technological Change." *International Social Science Journal* 25 (1973:2): 358-69.

——. *What Do You Want in* Which? London: Consumers' Association, 1965.

Morris, Ruby Turner. *Consumers Union—Methods, Implications, Weaknesses and Strengths.* New London, Conn.: Litfield Publications, 1971.

Norman, D.A. *Memory and Attention: An Introduction to Human Information Processing.* New York: John Wiley & Sons, 1969.

(Norway, Central Statistical Bureau). *Rapport fra kontoret for intervjuundersökelser Nr. 8, Undersökelse om Forbruker-rapporten, Vareundersökelser og reklamasjoner 1969.* Oslo: Statistisk Sentralbyrå, 1970.

Näslund, Hans. *Tre studier av konsumtionsprocessens måluppfyllnadsgrad och varudeklarationssystemet.* Lund: Institute of Business Administration, University of Lund, 1973. Mimeographed.

Organisation for Economic Cooperation and Development. *Consumer Policy in Member Countries.* Paris, 1972.

——. *Labelling and Comparative Testing.* Paris, 1972.

Organization for European Economic Cooperation. *Better Buying Through Consumer Information.* Paris, 1961.

Ölander, Folke, and H. Lindhoff. "Consumer Action Research: A Review of the Consumerism Literature and Suggestions for New Directions in Research." *Social Science Information* 14 (1975:6): 147-84.

Ölander, Folke, and Gerhard Scherhorn, eds. *Proceedings of the Second Workshop on Consumer Action Research, Berlin, April 9-12, 1975,* Berlin: Wissenschaftszentrum, 1975.

Raaij, W. Fred van, and Gery M. van Veldhoven. "Membership of the Dutch

Consumentenbond: An Investigation." Paper at First Workshop on Consumer Action Research, International Institute of Management, Berlin, 1974.

Rotenberg, Ronald H. "The Role and Importance of Non-Commercial Sources of Consumer Information as an Input in the Consumer Decision Making Process." Doctoral dissertation, Pennsylvania State University, 1974.

Rothenberg, Jerome. "Consumers' Sovereignty Revisited and the Hospitality of Freedom of Choice." *American Economic Review* (May 1962): 269-83.

Roberts, Eirlys. *Consumers.* London: Watts, 1966.

Sargent, Hugh. "The Influence of Consumer Product-Testing and Reporting Services on Consumer Buying Behavior." Ph.D. dissertation, University of Illinois, 1958.

Scherhorn, Gerhard. *Gesucht: der mündige Verbraucher.* Düsseldorf: Droste, 1974.

———. *Verbraucherinteresse und Verbraucherpolitik.* Göttingen: Otto Schwartz, 1975.

Smithies, R.J. *How to Double and Treble Your Membership.* Wellington, N.Z.: Consumers' Institute, 1974.

Stiftung "Im Grüne." *Der Konsument hat das Wort.* Schriftenreihe der Stiftung "Im Grüne" Rüschlikon-Zürich, No. 28. Düsseldorf: Econ-Verlag, 1964.

Stigler, George J. "The Economics of Information." *Journal of Political Economy* 69 (June 1961): 213-25.

(Sweden, Government Investigating Committee Reports). *Konsumentpolitik—riktlinjer och organisation.* Stockholm: SOU 1971:37.

———. *Konsumentupplysning—principer och riktlinjer.* Stockholm: SOU 1968:58.

———. *Reklam II: Beskrivning och analys.* Stockholm: SOU 1972:7.

———. *Reklam V: Information i reklamen.* Stockholm: SOU 1974:23.

———. *Varudeklaration—ett medel i konsumentpolitiken.* Stockholm: SOU 1973:20.

Thorelli, Hans B., and Sarah V. Thorelli. *Consumer Information Handbook: Europe and North America.* New York: Praeger, 1974. (Cited as *Handbook* in this work; reader is advised to get second printing, 1975).

Thorelli, Hans B.; Helmut Becker; and Jack Engledow. *The Information Seekers—An International Study of Consumer Information and Advertising Image.* Cambridge, Mass.: Ballinger Publishing Co., 1975. (Cited as *The Information Seekers* in this work.)

Thorelli, Hans B., ed. *Strategy + Structure = Performance.* Bloomington: Indiana University Press, 1977.

University of Missouri. *Freedom of Information in the Marketplace.* Columbia: Freedom of Information Center, 1967.

Warland, Rex H.; R.O. Herrmann; and J. Willits. "Dissatisfied Consumers: Who Gets Upset and Who Takes Action." *Journal of Consumer Affairs* 9 (Winter 1975): 148-63.

Warne, Colston E. "Consumer Interests in the Decade of the 1970's." In *Proceedings of the 6th Biennial Conference of the International Organization of Consumers Unions.* The Hague: IOCU, 1971.

———. "Consumers Look at Advertising." Address before the Advertising Age Creative Workshop, Chicago, July 30, 1970. Mimeographed.

Wilkie, William L. *How Consumers Use Product Information—An Assessment of Research in Relation to Public Policy Needs.* Washington: National Science Foundation, 1975.

Will, Michael. *Warentest und Werbung.* Heidelberg: Verlagsgesellschaft Recht und Wirtschaft, 1968.

Winter, Ralph K., Jr. *The Consumer Advocate versus the Consumer.* Washington: American Enterprise Institute for Public Policy Research, 1972.

Country, Journal, Organization and Person Index

389

Subject Index

advertising, 20, 50-51, 124-28, 214, 270-73, 281-82, 310; Code of, Practice (U.K.), 338; comparative, 357

alternativism, 41, 43, 67

antitrust, 25, 164, 220, 246, 287, 294

aspirations
for information, 264-70;
for product, 21

audience, 288, see Information Seekers

availability, see product availability

average consumers, 3, 65, 114, 125, 144-46, 251-55, 278-80, 288, 291, 319

best buy, see recommendations

brand, 25-27, 47, 158, 267, 310;
coverage, 82-84, 163;
degree of comparison, 114;
number of, tested, labeled, certified, 234-35, and by categories, 240;
proliferations, 18

budgets
of CI programs, 181, 234-45, 238-39, 310-16, 325;
of individual programs, see Appendix E

business, see producers, distributors

buying criteria, 20, 47, 50, 89, 90, 265-66

clientele
of programs, 114;

in model, 183, 241-43, 310, 324

command economy, 40-41, 44

comparative testing, 2, 28, 84-86, 103, 114-16, 234-41, 267

competition
between CI programs, 116-19, 293;
interproduct, 267;
policy, 44-46

complaints, 25, 47, 282, 284, 289, see also Central Consumer Complaints Board

compulsory programs, see obligatory programs

computerized CI utility, 4, 273-277, 367-74

consumer
democracy, 158-59;
expectations, 21;
interest, 35;
satisfaction, 41-42, 80, 146, 183, 282, 284, 289, 310
sovereignty, 37-42
strategy, 42-43

consumer advisory centers, 5, 280;
in Sweden, 210;
in U.K., 276, 335-37

consumer education, 5, 24-26, 47, 51, 131, 266-67

consumer information, see information

consumer information as protection, 1, 51-52, 67, 263

Consumer Information systems, 7-9;
defined, 137-38;

About the Authors

Hans B. Thorelli is the E.W. Kelley Professor of Business Administration at Indiana University. He directed the International Consumer Information Survey sponsored by that university. Previous products of the survey include the *Consumer Information Handbook*, co-authored with Sarah V. Thorelli, and *The Information Seekers*, co-authored with Helmut Becker and Jack Engledow.

His prior books include *The Federal Antitrust Policy: Origination of an American Tradition, International Operations Simulation, International Marketing Strategy* and *Strategy + Structure = Performance*. He is a member of the President's Consumer Advisory Council and the only academic on the Consumer Affairs Committee of the U.S. Chamber of Commerce. He also serves on a National Academy of Science panel evaluating the National Bureau of Standards in the consumer products area and on the National Advisory Council of the Small Business Administration. He is a former member of the Committee on Consumer Finance and Credit of the Consumer Federation of America and was vice president–public policy of the American Marketing Association and a member of the Consumer Advisory Committee of the Federal Energy Administration.

Dr. Thorelli holds a Ph.D. and an LL.B. degree from the University of Stockholm.

Sarah V. Thorelli is a free-lance researcher and scholar, interested in organization management and consumer affairs. She is co-author of *Consumer Information Handbook: Europe and North America*. She has participated in field surveys of consumer and business organizations in South America, Europe, South Africa and Thailand. Currently she is a consultant to the U.S. Federal Trade Commission and the National Science Foundation. She has been an official translator of legal documents for the Swedish Foreign Office and an intelligence research analyst for the U.S. State Department.

Dr. Thorelli holds an A.B. degree from the University of Georgia, an M.A. degree from the University of Alabama and a Ph.Lic. degree from the University of Stockholm.

We hear a lot about the information explosion in science and industry—indeed, in all walks of life. Yet our demands for information seem to grow even faster than its availability. In the marketplace, in particular, the *effectively* available data about the proliferating flora of products and services is insufficient.

We are faced with a serious *consumer information gap*. Only when consumers can make intelligent decisions among competing offerings can we meaningfully speak of consumer sovereignty. What is more: only when at least some consumers are making intelligent decisions some of the time can an open market economy serve the needs of modern society.

A counterpart volume to *The Information Seekers*, this book is about systems for the delivery of independent consumer information—present and future. Concerned with both content and context, the authors examine in detail the nature, anatomy and operating problems of Consumer Information (CI) programs. A systematic overview of the entire consumer policy area is developed for the purpose of relating CI programs to other mainsprings of product information, including advertising and other commercial sources, and to other aspects of consumer policy. Using an ecologic approach, the authors examine the interaction of consumer information systems with the specific social, political and economic environments in which they exist, setting the stage for a thorough analysis of international transfers of consumer information experience and technology. In the final chapter, content and context are synthesized within a discussion of future consumer information systems.

Hans B. Thorelli is the E.W. Kelley Professor of Business Administration at Indiana University. He directed the International Consumer Information Survey sponsored by that University. Previous products of the survey include the *Consumer Information Handbook*, co-authored with Sarah V. Thorelli, and *The Information Seekers*, co-authored with Helmut Becker and Jack Engledow.